# The Two Faces of Dixie

## Politicians, Plantations and Slaves

### By J. Christy Judah

# The Two Faces of Dixie
# Politicians, Plantations and Slaves

By *J. Christy Judah*
ISBN       1442134844
EAN - 13    978-1-4421-3484-3

*Published by Coastal Books*
*C. 2009 by Joyce C. Judah*
*All Rights Reserved.*

*Front Cover Design by J. C. Judah. Lady in Yellow Photography by John Muuss, Photographic Artist. Couple is unidentified but were employees of the Kendall Plantation in Brunswick County; date unknown. Lady with Basket is unidentified. She is standing in front of a Slave Pen in Virginia. Date unknown.*

*Title Page: Slave Auction. Richmond, Va. Date Unknown*

*Back Cover Photo Unidentified Slave. Date Unknown.*

**Other books by this Author:**
An Ancient History of Dogs: Spaniels through the Ages
Building a Basic Foundation for Search and Rescue Dog Training
Search and Rescue Canine Log & Journal
Search and Rescue Log & Journal
The Faircloth Family History
Brunswick County: The Best of the Beaches
The Legends of Brunswick County: Ghosts, Pirates, Indians and Colonial North Carolina
Buzzards and Butterflies: Human Remains Detection Dogs

**Contact Information:**
carolinakennels@2khiway.net

*Printed in the United States of America*

# *Dedication*

**This book is dedicated to my parents, Mr. and Mrs. Herman R. & Erika Faircloth, my daughter, Jennifer, my son-in-law Jonathan Fisher, and my grandsons, Isaih and Jacob.  I love you all.**

*Romans 8:31*
*If God is for us, who can be against us.*
*The Bible*

# *Thank You*

*Thank you to the following for their cooperation, sharing and encouragement during the development and research for this book:*

Gwen Causey and the Brunswick County Historical Society who are working tirelessly to preserve the history of Brunswick County and southeastern North Carolina,

The Lower Cape Fear Historical Society whose main office is the Latimer House in Wilmington; especially Erin Boyle, Archivist and Candace McGreevy, Executive Director, who allowed me access to all of their plantation files,

Mayor Eullis Willis, of Navassa, for his information regarding the Gullah/Geechee culture, and his documentation of the history of the Navassa area of Brunswick County, including the plantations in the Navassa area; Mamie Hankins Frazier for her family stories of slavery and past history;

Richard Triebe, author of *On a Rising Tide* and *Port Royal*, for sharing his Civil War photographs; Ouida Hewett, local historian and preservationist for the Lewis and Hewett plantation information; the North Carolina room staff at the New Hanover Public Library for allowing me access to their slave sketches;

Bertha Bell for her continued support, Linda Fisher for her research information on slaves, Edith Edwards, author of *The Ghosts of Turtle Nest* for her editing advice, Juliana Morgan, author of *Zach's Tracks*, for her editing skills; John Muuss, Photographic Artist for his spectacular photographs, Katie Stewart, of *Old South Tour & Carriage Company* in Southport, NC, for modeling in colonial regalia; Ken Campbell, author of numerous novels including The Fifth Degree for his innovative help in selecting a title,

Don Joyner, Harvey Robinson, Eva Robinson, John Hankins, Dr. Kevin Donald, Donnie Robinson, John Hobgood, and all of those persons who have preserved memories and documents throughout the years for those of us desiring to learn more about our past,

and, as always, my family.

*J. Christy Judah*

# Table of Contents

# *Introduction*

During the course of researching my first book about southeastern North Carolina, *The Legends of Brunswick County: Ghosts, Pirates, Indians and Colonial North Carolina*, I began to realize the vast resources available that detailed our coastal history. After *Legends* was complete, my research continued and a second book began to evolve. Without a clear definition of the scope or content of the book, I began to document more of the personalities, politicians, plantations and slave circumstances that occurred in southeastern North Carolina. Certain topics emerged and became the focus of this book.

This book is not intended to be a comprehensive description of the Revolutionary or Civil Wars. Only a brief background is included to flavor the times. The emphasis is to promote an insight and understanding of the life of Indians, negroes and whites, and, briefly outline how southeastern North Carolina developed from the earliest colonial settlements through the Civil War era. This taste of the period therefore demands an accounting of the slave era and the ugliness of those times.

Portions of this book are not easy to read, much less reconcile within the heart. It is my hope that I have portrayed an accurate picture of colonial life. It is not my intent to incite, condemn, inflame, or otherwise enrage a reader but offer another glimpse into our history; and perhaps deepen an understanding and appreciation for all facets of our past.

In this book slaves are referred to as *negroes* which was common terminology of the time. The more inflammatory names, also quite common, are not used in this document even though they appear in some official documents and court proceedings. This author has chosen to not include the "n" word in this work as a personal and deliberate choice. In those sections where the more inflammatory word is used in the original document, brackets are used and the word "*negro*" substituted; i.e. (negro).

This book provides an insight into the lives of early settlers in southeastern North Carolina; Indians, negroes and whites. This book includes a broad range of information including historical documents that may be offensive or tend to describe stereotypes. Such materials must be viewed in the context of the relevant time period and do not reflect the personal views of the author.

I have intended to provide a book that would record a picture of southeastern North Carolina history. I hope I have done so with an eye towards truth, honesty and integrity. May we always remember from whence we came.

Respectfully,

*J. Christy Judah, M. Ed.*

**Chapter One**

# *The Beginning*

The lower Cape Fear and southeastern North Carolina lands were first explored in the late 1400s. The Cape Fear area encompassed the present counties of New Hanover, Bladen, Brunswick and Pender.

Christopher Columbus discovered the New World in 1492. John Cabot went on to explore the Carolina coast in 1497. Many others followed as Spain, Italy and Great Britain sent their emissaries to claim a part of the New World.

*John Cabot*

Giovanni Da Verrazzano followed Columbus and Cabot in 1521, the same year that Francisco Gordillo and Pedro de Quejo visited. About five years later Lucas Vasquez De Allyon explored the Santee River area of South Carolina while Lucas Vasquez De Allyon began to settle the Winyah Bay area (Georgetown, SC). (The North Inlet-Winyah Bay Reserve, South Carolina is located about 30 miles south of Myrtle Beach and 50 miles north of Charleston, S. C. and contains 12,327 acres. The reserve is home to many threatened and endangered species, including sea turtles, sturgeons, terns and wood storks. Its resources range from tidal marshes to oyster reefs, beaches, inter-tidal flats, coastal island forests, and open waterways.)

In 1540 Hernando De Soto explored the Carolina coast followed by Juan Pardo about 1566-67. In 1584 Philip Amadas and Arthur Barlowe explored the Roanoke area. At about the same time Juan Ribaut settled in Charles Fort, SC (about 1562). Pedro Mendenez De Aviles settled in Santa Elena in 1566 and Sir Walter Raleigh sent settlements to the Roanoke area between 1585 to1587. By 1620 Marmaduke Rayner was exploring the Albermarle region of North Carolina along with John Pory (1622). William Hilton explored the Cape Fear region of southeastern North Carolina as well as Port Royal during 1662-1663. About the same time, settlements were begun in Albemarle, NC as settlers from Virginia moved south from 1653 to 1663. Charles Town was established in 1670, and Dorchester, South Carolina in 1696.

The early 1700s brought about the North Carolina settlements of Bath (1705), New Bern (1710), and Edenton (1715). Beaufort was settled in 1711, and Georgetown in 1729. All of these communities were being formed amidst the Tuscarora War (1711) and the Yamassee War (1715). The Europeans had officially christened the New World.

Each of the explorers created maps and most recorded their explorations giving detailed accounts of their voyages. The astute researcher will find all of these fairly accessible in university collections.

Most of the initial settlements and plantations were along the coast of the Cape Fear River on the east and west sides. This area provided ample water for the rice fields and picturesque views.

*CAROLANA* was first chartered in 1629 and increased in size by a second charter in 1665. The initial split between the northern and southern sections of CAROLANA took place in 1711 and was redrawn in 1729. Around this time the explorers began to visit the interior of the Carolana coastline.

A pamphlet was created in England, describing the New World, to encourage settlers to consider colonizing. Robert Horne published it although it is not confirmed that he was the author. In it *CAROLINA* was described as "*a fair and spacious Province on the Continent of America..... This Province lying so neer Virginia, and yet more southward, enjoys the fertility and advantages thereof; and yet is so far distant, as to be freed from the inconstancy of the weather, which is a great cause of the unhealthfulness thereof; also, being in the latitude of the Bermudas may expect the like healthfulness which it hath hitherto enjoy'd, and doubtless there is no plantation that ever the English went upon, in all respects so good as this: for though Bermudas be wonderful healthy and fruitful, yet is it but a prison to the inhabitants, who are much straight(e)ned for want of room, and therefore many of them are come to Carolina, and more intend to follow. There is seated in this Province two colonies already, one on the River Roanoak (now called Albemarle River) and borders on Virginia; the other at Cape Feare, two degrees more southerly; of which follows a more perticular description. . . ."*

## The Perticular Description of Cape Feare

"*In the midst of this fertile Province, in the Latitude of 34 degrees, there is a colony of English seated, who landed there the 29th of May, Anno 1664; and are in all about 800 persons, who have overcome all the difficulties that attend the first attempts, and have cleared (sic) the way for those that come after, who will find good houses to be in whilst their own are in building; good forts to secure them from their enemies; and many things brought from other parts there, increasing to their no small advantage. The entrance into the River, now called Cape-Feare River, the situation of the Cape, and trending of the Land, is plainly laid down to the eye in the*

*Map annexed. The River is barred at the entrance, but there is a Channel close abord the Cape that will convey in safety a ship of 300 tons, and as soon as a ship is over the bar, the river is 5 or 6 fathom deep for a 100 miles from the Sea; this bar is a great security to the colony against a forreign invasion, the channel being hard to find by those that have not experience of it, and yet safe enough to those that know it."*

## The Earth, Water, and Air

*"The land is of divers sorts as in all countryes of the world, that which lyes neer the sea, is sandy and barren, but beareth many tall trees, which make good timber for several uses; and this sandy ground is by experienced men thought to be one cause of the healthfulness of the place: but up the river about 20 or 30 mile, where they have made a town, called Charles-Town, there is plenty of as rich ground as any in the world. It is a blackish mold upon a red sand, and under that a clay, but in some places is rich ground of a grayer colour, they have made brick of the clay, which proves very good; and lime they have also for building.*

*The woods are stored with deer and wild turkeys, of a great magnitude, weighing many times above 50 lbs. a piece, and of a more pleasant taste than in England, being in their proper climate; other sorts of beasts in the woods that are good for food; and also fowls, whose names are not known to them. This is what they found naturally upon the place; but they have brought with them most sorts of seeds and roots of the Barbadoes which thrive very well, and they have potatoes, and the other roots and herbs of Barbadoes growing and thriving with them; as also from Virginia, Bermudas, and New England, what they could afford: They have indigo, tobacco very good, and cotton-wool; lime-trees, orange, lemon, and other fruit-trees they brought, thrive exceedingly: They have two crops of Indian-corn in one year, and great increase every crop; apples, pears, and other English fruit, grow there out of the planted kernels. The marshes and meadows are very large from 1500 to 3000 Acres, and upwards, and are excellent food for cattle, and will bear any grain being prepared; some cattle both great and small, which live well all the winter, and keep their fat without fodder; hogs find so much mast and other food in the woods, that they want no other care than a swine-herd to keep them from running wild. The meadows are very proper for rice, rape-seed, lin-seed, etc., and may many of them be made to overflow at pleasure with a small charge. Here are as brave rivers as any in the world, stored with great abundance of sturgeon, salmon, bass, plaice, trout, and Spanish mackrill, with many other most pleasant sorts of fish, both flat and round, for which the English tongue hath no name. . . .*

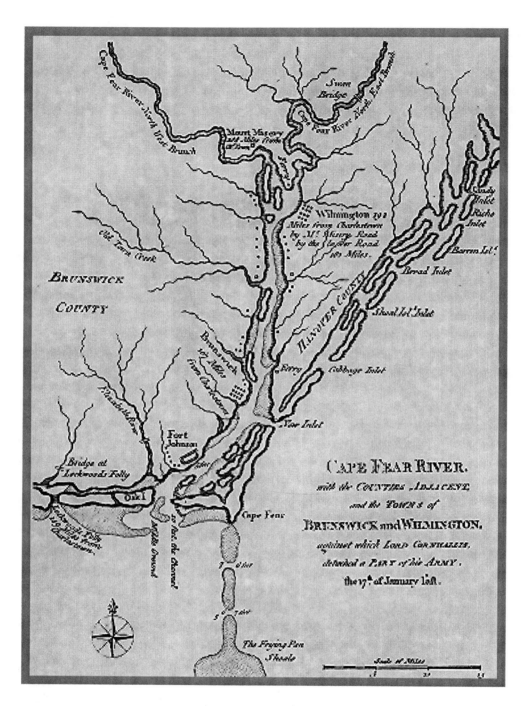

*Last of all, the air comes to be considered, which is not the least considerable to the well being of a plantation, for without a wholesome air all other considerations avail nothing; and this is it which makes this place so desireable, being seated in the most temperate clime, where the neighbour-hood of the glorious light of Heaven*

4

*brings many advantages, and his convenient distance secures them from the inconvenience of his scorching beams. The summer is not too hot, and the winter is very short and moderate, best agreeing with English Constitutions. . ."*

*"If therefore any industrous and ingenious persons shall be willing to pertake of the Felicites of this Country, let them imbrace the first opportunity, that they may obtain the greater advantages."*

## *The Chief of the Privileges are as follows:*

*"First, There is full and free Liberty of Conscience granted to all, so that no man is to be molested or called in question for matters of religious concern; but every one to be obedient to the civil government, worshipping God after their own way."*

*"Secondly, there is freedom from custom, for all wine, silk, raisins, currance, oyl, olives, and almonds, that shall be raised in the Province for 7 years, after 4 ton of any of those commodities shall be imported in one bottom."*

*"Thirdly, every free-man and free-woman that transport themselves and servants by the 25 of March next, being 1667, shall have for himself, wife, children, and men-servants, for each 100 Acres of land for him and his heirs for ever, and for every woman-servant and slave 50 acres, paying at most 1/2 d. per acre, per annum, in lieu of all demands, to the Lords Proprietors: provided always, That every man be armed with a good musquet full bore, 10 lbs powder, and 20 lbs of bullet, and six months provision for all, to serve them whilst they raise provision in that countrey."*

*"Fourthly, every man-servant at the expiration of their time, is to have of the country a 100 Acres of land to him and his heirs for ever, paying only 1/2 d. per Acre, per annum, and the women 50 acres of land on the same conditions; their masters also are to allow them two suits of apparrel and tools such as he is best able to work with, according to the custom of the countrey."*

*"Fifthly, they are to have a Governour and Council appointed from among themselves, to see the Laws of the Assembly put in due execution; but the Governour is to rule but 3 years, and then learn to obey; also he hath no power to lay any tax, or make or abrogate any law, without the consent of the colony in their Assembly."*

*"Sixthly, they are to choose annually from among themselves, a certain number of men, according to their divisions, which constitute the General Assembly with the Governour and his Council, and have the sole power of making laws, and laying taxes for the common good when need shall require."*

*"These are the chief and fundamental privileges, but the Right Honourable Lords Proprietors have promised (and it is their interest so to do) to be ready to grant what other privileges may be found advantageous for the good, of the colony."*

*"Is there therefore any younger brother who is born of genteel blood, and whose spirit is elevated above the common sort, and yet the hard usage of our country hath not allowed suitable fortune; he will not surely be afraid to leave his native soil to*

*advance his fortunes equal to his blood and spirit, and so he will avoid those unlawful ways too many of our young gentlemen take to maintain themselves according to their high education, having but small estates; here, with a few servants and a small stock a great estate may be raised, although his birth have not entitled him to any of the land of his ancestors, yet his industry may supply him so, as to make him the head of as famous a family."*

*"Such as are here tormented with much care how to get worth to gain a livelyhood, or that with their labour can hardly get a comfortable subsistance, shall do well to go to this place, where any man whatever, that is but willing to take moderate pains, may be assured of a most comfortable subsistance, and be in a way to raise his fortunes far beyond what he could ever hope for in England. Let no man be troubled at the thoughts of being a servant for 4 or 5 year, for I can assure you, that many men give mony with their children to serve 7 years, to take more pains and fare nothing so well as the servants in this plantation will do. Then it is to be considered, that so soon as he is out of his time, he hath land, and tools, and clothes given him, and is in a way of advancement. Therefore all artificers, as carpenters, wheelrights, joyners, coopers, bricklayers, smiths, or diligent husbandmen and labourers, that are willing to advance their fortunes, and live in a most pleasant healthful and fruitful country, where artificers are of high esteem, and used with all civility and courtesie imaginable, may take notice, that there is an opportunity offers now by the Virginia fleet, from whence Cape Feare is but 3 or 4 days sail, and then a small stock carried to Virginia will purchase provisions at a far easier rate than to carry them from hence; also the freight of the said provisions will be saved, and be more fresh, and there wanteth not conveyance from Virginia thither. If any maid or single woman have a desire to go over, they will think themselves in the Golden Age, when men paid a dowry for their wives; for if they be but civil, and under 50 years of age, some honest man or other, will purchase them for their wives."*

*"Those that desire further advice, or servants that would be entertained, let them repair to Mr. Matthew Wilkinson, Ironmonger, at the Sign of the Three Feathers, in Bishopsgate Street, where they may be informed when the ships will be ready, and what they must carry with them."*

*"Thus much was convenient to be written at present, but a more ample relation is intended to be published in due time."*

Source: Robert Horne, A Brief Description of the Province of Carolina . . . (London, 1666), reprinted in Alexander S. Salley, Jr., ed., Narratives of Early Carolina, 1650-1708 (New York, 1911), 66-73.

With these inviting descriptions, the first settlers made their way to the Cape Fear and southeastern North Carolina coastline. The first group arrived from England in 1663 and purchased thirty-two square miles of land along *Town Creek*, in

Brunswick County, from the local Indians. They left the area within two to three months and returned home to New England.

The following year, in 1664, Sir John Yeamans of Barbados led a second group to the same location and established *Charles Town* six years before the "South Carolina" Charles Town was established along the Ashley River. About 800 persons settled in this North Carolina settlement but by 1667 they were running out of supplies and a hurricane hit the area that August. The storm wiped out the entire settlement. Survivors left the area to head north, most into Virginia. For the next fifty years the majority of the settlers headed toward the Albemarle area or the Charles Town of *South* Carolina.

## Brunswick County

In May 1713, Landgrave Thomas Smith II (son-in-law of Mr. Roger Moore) was granted Barren Island (Bald Head Island). Shortly afterwards, Governor George Burrington began to distribute land along the Cape Fear (1724). Some of the settlers came from further south to settle here since the taxes in North Carolina were somewhat lower than those in South Carolina.

Maurice Moore (son of Governor James Moore) founded Brunswick Town and by June 1726 a map of the town was filed with the Secretary of the Province. The following year a ferry was opened to cross the Cape Fear in order to get to the eastern banks of the river.

*Maurice Moore*

## Brunswick Town

Brunswick Town was established in 1725 on part of the 320 acres of land given to Col. Maurice Moore, second son of Governor James Moore of South Carolina. Brunswick Town was officially begun in 1726 but *really* began to develop about 1731.

Brunswick Town was the county seat and remained so until 1779 after the beginning of the Revolutionary War.

Brunswick Town was also the county seat of New Hanover County until 1729 when Wilmington was established and named (in 1740). The settlement began to expand in 1725 as land grants were given (in addition to Maurice Moore) to Samuel Swann, Charles Harrison, and Eleazar Allen. Maurice Moore transferred many of his acres to his brother, Roger Moore, who developed *Orton Plantation*. Finally on March 9, 1764, Brunswick County was officially established and seceded from New Hanover County.

The residents of Brunswick Town evacuated their town in anticipation of a British attack during the Revolutionary War. They were right to leave as the British completely destroyed the deserted town and burned it to the ground in 1779. Four walls of the St. Phillips Church stand testament to a once grand structure.

Brunswick County became the home of three North Carolina Governors: Johnston, Dobbs and Tryon, and three acting governors, Rice, Rowan and Hasell. Its population peaked at four hundred and contained an overabundance of noted military and political men. Among those were Major General Robert Howe, Cornelius Harnett, Jr., General John Ashe, General James Moore, Judges Maurice and Alfred Moore, Attorney-General Archibald MacLaine, Chief Justices Allen, Hasell, Benjamin Smith and others; including Colonel Dry, the collector, and Mr. Richard Quince, a merchant, who were all noted to have a zealous interest in the completion of the St. Phillip Church building. (It was under construction about 1760.)

By the early 1800s Brunswick Town was mostly abandoned. The foundations of the original homes can be seen today.

## Two Major Churches and Burial Grounds

Churches in both Brunswick and Wilmington were authorized by the Act of 1751 although the establishment of a church in each was done several years prior. In Brunswick the majestic church was *St. Philips* and in Wilmington, *St. James*. As a general rule, the same ministers served both.

## St. James Church

The original *St. James Church* was not as large as St. Philips in Brunswick. It was plain and barn-like. The British officers used it as a barracks in 1781. It was located at the southwest corner of Market and Fourth Streets. There was also a graveyard at that lot. An Act in 1752 had allotted 30 feet across Market Street for this purpose.

The graveyard at St. James was in use until the *Oakdale Cemetery* was established in 1853. The first burial in Oakdale occurred on the 5th of February 1854. The politician, Cornelius Harnett, was buried in the St. James Cemetery in 1781. He lies buried in the northeast corner of the graveyard with this inscription on his tombstone:

*Cornelius Harnett,*
*Died 20th April 1781.*
*Aged 58.*
*Slave to no sect, he took no private*
*But looked through nature up to nature's God.*
*A worthy name of a worthy community.*

He is described by his biographer, Mr. Hooper, *"as being delicate rather than stout in person; about 5 feet 9 inches high; hazel eyes and light brown hair; small but symmetrical features, and graceful figure. Easy in his manners; affable and courteous; with a fine taste for letters, and a genius for music, he was at times a fascinating and always an agreeable companion."*

In a lecture by Col. James G. Burr in Wilmington in the opera house, in 1890, the Colonel related a condensed form of the following….a story regarding one of those buried at St. James Church as related in *History of New Hanover County, Vol. I.*

*"In March, 1810, Samuel R. Jocelyn, son of a distinguished lawyer of the same name in Wilmington, and himself a promising man-not long after conversing with his friend Alexander Hostler and others about the possibility of a man returning to earth after death and making his presence known, and after making an agreement with Hostler that the first of the two who died should, if possible, reveal himself to the survivor--was killed by accident, and buried in St. James' churchyard. Hostler was greatly afflicted by the death of his friend, and, while sitting alone in his room a day or two after the funeral, was overwhelmed by the sudden appearance of Jocelyn, who said to him: 'How could you let me be buried when I was not dead?' 'Not dead?' exclaimed the horror-stricken survivor. 'No, I was not,' replied his visitor: 'open the coffin and you will see I am not lying in the position in which you placed me,' and vanished immediately. Hostler, though greatly affected, believed he was the victim of delusion and tried to rid himself of it, but at the same hour on the next evening, and again at the same hour on the third evening, the apparition confronted him with the same mournful query. He then determined to exhume the body and see whether the fact was true or not. He told the story to Mr. Lewis Toomer, and asked his assistance in the disinterment, which he agreed to give. They went together at night and opened the grave, and upon removing the lid of the coffin and turning the light of a dark lantern on the body, discovered it lying face downward. Hostler communicated the facts to Colonel Burr's mother, who was his near relative, and between her and himself there was an affectionate intimacy, and Mr. Toomer told the facts of the disinterment in the presence of another venerable lady, Mrs. C. G. Kennedy, who put the statement in writing for Colonel Burr, who read it during the course of his lecture."* It was a chilling tale, just one of many originating in the Cape Fear region.

Generally the plantation owners and politicians were buried on their own plantations. Many of those burial grounds have wholly disappeared and the rest are mostly in ruins. However, even after the residents moved elsewhere, they sometimes continued to bury their dead in the St. Phillips Church Cemetery.

## St. Phillips Parish, Brunswick County

In 1741 all of the lands west of the Cape Fear River were incorporated into a parish called St. Phillips. Many of the members of St. Phillips Parish and Brunswick Town owned plantations in the surrounding lands but spent much of their time in the town.

In 1760, the following letter was written on behalf of the current minister of St. Philip's Parish by a group of Brunswick Town and Wilmington residents, including Rich Quince, John Davis, Rob Snow, Rich Eagles, Benj. Davis, Tho. Neale, John Davis, J.A. Murray, N.C. Watters, Jas. Watters and Will Dry:

*St. Philips Parish, Brunswick April 7, 1760*
*Right Hon. & Right Rev. Worthy Gentlemen*

*We, the Churchwardens and Vestry of St. Philips Parish, in New Hanover County, on Cape Fear River, in the Province of No. Carolina, humbly beg leave to recommend to your Society for a Mission the Rev. Mr. John Macdowell as a very good minister of the Church of England who has been in this Province since the year 1754 and has officiated in our neighboring Parish of St. James from the time of his arrival until May 1757 and for the next year did officiate in the town of Brunswick and Wilmington and from that time has been our Minister in this Parish, and by all the Vestries of every Parish, where he hath officiated.*

*We therefore humbly pray to recommend him to your favor for a mission. We are building of a very large brick church which is near done and soon hope to have a Glebe but at present we are obliged to hire a house, for him to live in, till we can do better, at present we are a poor parish, very heavily taxed on occasion of the present war with the French and Indians, therefore can't afford to give a competency, so as to maintain him and his young family in a decent good manner and we shall, as in duty bound, ever pray for a blessing on your most religious endeavours. We are*

*Right worthy Gentlemen*
*Your most dutiful and Obdt Servants*

Arthur Dobbs responded to the men certifying that he agreed with the foregoing recommendation that Rev. Mr. John MacDowell "is a person of unblamable life and conversation & deserving of the recommendation given him by the churchwardens & vestry." It is unclear what happened next. However....nine years later.....

A letter from William Tryon to Daniel Burton in 1769 talks of the Reverend Mr. Cramp who is the present pastor of St. Philips Church. Tryon says, *"He has promised me he will not stay in this government on any terms than induction from*

10

*me. I have urged him to accept of presentation to this parish, his answer was...'they will starve me, for none like the inducted parson.' I have offered to advance him what money he may want for his support till the right of presentation is determined in a course of law, and the salary that is detained recovered from the Church Wardens, as I told him I was sure he would have every support of the Society, on so important an undertaking. He is at present ill of the gout, and I hear inclined to return to England."*

Has the process of obtaining or keeping a preacher changed much over the years?

## Haule-over

In 1727 one of the court documents established a ferry to be created and conducted by Cornelius Harnett to connect the southern part of the Cape Fear River with the northern section. The place on the river to be used was to be called "Haule-over." For this ferry he would receive five shillings for a man and his horse and a half a crown for each person. No other ferries were allowed within ten miles of that location.

## New Hanover County

As early as 1730 settlers were on the east side of the Cape Fear River creating a place called *New Liverpool*. By 1733 John Watson received a land grant for 640 acres adjoining this settlement on the north. James Wimble, Joshua Granger, Michael Dyer, and others also obtained grants and worked together to layout the town.

James Wimble began selling lots in 1733 in a town he called *New Carthage* located along the east side of the Cape Fear River. The name changed several times to *New Liverpool* (1730), *New town*, *Newton* (1732), and finally incorporated as the town of *Wilmington* on February 25, 1740. Eventually the settlers along the western side of the Cape Fear seceded from New Hanover County and Brunswick County emerged.

Some of the older homes (pre-1900) in Wilmington include the *Latimer House* (1852, 126 South 3rd Street), *Slave and Servant Quarters* for the Latimer family slaves (1839, 215 Orange Street), *St. James Episcopal Church* (1840, 25 South 3rd Street), *First Baptist Church* (1859-70, 421 Market Street), *John Taylor House* (1847, 411 Market Street), *Four Porches Bed and Breakfast* (1837, 312 South 3rd Street), *Church Street Cottage* (1898, 210 Church Street), *Cumming House* (1897, 115 Church Street), and the *Hansen House* (1882, 114 Nun Street).

Robert B. Wood and John C. Wood built the Latimer House along with carpenter, James F. Post. It was built in 1852 for Zebulon Latimer (1810-1881).

*Latimer House, Wilmington, NC*
*Photo Courtesy of the Lower Cape*
*Fear Historical Society.*

## Settlements in the Waccamaw Area

Settlements in the Waccamaw area date to the early 1700s. There were two King's grants to Jonathan Calkins (Feb. 21, 1730) for 440 acres on the Waccamaw about 1.5 miles north of the South Carolina border. At least one of these lots was on the west side of the river. On April 26, 1730 Lewis John(s) received a grant for 1000 acres on the west side of the Shallotte River, which was listed as Bath County at that time. This was most likely in error as later in 1737 Johns sold some cattle on the west side of the Waccamaw River to Roger Moore.

John Swann sold 500 acres on the west side of the Waccamaw next to Joseph *Waters*, to Matthew Rowan in 1736 and in 1737 James Craven was granted 640 acres on the southeast side of the Waccamaw River, about a half-mile from the border.

In 1748 Jonathan Calkins of Prince Georges Parish in South Carolina sold Thomas Bell, then of New Hanover County, 420 acres bounded on the southeast by Little River. The Bell families were established permanent residents of Brunswick County. They also owned land in the Lockwood Folly community in 1728 where the courthouse was to be constructed later.

William Moore sold Edward Wingate, Jr. a tract of 320 acres in 1753 in an area known as *Piraway*, part of the former plantation of *Lewis Johns*. Also in 1753 Elisha Sellers received a grant of 200 acres on the southwest side of the Waccamaw at the Long Bluff. She and her five brothers, and a married sister, had moved here from Edgecombe County, North Carolina.

Nathan Benson received 100 acres in a grant in 1764 and sold the land the same year. It was located on the South Carolina border. He sold it to John Stevens. In 1765, James Marlow, Jr. was granted 200 acres on the west side of the Waccamaw "upon a swamp back of the river savannahs a little below his improvements" (NC Archive). He had been in the area as early as 1762 as he was listed on the tax lists at that time.

In 1767 John Stanley (Stanaland) received from HM Receiver General, for debts owed by Robert Halton, 640 acres on the east side of "*Waggamaw*" which extended southeastward along the South Carolina border. This was part of the original patent to Samuel Saban Plummer of 1737. He sold 200 acres of it to each of his brothers, Hugh and Gersham Stanaland the same year.

In 1767 Edward Wingate sold 320 acres of *Pyraway* property to Louis Dupree. Also that year William Grissett sold Wingate 640 acres on the Waccamaw known as *Rogues Harbour*, originally granted to Samuel Saban Plummer. It was on the west side of the river and possibly was in the Old Dock area.

Later in 1767 (December), just inside the South Carolina border, Ephraim and Joseph Frink were bequeathed land on the Waccamaw River that was originally owned by William Waters in 1736 and had been sold to Thomas Frink.

In 1770 John Stanaland sold 200 acres more of his 640-acre property to his brother Gersham Stanaland.

The following families were listed as heads of household in the Waccamaw River area in 1772:

| | | |
|---|---|---|
| Job Benton | John Hickman | Elisha Sellers |
| John Ethridge | William Hill | James Sellers |
| Samuel Ethridge | Enos Lay | Isaac Simmons |
| Needham Gause | John Lay | John Smith |
| William Gause | James Marlowe | Alexander Stevens |
| John Marlow | John Ward | William Gore |
| William Mooney | Edward Wingate | William Grissette |
| John Gnerette (Jenrette) | | |

(James Marlow of Southport compiled the above information on the Waccamaw Settlements.)

## *Lockwood Folly*

By 1779 Lockwood Folly was the county seat at the mouth of the Lockwood Folly River on the southwest bank. This was located on the plantation of John Bell, near the Lockwood Folly Bridge. By 1784 the seat was moved to the other side of the river and Walkersburgh, a new town, formed. It was named after John Walker on whose land it was established.

Walkersburgh included a jail, several homes and a tavern. The town never really developed, mostly due to the inconvenient location.

### Smithville Formed

In 1792, Joshua Potts requested that the NC General Assembly commission the town. Smithville was officially established and in 1808 the county seat was moved there where it remained for the next 169 years. The town was originally named Smithville, after Benjamin Smith, who had served under General George Washington during the Revolutionary War. He later became Governor of North Carolina. The townspeople of Wilmington had difficulty pronouncing Smithville and referred to it as "Smiffle." In 1812 Brunswick County contained six districts, Northwest, Town Creek, Smithville, Shallotte, Lockwood Folly and Waccamaw.

### Brunswick County Courthouse in 1865

*A northern artist's sketch of the Brunswick County Courthouse at Smithville in 1865.*

The sketch above appeared in an unidentified newspaper in the north on March 18, 1865 along with a description of Smithville: *"Smithville, one of the oldest and most dilapidated villages in the south, is situated on the Cape Fear River, about two*

14

*miles from the Atlantic. It has a population of about 600 persons, most of who are engaged in fishing. The courthouse will give our readers an idea of its general appearance. One of the apartments in the building was used as a shoe store, the rest being devoted to court offices. When our artist visited it, piles of public documents were strewn over."*

Another temporary courthouse was located at Deep Water point, a few miles east of Southport, below Bonnets Creek. In 1808 an act authorized the removal of the courthouse from Lockwood Folly to Smithville. Court records from 1805 - 1810 do not identify the location of the courthouse. From April 1810 to 1858 court was held in Smithville. *"Surveyed agreed to the original counses (sic) and distance. William Goodman, Surveyor. (Plantation of John Bell, Esq., upon Lockwood Folly, locations of Courthouse, prison and stocks.)"*

In the Wilmington Gazette (No. 646, 13th Year), on Tuesday the 23rd of May 1809, a notice was posted for the *"public auction to the lowest bidder, at the School-House in Smithville, on Thursday the 15th of June, at the hour of 1 o'clock, the building of a Court-house, Prison and Stocks, in that town, in the County of Brunswick at which time and palce, plans thereof will be produced and terms made known. Smithville, May 8, 1809."* (Note: lowest bidder??)

In 1887 Smithville was renamed Southport. The county seat was moved to Bolivia in 1977 where it remains today.

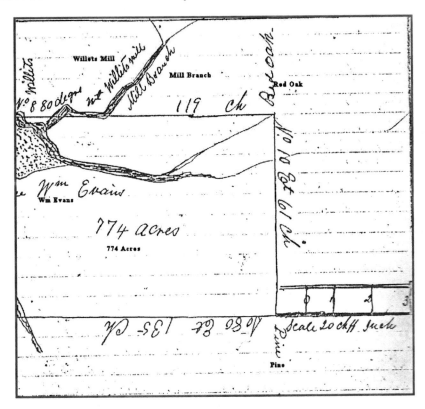

Notations on map: *Willets Mill, Mill Branch, 774 acres, Pine*
*Notations on map: (beginning in the upper left and moving around in a counterclockwise direction)*
*Ashe tree, Lockwood Folly, Old Bridge, COURTHOUSE, Graveyard, House of William Evans,*
*Willets.*

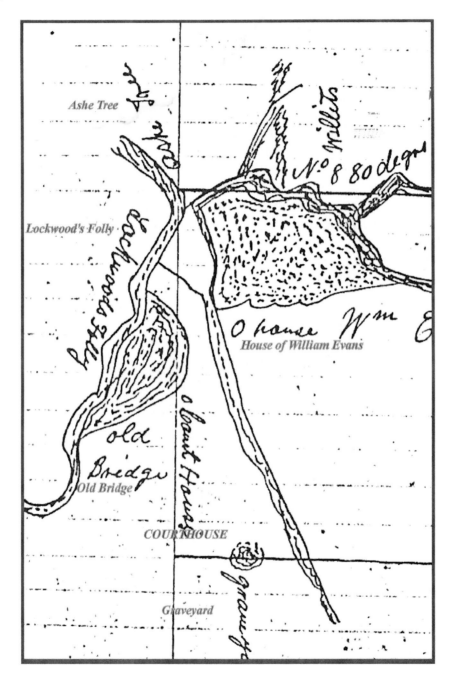

Mr. R. V. Asbury, Jr. wrote an article for the *Brunswick County Historical Society* in its very first newsletter, Vol. 1, No. 1, in September of 1961, describing Brunswick's Itinerant Courthouse. He said in the newsletter that: *"In 1696, (the) Bath precinct was organized under the English Crown. This precinct extended from Albemarle County to the Cape Fear and beyond. By an act of Assembly, July 1729, the southern part of this precinct was erected into the precinct of New Hanover. In 1734, Bladen County was also formed from parts of New Hanover County."*

*"Brunswick County was formed on March 8, 1764 from New Hanover and Bladen Counties. It was named in honor of the House of Brunswick of which the four Georges, Kings of England, belonged. It is located in the southern section of the state, and is bounded by the Atlantic Ocean, the Cape Fear River, Columbus, Pender, and New Hanover counties. The present (land) area is approximately 22,000."*

In a transaction between Schenking Moore and his wife, Mary, and Nathaniel Moore, in which they sold some land to William Evans, there is a map describing the location of the courthouse. This map places the location near the old Lockwood Folly Bridge, graveyard, and house. Sometime later the courthouse was moved from this location to the mouth of Lockwood Folly River near the inlet in the area now called Brown's Landing. The following sketch of the location of the courthouse was included in a deed. It is broken into two parts to make it more legible. Date: June 24, 1784.

*"The 774 acres noted, belonging to William Evans, was located on the west-side of Lockwood Folly River beginning at the ashe tree out to the next side of said rivers a small distance below the mouth of Doe Creek, running from thence No. 80 degrees west 119 chains to a Red oak on the south side of a knoll branch and from thence North 10 degrees, 61 chains to a pine, then south 80 degrees 135 chains to a ___and the branch of the rivers, then down the ____ ___...to the beginning including the plantation where on Schinkup Moore formerly lived."*

(Brunswick County historian, Gwen Causey, is of the opinion that this location is near the Concord Church presently located on highway 211 and near the intersection of highway 17. The graveyard would then be identified as the Concord Church Cemetery.) (There is another cemetery, the original Galloway Plantation Cemetery in the area, near the present Lockwood Folly Park, off highway 211. This cemetery may be the one indicated in the drawing, or, there may be yet another undiscovered cemetery in the near vacinity.)

The courthouse was described as a wooden frame building having several rooms, one being the jail and several more offices. It had a large stone chimney made of ballast stone. The road, which approached the landing where it was moved, is still called Stone Chimney Road. In 1789 there was a failed effort to move the courthouse to a more central location.

## *North Carolina in the 1800s - Census Data for Brunswick County*

| | | |
|---|---|---|
| 1810 - 4,778 | 1820 - 5,480 | 1830 - 6,516 |
| 1840 - 5, 265 | 1850 - 7,272 | 1860 - 8,406 |
| 1870 - 7,754 | 1880 - 9,389 | 1890 - 10,900 |
| 1900 - 12,657 | | |

## *The North and South Carolina Boundary*

The boundary between North and South Carolina was about thirty miles southwest of the Cape Fear River. The colonial records in 1729 described it as the "main branch of a large river falling into the ocean at the *Cape Fear*." At that time the Brunswick River was called the northwest branch of the Cape Fear. The boundary appeared to be just south of the present day Wilmington.

The eastern coast of North and South Carolina was colonized through hardship and determination with little more than the self-labor of the man, his wife, and perhaps a son or two. The practice of slavery in the New World was born out of a necessity to enlist the labors of others in order to cultivate the virgin lands. So began our journey.

Turpentine Distillery. Drawings signed by E. A. Abbey.
Photo Courtesy of the New Hanover Public Library.

# Chapter Two

# *Personalities and Politics*

**"Investment in knowledge pays the best interest." Ben Franklin, 1706-1790.**

The ancient town of Brunswick, once the seat of the Royal Government, was on the left bank of the Cape Fear River, about 10 miles from the present town of Smithville. It was nearly destroyed on the 7th of September 1769, by a hurricane, which is depicted in a dispatch from William Tyron. (Colonial Doc's from Rolls Office, London.). This is the storm that damaged the St. Phillips Parish Church roof and many other homes in southeastern North Carolina.

Tryon wrote to Wills Hill, Marquis of Downshire, on the 15th of September 1769: *"On Thursday the 7th instant we had a tremendous gale of wind here. It began about 10 in the morning at North East and blew and rained hard till the close of the evening when both wind and rain increased. The wind shifted before midnight to the North West. The gale became a perfect hurricane between twelve and two o'clock on Friday morning the 8th instant. The fury of its influence was so violent as to throw down thousands and I believe from report hundreds of thousands of the most vigorous trees in the country, tearing some up by the roots, others snapping short in the middle. Many houses were blown down along with the Court House of Brunswick County. All the Indian corn and rice leveled to the ground and the fences blown down, add to this upwards of twenty saw mill dams carried away with many of the timber works of the mills, and lastly scarce a ship in the river that was not drove from her anchor and many received damage. This, my Lord, is but the relation of what happened within fifty miles of this town. We are therefore in hourly expectation of receiving as melancholy accounts from other parts of the province. It is imagined that as the corn was within six weeks of its maturity, the planters may save about half a crop, but they have no hopes of recovering the rice lying at this period under water from the freshets that this gust occasioned. The country will I fear be greatly distressed this winter for provisions as far as this gale has extended, for the people will not only be short of corn, but the hogs which are the support of many families will lose the acorns and nuts in the woods which used to fat them for market, the wind having stripped every acorn from the trees before they were ripe. In short, my Lord, the inhabitants never knew so violent a storm; every herbage in the garden had their leaves cut off. This hurricane is attributed to the effect of a blazing planet or star that was seen both from Newbern and here rising in the east for several nights between the 26th and 31st of August, its stream was very long and stretched upward towards the South west."*

However, the town did survive and became home to many well-known individuals.

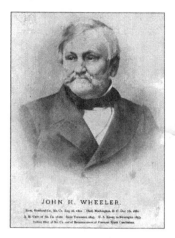

JOHN H. WHEELER.

John H. Wheeler was born in Hertford County, North Carolina about 1802 and died in 1882. He was an historian who provided us with his memories in the book *History of North Carolina and of Reminiscences of Eminent North Carolinians* where he described the personalities and practices of the colonial period. He felt that *"Tis well that a state be reminded of its great citizens."* These are the men and women who took us through the Revolutionary and Civil Wars; the founders of southeastern North Carolina.

*John Wheeler*

One of the major political movements came in July of 1775, as North Carolinians from southeastern North Carolina held their own uprising. They seized the Stamp Master and destroyed the stamps sent to them from England driving the Royal Governor Martin from the country. All this occurred while the northern states revolted for the same causes in the Boston Tea Party a few years later.

*"The **Stamp Act of 1765** (short title for Duties in American Colonies Act 1765; 5 George III, c. 12) was the fourth Stamp Act to be passed by the Parliament of Great Britain but the first attempt to impose such a direct tax on its American colonies. The act required all legal documents, permits, commercial contracts, newspapers, wills, pamphlets, and playing cards in the colonies to carry a tax stamp. It was part of an economic program directly affecting colonial policy that was initiated in response to Britain's greatly increased national debt incurred during the British victory in the Seven Years War (the North American theater of the war was referred to as the French and Indian War)."* (Wikipedia.)

History was in the making and the citizens of southeastern North Carolina did not stand idly by. Instead they took an active part in shaping our country, both from the top and the front lines. Smithville, the county seat at that time, was the home of Howe, Harnett, and Hill, where wealth, stately mansions, generous hospitality, gentle courtesy, and social harmony prevailed. Refinement was the norm amid the war.

## American Revolutionary War

The thirteen colonies that supported the American Revolution were referred to as Americans, Patriots, Whigs, Rebels or Revolutionaires. Colonists who supported the British were called Loyalists or Tories. The War of Independence began in 1775 and lasted until 1783. Involved in many of the historic conflicts were members of families who resided in southeastern North Carolina. Some of those Patriots and Tories are detailed in the mini-biographies that follow.

## Richard Quince

Richard Quince, the *first,* had two sons, *Parker* and *Richard, Jr.* He was a merchant doing business in Brunswick as Richard Quince & Sons that later became Parker Quince & Company. He was at one time a Commissioner of the town of Brunswick, Chairman of the Court of Pleas and Quarter Sessions of Brunswick County, a Church Warden of St. Philip's, a Judge of Vice-Admiralty, a Justice of the Peace, a member of the Wilmington Committee of Public Safety, and, with his son, Richard, a member of the general Committee of the Sons of Liberty. He was an active participant in the Revolution, died in 1778, and was buried in the churchyard of St. Philip's in Brunswick.

Quince was originally from Ramsgate, England, where he had a brother, John (who had apparently come to Wilmington before 1768 and set up a business as a merchant there where he owned a house. He was also a freeman of the Cinque Ports, of which, in 1741, "*he produced sufficient testimony*" and was therefore excused from jury duty.) (*Brunswick County Court Records, 1737-1741, p. 133.*)

Quince lived first at "*Orton*" plantation and later at "*Rose Hill*" on the Northeast, a plantation that he left to his son Parker. The latter and his brother Richard are said to have been "*gentlemen of great respectability and devoted Whigs, but quiet and unobtrusive in their characters and never mingled in public life.*" (*Lady of Quality.*)

## The Ashe Family

Most every member of the Ashe family was able to bear a musket in the army. They are well known as a distinguished family of English origin and first settled in Heightsbury, a borough on the river Willy in Wiltshire, England. Many of the descendents were named after their ancestors and it does become difficult to keep them aligned with the correct information. Every attempt has been made to do so in these accounts.

## John Baptista Ashe

John Baptista Ashe was the founder of the Ashe family in North Carolina in the early 18th century. He married Elizabeth Lillington Swann, the sister of Colonel Samuel Swann. He left these words in his will dated November 2, 1731. (Notice the *river* referred to as Cape FAIR River.)

# JOHN BAPTISTA ASHE WILL

*IN THE NAME OF GOD, AMEN. I, John Baptista Ashe, of Bath County, in the Province of North Carolina, Gent., being thro the mercy of Almighty God, of Sound Mind and Memory, Do make, appoint, Declare and ordain this and this only to be my Last Will and Testament, revoking and making void all former Wills by me heretofore made. The Lord have Mercy on my Soul for Christ's Sake.*

*Imprimis. I will that all my just and lawful debts be duely paid by My Executors hereafter named; particularly that one hundred pounds, North Carolina Money, or the Value thereof be remitted paid to the heirs, Exors. or Admins. of James Nolan, of Boston, Mariner, deceased; the Sum of Sixty pounds of thereabouts having laid in my hands for some years, the Widow who claimed not Complying with the Statute (in that Case provided) for giving Security to Admtors: but I now direct that if they cannot Comply Strictly with the Law, Yet rather than faile, their own bonds to whom the money is payable, May be taken when the money is paid, to indemnify my Estate against any Creditors which may claim in this Province. Also, I will that there be paid as of Debt, to Daniel Hendrick, of South Carolina, Shoemaker, his Exors. or assigns, the Sum of fourty pounds, Current money of this Province. Furthermore, I will that there be paid to the Exce. or heirs of Robert Gamsby, of Boston, Mariner, deceased, if such be to be found, the sum of fourty pounds, Current money of this province.*

*Item. I give, bequeath and devise (after payment of debts & legacies) to my three Children, John, Samuel, and Mary, all my personal Estate, to be Equally Devided amoungst them.*

*Item. I give, devise, and bequeath unto my Son, Samuel, and unto my daughter, Mary, my Lands up the north west branch of Cape Fair River, called Ashwood, which are scituate lying and being on the South side of the Said River between the lands of John Porter, of Virginia, Mercht., and the Plantation whereon Daniel Donaho, lately deceased, dwelt, Together with my other Lands on the north Side of the River directly opposite to those aforementioned, to be equally divided betwixt them, the Said Samuel and Mary, to them, their heirs and assigns forever.*

*Item. I give, devise, and bequeath unto my Son, Samuel, a tract of land containing six hundred and fourty Acres lying on Stumpy Sound, called Turkey Point; also one other tract Containing one thousand Acres, called Stump Island or New River Banks, to him, his heirs or assigns for ever.*

*Item. I give, devise, and bequeath unto my Son, Samuel, four hundred Acres of Land lying above William Lewis's plantation on the Main Branch of Old Towne Creek, to him, his heirs and assigns forever: unless John Russell shall personally come and demand of My Exors. a Bill of Sale for the last mentioned four hundred acres of Land, and Shall pay the ballance of Accounts betwixt us, amounting be about fourty pounds money of South Carolina, Then my Exors. are hereby directed and empowered to Convey the said four hundred Acres of land to the said John Russell, to him, his heirs and Assigns for ever.*

*Item. It is my will that my Sons have their Estates delivered to them as they severally arrive to the age of twenty and one years, and that my daughter have her Estate at the day of Marriage, or age of Twenty and one Years, which shall first happen.*

*Item. I will that my Slaves be kept to work on my lands, and that my Estate may be managed to the best advantage, so as my Sons may have as liberal an Education as the profits thereof will afford; and in their Education I pray my Exers. to observe this method: Let them be taught to read and write, and be introduced into the practical part of Arithmetick, not too hastily hurrying them to Latin or Grammar, but after they are pretty well versed in these let them be taught Latin & Greek. I propose this may be done in Virginia; After which let them learn French, perhaps Some French man at Santee wile undertake this; when they are arrived to years of discretion Let them Study the Mathematicks. To my Sons when they arrive at age I recommend the pursuit & Study of Some profession or business {I could wish one to ye Law, the other to Merchandize), in which Let them follow their own inclinations.*

*Item. I will that my daughter be taught to write and read & some femanine accomplishments which may render her agreable; And that she be not kept ignorant as to what appertains to a good house wife in the management of household affairs.*

*Item. I give to each of my Exors. a Gold Ring as a token of the respect which In my life I bore them.*

*Item. I will that a Brick Vault may be built at Groveley, and my Dear Wifes body taken up out of the Earth & brought and laid therein; and if it should be my fortune to die in Carolina so as my Corpse may be Conveyed thither, I desire that one large Coffin may be made, and both our body's laid together therein and lodged in the said Vault.*

*Item. I give, devise and bequeath unto my honoured friend, Edward Mosley, Esqr., the one half or moiety of my Lands, lying near Rock Fish Creek, on the North West branch of Cape fair River, being twenty five hundred and Sixty Acres, to be equally divided between him and my heir, to him, his heirs & Assigns forever.*

*Item. I give, devise and bequeath unto my Loving Brother, John Swann, Six hundred and fourty Acres of land lying on the North East Branch of Cape Fair River, which he bought of, and of which I have not as yet made him any Conveyance, it being land adjoining below that whereon my Brother, Samuel Swann, dwells, to him the sd. John Swann, his heirs & assigns forever.*

*Lastly, I nominate, Constitute and appoint my honour'd friends, Edward Moseley & Nathaniel Rice, Esqrs., my good friend Mr. Roger Moore, my loving Brothers, Samuel Swann and John Swann, my good friends, Messers. William Downing and Edward Smith, to be Executors of this my Last Will, Testament, hereby desiring & praying them to see the same duly Executed. In witness whereof, I have hereunto set my hand & Seal, this second day of November, Anno Dom., 1731.*

JNO. BAPTA. ASHE. (Seal)

Signed, Sealed and Published in the Presence of us:

MEHITTOBDE X RUTTER
JOHN HAWKINS
CORNELIUS DARGAN
MICH. RUTTER

*NO. CAROLINA, SS. I do hereby make a Codicil to be annexed to this my Last Will and Testament, and do hereby appoint my Loving friend, Job Hows and Thomas Jones, Executors to my Last Will and Testament, and this codicil thereunto annext, together with the several persons before named in my said Last Will and Testament as my Exors. And whereas their is a certain Saw Mill in Building between Mr. Mathew Rowan and my Self, It is my will that my part of the Said Mill together with my part of the lands of belonging be sold by my said Exors. for the use of my three children and the money arising by the Sale thereof to be Equally divided amongst them. In testimony whereof, I have hereunto Set my hand and seal this Sixteenth Day of October, 1734.*

JNO. BAPTA. ASHE. (Seal)

Signed & Sealed In the Presence of, and annext:

JAMES INNES
JOSEPH WALTERS
ED'D SMITH
NORTH CAROLINA.

*Before his Excelly., Gabriel Johnston, Esq., Captain General, Governor in Chief of the Province of North Carolina, and Ordinary of the Same. Personally came before me Michael Rutter, one of the Witnesses to the within Instrument, being the Last Will and. Testament of John Baptista Ashe, Esq., who being duely sworn on the Holy Evangelists, declared that he was present and saw the said John Baptista Ashe, Esq., Sign, Seal, publish and declare the same to be his Last Will; and that he was at the same time of sound and disposing mind and memory and understanding, to the best of this deponents knowledge; and that he saw John Hawkins, Cornelius Dargan & Mihitobade Rutter, three other signing witnesses, present at the execution of the said Instrument and sign their names or mark thereunto. Likewise, Personally appeared James Buis, Esq., one of the witnesses to the Codicil annexed to the said Instrument or Last Will and Testament Afforsd, who being duely sworn on the holy Evangelists, saith, that he saw the Said John Baptista Ashe, Esq., duely execute and publish the said Codicil as the codicil of his last Will and Testament, and that he was at the same time of sound mind and memory to the best of this deponents knowledge, and that he saw Joseph Waters and Edward Smith, the two other signing Witnesses present at the Execution of Given under my hand at Brunswick, the 15th day of November, Anno Dom., 1734.*

GAB. JOHNSTON
November ye 30th, 1734

Personally appeared before me Edward Moseley, Roger Moore, Samuel & John Swann, Esqrs., & took ye oath appointed by law to be taken by Executors.

W. SMITH, C. J.

## General John Ashe

John Ashe was the son of John Baptista Ashe. He was born in North Carolina in 1720 at *Gravely*, in Brunswick County, N. C. and was educated at Harvard College (and possibly finished at an English University.) He married Rebecca Moore (the daughter of General Maurice Moore, and sister of General James Moore and Judge Maurice Moore) and had the following children: John (a Major in the NC Troops), Samuel (who commanded a horse unit during the War of '76), Harriet (who first married Davis and second married a Laspiere), Elizabeth (who married William H. Hill, a member of the Assembly in 1794 and of Congress from 1799 to 1803. His father was William Hill, from Boston, who settled in Brunswick County and taught school. William H. Hill was the speaker of the Assembly from 1762 to 1765. He opposed the Stamp Act and was active in the cause against it. President Adams appointed him to the Federal bench.) Mary married William Alston of Waccamaw, *South Carolina*, whose son married Theodosia, daughter of Aaron Burr. William was lost at sea and drowned. Two additional children were A'Court, and Anna.

Elizabeth and William H. Hill had the following children: Joseph Alston Hill, William Henry Wright, Griffith J. McRee, and Judge Samuel Hall.)

General Ashe was *"five foot ten inches tall, had an olive complexion, brown hair, dark hazel eyes and well-defined features with a slender figure he carried most graciously."* None of his sons had children. He died in 1781.

Colonel, John Ashe, then Speaker of the House of the Colonial Assembly, boldly proclaimed to the Royal Governor, surrounded by his satraps, that he *"would resist the execution of the act to death!"* (A satrap includes a governor, his advisors and others who surround him.)

His role in history is noted in 1765. The English ship, the *"Diligence"* entered the harbor. The flag of England was flying and her cannon loaded and ready. She dropped her anchor. Governor Tryon announced the arrival by proclamation on the 6th of January. The citizens of Wilmington prevented anyone from the ship to come ashore, intimidated the commander, seized the ship's boat, mounted it on a cart, raised a flag on it and marched in triumph to the residence of the Governor at Wilmington. The whole town was "wild with excitement."

The next morning Colonel Ashe went to the Governor and demanded the Stamp-master (William Houston) be delivered to him. The Governor refused. Ashe began to make preparations to burn the house. Terrified, the Governor gave up the Stamp-Master and others. There was no bloodshed but Houston made a pledge in writing to *"never receive any stamped paper which may arrive from England, nor officiate in any way in the distribution of stamps in the Province of North Carolina."*

The Stamp Act was dead in North Carolina eight years before the Boston Tea Party, and a full ten years before the signing of the Declaration of Independence. The daring acts of the Cape Fear residents were a solid demonstration by men of character and courage.

The pledge made by Houston was recorded in the Rolls Office, London as an extract from Governor Tryon's dispatch, dated the 26th of December 1765.

*"I do hereby promise that I never will receive any stamp paper which may arrive from Europe in consequence of any act lately passed in the Parliament of Great Britain, nor officiate in any manner as Stamp-master in the distribution of stamps within the Province of North Carolina, either directly or indirectly."*

*"I do hereby notify all the inhabitants of His Majesty's Province of North Carolina that notwithstanding my having received information of my being appointed to said office of Stamp-master, I will not apply hereafter for any stamp paper, or to distribute the same, until such time as it shall be agreeable to the inhabitants of this Province."*

*"Hereby declaring that I do execute these presents of my own free will and accord, without any equivocation or mental reservation whatever."*

*"In witness hereof I have hereunto set my hand this 16th November, 1765.*

"WILLIAM HOUSTON."

However, Ashe knew when to push and when to temper his actions as is demonstrated just three months later when he mended the insult to the Governor in the following note:

*"February 19, 1766.*

"TO GOVERNOR TRYON:
   *"SIR: The inhabitants, dissatisfied with the particular restrictions laid upon the trade of this River only, have determined to march to Brunswick, in hopes of obtaining, in a peaceful manner, a redress of their grievances from the Commanding Officers of His Majesty's ships, and have compelled us to conduct them. We, therefore, think it our duty to acquaint Your Excellency that we are fully determined to protect from insult your person and property, and that if it will be agreeable to your Excellency, a guard of gentlemen shall be immediately detached for that purpose.*
   *"We have the honor to be, with the greatest respect, sir,*

Your Excellency's most *"Obedient, humble servants,*
JOHN ASHE, THOMAS LLOYD,
ALEXANDER LILLINGTON

The Governor knew the power of John Ashe. He tried to build a bridge with the people of Wilmington and the muster of militia there and prepared a great feast, with much liquor for them. The residents of Wilmington rushed to the tables but then poured the liquor in the street and the uneaten foods into the river. This was their way of reminding the Governor they that they could be neither cajoled or intimidated. *This was John Ashe's home.*

In the *Defense of North Carolina,* by Jones, the Ashe family is described as having *"contributed more to the success of the Revolution than any other in the state. General John Ashe and his sons, Captain Samuel Ashe and his son William, Governor Samuel Ashe and his son Samuel, and Colonel John Baptista Ashe were all in constant service."*

## Governor Burrington

Colonel Ashe was not well regarded by Governor Burrington. In a note dated the 20th of February 1732, he said, *"Immediately before the Assembly met, Mr. Price, the Secretary, and Mr. Ashe, came together from the Cape Fear to Edenton, the seat of Government. Mr. Ashe, when qualified, began immediately to oppose me in the council. He gained Mr. Smith and Mr. Porter to join him. Mr. Ashe is altogether bent on mischief. I have been a great friend to him. My benefits he has returned with ingratitude." "He is a great villain, and is unworthy of sitting as Councillor in this Province."* Ashe had written and published information meant to defame Governor Burrington, much to the Governor's dismay.

Governor Burrington also held Colonel Maurice Moore in poor regard when he quarreled with him about a title to lands at Rocky Point, which the Colonel was about to *settle*. In 1731 he tried to "square accounts" with him, but said in other arenas "*About 20 men are settled on the Cape Fear from South Carolina---among them are three brothers of a noted family whose name is Moore. These people were always troublesome where they came from, and will doubtless be so here.*"

Ashe and others effectively pressured Burrington to resign and the Governor sent the following to his sovereign King:

"MAY IT PLEASE YOUR GRACE:
*Having lived in this Province for some years without receiving any money from the King, or the country, I was constrained to sell not only my household goods, but even my linen, plate and lands and stocks. The many sicknesses that seized me and their long continuance have greatly impaired my constitution and substance. My affairs and health being in a bad condition, I humbly desire my Lord Duke, will be pleased to obtain His Majesty's leave for my return to England.*

*I am with profound duty, My Lord Duke Your Grace's most humble and most devoted servant.*

GEORGE BURRINGTON

Burrington returned to his residence at Rocky Point about 1781, with a broken body and mind. He hid in the recesses of Burgaw Swamp and only sporadically and carefully visited his family. Manuel, his confidential servant, had betrayed him and given Major Craig his location. A party of Dragoons was dispatched to capture him. In the fray he was shot in the leg and captured. He was eventually paroled from the prison in Wilmington and died at the home of Colonel John Sampson in October of 1781. (He was in Sampson County trying to move his family into the back country when he died.)

## *Governor Samuel Ashe*

Governor Samuel Ashe was born in southeastern North Carolina in 1725. He studied law at Harvard University. He was the speaker of the Senate in 1777 and one of the first three judges after the adoption of the Constitution. He married Mary Porter (daughter of John Porter who was one of the incorporators of Wilmington.) He had three sons, John Baptista Ashe, Cincinnatus, and Samuel, with his first wife Mary. He was elected Governor of the State in 1795 after being a Judge and public servant for twenty years. This Samuel died at the age of 88 in 1813. He was buried at the Neck Plantation with other descendents. He also lived on the Sloop Point Plantation. Governor Ashe was instrumental in the founding of the University of North Carolina and became President of the University's Founding Board of Trustees.

After the death of Mary, he married Elizabeth Merrick and had several more children. They included Thomas who was the only one who grew to adulthood. Governor Samuel Ashe died in 1813. He is buried in the Ashe Family Cemetery in Rocky Point on the grounds of his plantation "The Neck".

Thomas, the son of Samuel and Elizabeth Merrick Ashe, married Sophia Davis and had a child named Pascal Paoli Ashe who married Elizabeth Strudwick. Pascal was the father of Judge Thomas S. Ashe.

Cincinnatus died at sea with his cousin, William, was on a privateer. (A privateer was a privately owned ship, authorized by its' country of origin, to attack any incoming foreign shipping vessels.)

## Samuel Ashe, Son of Governor Samuel Ashe

Samuel Ashe was born in 1763 and died in 1835. He enlisted in the army at sixteen years of age and was captured at Charleston with General Lincoln. He married Elizabeth, a daughter of Colonel William Shepperd. His children included Betsy (who married Owen Holmes), Mary, John B. and William S. (born 1813 and died 1862) who married Sarah Ann Green and had children named Samuel A'Court, John Grange, and others.

He served throughout the War and was described as *"brave, modest and unobtrusive."* He was a Lieutenant during the Revolution and received that commission at seventeen years old serving in the 1st North Carolina Regiment.

## John Baptista Ashe, Son of Samuel Ashe

John was born in 1748 and died in 1795. He served throughout the war of 1776, was a Lieutenant Colonel of the North Carolina Troops, Speaker of the House in 1785, a member of the Continental Congress in 1787, the United States Congress 1789-1791, and elected to the next Congress (1791-93). He died before he could be inaugurated as the newly elected Governor and before qualifying for the Governor position. He married Miss Montford (sister of Mrs. Willie Jones).

His political views were not unlike many of the Cape Fear region, antagonistic. When others said "aye", John said "nay".

His son Samuel Porter Ashe married Mary, a daughter of Colonel William Shepperd.

## John Porter

As an infant, about 1711, his mother rescued him from an Indian who was in the process of "dashing his brains out against the house". His daughter, Mary, married the future Governor Samuel Ashe.

John Porter received a land grant for 640 acres below Brunswick Town on July 14, 1725 but sold it the following year to Governor Burrington. This tract was called Governor's Point and Sturgeon Point.

## Governor Josiah Martin

Governor Martin followed Tryon and inherited the difficulties with other coastal Carolinians. He tried every means to get them to reconcile with the mother country. In 1775 (July 20), he took refuge on one of the English ships, the *Cruiser*, docked in the Cape Fear River. It is from here he relayed the information that "Fort Johnston has been burnt, and that Mr. John Ashe and Mr. Cornelius Harnett were the ringleaders of the savage and audacious mob." The *Cruiser* left the area and headed for Charleston.

Finally, the North Carolina Constitution was adopted, on the 18th of December 1776, and among the committee was W. Avery, John and Samuel Ashe, Thomas Burke, Rich'd Caswell, Cornelius Harnett, Joseph Hews, Robert Howe, Willie Jones, Thomas Jones, and others.

*Willie Jones*

## General Robert Howe

Robert Howe was born in North Carolina in 1730, the third son of Job Howe (or Hows). His grandfather was also named Job. He came with the Moores from South Carolina and was related to the Moores, Drys, and others through his grandmother, Mary Moore.

Colonel Robert Howe was the commander of the 2nd Regiment of NC Troops in the Continental Army. He was one of the patriotic sons of Brunswick County and a descendent of the noble house of Howe in England but lost both of his parents at a young age. He was raised by his grandmother who so indulged him that his education was somewhat neglected. He married Sarah Grange, daughter of Thomas Grange, but separated from her in 1772 and never remarried.

He visited and remained in England for about two years before returning to North Carolina. Robert Howe, Esq., was also the Captain of Fort Johnston from 1732 to 1785.

Governor Martin charged him with "misapplication of the public money" and with endeavoring "to establish a new reputation by patriotism." Quincy thought better of him and described him as "a most happy compound of the man of sense, the sword, the senate, and the buck. A truly surprising character." He was devoted to the revolutionary cause. He died in 1786 at fifty-six years old.

*Robert Howe*

## *Josiah Quincy Journal*

Josiah Quincy left a journal dated from 1744 to 1775. In his memoirs, he made remarks about various southeastern North Carolina people. Some of those entries provide us a glimpse of life and include: *"Lodged the last night in Brunswick, N. C. at the house of William Hill, Esq., a most sensible, polite gentleman, and though a crown officer, a man replete with sentiments of general liberty, and warmly attached to the cause of American freedom."*

*March 27, 1773. "Breakfasted with Colonel Dry, the collector of the customs, and one of the Council, who furnished me with the following instructions given Governor Martin, and, as Col. Dry told me Governor Martin said, 'to all the colony governors likewise. Colonel Dry is a friend to the Regulators, and seemingly warm against the measures of British and Continental administrations. He gave me an entire different account of things from what I had heard from others. I am now left to form my own opinion, and am preparing for a water tour to Fort Johnston.*

*Dr. Thomas Cobham*

*Yesterday was a most delightful day. Fort Johnston is a delightful situation."*

March 28, 1773. *"I go to church this day at Brunswick: hear W. Hill read prayers; dine with Col. Dry; proceed tomorrow to Wilmington, and dine with Dr. Cobham with a select party. Colonel Dry's mansion is justly called the house of universal hospitality."*

March 29, 1773. *"Dine at Dr. Thos. Cobham's in company with Harnett, Hooper, Burgwin, Dr. Tucker, and (company) in Wilmington; lodged also at Dr. Cobham's, who treated me with great politeness, though an utter stranger, and one to whom I had no letters. Spent the evening with the best company of the place."*

March 30, 1773. *"Dined with about twenty at Mr. William Hooper's; find him apparently in the Whig interest; has taken their side in the House--is caressed by the Whigs, and is now passing his election through the influence of that party. Spent the night at Mr. Harnett's--the Samuel Adams of North Carolina, Robert Howe, Esq., Harnett and myself made the social triumvirate of the evening. The plan of continental correspondence highly relished, much wished for, and resolved upon as proper to be pursued."*

Quincy then visited with Mr. Harnett, Judge Howard, Colonel Palmer, and Colonel Richard Buncombe of Bath and Tyrrell Counties. He decided not to remain in that area long after hearing the following tale from some of the local lawyers of Edenton: *"D. Samuel Cooper of Boston was generally (they said universally) esteemed the author of 'Leonidas,' who together with Marcius Scaevola, was burnt in effigy under the gallows by the common hangman. There being no Courts of any kind in this province, and no laws in force by which any could be held, I found little inclination or incitement to stay long in Edenton, though a pleasant town."* Quincy left and headed into Virginia.

April 5, 1773. *"The soils and climates of the Carolinas differ, but not so much as their inhabitants. The number of negroes and slaves is much less in North than in South Carolina. Their staple commodity is not so valuable, not being in so great demand as the rice, indigo, & of the South. Hence labor becomes more necessary, and he who has an interest of his own to serve is a laborer in the field. Husbandmen and agriculture increase in number and improvement. Industry is up in the woods at tar, pitch, and turpentine; in the fields, ploughing, planting, clearing, or fencing the land. Herds and flocks become more numerous. You see husbandmen, yeomen, and white laborers scattered through the country, instead of herds of negroes and slaves. Healthful countenances and numerous families become more common, as you advance north. Property is much more equally diffused in one province, than in the other, and this may account for some, if not for all the differences of character in the inhabitants. However, in one respect I find a pretty near resemblance between the two colonies (New Hanover/Brunswick and the colony of Bath around Edenton); I mean the state of religion. It is certainly high time to repeal the laws relative to religion, and the observation of the Sabbath, or to see them better executed. Avowed impunity to all offenders is one sign at lest, that the laws want amendment or abrogation. Alike as the Carolinas are in this respect, they certainly vary much as to their general sentiments, opinions and judgments. The staple commodities of North Carolina are all kinds of naval stores, Indian corn, hemp, flax seed, some tobacco, which they generally send into Virginia and c. The culture of wheat and rice is making quick progress, as a spirit of agriculture is rising fast. The favorite liquors of the Carolinas are Claret and Port wines, in preference to Madeira or Lisbon. The commerce of North Carolina is much diffused through the several parts of the province. They in some respects may be said to have no metropolis, though New Bern is called the Capital, as there is the seat of government. It is made a question which carries on the most trade, whether Edenton, New Bern, Wilmington, or Brunswick. It seems to be one of the two first. There is very little intercourse between the northern and southern provinces of Carolina. The present state of North Carolina is really curious; there are but five provincial laws in force through the Colony, and no courts at all in being. No one can recover a debt, except before a single magistrate, where the sums are within his jurisdiction, and offencers escape with impunity. The people are in great consternation about the matter; what will be the consequence is problematical."* As noted, Quincy was very concerned with the politics of the day.

## The Moore Family

The Moore family was of Irish descent and claimed to belong to the Chiefs O'More. An early known American Moore was James, who came into Charleston and married a daughter of Governor Yeamans in 1665. Gov. Yeamans was the Governor of Carolina in 1671. James died in 1706. (The Yeamans colony was established in 1664-1665 as a temporary colony before the establishment of Brunswick Town.) James I had ten children with Miss Yeamans. This James Moore became the Governor of (South) Carolina from 1700-1703 upon the death of Joseph Blake and from 1719 to 1721. He was reported to be the grandson of Roger Moore, leader of the Irish Rebellion of 1641.

Some of the ten children of James I included: General James Moore, II, Colonel Maurice Moore, and Rebecca Moore.

The oldest son of *James Moore, the first*, was also named James, (the second) and became noted in the military. He participated in numerous campaigns against the Indians who were considered fierce and troublesome. In 1703 he marched to North Carolina and had a skirmish with the Appalachian Indians who were involved in a murder in the Cape Fear region. James, the son, completely subdued them. In another conflict with the Tuscarora in 1713 he stopped the Indians in a severe engagement near Snow Hill in Greene County. These were the tribes that had massacred many colonists including John Lawson, one of North Carolina's first historians. James remained in North Carolina about seven months before returning home to South Carolina. (Note: North and South Carolina was the same province until 1693.) By 1719 James was presumed to have returned to the Cape Fear region after his service as the Carolina's Governor of 1719. He never married.

*Colonel Maurice Moore*, the son of James Senior and Miss Yeamans, had several children. Maurice was a soldier, brave, energetic and successful. He married a Miss Porter. His children included Judge Maurice Moore, General James Moore, and Sally Moore. (He was known to have a few skirmishes with the local Coree and Tuscarora Indians in southeast North Carolina. In one instance, he and his favorite domestic, Tony, were watching the Indians through a spyglass as far away as Sugar Loaf (on what is now Carolina Beach) where several Indians were standing. He and Tony ended up tying up the Indians and bringing them back to the colony. We aren't told what happened next.

In another situation there was an Indian encounter when he and Tony were about to cross the river, seemingly blocked by the natives. Without a firearm, Moore began to slash his whip, whipping the Indians. This frightened them and they ran away panic stricken jumping into the river and the adjoining swamp. The Indians believed *he* could only be killed with a "silver bullet."

A memorial to Colonel Maurice Moore hangs on the inside walls of the St. Philips Church in Brunswick Town.

*Rebecca Moore* was the daughter of James Senior and Miss Yeamans. She married John Ashe.

The grandsons of *Roger Moore* (who led the Irish rebellion in 1643) were Roger, Maurice and Nathaniel. One other brother, Colonel James Moore remained in South Carolina and became Governor, like his father in 1701.

The three brothers, Roger, Maurice and Nathaniel joined about 17 others and were the founders of the settlements in the Cape Fear area by 1735. A Mr. Davis (George?) described the brothers as *"No needy adventurers, driven by necessity to seek a precarious living in a wild and savage country, but gentlemen of birth and education, bred to the refinement of society, and bringing with them ample fortunes, polished manners, and cultivated minds."*

The Moore family is well known for their integrity, intellectual capabilities, and allegiance.

## *Judge Maurice Moore* (Died 15 Jan 1777)

Judge Moore was the oldest son of Colonel Maurice Moore and Miss Porter. He was a lawyer, very much esteemed, and was appointed an Associate Justice in 1768. He traveled bad roads and had uncomfortable accommodations as he provided services on the circuit that was eleven hundred miles long.

Governor Tryon recommended his removal in 1766 but this did not happen and he continued on the bench until the Revolution closed the courts. He was considered a military genius.

He married Anne Grange and had two children, Alfred and Sally. Judge Maurice Moore died in 1777, at home, just an hour before his brother, General James Moore.

## *Alfred Moore* (21 May 1755 - 10 October 1810)

Alfred was the son of Judge Maurice Moore. He married Susan Eagles and had four children: Maurice (Colonel in the War of 1812), Alfred, Anna (who married Hugh Waddell, son of General Hugh Waddell), and Sally (unmarried).

Judge Alfred Moore was elected to the House of Commons but lost his *certification of election*. While attending his first session he would have to defend his presence without having the required documentation to prove that he *was* the elected representative. His first speech was memorable with his polished and melodic voice. He described the history and method of election and argued his right to be there without the documentation. His ornate and elegant manner convinced the members of the house and he was admitted as a full member. It is said that Alfred Moore was more eloquent and convincing than even Clay, Calhoun or Webster....noted speakers of the time. Moore was further described as having *"courtly elegance of manners, simplicity, and modesty of demeanor."*

In 1782 he was elected as the State Attorney-General despite having never read a law book. He was appointed to the state bench in 1798 and the following year appointed by the President to the United States Supreme Court. He remained there for six years. His health began to fail so he resigned and died in 1810 at the home of Major Waddell in Bladen County at 55 years of age. He was once described as *"graceful, charming, having had a brilliant wit as a model of a North Carolina gentleman."* His gravestone is in the St. Philips Church Cemetery at Brunswick Town.

## General James Moore  (Died on 15th January 1777)

General Moore was the son of Maurice Moore and Miss Potter, and brother to Judge Maurice Moore.  He died in 1777, at home, just an hour after his brother, Judge Maurice Moore. He married Anna Ivey and had four children, Duncan, James, Mrs. Swan, and Mrs. Waters.

*Sally Moore* was the daughter of Colonel Maurice Moore and Miss Porter, and married General Francis Nash who subsequently died in a battle at Germantown.

The Moore family members were but a part of the notable settlers taming the new lands.  Other notable colonists included:

## Edward Mosely

*Edward Mosely* was reported to have settled near the Cape Fear about 1723.  He is mentioned in colonial records as early as 1707 where he wrote depositions regarding the boundary of the North Carolina and Virginia line. He was a surveyor for the colonies.  He worked with Samuel Swann, who was Mosely's nephew but had no surveying experience.  Together they attempted to survey the line about 1710 - 1728 often arguing with the Virginia surveyors working the same properties.  In the end, some plantations were cut in half and the survey extended from the Dismal Swamps to the Appalachian Mountains.

The Dismal Swamp earned its name from the spongy terrain, with reeds twelve feet high laced with briars.  As Mosely and Swann walked through the swamp, each footprint was instantly filled with water.  Mosely and Swann complained of the tall cypress trees that were blown over and lying across the terrain.  Sharp snags grew out of them forming treacherous walking.  Overall over 245 miles of chain line was laid forming the boundary in 1828.

Note:  "The Great Dismal Swamp is a marshy area on the Coastal Plain of southeastern Virginia and northeastern North Carolina between Norfolk, Virginia, and Elizabeth City, North Carolina in the United States. It is located in parts of southern Chesapeake and Suffolk in Virginia, as well as northern Gates, Pasquotank, and Camden Counties in North Carolina." (Wikipedia.)

## Benjamin Smith  (1756 - 1826)

Benjamin Smith was born on the 10th of January 1756 in Brunswick County and died in January 1826 in Smithville, the center of Brunswick County, which was named after him.  His burial place is debatable.  Some think he was buried in Southport, but the exact location is in doubt. He was the 13th Governor of North Carolina, from 1810 - 1811.

Governor Smith was very wealthy and owned large tracts on the Cape Fear River. He actually donated 20,000 acres of land to a university in 1789 showing his support for education. He was described as "*sudden and quick in a quarrel*" and was involved in more than one duel. In one of those duels he received a ball (bullet) in the hip that remained with him throughout his life. That was courtesy of a man by the name of Leonard. *(There is a Leonard Family Cemetery located one block off Main Street in Shallotte, N. C.)*

Benjamin Smith was elected to the State Senate fifteen times. He was elected Governor in 1810. He owned the *Belvedere Plantation*, the *Blue Banks Plantation*, the *Orton Plantation*, and also a three-story brick building in Wilmington, on Dock Street, which he used as a town house.

He was penniless when he died. According to the newspaper, the *Observer*, in Raleigh, he was buried the same night he died, under cover of darkness to avoid having a debt levied on him and forcing his friends to pay it before burial was allowed by the sheriff.

A memorial stone rests at St. Philips Church in Brunswick Town. "To the Memory of......"

## *Cornelius Harnett* (20 April 1723 – April 28, 1781)

Harnett was a merchant in Dublin who settled in the Cape Fear area. He married Mary Holt, daughter of Martin Holt. He had one son who married Mary Grainger, Jr. but they had no children.

He first became involved in politics in 1750 and was elected a Wilmington town commissioner. He was also appointed the first Sheriff of New Hanover County (1739-1741). He also served as the Justice of the Peace for New Hanover County and later represented Wilmington in the NC General Assembly in 1754. In 1765 he became the Chairman of the Sons of Liberty and led in the resistance to the Stamp Act. He served in the Continental Congress from 1777-1779.

The British captured him in January of 1781. He died shortly after being released from prison in April 1781, and is buried in the St. James Church cemetery in Wilmington.

## Daniel Lindsay Russell    (1845 -1908)

Daniel Russell, a Brunswick County native, served North Carolina as Governor from 1897-1901. Daniel Lindsay Russell was born on the Winnabow Plantation on August 7, 1845 and died May 14, 1908. That home was located on Governor's Road in Winnabow. There is a historical marker on Highway 17 at the intersection of state road 1521. He was buried in Hickory Hill in Onslow County, NC.

His mother, Carolina Sanders Russell, died soon after her son was born leaving him to be nursed and cared for by a black woman, one of twenty-five slaves she had received with her dowry. He spent some time with his grandfather in Onslow County and was sent to the Bingham Academy at twelve years of age. *"Some family records indicated that he did not enjoy having a warm lunch brought to him by a slave since his classmates did not have the same."* (Brunswick County Historical Society Newsletter, May 1985.)

His father, D. L. Russell, owned about 25,000 acres and ran a turpentine plantation in 1855. It grossed over $25,000 per year with a work force of 150 persons. He also had 1,000 acres cultivated in corn, cotton, and other food crops.

Russell was first elected to the Legislature in 1864 from Brunswick County and re-elected in 1865. He was a superior court judge for six years from 1868 till 1873. He beat Alfred M. Waddell for the 46th Congress as a Republican.

Russell was indeed deemed a "maverick." As a congressman he embraced the cause of currency reform and the regulation of corporate enterprise. As a superior court judge in 1873, he ruled that in the Wilmington Opera House case that blacks could not be denied accommodations on account of their race. He stressed equality under the law for all men.

Russell was sensitive about personal honor and the obligations that accompanied his privileged position in society. However, he had an unruly temper and that created an image of arrogance. Louis Goodman, his law partner, characterized him as a *"smart man who could not tolerate the unsound reasoning of those less intelligent than he."* He was known to be very gentle with children, though he had none of his own. He weighed nearly 300 pounds, wore a wide-brimmed hat and carried a walking cane.

After completing his political career as Governor, he returned to his home in Brunswick County. His plantation had no white neighbors nearer than one family located a half-mile to the south. On the west, along River Road, which ran on the backside of his plantation, was a settlement of negroes who furnished labor for the

Belleville Plantation. On his plantation, there were no negroes except "Aunt Lou" who took care of the chickens and fed the boys who did the milking. Mrs. Russell had accumulated 75 cows by 1908.

Daniel Russell's eyes were described by his eleven-year-old niece as *"beautiful strong and clear blue."* In the last year of *his* life he coached her in mathematics. He died that May in 1908 about three o'clock in the afternoon. He had never given up on the possibilities of making human life better.

Many other names such as Thomas Allen, Archibald McLaine, William Lord, Thomas Leonard, William R. Hall, Parker Quince, John Rowan, Colonel Waddel, and William Gause (originally from Arkansas) deserve recognition in accounts of early southeastern North Carolina history. Their lives certainly shaped the development of our coast and the state and some of their Last Will and Testaments are included in the appendix of this book.

The colonists weathered the storms, the Indians, and toiled the land; some with slaves and some without, clearing land to establish settlements in southeastern North and South Carolina. Some, like John Porter, appeared on the Corn Lists in Beaufort and Hyde Precincts as early as 1715.

## A Corn List
## For Beaufort and Hyde Precincts 1715

In 1712 the government of North Carolina imposed a levy of corn, wheat and money on every tithable in the colony to provide money and provisions for a small army of Yamassee Indians from South Carolina. This effort was implemented to protect the settlers. It was in response to the early morning massacre on September 22, 1711 in the region of North Carolina. Eastern *1679-1754.*

Below is a portion of a corn list of 1715 found in the *Colonial Court Records; Box 190; 1715-1716"; Taxes & Accounts,*

| | | | |
|---|---|---|---|
| John Adams | M'r Drinkwater | James Shingleton | Tho's Worsley |
| Rich'd Albeen | John Foreman | Giles Shute | |
| Robert Aldershire | Cull Flynn | William Sidley | |
| Rob't Banks | Simon Foscu | Gilford Silverthorne | |
| Cor Bell | Col Gale  Fra. Gerganeos | Benja Slade | |
| Tho's Blount | Thomas Gidians | Henry Slade | |
| Ro't Borr | James Hall | John Slade | |
| James Bright | Joseph Hall | Sam Slade | |
| John Bright | Abra | Charles Smith | |
| Edw'd Carter | Porter Price | Henry Smith | |
| Coll Cary | Peter Prichard | Oliver Smith | |
| Tho's Cealy | Phillip Prichard | Rob't Spring | |
| John Chester | Tho's Proctor | Wid Tice | |
| John Clark | Pundant | Tho's Tooly | |
| Coll'o Cleeves | Mr. Reading | John Trip | |
| Dan'l Cocks | Ben Sanderson | James Welsh | |
| Jos Cook | Joseph Shackleton | Abraham Wilkinson | |

*Africans of the Slave Bark Wildfire. Brought into Key West on April 18__. Library of Congress.*

# Chapter Three

# *The Plantations*

The plantations of the Cape Fear encompassed the most beautiful lands along a rich river. Likewise adjoining lands in Brunswick County, Bladen County and Pender County became the home places of many European settlers. Many of these plantations are listed in the Last Will and Testaments contained in the appendix of this book.

The height of plantation life was from 1730 to about 1812. By the mid to late 1800s many of the grandest colonial homes were already disappearing. The rice plantations were malarial and the owners preferred to stay "in town." The deserted houses soon came into disrepair and this new way of life began to diminish from the original fashion.

In a few cases, more detailed information is known about the larger and more grandiose plantation; in other cases, little, except perhaps an owner or two, is known as they passed from one planter to the next. Last Wills and Testaments and land deeds do allow us to track some of them.

The reader must keep in mind that any amount of land "could" be referred to as a plantation. A plantation was only a tract of land used for planting. However, this author has attempted to list any tract of land referred to as a plantation in a Will or deed and indicated the amount of acres, if known. (This list is intended to be comprehensive, albeit, not all inclusive one of "all tracts" in the colonial records.) In addition, as deeds are reviewed and Last Will and Testaments surveyed, it becomes readily apparent that the same tract of land would change names with a new owner. This is noted in the plantation list which follows some of the known maps identifying locations of the plantations.

*R. V. Asbury drew the following map in 1961 showing the old plantations in the Lower Cape Fear area.*

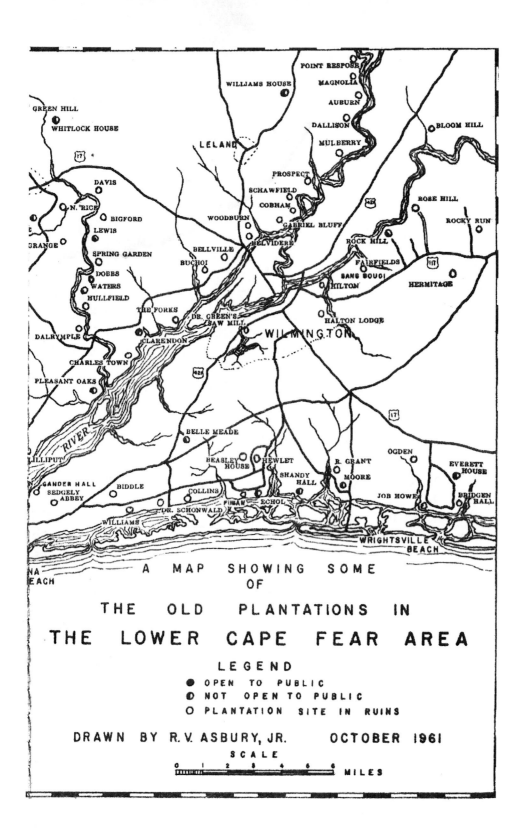

A MAP SHOWING SOME
OF

THE OLD PLANTATIONS IN
THE LOWER CAPE FEAR AREA

LEGEND

● OPEN TO PUBLIC
◑ NOT OPEN TO PUBLIC
○ PLANTATION SITE IN RUINS

DRAWN BY R. V. ASBURY, JR.     OCTOBER 1961

SCALE

0  1  2  3  4  5  6     MILES

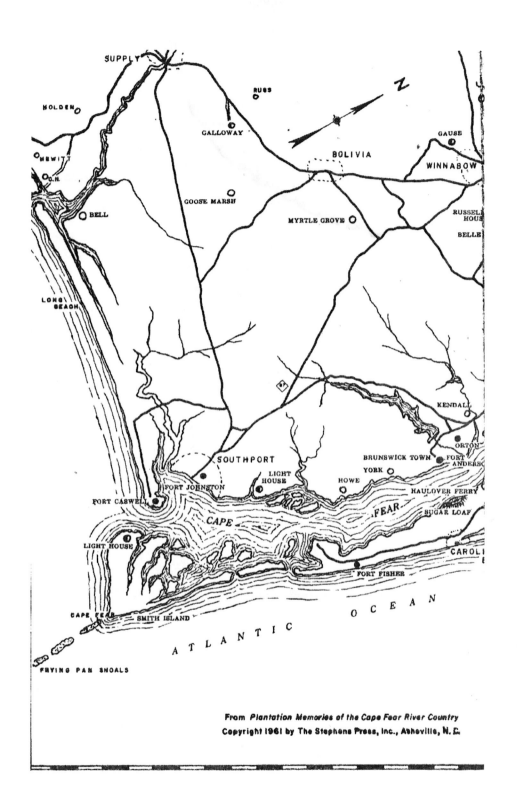

From *Plantation Memories of the Cape Fear River Country*
Copyright 1961 by The Stephens Press, Inc., Asheville, N. C.

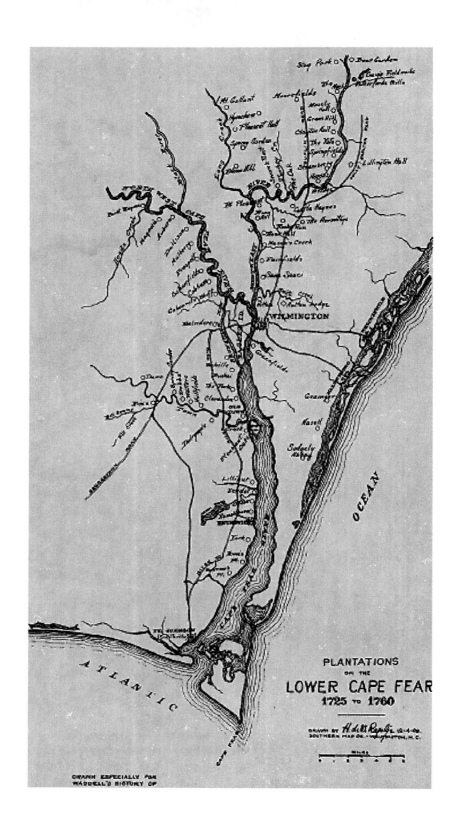

PLANTATIONS
on the
LOWER CAPE FEAR
1725 to 1760

DRAWN BY *H. McB. Ropp*
SOUTHERN MAP CO. · WILMINGTON, N.C.

DRAWN ESPECIALLY FOR
WADDELL'S HISTORY OF

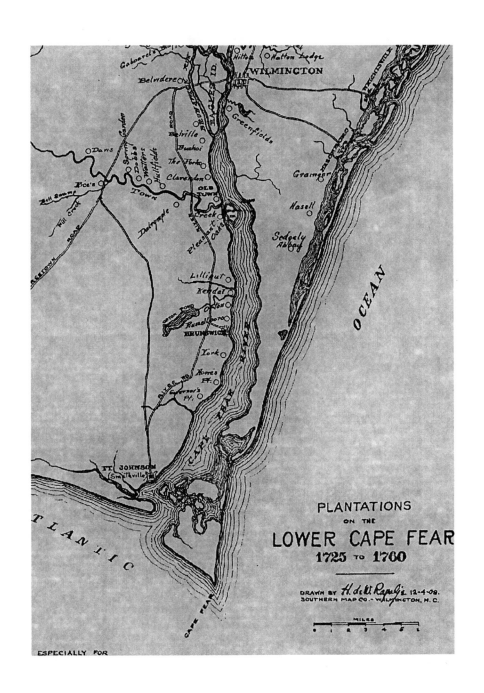

PLANTATIONS
ON THE
LOWER CAPE FEAR
1725 TO 1760

DRAWN BY *H. deR. Raper Jr.* 12-4-08.
SOUTHERN MAP CO. - WILMINGTON, N.C.

ESPECIALLY FOR

45

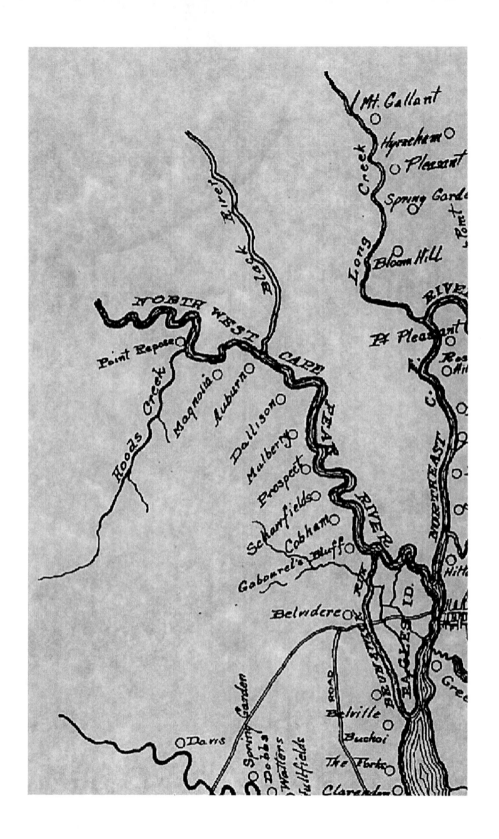

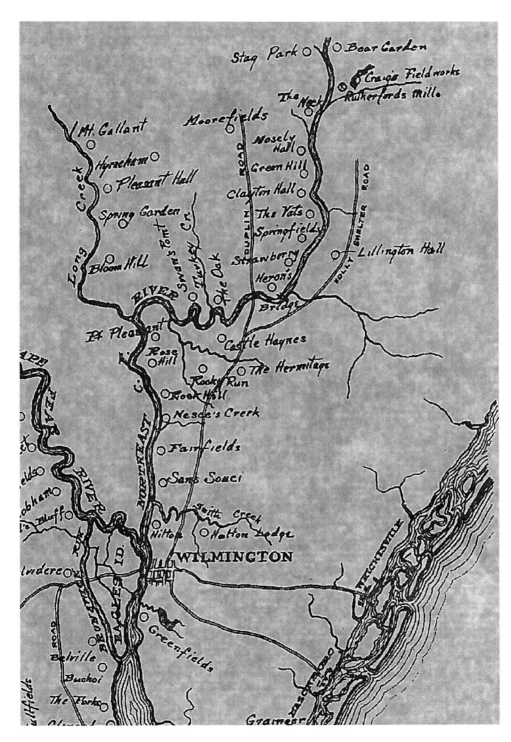

*Northwest Cape Fear River Plantations*

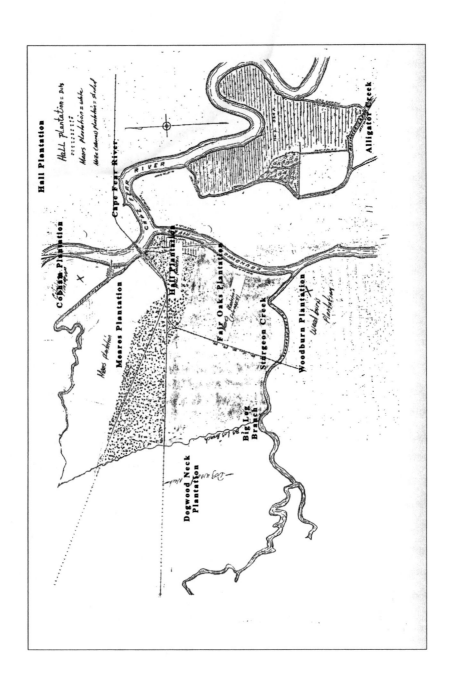

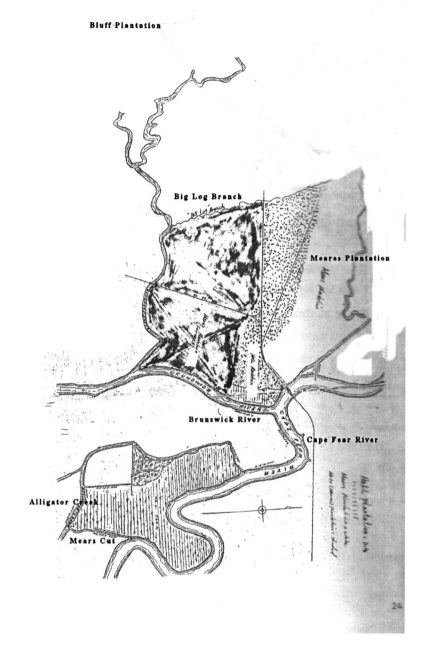

Bluff Plantation

Big Log Branch

Meares Plantation

Brunswick River

Cape Fear River

Alligator Creek

Mears Cut

49

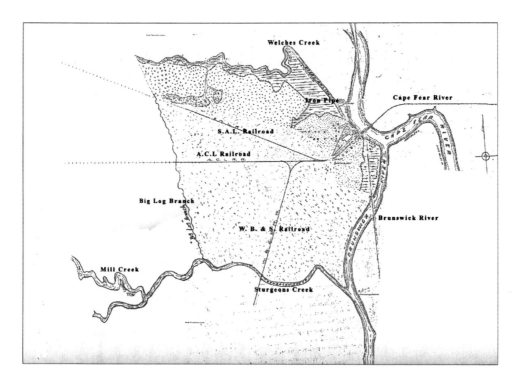

The following plantations are those known to be in the Brunswick, New Hanover, Pender, Columbus, Bladen, and southeastern coastal North Carolina areas:

***Ashe Plantation:*** The Ashe family owned several plantations also called by other names. See complete listing of plantations.

***Aspern Plantation:*** (Asperne) was owned by Col. Maurice Moore. By 1860 it was owned by T. McIhenny and valued at $83,600.

***Auburn Plantation:*** was owned by the Watters family. A news release on August 20, 1833 announced that Samuel Paxson Watters, one year old, died on that date. He was removed from the *Auburn Plantation*, Brunswick County, NC, on December 3, 1859 to the Oakdale Cemetery in Wilmington and placed in the lot owned by Mrs. Mary E. Watters. Another announcement said, "Dr. John William Watters, 32 years old, died on April 14, 1836 at Lillington Hall in New Hanover County, NC. He was buried at *Auburn Plantation*, Brunswick County, NC. He was removed from this location on December 3, 1859 and buried at the Oakdale Cemetery in Wilmington in a lot owned by Mrs. Mary E. Watters."

***Baldwin Plantation:*** was located near Whiteville, in Columbus County. James Baldwin owned it.

**Barn Plantation:** was noted in the *Wilmington Gazette*, on April 4, 1799 as for sale and belonging to the late Henry Toomer. It contained rice fields, range for stock and 40-50 negroes.

**Beau Hill Plantation:** James and Ann Rutherford first owned the *Beau Hill*. They were brother and sister of John Rutherford, in 1750. Another brother, Thomas Rutherford, lived on a plantation in Cumberland County called *Tweeside Plantation*. John Rutherford lived on his *Bowland Plantation* in New Hanover County.

James was a merchant in Wilmington in 1743 and 1749. In 1754 John Rutherford sold James Rutherford 640 acres in Cumberland County.

**Bell Plantation:** was located on the east side of the Lockwood Folly River south of Supply.

**Belle Meade Plantation:** was located on Turkey Creek and owned by William Davis, Esq.. (1809)

*Bellmead Plantation House*

**Bellmead Plantation:**

The main home was built in 1826 according to the *Wilmington News*, March 25, 1953. "It was a one and a half-story home built of hand-hewed cedar and was located five miles out of Wilmington on Carolina Beach Road, about 1/2 mile from the highway. To the left of the front door are three visible bullet holes, which are said to have been put there by Union soldiers during the War Between the

States when they raided the plantation." The weatherboarding was made from hand-hewn cypress collected from nearby swamps.

***Belfont Plantation: (Bellfont) (Bellefont, Belle Fonte)***
Gen. Hugh Waddell and his wife, Mary Haynes, owned several plantations; Belfont was one of them. Gen. Waddell is buried on land in Castle Haynes on the Northeast River. Bellfont was located in Bladen County.

*Hugh Waddell*

***Belgrange Plantation:*** was located on Old Town Creek and contained 2,500 acres. It was owned by Chief Justice Hasell and subsequently conveyed to James Murray in a marriage settlement between Hasell's son, James Hasell Jr., and Sarah Wright on the 20th of February 1750.

***Bellefont Plantation:*** was offered for sale in 1788 and was located on both sides of the Northwest joining and below *Blue Banks*. It contained about 3,000 acres. On the premises was a brick house containing four rooms, a kitchen, barn, and other necessary outbuildings. *(See also Bellfont, Belfont)*

*James Murray*

***Belvedere Plantation:*** Col. William Dry owned this estate and later sold it to Governor Benjamin Smith, his son-in-law. It was located on the west side of the river (on what is now the Brunswick River but in earlier times was called the Northwest Branch of the Cape Fear River). He operated it as a rice plantation.

In 1796 (April 26th), President George Washington had breakfast at *Belvedere* with Benjamin Smith. (Other accounts state it was 1791.) Thirteen young ladies, representing the thirteen colonies, greeted Washington and escorted him down a flower-strewn path to the main residence. Smith had served as an aide-de-camp to General Washington during the retreat from Long Island after the defeat of the American Army in August of 1776.

However, by 1812, Benjamin Smith, prior to his death, mortgaged his *Belvidere Plantation* along with a few other properties to William B. Meares and John R. London, trustees, for $26,000. On June 21, 1816, the Bank of Cape Fear sold Smith's mortgaged holdings to John F. Burgwin for $19,653.

Burgwin probably never lived on the plantation but began selling off 100-acre lots by 1818. Lot No. 4 was sold to John Swann Jr. for $5,000. He kept this lot until his death, 38 years later in 1856. He had married Frances M. Waddell, daughter of Hugh Waddell. He had renamed the place, *Woodburn Lands*. After Swann's death, the property was sold to William E. Boudinot in April of 1857. Boudinot held the land for thirteen years and eventually lost the property through legal maneuvers (payment of taxes or mortgage debt?) It was sold on the courthouse steps and bought by William B. Giles in 1870. Giles maintained ownership of these lands for three years and divided the parcel into two sections...the *Sturgeon Creek* and *Woodburn* areas. He eventually sold both tracts to John MacRae, Senior who paid $6,000 for them in 1873. In 1876 he sold 640 acres to James Dickson McCrae for $1200. The land was then called *Dogwood Neck*. McCrae died in the early 1890s and his family moved to Georgia. Godfrey Hart then purchased this land in an auction in 1896 for $1,000. (*Eulis Willis, in his Navassa, The Town and Its People, outlines the deed transactions and references.*)

In 1831 a for sale notice in the *Cape Fear Recorder* of Wilmington describes the plantation as being located on the *Stage Road* leading from Wilmington to Fayetteville and the road leading to Georgetown, S. C. It further describes the property as having at least "*200 acres of tide swamp, 160 acres of which are banked and ditched and now under cultivation. In fertility, I don't know that it is superior to other lands in the neighborhood but in every other respect it combines more advantages than any other rice plantation in this state. In the first place, it is situated precisely in that pitch of the tide which exempts it from the effects of the salt water and freshes, and it is also protected by woodlands adjoining, that may (sic) losses by storms have been very inconsiderable which renders a crop certain, let what will happen.*"

William Dry was called "the collector" and was the 4th descendent of Robert Dry or Drye, who originally settled South Carolina about 1680; his grandfather and father were all called William. He first married Elizabeth, daughter of Benjamin Blake. He also owned the *Oak Grove Plantation* down in Charleston, S. C. William Dry II was one of the original landowners in Beaufort Town in North Carolina. He had a second plantation two miles above Goose Creek Bridge where he lived with his son, William the III (The Collector) who was born in 1720. He offered both plantations for sale in 1734 in the *South Carolina Gazette*, July 28th, 1733 and again in 1734 and '35. He finally left the colony with his family soon after August 1735. He had married Rebecca, sister of Roger, Maurice, and Nathaniel Moore, and it was undoubtedly through his interest in their Cape Fear project that he joined them in the enterprise.

Either before his arrival or immediately after, he bought lots in Brunswick and lived there as a merchant, Justice of the Peace, and Captain of Militia until his death, which occurred in 1746 or 1747. His wife survived him about ten years.

*"The son, William Dry, the third, was fifteen years old when he went with his father to the Cape Fear. He first became prominent in September 1748, when, at the age of twenty-eight, as Captain of the Militia, he led the attack (aided by men from Wilmington) on an invading force from two Spanish privateers, which had landed*

*and obtained possession of (?) in Brunswick. He became a colonel in 1754, was appointed collector in 1761, was named one of the charter aldermen of Wilmington in 1760, served in the Assembly from 1760 to 1762, became a member of the council in 1764, and continued in the latter capacity under Dobbs, Tryon, and Martin. (In) July 1775 Governor Martin suspended him on the ground of being disloyal to the crown. He took the side of the Revolution, though he was never particularly active in its behalf; and when the new constitution was adopted, accepted a seat on the Revolutionary Council."* (*Lady of Quality.*)

In February 1746, Dry married Mary Jane Rhett, granddaughter (through her father) of William Rhett and (through her mother) of Nicholas Trott of South Carolina, and (as the marriage notice states) *"a lady of great fortune and merit"* (*South Carolina Gazette, February 24, 1746*). He had a large plantation, *"Belleville,"* on the north side of the road leading from Wilmington across Eagles Island southward, and at his death left this plantation to his daughter, Sarah, *"one of the finest characters in the country,"* who married Benjamin Smith, later Governor of the State and the founder of Smithville (now Southport), who was of the Landgrave Thomas Smith family of South Carolina. He died in 1781, aged sixty-one, and was buried in St. Philip's churchyard. His wife survived him until 1795, when she died at the age of sixty-six. She must have been married at seventeen.

It was at Dry's residence in Brunswick that Josiah Quincy dined in 1773, and enjoyed it so much that he called it *"the house of universal hospitality"* (*Journal*, p. 459).

William Watts Jones continues his description of the *Belvedere Plantation* with: *"Last though not least, it is intersected by creeks in such a manner that it can be harvested in one-third less time than it would otherwise require. There are about nine hundred (900) acres of pineland which is poor and will remain so forever, except some fifty (50) or sixty (60) acres perhaps which has a clay foundation, the rest would require manure every year and with such lands I never meddle."*

He went on to say that, *"on the premises are a comfortable and convenient two-story dwelling house and a building one and half story with kitchen."*

*"It is well-watered, having many good springs; and a well of as good and as cold water as can be found in the lower part of the country. Improvement - On the premises are a comfortable and convenient two-story dwelling house and a building one and one half story with kitchen, washhouse, stable, carriage house, smokehouse, etc. A barn, 110 feet long, 40 feet wide, two story's high contained a threshing machine and other machinery. Also overseer's houses and kitchen, all of which buildings are of brick, put up in the most substantial manner. There is another barn built of wood directly at the river from whence the rice can be conveniently thrown into a flat or vessel and any vessel that can come over the bar can come to the barn."*

*"I have endeavored to render as permanent as possible all the repairs and improvements. I think it is upon the whole the handsomest and most pleasant residence in this part of the country."*

*"The improvements were made with the expectation that it would be my chief residence all my life, but the state of my health requires that I should reside more permanently in a high and dry part of the country."* Later Mr. John Waddell is reported to have lived on this estate.

*Belvedere Plantation House Road*

*Belvedere Plantation House*

The Evans family owned it in 1947. In 1958 only one brick building remained which was a one-story with a basement and a wooden addition to the rear. It is believed to have been the overseer's house.

At that time there were three enormous oak trees believed to be over 200 years old in the area amidst over 2000 old ballast stones.

Several interesting news articles have been preserved which provide us with a view of the *Belvidere Plantation* over the years. These are quoted precisely as documented by Gwen Causey, local historian.

*4-17-1874   We visited the noted truck farm, Belvidere, owned by Messrs. Willard Brothers, and located on Brunswick River. Here we saw 20 acres in English peas, 6 acres in cucumbers, a field of 30,000 cabbage plants, and other vegetables in almost endless profusion. We also saw here what may be done with our rice lands by a thorough system of drainage. About 10 acres of the Belvidere tract, immediately on the Brunswick River, were formerly cultivated in rice; but that crop has long since been abandoned, and by the aid of a pump, worked by a wind-mill, the land is kept sufficiently dry, even during the heaviest freshets in the river (when the natural drainage is entirely stopped), to produce the finest cabbage, oats, corn, and in fact every crop that has yet been tried. The soil is as loamy and friable as that of a well-cultivated garden, and presents an incontrovertible argument in favor of the dry-salure system.* Wilmington Weekly Star.*

*1-9-1880   At the Belvidere Plantation, on Monday night, 3 or 4 miles from Wilmington, Robert and George Everett, both colored, and half-brothers, got into a probable fatal cutting affray about some meal belonging to George, who accused Bob of appropriating it to his own use. The wounded man was loaded into a boat and brought to Wilmington. Dr. W. W. Lane examined the injuries and thought them to be very serious. He was taken to his home. It is very unfortunate that Wilmington has no hospital to which such cases as the above can be taken.* Wilmington Star.*

*5-25-1889   We have seen fine cabbage growing on the rice field of the old Belvidere Plantation, in Brunswick County, now owned by Mr. J. D. McRae. By means of a pump operated by a windmill, the field was kept sufficiently dry, and the soil was as mellow and friable as that of a highly cultivated garden.* Wilmington Star.*

*4-28-1893   J. Dickson McRae, of Brunswick County, who has heretofore cultivated rice quite extensively every year, has not planted any this year, has not planted any this season, and will give his whole attention to other, and he thinks, more profitable crops. He will keep his rice fields "flowed" until next fall, in order to kill out the grass, when he expects to experiment with oats on these lands. Mr. McRae has no doubt acted wisely. Mr. McRae is devoting his upland field to corn, peas, strawberries, and other crops; and just here it may be noted that some years ago when his farm was known as Belvidere, fine cabbages were made on some of the rice lands on the west side of the Brunswick River, the soil being kept free from excess of moisture by means of a pump operated by a windmill.* Wilmington Weekly Star.*

*2-7-1902   On Sunday morning last, at the home of the bride's father on Town Creek, Miss Nancy Walker was married to Mr. Eugene V. Evans, Rev. T. J. Browning performing the rite. The bride is the daughter of Sheriff Daniel R. Walker.*

*Mr. Evans is the successful merchant, now at Belvidere, two miles from Wilmington.* Wilmington Star.

_____ *The Belvidere Heights Development of beautiful homes is located on the old Belvidere Plantation, once the home of Benjamin Smith. Blake.*

**Belville Plantation: (Belleville)** Mr. John Wadell owned this and three other plantations further up the river. The Town of Belville, which borders the Brunswick River, is home to Brunswick River Park. The site was once part of the 280-acre *Belville Plantation*, and was also owned by the family of Daniel Lindsay Russell, who served as Governor of North Carolina from 1897 – 1901.

The plantation stretched along the Brunswick River for a mile, with rice fields bordering it on the east and wooded tracts running along the road to the west, with the cultivated fields in the middle. There was additional land belonging to this plantation located on Eagle Island on the other side of the river.

The dairy and the lot were located toward the southern end of the plantation. There were at least two houses, long since destroyed. There was also a plantation racetrack on this estate. The home was about two hundred yards from the lot in an open field to minimize the danger of mosquitoes. For safety it was built on a one-story high brick column. The space underneath the columns became a grandchildren's playground.

*Belville Plantation House in 1896*

Underneath, towards the center of the house was a furnace pumping hot air in the winter. The house faced east and was built as a rectangle to allow access to the summer breezes with the prevailing southwest winds.

The front had a narrow porch running the width of the house, with a view of the river. Upon entering the house you were in the reception room with a study on the left. Russell would sit in this study in a large leather upholstered rocker in front of the fireplace, which had a painting of his grandfather above it. In the corner was his father's desk and a Windsor-type chair made on the *Winnabow Plantation*. Three broad bookcases reached from the ceiling to the floor holding the family books. The dining room could easily seat 20 guests. Near it was a large bedroom and bath.

The *Belville Plantation* was a valuable rice plantation on the Cape Fear. The name has been spelled in a variety of ways including Belville or Belleville. It was located about 6.5 miles from Wilmington and contained about 200 acres of land.

Benjamin Smith sold 160 acres of this site to Archibald McAlester of Belville, which adjoined his *Belville Plantation*. (McAlester fought in the American Revolution in Charleston, S. C. After moving to North Carolina, he married Mary Moore, widow of Roger Moore, grandson of the first Roger Moore.)

By the 17th of October 1793 McAlester had died and left his plantation with all of its *slaves* to his wife, Mary. At her death it was to pass to his brothers and sisters, namely John McAlester (wife Elizabeth); Henry Bush (wife Eliza); Alex King (wife Sarah); and Nancy McAlester.

Mary McAlester died on the plantation on the 17th of October 1807 and it was then sold for $9,000 to John Waddell. Mr. Waddell owned this and three other plantations further up the river. There were reportedly *70 slaves* working for Mr. John Waddell around 1790.

According to the *Wilmington Chronicle* in November 20, 1844, this property *"will be sold at auction in Wilmington on the first day of January next, that well-known rice plantation, "Belleville" situated on the west branch of the Cape Fear River, nearly opposite the town of Wilmington." "The high land settlement is a most advantageous one, fronting one mile on the river." "Upon the premises is an excellent dwelling house, containing eight rooms, as also all necessary outbuildings, a large barn, winnowing house, etc."*

The land was described in 1846 as *"prime rice land as is to be found in the states of North or South Carolina or Georgia, and at the very best pitch of the tide."*

*"The uplands consist of between 300 and 400 acres of most excellent Provision Lands, yielding abundant crops; the entire tract contains ___ acres, more or less. The improvements consist of a commodious dwelling house, kitchens, barns, stables, negro houses, sufficient for a large gang of negroes, and a rice thresher."* Belleville Plantation was listed for sale on the 21st of December 1846 in the *Wilmington Commercial*.

The site was once part of the 280-acre *Belville Plantation* that was also owned by the family of Daniel Lindsay Russell, who served as Governor of North Carolina. In November of 1900 a news story announced that Governor Russell's new dwelling is rapidly nearing completion. Painters and tinners are at work on it this week. The dwelling should be complete in three weeks in all its appointments, heated by furnaces and equipped with a *full set of water works*. The rooms are to be furnished in hard wood, a different variety to each. The total cost was $6,000 to $8,000.

By January of 1901, Governor D. L. Russell was living in his new country home where he drove his buggy to and from his law office. An interesting note: In July of 1897, Mr. W. R. Boyd, the superintendent of Governor Russell's rice plantation, "*drowned out*" an army of worms that attacked the rice fields on Eagles' Island (which was leased by Governor Russell.) The worms had stripped a whole section of the rice field and done considerable damage there and to the Butters-Russell rice fields lower down on the island. This field had been leased out to a group of colored farmers known as "the syndicate."

**Benevento Plantation:** was offered for sale in the *Wilmington Gazette* on the 27th of April 1815 in a public auction. It was to be put up for sale on the 2nd of May by Benjamin Smith, Esq. It was located on Malary Creek and the Cape Fear River in Brunswick County and was the property of the late James Read who lived there prior to his death. It included a sawmill, gristmill, and 850 acres located eastward of the Cape Fear River. Several more tracts of land adjoining this plot were also offered for sale adding another 1100 acres.

*Benevento* and *Kendall Plantations* were sold on the 15th of May 1815 on the Court House steps with a deed from Benjamin Smith to James Smith who had originally bought this land in March of 1807.

**Bernard's Creek Plantation:** In the Last Will and Testament of Catherine Young, she left her son, Henry Young, a "*tract of land in dispute between my son, Henry, and Colonel Alfred Moore.*" This was in June of 1794. She was the widow of Henry Young and the daughter of Joshua Grainger.

By October 1785 a guardian was appointed for the children, her son, Henry, and daughter Catherine. The tract was *Bernard's Creek Plantation*, on the east side of the Cape Fear River about five miles below Wilmington. The father, Henry had paid 1500 pounds for this land. The original patent was to Moore on the 29th of January 1729 and stated the land was 1500 acres on Barnard's Creek.

By 1736 Richard Evans had 300 acres on Barnett's Creek in the New Hanover Precinct. Col. Maurice Moore disputed this in 1737 with his version of the ownership patents. To complicate matters, in April of 1736, Richard Evans (a tailor) sold 320 acres to John Montgomery of Chowan Precinct....land on the head of Barnett's Creek in New Hanover. (Whew...confuses me!!)

On the 8th of June 1794, Catherine Young listed *Bernard's Creek Plantation* in her Last Will and Testament.

In 1802 Henry Young sold *Bernard's Creek* to James W. Walker, of Wilmington, for 500 dollars. By 1820 Henry Young had moved to Brunswick County with his wife, Eliza.

By 1806 it belonged to the family of General Joseph Gardner Swift and contained 4,000 acres. It was located about four miles from Wilmington on the Cape

Fear River. Later in 1806 newspaper notations indicated that Mr. James Walker had to move away from the *Bernard's Creek Plantation* because of ill health and returned to the Fort (?). By the 8th of September he recovered and was able to return to Wilmington. (Probably Fort Johnston?)

Bernard's Creek Plantation was a rice mill. In 1847 John S. Fyler, Esq., posted the following advertisement in the Wilmington Chronicle (6 July 1847): *"Bernard's Creek is now prepared to receive rice on Toll, at the usual terms."*

**Bevis Land:** Rev. Christopher Bevis owned this estate and was one of the early ministers of St. Philip's Church at Brunswick Town. About 1750 it was located two or three miles below Wilmington on the east side of the river.

By 1771 Dr. Samuel Green left a tract of land known as *Bevis Land* to his son, John Green. It was located just south of *Trapland Plantation*.

**Biddle Plantation:** No additional information is available.

**Bigford Plantation:** No additional information is available.

**Blue Banks Plantation:** or the Roger Moore Plantation as it was called, was located beyond the *Captain Gabriel Plantation* on the Black River. He bought 640 acres from John Marshall, of Bath County, on the 10th of April 1733. Prior to that time it belonged to Seth Pilkington (March 1728) who originally named it *"Bleu Banks."* It was located on the Northwest River of the Cape Fear.

On the 19th of July 1746 Roger Moore (now at *Orton Plantation*) gave this and eight other tracts of land to his son, George Moore. It contained 640 acres and was called *"Blue Banks."* On April 7, 1784, William Watters sold Benjamin Smith about 210 acres of *Blue Banks*. Smith later sold 43 acres to Drury Allen on the 1st of July 1784. The deed identified it as part of a track originally granted to Joseph Watters on 5 November 1729. Part of the share of William Watters, grandson of Joseph Watters, included his part of the 320 acres that was given to them previously.

*Blue Banks* was again offered for sale in 1788 and described as situated on both sides of the river, below Smithfield, and containing 2,331 acres.

Another reference stated that the *Blue Banks Plantation* was owned by A. A. Wannett (Wanet) in 1860 and that he had 2,000 acres and *39 slaves*. He did *not* produce rice.

By July 2, 1788, the *Wilmington Centinel* (sic) reported that *Blue Banks* would be sold, *"2,331 acres of land, 410 of which is rich swamp, about 130 acres being cleared of which 80 acres may be watered at any time with great ease."* *"The uncleared swamp contains a vast body of cypress timber, and the high land has two streams fit for grist-mills running through it; between 200 and 300 acres are cleared, part of it being very good corn land. There is a dwelling house, containing a hall, parlour, four chambers and three closets, a kitchen, stable, and large brick barn. The beauty and healthiness of this place is too well known to require further description.*" For further particulars, the reader was to contact Benjamin Smith who resided at the *Belvidere (sic) Plantation.*

The bluff is at least one hundred feet above sea level and has a large meadow on the opposite side of the river. One side of the river is high while the other is subject to flooding. The Moore's reportedly grew *four score* bushels of corn on every acre. In 1734 a traveler made reference to this plantation stating that Mr. Moore is planning to build "*another very large brick house.*"

The *Blue Banks Plantation* became a tree farm and was owned by the Blake brothers, Wesley and Anthony.

**Bluff Plantation:** was located on the Northwest River just above Wilmington about four miles. It was originally called *Gabourel's Bluff* for its owner Captain Joshua Gabourel (1734). He was an English traveler from South Carolina. He described the area in 1734 as: "*we reached the forks where the river divides into two very beautiful branches called the Northeast and Northwest. We proceeded up the Northwest branch and when we got about four miles from thence, we came to a beautiful plantation belonging to Captain Gabriel.*" This was also the location of the ferry from there to Newton (Wilmington).

This land was originally granted to Roger Moore on the 10th of September 1735 and contained 500 acres on the southwest side of the Northwest River called *Welshes Bluff.* In 1737 he sold it to Amice Gabourel, an heir of the now deceased Joshua Gabourel. He bought the 300 acres for 200 pounds of sterling. Amice sold it to Jerome Rowan about 1738 and he owned it for the next 25 years. Jerome Rowan also owned the government mansion/building located at Brunswick Town. He was a temporary Provincial Governor. He died about 1770 without leaving a will. He had four daughters. The courts awarded *Rowan's Bluff Lands* to his daughter Elizabeth. She was married to Archibald Maclaine who died around 1792. He left this property to his daughter, Catherine. This is the site that eventually became the home of the Navassa Guana Company.

It was also called *Maclaine's Bluff.* Maclaine is buried there. He was described as having a "*sanguine temperament and irritable passion,*" according to *McRee's Iredell*, Vol. I, p. 370.

Catherine married George Hooper who was a Loyalist. They eventually gave this land to their two children, Mary Hooper Flemming and Archibald Maclaine Hooper in 1797. In 1806 Archibald Hooper married Charlotte Deberniere and had six children.

In 1822 Archibald and Mary contracted with William B. Meares, a Wilmington lawyer, to divide the lands. Meares ended up buying one of these tracts owned by Archibald (about half of the plantation.) This was the beginning of the *Meares*

*Plantation*, which later became *Five Oaks* or *Meares Bluff* and eventually the Guana Company.

Archibald Hooper died in 1853 after losing his fortune through a lifetime of failing business ventures.  T. Meares owned it by 1860 and it was valued at $27,000. (*The Bluffs*.)

**Bowlands Plantation:**  John Rutherford owned this plantation.   He also owned *Stoney Creek* and *Bear Garden Plantation* in addition to land in Bladen and Duplin Counties.   In Stoney Creek and Bear Garden he established mills known as *Rutherford Mills* and later *Ashe's Mills* (1763 - 1781.)   After the Civil War the British used these mills to grind the grain robbed from neighboring fields.

Rutherford lost *Bowlands* to the Murray family for debts due them.  Then he acquired a large estate up the North East River called *Hunthill*.

**Brighton Plantation:**  was located at Carver's Creek, near Elizabethtown, and owned by Gov. Gabriel Johnston according to a Will Abstract dated 1790.

**Brompton Plantation:**  was owned by Governor Gabriel Johnston.  His brother, Gilbert, also lived there.   It was located in Bladen County near the river.

**Brush Hill Plantation:**  was owned by James Moore, son of Brig. General James Moore.  It was located on the east side of Rileys Creek, in the early 1820s, in then New Hanover County and what is now Pender County.

**Buchoi Plantation:**  Judge Alfred Moore, an Associate Justice of the United State Supreme Court, owned this rice plantation.  The name may have come from an old *Moore Plantation* in Goose Creek, South Carolina, called *Boo-Chawee* (an old Indian word).  Both names are pronounced the same.  All of the Moore's of the Cape Fear originally came from Goose Creek, S. C.

The Fayetteville Observer reported on the 31st of March 1825 that the house of Alfred Moore, Esq. was burned to the ground on the night of the 17th.  It was re-built and then offered for sale in the *Wilmington Advertiser* on November 16, 1838 and described as located on the west side of the Brunswick branch of the Cape Fear River, about four miles from Wilmington.  "*It contained two hundred acres of tide swamp, 110 of which have been cultivated--also, forty acres of upland of which has been cleared, and on which is a dwelling house, with necessary outhouses, a large brick barn, and other improvements.*"  Interested persons were asked to respond to W. C. Lord.

By April of 1842, John Brown, Commissioner in Equity, was offering to sell for cash at a public auction at the court house in Smithville, on the 7th day of June, "*that valuable rice plantation, on the Cape Fear River, formerly the property of John*

*Waddell, known by the name of Buchoi Plantation, lately purchased by John L. Hewett from F. N. Waddell and his wife."*

In 1860 Frederick K. Lord and Samuel Frink owned this estate. Lord had purchased it from T. C. McIlhenny on the 17th of May 1858. Lord owned 870 acres, had *53 slaves* and produced 180,000 pounds of rice. Frink, at the same time, owned 3,723 acres, had *53 slaves*, and produced 1,080 pounds of rice.

Lord later sold the estate at an auction on the 25th of July 1874. At that time he also owned some land in Smithville at the intersection of Bay and Garrison Streets, which he offered for sale.

*The Messenger*, in Wilmington, on December 3, 1903, conveyed the message that Mr. Augustus W. Rieger, of Brunswick County, from the *Beauchoix Plantation* had died unexpectedly at his country home. He was married to a Miss Thompson of Southport and had one son and two daughters. He was 54 years old when he died and was buried in Southport.

**Cain Tuck Plantation:** was located in New Hanover County and owned by Fredrick J. Swann who sold it to Robert H. Cowan in November of 1834 for $1800. It contained 97 acres.

**Castle Finn Plantation:** was located between Bradley's and Hewlett's Creek on the sound in New Hanover County.

**Castle Haynes Plantation:** was located on the north side of *The Hermitage* and owned by Capt. Roger Haynes. Haynes married the daughter of Rev. Richard Marsden.

Peter Portevint, of Bath County bought it (1000 acres) on the 22 of October 1728.

**Cedar Grove Plantation:** The DeRosset family owned the *Cedar Grove Plantation.* Dr. Armand DeRosset, his wife and two sons, came from England about 1735. They originally came from France. His oldest son, Louis Henry, was a Justice of the Peace in 1751. As a merchant and planter he accumulated a rather large fortune. In 1779 he was banished from the Province of Carolina "on the threat of death if he returned" (due to supporting the English and Royal Governors.) He died in London in 1786. He had lost it all.

*(Shown: Dr. Armand John De Rossett, II (1807-1897), physician, philanthropist.)*

The younger brother, Moses John DeRosset, became a prominent physician. During the Stamp Act era he was the Mayor of Wilmington. He supported the rights of the colonies against his older brother. He died in 1767.

***Cedar Hill Plantation:*** was formed from part of the *Bluff Plantation* coming from George Hooper who gave part of this estate to his daughter, Mary. Mary married James Flemming who owned the *Cedar Hill Plantation*. James died in 1811 after being thrown from a horse during a horse race. Sometime later Mary moved to Hillsborough in Orange County, NC. In 1826 she deeded this land to her daughter, Mary.

Mary II had married Haynes Waddell, son of John Waddell who owned *Belville Plantation* at the time. The land was then divided into two plantations, one called ***Moze*** which was bought by Armard deRossett, physician and grandfather of the Navassa deRossett who immigrated to Wilmington from France prior to 1735. John deRossett was also a doctor. Moses had a son named Armand John deRossett (1767-1859) who had a son named Armand John deRossett (1807-1897). All were doctors. The deRosset's were some of the largest *slaver owners* in the Cape Fear region. An overseer ran their operations. The deRossett house is still standing in Wilmington as a historical residence.

In 1851, deRosset gave his *Moze lands* to his son, Armand John deRossett along with *23 slaves*. In 1855 the land was sold with *39 slaves* to James Moore for $21,500. This Mr. Moore was born in 1807 and married Sallie Davis. The "Moze" name is thought to have come from "Moore."

In 1870 the plantation was sold for delinquent taxes. Daniel B. Baker was deceased by that date (Jan 1, 1870) and owed $64.50. *(Wilmington Star.)*

***Charles Town Plantation:*** was built by Sir John Yeoman around 1665.

***Chauncy Plantation:*** was located in the Bogue Township of Columbus County.

***Clarendon Plantation***: was located next to Old Town and owned by Mr. Campbell who later sold it to Mr. Joseph Watters. Mr. and Mrs. D. H. Lippett of Wilmington (who sold it in 1945 to the now deceased Mr. Cornelius Thomas) later owned it. It is located between N. C. 133 and the Cape Fear River, south of Mallory Creek and north of Town Creek. It is listed on the NC inventory of State Historical Resources.

Fanny Watters described the western porch of the *Clarendon Plantation* in the following essay: *"From the western porch at Clarendon we stepped into the flower garden that opened into the lane, where we took the carriage when we went to Wilmington by land, which was eight miles. Marsden drove Tom and Jerry. Now and then we went in a row boat by water, which was five miles."*

*"On the east was an upper and lower porch. At one end of the lower porch was a yellow jasmine vine, and at the other end an English honeysuckle the humming*

birds loved. Dr. John Hill was a near neighbor and frequent visitor. He was sitting with us one day and noticed the birds. He asked Mother to give him a teaspoon of brandy or whiskey and a little sugar. He mixed it thoroughly and we went to the upper porch where the railing was covered with the two vines, and put the mixture in the honeysuckle blooms."

"In a short time the humming birds were enjoying their treat and not long after they were too drunk to help themselves. Dr. Hill took one or two in his hand very carefully to let me see the exquisite little things near. They soon got over their treat and flew away unharmed."

The plantation was described in *The People's Press* and *Wilmington Advertiser* in 1834: *"For Sale: The rice plantation on which I reside in Brunswick County five miles below Wilmington called Clarendon. It contains 335 acres of tide swamp, 654 acres upland and 229 acres in a high state of cultivation, averaging 72 bushels of rice per acre. On the premises is a comfortable dwelling house and brick barn with a framed mill house attached and two threshing mills. Negro quarters, capable of containing 100 hands, well built of brick and covered with Dutch pantile. A comfortable house for the overseer and a gristmill with a plentiful supply of water. Also will be sold with this plantation, or separate, 300 acres of land on Masonborough Sound, New Hanover County, and the family summer retreat. The distance is eight miles from Wilmington and about the same distance from the plantation. The home is well planned for comfort and elegance, containing a parlor, and a drawing room, six bedrooms, pantries, cellar, with double piazzas front and rear, 14 feet wide, and is situated in an agreeable neighborhood. The sound is within 100 yards of the house, affords an abundant supply and variety of fish, oysters, and with a beautiful sheet of water for fishing, sailing, and boating. Apply to Marsden Campbell."*

By 1860 it was owned by H. N. Howard and valued at over $10,000. In 1883, the *Wilmington Star* stated *"Two specimens of beautiful machinery could be seen yesterday on Wilmington wharves. They are rotary pumps for draining the Clarendon rice field, about five miles below this city, which is planted by Messrs. Preston Cumming and Company. They seem perfectly adapted to the purpose intended and are so perfectly balanced that a man can turn them with his finger. The water comes out in a 3-inch stream and is thrown off through a pipe."* Later in December of 1884 they reported that, *"A large rice barn of Messrs. Preston Cumming & Co., at the Clarendon Plantation, about four miles below this city, was destroyed by fire yesterday morning, including a quantity of rice and machinery for cleaning the same, etc. The most of the crop had been sold, and much of it delivered. The fire is said to be the work of an incendiary. The building was a substantial and valuable one. The loss was covered by insurance."* Wilmington Weekly Star.

By July 27, 1894 the Star reported that a *"few stalks of rice-the first of the season, from the Clarendon Plantation, were shown in Wilmington."*

*On January 25, 1906, "Mrs. Josephine E. Hardy died at the home of her son, H. B. Hardy, in Raleigh, NC on Tuesday. She was born in Brunswick County and was 76 years old. She was a daughter of the late Joseph Watters, a wealthy rice planter, who owned the Clarendon Rice Plantation near Wilmington. She was married in 1846 to Mr. H. B. Hardy, a brilliant lawyer of Windsor, Bertie County, who died in 1868. Her brother, the late William Watters, of Wilmington, died two years ago. Funeral from the Catholic Church in Raleigh and interment in Jackson, NC beside her late husband."* Wilmington Star.

Several additional articles have appeared through the years that have referenced the Clarendon Plantation.

10-1-1916    *Mr. J. E. Cowell, who for five years has operated two of the most popular barber shops in downtown Wilmington, has disposed of his interests in the business to operate Clarendon farm on the Lower Cape Fear River, which he purchased yesterday.* Wilmington Star.

8-5-1925    *Mr. and Mrs. Devereau H. Lippitt, and son, D. H., Jr., moved today to their estate "Clarendon" on the Cape Fear River, where they will spend the rest of the season. Maxwell Lippitt, of The Hague, Holland, is expected to arrive in the near future for a visit to his parents at Clarendon.* Wilmington News-Dispatch.

10-4-1934    *The entire estate of Devereaux H. Lippitt, who died June 29, is bequeathed to his widow, Mrs. Margaret W. Lippitt, in the will of the late cotton exporter.* Wilmington News.

4-16-1944    *Miss Fanny C. Watters, 89, of Asheville, NC, who was born at Clarendon Plantation, the sister of Miss Nammie E. Watters, 505 S. Third Street, is the author of a little book soon to be released, "Plantation Memories of the Cape Fear River Country". It is a series of very short intimate sketches about people and things that impressed her so deeply in her youth that memories of them are still vivid. Some of the titles are "Ploughing in the Rice Fields", "The Tipsy Hummingbirds", "Bullfrog Hunting", Spanish Moss", "Soap Boiling", and "Feeding the Hounds". Each story is accompanied by a small drawing.* Wilmington Star.

7-19-1944    *Cornelius Thomas had recently purchased the Clarendon Plantation.* State Port Pilot.

8-13-1944    *Mr. and Mrs. Cornelius Thomas, of Clarendon Plantation, and Wilmington, announce the engagement of their only daughter, Wilna Victoria, to Lieut. George Edward Pickett, IV, U. S. Army, son of Mr. and Mrs. George E.*

*Pickett, of Fayetteville and Washington, D. C. Lieut Pickett is the great-grandson of General Pickett of Civil War fame.* Wilmington Star.

3-5-1974     *Flames gutted a 200-year-old historic mansion late Monday night. The destroyed structure was known as the Watter's House and is located on a 1,000 acre plantation on the Cape Fear River. The fire was reported by the plantation owner, Mrs. Cornelius D. Thomas.* Wilmington Star.

*Clarendon* is a private residence today and owned by the Thomas and Pace families. In December of 2008, the owners placed a 400-acre tract of land and a second 325-acre tract under a working forest landowner agreement. The agreements mean that, while the property will remain in private hands, its management will protect natural resources that benefit the public.   A press release by the NC Coastal Land and Trust stated that, *"We've always recognized Clarendon's critical importance to the tapestry of conservation lands on the western banks of the Cape Fear River. These are lands of national significance," said Camilla M. Herlevich, Executive Director of the Coastal Land Trust. "Wildlife needs corridors along rivers to travel as they forage for food—the wider the better. Not only does Clarendon add to the thousands of acres that neighboring private land owners have set aside for wildlife to use, it boasts miles of buffers for water quality, expanses of marsh, and productive forestland, which helps everyone in the community."   "Clarendon is considered to be the "keystone" tract of the Coastal Land Trust's Cape Fear Corridor Conservation Initiative because it is the northernmost of a series of properties in eastern Brunswick County – almost 11,000 acres in total – that have been protected since 1995. That acreage includes a 900-acre tract near Clarendon that will eventually be donated to Brunswick County and operated as a nature preserve open to the public."   "My family has worked toward conserving and protecting our land for at least ten years now. We are thankful that the Coastal Land Trust has had the vision, perseverance and expertise to achieve our mutual goal of being good stewards of the land," said Rachel Pace."*
*"Clarendon's water quality landowner agreement calls for buffering more than 3 miles of water including the lower Cape Fear River and its tributaries Mallory Creek and Little Mallory Creek, which serve as the northern boundary of Clarendon Plantation. The brackish marshes and river are home to native sturgeon and the American alligator, and numerous birds, shellfish and other wildlife. "The conservation of Clarendon Plantation is an important addition to a significant water quality and natural resources conservation effort underway along the lower Cape Fear River and Town Creek," said Richard Rogers, Executive Director of CWMTF.*

*"The working forest landowner agreement is designed to protect Clarendon's forests of longleaf pine and mixed pine hardwoods. The uplands also feature special limesink ponds, which are of great interest to biologists because of their unusual plant life."*

*Clarkmont Plantation:* on March 17, 1830, the Cape Fear Recorder reported that Mrs. Christian Fleming, consort of James Fleming, Esq. had died on the 16th at *"Clarkmont"* in Brunswick County.

*Clay Fields Plantation:* was sold by Bryant Buxton to Moses Ritter in February 1787 for 100 pounds. It was 250 acres on Poplar Swamp near the Widow Moores Creek in New Hanover County.

An interesting note appeared in the True Republican or American Whig (Vol. 1, No. 16) on Tuesday, the 18th of April in 1809. It said, "Notice, my wife, Hannah, has deserted my Bed and Board, without any provocation. I do hereby forward all person whatever, from dealing with her, as I am determined not to pay, or answer any of her contracts, to which I request all persons to take due notice. Nevertheless, if my said wife Hannah will return to me, I will support her as usual, or procure a good house for her reception. Signed, Moses Ritter, April 17, 1809."

*Clayton Hall Plantation:* was owned by Francis Clayton. It passed to Col. Sam Ashe, son of Governor Sam Ashe. He was the grandfather of Capt. S. A. Ashe who wrote a history of North Carolina in 1908.

*Cobham Plantation:* was owned by Dr. Thomas Cobham, a prominent physician in Wilmington. Interestingly, he witnessed the Will of Lieutenant Whitehurst of H. M. S. Viper, who in a duel with Alexander Simpson fought and died from his wounds. Cobham settled in the Cape Fear in 1766 practicing medicine with a partner, Dr. Robert Tucker. Dr. Cobham actually treated the wounded Loyalists in the Battle of Moores Creek.

Cobham and his wife, Catherine Mary Paine (widow of John Paine of Brunswick County) had bought land on Old Town Creek but sold it in 1771 and acquired the *Cobham Plantation* that had 1300 acres and contained two sawmills. He also rented a house in Wilmington (1772) where Josiah Quincy dined in the company of Harnett, Hooper, Burgwin, Dr. Tucker, and others. It was not unusual to have a plantation and another home in town.

Cobham purchased another home in Wilmington about 1775 for 840 pounds (from George Moore). In 1778 he exchanged this house for a plantation of 500 acres in the Wilmington area, probably near *Schawfield*. This plantation was referenced in a deed in 1779 when John Rutherfurd sold it to him. It was located on both sides of the main branch of Long Creek adjoining the lands of Cobham.

Mrs. Cobham died sometime before 1777. She had one daughter, Catherine Jane. Dr. Cobham left his furniture and his daughter, Catherine, in the care of a lady in Wilmington when he went to Charles Town. He made provisions for her in his

Will leaving her 400 acres on the west side of Northwest, next to *Schawfield* on Indian Creek.

Dr. Cobham was still living in 1797.

In 1830 *32 slaves* worked this land. Later in 1860 only *29* remained on this plantation.

At some point later a Mr. June Davis owned it. It was sometimes referred to as "Royster" about the 1830s - 1860s. On November 25, 1846 the Cobham Plantation was offered for sale in the *Wilmington Commercial*. It was described as a rice plantation on the north branch of the Cape Fear River.

*Collins Plantation:* This may be the *Josian Collins Plantation* in northeastern North Carolina.

*Dallison Plantation:* was owned by Col. John Dallison.

*Dalyrmple Place Plantation:* adjoined John Baptista Ashe's plantation (*Spring Garden*). In 1742/43 "the land was left to my wife, Martha, containing 420 acres, cattle and *slaves*." (Joseph Watter) This estate contained 550 acres and was sold to John Dalrymple by the Joseph Watters descendents in 1744. It was located on the north side of Old Town Creek.

By 1860, Henry N. Howard owned it and it was valued at $10,445 as a rice plantation with an annual income of $2,943. It contained 3,045 acres and had a rice production of 143,532 pounds. At that time it had 42 slaves.

*Davis Plantation:* consisted of 750 acres on the Old Town Creek. Eleazer Allen sold it to John Davis in 1744. Eleazer Allen, Esq., also owned a brick home about a half a mile from Roger Moore.

*Dobbs Place Plantation:* was located on Old Town Creek and owned by Governor Dobbs where he is supposedly buried. The location is unknown. The Ashe family originally owned this plantation.

*Dogwood Neck Plantation*: (see also the *Belvedere Plantation*.) was originally owned by W. E. Boudinot and also referred to as *Westfield. Ten slaves* worked this plantation in 1860 and it was valued at $10,500. By 1880 it contained 60 acres and valued at $2000.

*Drunken Run Plantation*: was mentioned in Gen. Thomas Brown Will abstract, 1814. It was located in Bladen County, NC.

***Fairfield Plantation***: was mentioned in the Wilmington Gazette (Number 636, 13th Year) on Tuesday, 14 March 1809 on page 3. )

*"Cyprus Wreath. On Tuesday last the friends and relations of Mrs. Elizabeth Hall, wife of John Hall, Esq., assembled at Fairfield Plantation to perform to her the last sad duties of humanity by attending her obsequies...she now participates in the joys of the virtuous in Heven."*

***Fishing Creek Plantation:*** is mentioned in a deed when *Negro Head Point* was sold to Peter Mallett in 1787. It was located next to *Negro Head*.

***Flowers Plantation:*** was owned by the Flowers family and was located along Carver's Creek in Bladen County, NC.

***Forceput Plantation:*** was located on the river near Wilmington. William Hill's Will refers to this plantation in September 1788. His wife Margaret, acknowledged this land would go to her son, William Henry Hill for 2,234 pounds. This was just a part of the estate, which also included *the slaves.*

William Hill was originally from Boston, then moved to Brunswick Town in 1778. This land came to the late William Hill in a deed from Roger Moore and his wife, Mary, on the 21st of April 1778. It was 200 acres of swampland and 200 acres of highland near the *"Bluff."*

*William Henry Hill*

By January of 1791 John Hill, William Hill, and Nathaniel Moore sold *Force putt*, which had been in the possession of Thomas Hill, for 1200 pounds. It contained 400 acres on the west side of the Northeast Branch of the Cape Fear.

***Forks Plantation:*** Richard Eagles owned this estate in 1736. It was later owned by John Davis, Esq., and then Mr. Joseph Eagles. An abstract of Richard Eagles Will:

### Richard Eagles Will - 1769

March 23, 1769. March 31, 1769. Son: JOSEPH ("House, plantation, saw and grist mills"). Daughter: SUSANNAH EAGLE. Wife: MARGARET HENRIETTA

EAGLE (formerly BUGNION). Cousins: JEAN and ELIZABETH DAVIS. Sister: ELIZABETH DAVIS. Other legatees: JEANET MCFARLING, JOHN EAGLESON. Executors: JOHN GIBBS, ROBERT SHAW, JOHN ANCRUM and THOMAS OWEN. Witnesses: JOHN WALKER, JOHN FERGUS, MARY WALKER. Will proven before WM. TRYON. Codicil to this will, of even date. Confirms title to MR. WM. DRY in and to a tract of land "bought of my father, RICH'D EAGLES."

*(Source: Abstracts of North Carolina Wills, Secretary of State, 1910, Page 106)*

Richard Eagles was originally from Bristol, England and lived in South Carolina until 1735 when he came into Brunswick County. He also owned a plantation, *Eagles,* in Charles Town, *South Carolina* that he advertised for sale in 1734. It included a dwelling house, large store, stable, and chaise house. He married Sarah _____. He died in 1791, leaving two children, Richard, 3rd, and Joseph, 2nd, the first of whom died before 1811 and the second in 1827, each without heirs. As only an aunt remained, the wife of Alfred Moore, the disappearance of the family name from the annals of North Carolina is readily accounted for and recorded by the *Brunswick County Records, Conveyances, B, 84, 189, 327, 341, 368; North.*

Eagles's plantation was inherited from his father, who was living upon it at the time of his death. It was situated a short distance above Old Town Creek, on the road from Brunswick to *Schawfield*, was bounded on the south by Eagles Creek, and lay a little below Eagles Island opposite Wilmington--an island that received its name from Joseph's grandfather, who owned land there. The plantation was of considerable size, containing a house, a sawmill, and a gristmill.

*Fair Oaks Plantation:* was also called "*Moze*" plantation (after Moore) and owned by J. Moore in 1860 where *56 slaves* worked. It was valued at $13,000. By 1880 F. N. Moore owned it and it contained only 170 acres valued at $6,000. (*See the Meares Bluff Plantation information.*)

*Fulford Plantation:* John Gerrard granted land

"in Core Sound on ye west side of Nelsons Creek, joining ye Mouth of a Gut, James Dauge, Joseph Fulford, another gut from the head of the mouth, and the main Creek." (*Patent Book One*, #889, p. 293.) Nov. 11, 1719.

### John Fulford Will - 1712

Know all men by these presents yt: I John ffulford of ye: County of **Bath** and In ye: prect: of **Craven** and In Coresound out of __e & affection I have to My well be Loved Sonn Jos: ffull    being My youngest Sonn and finding him very Dutyfull & Tendr: of Me Now In My old age and Pecving how subject Mankinde is to a Soden and unprovided Death Doe ffreely give him My sd: Son

*My Now Dwelling Plantation* and Land Cituated and lying and being Upon ye: hed of ye: **Straits in Core Sound** Containing one hundred and Eighty acres to him and his Hairs for ever ye: sd: land I freely give unto him My sd: Sonn Jos: ffullford to use Occuply & __joy free from Me or any other P:son or P:sons Whats_ever In Wittness yt: ye: sd: P:mises is a free gift to __sd: Son I Doe hearunto Sett My hand and Seal_ 21st: Day of Janry: 1712. George Bell Alexandr: Goodgroom Jos: ffullford (Se__) (Craven Co. court minutes) Jan. 21, 1712.

Joseph Fulford, "planter of Core Sound," was named in a dispute of the ownership of a slave: "Fomvile v. Fullford. "John Fomvile Administrator of Peter Fomvile deceased . . . to prosecute his Suite aforesaid against Joseph Fullford of Core Sound Planter in a plea of Tresspass on the Case Sur Trover and Conversation for *One Indian Male Slave* named Harry of the age of Sixteen Years or thereabouts of the price of Sixty Pounds Sterling money of great Britain which Said Slave he declares to have been part of the proper Estate of the said Peter . . . . And the Defendante [torn] his Attorney appeared and pleaded not Guilty . . . ." (Price, *NC Higher-Court Records*, Vol. V, p. 263) Mar. Court 1722.

"Fomvill etc. v. Fullford. On Motion of the plaintiffe's Attorney of the said Joseph Fullford in Court confess't that the said John Fomvill demanded the Indian Slave now in dispute before Action was brought and that he refus'd to deliver him." (Price, *NC Higher-Court Records*, Vol. V, p. 322) Oct. Court 1722.

A *negro slave*, Adam, property of William Jones, was indicted for the murder of Joseph Fulford, husband of Hannah Ward, sometime during October or November 1804. The jury found the slave not guilty. Several more court sessions were held to determine who would pay what fees associated with the death and trial. One expense submitted included payment of a midwife's fee to a *negro woman*, Dorcas, on January 2, 1805. Hannah remarried Joseph Corbet Bell on January 25, 1806. Carteret County, NC.

**Fullwood Plantation:** was mentioned by Mr. Harvey Robinson, at 100-years of age, as he described the Civil War era through his father's eyes. The *Fullwood Plantation* was located in the Zion Hill area near the present Sunset Harbor, just north of Holden Beach. It is also referenced in the Judge Ernest Fullwood Family History.

Many of the local black Fullwoods worked on this plantation according to Harvey Robinson, currently 100 years old. Mr. Robinson recalled the three Fullwood brothers, Joseph, Jacob and Benjamin. He and Mr. Don Joyner, who has completed an extensive family history, told the Fullwood story on a Sunday afternoon in March of 2009 sitting in Mr. Robinson's home on Middle River Road off of Highway 211. The white Fullwoods owned the three black Fullwood brothers., Joseph, Jacob and Jack.

Joseph Fullwood (later taking the name of Joseph Monroe), joined the army about 1862 at 15 years of age. He was listed in the 37th Regiment of the United States Colored Troops in March 1865 where he signed up at the Fiason Station in Wilmington, NC. He was also at Ft. Monroe, Virginia and some family thought he changed his name at that time to Monroe to avoid being connected to the family back in Brunswick County. At that time, family members were in danger of retaliation when a free black joined the ranks to fight in the Civil War. Joseph is mentioned on a monument in Washington, DC where the colored troops were honored long after serving in the army. Other accounts suppose that he changed his name to Joseph Monroe when he was sold to the Monroe family of Shallotte, NC.

Joseph's brother, Jack Fullwood married Hollan _____ who would later pass away at a funeral, so overcome with grief that she died right at the funeral. Their son Fred Fullwood, became a minister. Benjamin Fullwood, the third brother, became the wealthiest of the black Fullwoods making his money by lending it to his brothers for land. They in turn, were said to like the liquor and did not amass the land holdings of their wiser brother. Benjamin could not read or write but made sure his children were schooled. Benjamin was one of the few blacks in Brunswick County who left a Last Will and Testament, written about a year before he died. His son, also named Benjamin, along with Smart Monroe, followed the Turpentine jobs into Florida and later died there.

Jacob Fullwood was sold to the Green family when the Fullwoods were in a financial crunch. Nothing more is known about him at this time. The Green family lived in Brunswick County.

***Gabirel Plantation:*** was located on the Northwest branch of the Cape Fear River about two miles up river from the *John Davis Plantation*, about twenty-two miles from the bar.

Four miles up the river from Captain Gabriel at an opening in the Northwest branch, called the Black River, was a good meadowland but no one settled there.

***Galloway Plantation:*** was located just off the road on the south side from Supply to Bolivia. It was almost across the street from the *Russ Plantation*. An old Galloway ancestor cemetery is located just off of a dirt road, off of highway 211 very near the Lockwood Folly Park. Gravestones date this cemetery to 1874 and earlier. It is presently uncared for and unmarked. Members of the Brunswick Search and Rescue Team have marked the path to it with flagging tape from the more recent Galloway Cemetery that is nearby. This cemetery needs a caretaker to preserve its history. Within a quarter mile, in the same patch of woods, a small cabin is deteriorating which was the residence of Uncle Perdy (described by Mrs. Mamie Hankins Frazier). This residence appears to be a leftover slave quarter, barely 20 X 20 feet, no kitchen, no bathroom, no electricity…whole log rafters with a tin roof. If not a previous slave quarter, one built in the same fashion of the time.

***Gander Hall Plantation:*** was owned by James McIlhenney. The tale is that it got its name because Mr. McIlhenney decided, "to go into the business of raising geese for their feathers, which he was going to sell. He purchased a very large flock from up country and when the season, eggs hatching, etc. came, there were no eggs. Mr. McIlhenney called in a neighbor who informed him that he had nothing but ganders. So for the balance of time, it was called *Gander Hall*." (*Fanny Watters.*)

***Gause Plantation***: John Julius Gause (1774-1836) was buried in a brick burial tomb in the present Ocean Isle area, off highway 179, about five miles from Shallotte. It is located about 500 feet eastward from State Road No. 1154 and about the same distance south of the run of Jinnys Branch. His plantation was within that area, reaching all the way to the coastline. He owned more land in Horry County, South Carolina in addition to his Ocean Isle area holdings. There is also a mention of an adjacent cemetery.

John Julius Gause left a description in his will of who was to be buried in this tomb: "Reserving from a sum sufficient to build a family vault for the interment of my remains and that of my family as hereinafter directed. It is my request that my body should be placed in the vault with my two dead wives until a new one can be built at the old family grounds on the plantation late the residence of Samuel Gause, deceased, estate, then I request my executors to have my own remains interred therein, those of my two wives, Mr. and Mrs. Bruards, and my children that are within the vault or lie interred in the old burying ground. This I enjoin on my executors to have carried into effect immediately after my death." Son, Frederick B., Friend and kinsman, Samuel Frink, sons John P., Samuel S., and George W. Gause, Executors, 3 May 1836….John J. Gause.

John's father was William Gause. William had six sons, Needham, Charles, Benjamin, Bryan, John Gause and William, Jr. John and William Jr. were active in local government and the Revolutionary War. William, Jr.'s home was near the present Gause Landing site. His home was a stop for George Washington where he is said to have taken a dip into the ocean and hung his "underwear" on a massive oak to dry. Washington had breakfast with William.

John Gause, the Revolutionary War vet, was the father of John Julius Gause, who erected the tomb. In his Will, dated 3 May 1836, he authorized the building of the Gause tomb. He married first, his cousin, Elizabeth Bacot Gause, daughter of William Gause, Jr. but she died young. Then he married Maria Theresa Bruard, and later married Emily R. Miller.

William was wounded and lost a leg in the Revolutionary War. He later served in the House of Commons from Brunswick County in 1778 at 33 years of age. He lived at or near Gause Landing Road.

Gause Landing Road is lined with oaks forming a canopy and is one of the most beautiful locations in the area. Another *Gause Plantation* was known to exist in the Winnabow area just north of the road leading from Supply to Winnabow.

*Gibbs Plantation:* was adjoining Mr. Moore's Plantation and owned by Captain Gibbs.

*Goose Marsh Plantation:* was located on the old Smithville and Georgetown, S. C. Road about fifteen miles from Southport and about six miles southwest of Bolivia. It was owned by Nathaniel Galloway, Senior, and had been in the family nearly 150 years.

The "old house" was a large two-story building with dormer windows. It was built of "squared" logs, dovetailed together with pins, plastered between the cracks, lathed, and plastered inside. It was shingled on the outside.

It had a large fireplace and mantel, panels in the shutters at the windows, and was probably built between 1770-1800. The house has now been torn down. The plantation primarily earned income from turpentine, tar, corn, cotton, and potatoes. The plantation was self-sustaining with cattle, sheep, hogs, etc., which were used for food and clothing.

On July 27, 1976 the following note ran in the *Wilmington Star newspaper*: *"Mrs. Erla Roberts Swain Stone, widow of Robert Rollo Stone, died in Wilmington Sunday night. She was born here on November 19, 1886, the daughter of the late Luke Peyton Swain, and Mary Ida Prigge Swain. She was the fifth generation to live on his plantation (Goose Marsh in Brunswick County). Her husband, R. R. Stone, died on February 21, 1955. Interment in Oakdale Cemetery."*

*Goutier's Plantation:* was noted in a sale of property on the 12th of April in 1798. \_\_\_ter Goutier owned it.

*Governor's Point Plantation:* was located on the southernmost part of the river. Governor Burrington bought it from John Porter about 1723. He died in Rocky Point in 1734. Members of his family married those from the Moores, Ashes, Lillingtons, and Moseleys.

*In a Cotton Field. Drawn by Horace Bradley for the Harper's Weekly,*
*Vol. XXXI, No. 1600; after 1884.*

***Gray & Carter's Plantation:*** was formed when the patent was given to William Gray and William Carter in June of 1736. *(See Red Banks Plantation for more information.)*

***Green Banks Plantation:*** was owned by Michael Bryan in 1860 and valued about $5,500. Along with rice, Bryan produced turpentine. The *Peoples Press* of Wilmington reported on May 29, 1833, "*Died - At Green Bank Plantation in Brunswick County on thee 23rd inst., in the 67th year of his age, William Bryant, Esq., a native of Jones County but for the last 31 years a resident of Brunswick County.*"

***Green Hall Plantation:*** was located on the west side of the Black River about 49 miles from the mouth of the Cape Fear. William Gill received a patent for 150 acres in February 1837. He then sold it to Gov. Mathew Rowan in 1751. Later it was sold to John Lyon who resold it in 1787 to Enoch Herring.

**Green Hill Plantation:** General John Ashe lived on *Green Hill* next to *Clayton Hall*. His family cemetery is on this plantation but he is buried under an oak tree on the John Sampson farm in Clinton, N. C.

*Green Hill* is located just northeast of Winnabow barely east of the *Gause Plantation*.

**Greenfield Plantation:** was owned by Tom McIlhenney. Dr. Green had a sawmill at this location and owned *Greenfield Gardens*. Before the arrival of white men, the Indians had a settlement here. Archaeologists have found pottery in the area around the lake on the property, and date those remnants to 500 A. D. - 2000 B. C.

In 1735, in William Smith's Will, Greenfields was given to Gabriel Johnston and Robert Halton.

In 1750 Dr. Samuel Green bought 500 acres just north of Mill Creek. He added another 500 in 1758 and continued to add to it, eventually naming it *Greenhall Plantation*. He died about 1771 and left his property to his wife, Hannah. He left her the choice of *Greenfields* or the *Greenhall Plantation*. His young daughter, Hannah, was to receive the *Trapland Plantation* of 640 acres, which was a little more south. His son, John, was to receive 640 acres known as *Bevis Land*. His son, William, was to receive the *Greenhall Plantation* containing 1300 acres and the sawmill. In the final settlements in 1782, William Green inherited the *Greenfields Plantation*. It remained in the Green family until the 1840s. In 1844 it was offered for sale and described as between the Mill and Jumping Run Road. By then, William M. Green was living in Chapel Hill, NC.

In 1834 William M. Green sold Governor Edward B. Dudley a part of *Summer Hill,* which was on Green's Creek, and another tract in 1844 that he deeded to his son, Christopher H. Dudley (1441.75 acres).

By 1869 there was a court dispute over this land between Mary Hewett (husband John) and Miles Costin in the New Hanover County Courthouse. It was described as the land on the road from Wilmington to Fort Fisher crossing Jumping Run and Mill Pond. It would later be auctioned off, 387.5 acres, and the money owed to John F. Gafford paid off.

**Groveley Plantation:** James Walker bought Groveley from Samuel Ashe in 1791. He then sold it to Richard Quince. Later his "in-law" Nancy Quince, sold it to John Moore. Moore sold it to Thomas A. Smith in November of 1837.

Quite the stir, the *Wilmington Star* reported on January 10, 1879 *"The blacks on the plantation of Dr. J. D. Bellamy, in Brunswick County, were excited over two elopements in "high colored life" which occurred there recently. John Davis, the overseer of the plantation, ran away with a "dusky damsel" and left a wife and three children to scuffle for themselves, and a laborer on the place eloped later the same day, also leaving a wife and several children to fight the battle of life."*

On November 7, 1901, the *Star and Wilmington Messenger* reported that *"Miss Bessie C. Bellamy, daughter of Mr. and Mrs. George H. Bellamy, of Grovely, the county home in Brunswick, married Mr. S. Paul Venters, a prosperous young planter and businessman of Onslow County, on 11-6-1901. The ceremony was conducted by Rev. Mr. Browning. The couple will reside in Richlands, Onslow County."*

***Hail Point:*** The Cape Fear Recorder documented on April 21, 1830, that Margaret E. Giles, daughter of William Giles, Esq., at the residence of Robert Gibbs, Esq., at *Hail Point*, Brunswick County, was married to Philip Yonge, of Rocky Comfort, Middle Florida.

***Hall Plantation:*** In 1841, William L. Hall deeded 116 acres located on the west bank of the Brunswick River to John G. Hall, his brother, for the sum of $12,387. It contained 71 acres on *Eagles Island*. Hall was a former Sheriff and slave trader with a large plantation on Indian Creek (now the Phoenix area). References note that W. L. Hall bought and sold in excess of *1500 slaves* during his lifetime (*E. Willis*). It was valued at $6,000 in 1830 and had 45 working *slaves*. By 1880 it contained 50 acres and was owned by J. G. Hall (heirs? as he died in 1841). It was still listed as owned by J. G., perhaps by his wife, Sarah. Sarah moved to Granville County and sold 55 acres of this estate. In 1890 she sold one acre to the AME Church for religious purposes only. The site is now Mount Calvary's Cemetery. The remaining property was sold in 1899 to Francis M. Moore for $2,000. He left the property to his daughter, Viola A. Robbins. The plantation house was torn down in 1917 to make room for another Guano Company, a fertilizer factory; (*Morris Fertilizer*). It was also sometimes referred to as *Armour* (from the Armour Fertilizer Factory).

***Halton Lodge Plantation:*** Next to the Hilton plantation on the east side of Smith's Creek (which was named for Chief Justice Smith) was Halton Lodge. It was owned by Col. Robert Halton and contained 640 acres. He was one of the founders of Wilmington. Halton obtained this estate from Thomas Clark, after his death.

Robert Halton, in a Will dated 15th of April 1749, left *Halton Lodge* to his wife, Mary, who resided in England. Halton was also referred to as the *Laban* tract on Mill Creek and *Brown Marsh* on the Northeast Cape Fear River. In 1754 it was conveyed to Daniel Dunbibin. Robert Halton died 2 December 1766 and the remaining land was sold to Cornelius Hewett (640 acres) by the sheriff of New Hanover County, Arthur Benning, at the courthouse steps.

There is one other notation of 350 plus acres on the south side of Smith's Creek that was originally owned by William Dry, conveyed to Thomas James, a tailor. Another notation states that John Maultsby bought it from Roger Moore. Dates of these transactions are unknown.

***Harmony Hall Plantation:*** was located in the White Oak area of Bladen County, NC and owned by Col. Richardson.

***Hasell's Place Plantation:*** was owned by Judge Hasell on the north side of Sedgely Abbey. This was located just above the present Carolina Beach and opposite Cabbage Inlet. He died in 1786 and his estate passed to his family.

***Haw Fields Plantation:*** was identified in February of 1735 as 150 acres belonging to Jere Bigfurd, in New Hanover County in the precinct of Town Creek. It was later called *Mount Pleasant* by Jere Bigfurd when he and his wife, Magdalen, sold it (140 acres) to Josiah Bell on the 13th of June 1737. He originally was awarded 320 acres on September 11, 1735. In other documents it is sometimes referred to as *Pleasant Oaks.*

***Haw Hill Plantation:*** The Wilmington Star newspaper ran the following ad on June 11, 1882: *Rice Farm for Sale - I will sell that valuable rice farm, formerly owned by Col. Henry N. Howard, and known as Haw Hill Plantation. Situated near the mouth of Town Creek, in Brunswick County, containing about 200 acres of farmland, of which 125 acres is rice and balance upland, of a light gravel surface with heavy subsoil, and about 300 acres of woodland. These lands are secure from river freshets; less expensive to cultivate than the river lands, while they are as productive as any to be found on the Cape Fear River. (Signed) D. L. Gore.*

*River Scene. A Scene on the Tributary of the Cape Fear River, North Carolina. Market Boats on their way to Wilmington. Dated about October 30, 1869.*
*Drawing Courtesy of the New Hanover Public Library.*

On November 28, 1901, the newspaper ran another story on the *Haw Hill Plantation*: *"three thousand bushels of rice belonging to Gilbert Hollins, who lives at Haw Hill Plantation, about two miles inland on the Cape Fear River, in Brunswick County, were destroyed by fire, which originated from an unknown source Monday of this week. The loss is about $2,700, fully covered by insurance."*

*John Burgwin*

***Hermitage Plantation:*** was owned by Mr. John Burgwin, a merchant in Wilmington. His plantation (shown below) was located on Prince George's Creek near Wilmington. The drawing of the *Hermitage Plantation* house was drawn about 1795 - 1805.

*The Hermitage*

***Hewett Plantation:*** There were several *Hewett Plantations* in southern Brunswick County. One was located near the Holden Beach area and owned by Joseph Hewett, Sr. and his wife, Mary. At some point Joseph had died and Mary remarried a Mr.

Hemingway. In her Last Will and Testament she was known as Mary Hewett Hemingway. She had a large number of *slaves*, as evidenced by her will, and her plantation extended for hundreds of acres. (In her will she bequeathed a hundred acres to Job Holden. He is buried in the Holden Cemetery just off of Seashore Hills Road about a mile away from the grave sites of Joseph and Mary who are buried on Kinston Street just off of the Holden Beach Causeway.)

On Stone Chimney Road is a *slave* cemetery where it is assumed many of Mary Hemingway's slaves were buried. It was common for neighboring plantation owners to use the same graveyard for their *slaves,* which were mostly buried at night to avoid losing any work time.

Randall Hewett had two sons, Jonah and Tom who also owned a Hewett Plantation. They were also *slave owners.*

Mathias Hewett had a plantation in the Boones Neck area but was not known to have any slaves working there. Mathias Hewett and his wife, Elizabeth Morgan Hewett, owned this plantation, which consisted of about 200 acres. It was later known as the *Fulton Robinson Estate* in the 1800s. Their children were Anzie, Sarah, Enoch, Isaiah, Catherine, and Frances. The great land dispute was not settled among the heirs until the 1980s.

Mathias was a grandson of Joseph Hewett, Sr., and inherited the property from his father, Phillip Hewett, as part of the more than 1,000 acres that Joseph Hewett, Sr. owned in partnership with the Henry Leonard family. (The Leonard Cemetery is located off Main Street in Shallotte.)

Mathias was a farmer, trader, and well known for the establishment of the Silent Grove Missionary Baptist Church on Oxpen Road, where the Brunswick County landfill is located today. (*Note the German spelling of Matthew as Mathias.*)

The Silent Grove Cemetery still stands and many of the Mathias and Elizabeth Hewett heirs are buried there. His granddaughter, Viola Hewett, now 80+ years of age, is still living not far from the original plantation. (*Mathias and Elizabeth Morgan Hewett Plantation information is courtesy of Ouida Hewett.*)

***Hewitt Plantation:*** The Last Will and Testament of Thomas Hewitt, a planter, left his plantation to his wife, Elizabeth. It was written in 1776 in Onslow County, NC and proved in April of 1777. He mentioned his sons, John and Goldsmith Hewitt, and the location of the plantation on the New River. His plantation was bequeathed to John. He also bequeathed the plantation that "he now lives on" to his son Goldsmith after the death of his mother. Thomas had the following daughters: Christian [na?] Hewitt, Elizabeth Hewitt, Judah, and Mary Hewitt. Thomas had originally purchased the land from Mr. John Morris. (This Hewitt Plantation is included because of the large number of Hewett families now living in southeastern North Carolina, particularly Brunswick County.)

Thomas Hewitt was mentioned in a deed from Adam Scott to Phelps on 18 Aug 1784 in Onslow Co., NC; "60 acres which is the homestead where Thomas Hewitt lately lived which I purchased of him and is between land of the heirs of William Conoway deceased, land of John Hewitt,
and is on Whiteoak River. Teste: John Hewitt." He was a Constable in 1787. He signed as a witness for the Will of Isaac Gibson on 13 Aug 1789 in Onslow Co., NC. He died before 1790.

The *Brunswick County Hewitt Plantation* was located south of the *Holden Plantation*.

**Hickory Hall** is located in the area of the present town of Calabash. Some of the bricks have the imprint of the date 1812 in them so this is presumed to be the time period it was built. Samuel Frink (September 1786 - November 1862) built this house. His great-grandfather was Nicholas Frink, one of the first settlers in the Brunswick area.

Samuel Frink produced primarily indigo, rice, and the long leaf pine tar and pitch for naval stores. The house was built over a huge hickory stump that was used as a table in the home.

*Hickory Hall Plantation, c. 1850; Artist Unknown (. D. '71?).*

The stump eventually decayed and was removed.

Architectural features included two chimneys built from ship ballast stones. The foundation contains oyster shells that were burned into lime-like substances used in the mortar. It contained five fireplaces used for cooking and heating. The ceiling and walls were made of bead paneling, possibly imported from England. The original floors were native long leaf pine planking. Some are still remaining today.

***Hilton Plantation:*** Cornelius Harnett, John Gardner Squire, John Maultsby, and John Hill owned this site through the years beginning about 1730.

Later William H. Hill acquired it. He said in his will that he named it Hilton after his family but left out an "l". It was originally called *Maynard* by Cornelius Harnett and was located on Smith's Creek.

The interior of the home was described as rooms paneled in Georgian style. The exterior shows a Georgian architecture. One writer described it as "in all my life I never saw a more glorious situation." *(Janet Schaw in 1775).*

*Interior of the Maynard, later the Hilton, showing wood paneling. The doors appeared to be at least twelve feet tall. Maynard & Hilton, c. 1855. Sketch featured in Ballou's Pictorial Drawing-Room Companion.*

*Hilton Plantation when Cornelius Harnett owned it.*

*Hilton Plantation Grounds facing away from the river. C. 1892.*

When the home was demolished, no effort was made to measure or photograph it. The following photograph was taken on demolition day.

*The Maynard Plantation Home,*
*later called the Hilton Plantation at the time of demolition.*

***Holden Plantation:***   "At the going rate, (of fifty shillings per hundred acres), Benjamin Holden bought four tracts of land for his mainland plantation in 1756. He also paid for and was granted by Governor Dobbs, the island between his plantation and the ocean. By this purchase he acquired the 100-acre island extending from Lockwood Folly Inlet to Bacon Inlet for fifty shillings." (John. F. Holden, *The Beginning and Development of Holden Beach.*)

"In Benjamin Holden's Last Will and Testament, dated February 19, 1778, he bequeathed the eastern half of my beach to his son Amos, and the western half to his son James. By later transactions the whole island became the property of another son, Job, from whom it passed to his son John and later to grandson John, Junior. The lattermost owner made the initial efforts toward developing a resort." (John F. Holden.)

The *Holden Plantation* was located just inland of the *Hewitt Plantation* in the Brunswick County/Holden Beach area, in the present Sierra Estates. Benjamin Holden's home and the family cemetery were located there. The Job Holden

Cemetery is the final resting place for John Holden, Sr., Benjamin Holden, and Job Holden, among others.

The *Holden Plantation* was subsequently deeded to Thomas Holden. When Thomas moved to Hillsboro, he sold the old home place to Wallace Styron but designated a small tract as the cemetery.

***Howe's Point Plantation:*** was located beside Governor's Point and owned by Job Howe, father of General Robert Howe. His father was also the Job Howe who was the grandson of the first Governor of South Carolina, Gov. James Moore. It was located at the rear of an old fort used for protection against pirates.

About a half mile behind this location is Liberty Pond where a bloody battle ensued during the Revolutionary War. The blood of fallen soldiers is said to have reddened the pond.

The residence was a large three-story building on a stone or brick foundation near the old colonial, just below Old Brunswick town. The area is presently owned by the federal government and located at Sunny Point. General Robert Howe, the son, eventually lived on this plantation that was largely destroyed by the British on May 12, 1776.

***Hullfields Plantation:*** was located next to *Belgrange* and owned by Schencking Moore, son of Nathaniel Moore. He sold it to John McKenzie.

***Hunthill Plantation:*** Rutherford lost *Bowlands Plantation* to the Murray family for debts due them. Then he acquired a large estate up the North East River called *Hunthill.*

***Hyrneham Plantation:*** was located the farthest west from the river and owned by Captain Edward Hyrne. He received it from Col. Maurice Moore in 1736 as a gift. It passed to his son, Henry Hyrne upon his death, then to his nephew, Harry Hyrne Watters (who married the daughter of one of the signers of the Declaration of Independence, William Hooper.)

***Indian Creek Plantation:*** was located on the North-west river and owned by Joshua Bradey in 1809 as is evidenced by the following advertisement in the Wilminton Gazette.

**March 14, 1809.** The Wilmington Gazette (Number 636, 13th Year).
"Fifteen dollars reward! Ran away on the 2d instant, a stout likely negro fellow named Jacob, formerly the property of Joshua Bradey deceased, quite black about six feet high, plausible in conversation and very artful. He has a down look, is well known about the plantation of Joshua Bradey's called Indian Creek, 8 miles from

Wilmington on the North-west river. A more particular description of him will be given next week. Whosever will apprehend the said fellow and lodge him in jail, so that I can get him, or deliver him to me in Wilmington shall receive the above reward. Hillory Moore, Es'r. January 31."

***Indian Island Plantation:*** is mentioned in February 1739, in New Hanover County in a deed where Lewis Bryan (now of Craven County) sold it to William Gray for 100 pounds. It contained 185 acres on the east side of the North East branch of Cape Fear River including the island in the river called Indian Island. Lewis Bryan got the original patent in 1736.

***Kendall Plantation:*** James Smith owned Kendall, which was located next to the *Orton Plantation.* This was Governor Smith's brother, who assumed the name of Rhett when he moved to South Carolina. (Hummmmm...) *Kendall* first belonged to Col. Maurice Moore in 1725 (640 acres). It then passed to Roger Moore in March of 1726, then to Roger Moore through a will for 440 acres, then to George Moore in 1765. It eventually went to John Davis, Jr. Owen Holmes also owned it at one time. Later the McRee family acquired it.

The main house was brick and already standing by 1734 as a traveler from Georgia stated in his memoirs. While owned by John Davis, it was described as "this house is built after the Dutch fashion, and made to front both ways -- on the river, and on the land. He has a beautiful avenue cut through the woods for about two miles, which is a great addition to the house."

John Davis sold it to General Robert Howe, in 1794, who passed it to his son, Robert Howe. Robert Howe Jr. sold it to James McAlister (heir of Archibald McAlister) for 1200 pounds. This was 400 acres, more or less.

James Sprunt purchased it in 1920 from the Frederick Kiddere estate.

*Kendall Rice Fields. Photo Courtesy of the Lower Cape Fear Historical Society, Image Archives.*

*Kendall Plantation. Date Unknown.*
*Photos Courtesy of the Lower Cape Fear Historical Society, Image Archives.*

*Kendall Plantation. Date Unknown.  Lady in dark coat leaning against the post is thought to be Annis Kiddere (Smith).   This photo is thought to have been taken when Fred Kiddere owned Kendall Plantation.  Photo Courtesy of the Lower Cape Fear Historical Society Image Archives.*

*Kendall Plantation. Date Unknown.  Presumed to be* **Frederick Kiddere.**
*Photo Courtesy of the Lower Cape Fear Historical Society, Image Archives.*

On March 9, 1909, the Wilmington Star news reported that "*Mr. Arthur Hill Holmes, 47, died in his store in Wilmington from apoplexy. He had been a grocer for 24 years. He was born at Kendal Plantation on the Cape Fear River, a son of Own Holmes. He moved to Wilmington at an early age. About 25 years ago he married the former Miss Caroline Greene Hall, and she and five children survive the deceased. Interment in Oakdale Cemetery.*"

***Laurens Plantation:*** was owned by Col. James Morehead. A tall, thin man, he died in 1807 and is buried at *Owen Hill*. Laurens was located near Elizabethtown.

***Lebanon Plantation:*** was located in Bladen County on Carver's Creek. The Gillespie and Flowers families owned it.

***Legares Neck Plantation:*** was located on the Northeast River between Prince George's Creek and the Northeast branch of the Cape Fear River where the mouth of Prince George's Creek empties into the river. It is mentioned in a court case in the mid 1850s and was to be sold. Another snippet mentions a court case where there was the sale of *L. N.* and *Castle Haynes* on the NE River for $6,500.

***Lewis Plantation:*** was also called the *George Washington Lewis Plantation* and was located in Shell Point on the Shallotte River. It was also known as *Monogram*.

George Washington Lewis and his two sisters arrived in Brunswick County from Carteret County about 1871. George fell in love with Lydia Ann Hewett, daughter of Robert Hewett and Helen (unknown), and was married. He purchased about 200 acres, more or less, of land from Robert and Helen Hewett for one hundred and fifty dollars. He and Lydia Ann built a home there that stood until recent years. He sold this piece of land and purchased two more tracts even greater than the first one. This turned into a plantation located on the Shallotte River, better known today as *Shell Point*. Their children are: Riley Lewis, Simproneuas; James Harker, George Washington, Jr.; Samuel Asbury, Joe Cephus, William Edward, Henry Johnson, Anna, and Robert Fulton.

The Lewis family farmed and fished, worked as boat captains, and was very successful. They planted a variety of crops, canned, stored, dried, and sustained their family well.

George Washington Sr. and wife Lydia Ann were two of the founders of *Sharon Methodist Church* and are buried in the church cemetery. They also founded "The Lewis School" in Shell Point or Monogram as most locals called the area at that time. The local people called it "Frog Pond School", but it is listed as Lewis School (Academy) on state records.

When the state consolidated the county schools and built district ones, in the early 1920s, Samuel Asbury Lewis traveled from Carolina Beach where he had relocated his family, to the Lewis School to sign legal transfer papers with the state of North Carolina concerning the school.

The *Lewis Plantation* was divided among heirs of the family. The Harold Robinson family still has a hay field on what was once a thriving plantation. (*Lewis Plantatin information courtesy of Ouida Hewett.*)

**Lillington Hall Plantation:** was located on the east side of the Northeast River about four miles above the *Vats*. Gen. Alexander Lillington, who fought at Moores Creek Bridge, owned it. Lillington Hall was a large brick house as described by Sarah William Ashe, sister of Captain Samuel A. Ashe, in 1866. She talked about the burial ground with white tombstones. The cemetery was surrounded by a wall and located near the house. She said that on some of the panes of the windows were the names of Revolutionary soldiers. (*See Alexander Lillington Last Will and Testament in the appendix.*)

**Lilliput Plantation:** North of *Kendall* was the *Lilliput* granted in 1725 to Eleazer Allen. He is buried there with the headstone that says "Chief Justice of North Carolina." Sir Thomas Frankland, the great-grandson of Oliver Cromwell, also owned this estate. Dr. John Hill owned it at some point according to Fanny Watters. Later the McRee family owned it. James Sprunt purchased it from the Kiddere estate. The great house was made of brick.

On February 21, 1893, the *Wilmington Messenger* reported that Dr. John H. Hill, 86 had died Sunday "at the residence of his son, J. H., Jr., in Goldsboro. He was a native of the Cape Fear section, and after becoming a physician, he developed a fine rice plantation at *Lilliput*, near Orton, now owned by Col. K. M. Murchison." He was born in New Hanover County on April 28, 1807.

**Louisiana Plantation:** This plantation was once owned by the Lock and Robbins families. It was located near Hood's Creek in Brunswick County.

**Ludlow Castle:** was also referred to as *Bridgen Hall*. It was located in New Hanover County and was owned by Samuel Bridgen. It was north of *Howes Point* and contained 640 acres in the grant dated 30 June 1757. It was also sometimes called "*Bridgen's Pastime*". Bridgen was married to Sarah and had a son, Edward, who was a merchant in London. In his will, Samuel Bridgen gave 960 acres to Job Howe Sr. and Job Howe Jr, and requested that they set up a trust for his son, Edward.

The original part of this tract, 2500 acres, belonged to Samuel Swann (on the 15th of July 1725) who bought it from Col. Maurice Moore.

**MacKnights Plantation:** was mentioned in the Will of Edward Mosely and bequeathed by him to his son, John. It was located "below Brunswick".

*Magnolia Plantation:* was owned by the Hall family.

*Mallory Plantation:* was sold by Benjamin Smith to William B. Meares on the 25th of December 1815. Benjamin Smith was authorized to sell the property of George Hooper to the highest bidder on the 25th of September 1815 for a lot in town valued at $500 and another in town valued at $500, and *Mallory Plantation* valued at $1,000. It was located in Brunswick County on the Cape Fear River.

It was sold again in the following ad: "Mallory Plantation is located about four miles below the *Belvedere Plantation* and contained about 400 acres of tide swamp; of which 40 acres are under bank and ditch and in cultivation and 160 acres of well timbered pine land lying on both sides of an excellent stream on which once stood a saw mill; albeit little used. The mill has been down for some time, but the foundation is perfect, and the milldam is entire, so that it can be erected again at a very trifling expense. In addition to the pine timber, there is a quantity of cypress above and below the mill. A pounding mill can be erected and a threshing machine with great advantage."

"A great deal of the high land may be very profitably cultivated and a part of it may be converted into a brickyard. It is so situated as to admit of its being divided into two fine settlements of equal value and similar advantages."

"The advantage of the pond to the rice field is that when the tides are short or the water brackish, they can be supplied with water. The soil of the tide swamp is of first quality, elegantly situated for cultivation and I am informed not a creek in it except the one on which the mill stood."

"I will sell either or both of these plantations (the other being *Belvedere Plantation*) on an extensive credit and on reasonable terms upon the payment being satisfactorily secure. Enquire in my absence of Mr. John Walker". SIGNED William Watts Jones. *(Listed as a plantation for sale in the Cape Fear Recorder, Wilmington, NC 1831.)*

*Masonboro Area:* contained several residences owned by well-known citizens like Hooper, Harnett, Lillington, and Maclaine. Hooper's place was called *Finian*.

Further north of Masonboro was Deep Inlet Creek (Hewlett's Creek) where more prominent families had some larger tracts. William Nichols and George Moore had homes there. Further north at Lee's Creek (Bradley's Creek) Martin Holt had a residence. North and eastward of Lee's Creek were the homes of Governor Gabriel Johnston, and beyond toward Wrightsville was Job Howe's home at *Howe's Point,* below Brunswick. Other places nearby were *Royal Oak Point, Bridgen's Pastime, Bridgen's Hall,* and *Ludlow Hall.*

Additional locations up toward *Sloop Point* included the home of Mr. Whitfeld, which was later owned by the McMillan family. Prominent homes in the area included the *Whitlock House* and the *Williams House*. Many of these were the "summer homes" of the plantation owners.

***Masonborough Plantation:*** was owned by Caleb Grainger and located in the Wilmington area.

***Meares Bluff Plantation:*** was located in Brunswick County and owned by Sen.

William B. Meares. He had purchased part of the *Bluff Plantation* about 1822. Meares (1787 - 1841) was a member of the NC House of Representatives from 1818 - 1819 and a member of the Senate from 1828 - 1834.

Meares was also the founder of the Bank of the Cape Fear. He and George Hooper, another bank founder, ultimately "proved to be the undoing of Benjamin Smith and the *Belvidere Plantation*."

W. B. Meares took control of the *Bluff Plantation* in 1824 until 1869 when it was sold to the Navassa Guana Company (fertilizer company). In 1830, the census showed W. B. Meares was the second largest slave owner in Brunswick County, with 61 *slaves*. Another source indicates 96 *slaves* in 1830.

*William Belvedere Meares*

The largest *slave owner* was listed as John Swann, Jr., owner of *Woodburn Plantation* and *Dogwood Neck*.

Mears died in 1841, and his son, Thomas Davis Meares took control of the Bluff lands. Meares cemetery is named after him. He was born in Fayetteville at the home of his maternal grandfather, General Thomas Davis, in 1818. He was the second son of William B. Meares and Katherine Davis.

The plantation of Thomas D. Meares (Colonel) was described as: "having only the fifth largest improved acreage on the river with 346 acres. In 1859 it produced 864,000 pounds of rice (20,000 bushels), the largest crop ever recorded on a single plantation on the Cape Fear, a yield in excess of sixty bushels per acre. The *slave* plantation population was 107, third largest among the rice plantations. Some of the fields had been planted regularly for over forty years and still produced luxuriantly." Thomas D. Meares died at his home in Wilmington in 1871.

***Mill Point Plantation:*** was sometimes called the *John Davis Land* or *Sandy Hill*. This was located just north of the land owned by J. LaPierre (of *Sandy Hill Plantation*).

Originally, Nathaniel Moore was granted 500 acres on the west side of the Cape Fear in October 1728. He assigned this land to Benjamin Laws who in turn deeded it to John Davis, nephew of Nathaniel Moore. John Davis settled there about 1728/30.

In 1765 John Davis left this tract in his Last Will and Testament; 500 acres to his son, Roger Davis, called *Mill Point*. He reserved 1/4 acre for the burying place. He also left him a tract called *Planters Delight,* which was another 640 acres. He also left his son John Davis, his stock; his daughter, Mary Paris Moore, 50 pounds; his daughter, Justina Dobbs, his slaves; his son, William Davis, (?). It was also his desire that "his daughter, Justina Dobbs, should have use of his dwelling house at Mill Point where he now lives until her brother, John Davis, provides a house for her and that she should have use of all stock, etc. and at his death on the plantation, during her stay in said house."

In 1779 640 acres were sold to John Lassiere (Lapiere). In 1832 John J. Green of Georgetown, S. C. sold 500 acres to John C. Baker for $500, which may have been part of this land.

A deed in 1821 calls this land *Sand Hill Plantation*. Later deeds combined these lands (*Sandy Bay* and *Mill Point*) to call it *Sand Hills Plantation*. It then became a part of the *Pleasant Oaks Plantation* in 1934 when purchased by F. B. Adams.

**Moore, F. M.:** Although not referenced as a plantation, the *Wilmington Star* reported in September of 1880 that the correspondent *"writing from Brunswick County, says he has just had the pleasure of going around the rice farm of F. M. Moore, Esq., with Mr. Samuel Hall, the manager, and that it made him feel proud of old Brunswick once more, to see the beautiful sight of 9,000 bushels of waving grain, now about ready for the sickle, the result of good management, energy and industry."*

**Moorefields Plantation:** George Moore owned this plantation and was a very wealthy man. He was the father of 28 children by two wives. There was a road from his home leading to the Masonboro Sound, perfectly straight, about 15 miles long. His *slaves* prepared that road.

**Moseley Plantation:** Col. Sampson Moseley, the son of Edward Moseley, owned this estate.

**Moze Plantation:** This area was a portion of the *Cedar Hill Plantation* and valued at $9,000 in 1830 with 28 *slaves*; owned by A. J. DeRossett. In 1860, James and Sallie Moore were the residents. James, 53 years old, and Sallie, 48, had three sons, John, Alexander Duncan and Francis M. James sold this property to George R. Griffith of Alabama after the Civil War and moved to Chatham County.

An ad was posted in the Wilmington Gazette (No. 646) on May 23, 1809 seeking the return of a slave named Peter. "Peter, a mulatto boy, belonging to A. J. DeRosset, about 18 or 19 years of age, low of stature, but sturdy made, bushy hair seldom combed, and inclined to generally be dirty, dressed in striped cotton homespun, tho' he may have other clothes. Bryant Sullivan belonging to James Telfair, about 16 years old, also a mulatto, stutters when questioned, a scar across his nose, habited in homespun, but has also other clothes. Both these boys have worked several years at the Brick laying business. A reward of ten dollars will be paid by the owner, of the above boys respectively, if taken within the state, and thirty of without the same, and all charges paid, on delivery in Wilmington on their being so secured as that the owners shall get them. Masters of vessels are particularly cautioned against taking them off or harboring them under the penalty of the law, which will be rigidly enforced. A. J. DeRosset, James Telfair, May 18, 1809.

Francis married Louisa J. and in 1874 re-acquired the 600 acres of the *Moze* tract land from Griffith for $20,000. By 1895, Francis married Mary Agnes Groves, the daughter of William and Mary Groves. He added several more hundred acres by 1899. He became the first Navassa postmaster. (*See the Cedar Hill Plantation description.*) (Note: Moores--Mors--Moze).

**Mount Pleasant:** See *Haw Fields Plantation.*

**Mt. Gallant Plantation:** was owned by Col. John Pugh Williams, a Colonel of the 9th Regiment, Continental Line.

**Mulberry Plantation:** William Watters father left him the Mulberry estate in his Will in 1751. By 1788 it belonged to John Davis and later the Hall family. John G. Hall owned it by 1860 and the rice value per year was $5,946. The plantation itself was valued at a little over $9,000.

**Myrtle Grove Plantation:** was located in Brunswick County just south of Bolivia.

**Neck Plantation:** (*Porter's Neck*) was home to Governor Sam Ashe who is buried there in his family cemetery. (*Porter's Neck*...previously owned by John Porter.) His son, John Baptista Ashe, was also elected a governor but died before taking his seat.

   *Oakley Plantation* and *Porter's Neck Plantation* were mentioned in the Will of Thomas Cowan on the 15th of January 1831 as land purchased from Thomas F. Davis.

   George Davis, the son of Thomas Fredrick Davis (5 Sept. 1778 - Dec. 1846) and Sarah Elizabeth Eagles Davis, was born on the *Porter's Neck Plantation,* which his father owned on 1 March 1820. He married Monimia Fairfax and died on 9 May 1866. George is buried in Oakdale Cemetery in Wilmington.

***Negro Head Point Plantation:*** was owned by Col. Peter Mallett. This plantation was also called *Point Peter.* It was so called because a negro's head was said to have been stuck up there at the time of the Nat Turner insurrection in 1831 but this is in error since the name was in court records as early as 1764. (Perhaps another incident?) It adjoined a plantation called *Fishing Creek*, on the west side of the Northeast branch of the Cape Fear River.

Arthur Magill sold this land to Peter Mallett on 16 September 1779. There were several disputes over who owned this land involving Roger Moore and his wife, the Magills, Mallett and Margaret Hill, widow of William Hill.

## A brief Account of the Nat Turner Insurrection of 1831

In 1831 the slaves banded together to murder whites. Over 55 whites were murdered in Virginia and word spread quickly as did the rebellion throughout the south. " North Carolina, Raleigh and Fayetteville were put under military defense, and women and children concealed themselves in the swamps for many days. The rebel organization was supposed to include two thousand."

"Eventually forty-six slaves were imprisoned in Union County, twenty-five in Sampson County, and twenty-three, at least, in Duplin County, some of whom were executed. The panic also extended into Wayne, New Hanover, and Lenoir Counties. Four men were shot without trial in Wilmington, -- Nimrod, Abraham, Prince, and "Dan the Dray-man," the latter a man of seventy, -- and their heads placed on poles at the four corners of the town. Nearly two months afterwards the trials were still continuing; and at a still later day, the Governor in his proclamation recommended the formation of companies of volunteers in every county." Nat Turner was still at large.

"It is said the negroes intended to rise as soon as the sickly season began, and obtain possession of the city by massacring the white population. The same letter states that the mayor had prohibited the opening of Sunday-schools for the instruction of blacks, under a penalty of five hundred dollars for the first offence, and for the second, death."

"The arrest took place on the thirtieth of October, 1831, the confession on the first of November, the trial and conviction on the fifth, and the execution on the following Friday, the eleventh of November, precisely at noon. He met his death with perfect composure, declined addressing the multitude assembled, and told the sheriff in a firm voice that he was ready. Another account says that he "betrayed no emotion, and even hurried the executioner in the performance of his duty." "Not a limb nor a muscle was observed to move. His body, after his death, was given over to the surgeons for dissection." Nat Turner was dead.

"Nat Turner came to symbolize the radical struggle against slavery in the decades prior to the Civil War." He was hanged for his actions. (*The Atlantic Monthly, August 1861*.)

***Nesses Creek Plantation:*** was mentioned in 1759 in the New Hanover Court Minutes when Mr. James Gregory was authorized to build a mill at his plantation on *Nessis* Creek. He then sold it to Mr. Arthur Mapson (1000 acres) in 1762 and noted it was formerly owned through a patent obtained by William Forbes who received the patent in September 1735 and sold it in 1750 to Maurice Moore. Moore sold it to Nathaniel Moore who sold it to James Gregory. (Did you really follow all that?)

It eventually came to be owned by Gabriel Holmes, Junior and his wife, Mildred, and James B. and Louis Laroque. They sold it to John F. Burgwin and George C. Clitheral for $4,000 on the 17th of January 1810. It was located on Nesses Creek on the eastern side of the Northeast River formerly belonging to Arthur Mabson, who was deceased by 1810. It contained 860 acres of highland, 150 acres of tide swamp, and 90 acres of Cat Tail for an estimated 1100 acres. Later, this plantation became known as the *Oakley Plantation*. (Nathaniel Moore was from *Oakley*.)

***O. M. Plantation:*** was located on the coast in the Holden Beach area just below the *Hewitt Plantation*.

***Oakland Plantation:*** was located in Bladen County and owned by Gen. Thomas Brown about 1812. He also owned a place called *Ashwood*, where he actually lived.

***Oakley Plantation***: was originally patented to William Forbes on the 10th of September 1735 for 1000 acres. It was located in New Hanover County on Nesby's Creek on the Northeast River of the Cape Fear. When Forbes sold it to Maurice Moore, he asked for a re-survey, as it did not appear to be a full 1000 acres. The original patent could not be located and there was a doubt about the exact location of the 1000 acres, or if it was 1000 acres. Maurice was the son of Nathanial M. Moore and obtained the *Oakley* on 3 December 1750 for 500 pounds. It included all the rights for hunting, hawking, fowling, fishing, all woods, waters, and rivers.

Maurice left it to his daughter, Mary, in his Last Will and Testament of 1753 and described it as on Nesses Creek, three miles above Wilmington, "unless my brother, Nathaniel Moore, who is now improving the land shall give my daughter, Mary - *York Plantation*...then Nathaniel will receive *Oakley*." Nathaniel and his wife, Margaret Moore, did give Mary the *York Plantation* and assumed residence at *Oakley*. He later sold it to James Gregory, a merchant in Wilmington, in 1762. Gregory sold it to William Arthur Mabson, a planter who left it in his Will (17 Nov 1777) to his son, Arthur all lands and 1/6th of the slaves, cattle, hogs and estate.

In 1808 the *Wilmington Gazette* (22 November) had the following advertisement: "*Whereas the Plantation on the NE River, 4 miles above Wilmington, belonging to the heirs of Mr. Arthur Mabson, deceased, having sustained great injury from persons trespassing thereon, this therefore is to inform all persons from hunting or destroying timber on the same; as I am determined to prosecute the offenders on detection.*" George Holmes.

Gabriel and Mildred Holmes and James and Louisa LaRoque sold it to Jon. F. Burgwin and Geo. Cletheral on 7 Jan 1810 for $4,000. At that time there were 860 acres of high land, 150 acres of tide swamp and 90 acres of Cat Tail. It was then sold to Parker Quince in 1845 who sold it to Richard Quince for $2400 and included two tracts....*Oakley* and 26 more acres above the corner of Stanley's Bank.

The northern most part of Oakley was bordered by the *Rock Hill Plantation*. On the south it was bordered by *Fairfields Plantation*.

Convenances: Nathaniel Moore (1759), James Gregory (1762), Arthur Mapson (1762), McArthur Mapson (1777), Mary Mabson & Gabriel Holmes & wife, and James B. Laroque and wife (1792), John F. Burgwin (1810), George Clitherall (1810), John F. Burgwin (1813), Frederick J. Hill (1817), Parker Quince (1827), Richard Quince (1845), Mary Quince (1857), Samuel Watters (1867), to Mary Watters, John Brown, John D. Bellamy, D. L. Gore (1897), Heirs of Gore, Gore Estate Corporation, L. B. Rogers (1927), etc. (See the description for *Nesses Plantation*.)

***Oaks Plantation:*** was the home of Samuel Swann, an attorney. This estate was located near the mouth of Turkey Creek. His plantation was known to be the 'finest' in the Cape Fear. It was near the bend to the eastward near the lower end of the Rocky Point area. Swann was one of the surveyors who ran the dividing line between North Carolina and Virginia in 1729. He was the first white man to cross the Dismal Swamp. His only son, Sam Swann, an officer in the Revolution, was killed in a duel with a Mr. Bradley in Wilmington in 1787.

The mansion, great house, on this plantation was described by Dr. John Hampden Hill as "probably the finest and most stately in the whole Cape Fear region." He applied the same description to the *Swann Point Plantation* next door. The residence had mahogany stairs and carved woodwork. It was destroyed by fire after Mr. Duncan Moore bought it. He rebuilt it in 1816 but it was in ruins again by 1858. It was said that the old house had a fishpond on top of it (which may have been a cistern system or cupola.)

The house was sold in 1808 and described as brick, 60 X 40 feet with a view of the river 200 yards away. Defensive embankments were entrenched here during the Revolutionary and Civil Wars. The original tract of 640 acres (part of the acreage of *Hyrneham*) was a gift in 1736 to Captain Edward Hyrne by Colonel Maurice Moore.

Later it was advertised for rent as a *"large commodious house having four good rooms on a floor with four dry cellars."* It was a large brick, two-story home.

Col. John Taylor reportedly owned it at one point.

The *Oaks Plantation* was offered for sale in the *Wilmington Star* on October 10, 1880 as: *"Sale of valuable Lands in Brunswick County - Public Sale - Courthouse door at Smithville - December 6, 1880. The tract embracing a portion of the two tracts, formerly known as the Oaks Plantation and the Hill Tract, containing 144 acres of swamp land and 956 acres of upland, and which was conveyed by John D. Taylor and wife to the late Delia H. Badger by deed of mortgage, dated 1st January 1870, and registered in Brunswick County Register of Deeds office in Book U., pages 233-235."*

In 1901, on September 4th, *The Oaks* was mentioned by the *Wilmington Messenger* in the following notice: *"James Dixon McRae, 51, died yesterday at 508 South Third Street, Wilmington. For the past three years he has been manager of James Sprunt's rice plantation, The Oaks, in Brunswick County. He was a farmer earlier in Brunswick County."*

In August of 1907, the Star noted that *"a bundle of exceptionally fine new rice, grown this season on The Oaks Plantation by Messrs. Robbins and Harrelson, who bought the plantation the first of this year, was shown in Wilmington yesterday. Old planters say they have never seen a finer prospect for rice and with good luck from now on, a large and profitable crop will be harvested. Messrs. Robbins and Harrelson have 130 acres of rice like the sample brought to the city, all exceptionally well headed and with no set-back they will gather between 7 and 8 thousand bushels on the plantation."* By October of that same year, they were expected to reap 15,000 to 20,000 bushels.

By February 9, 1917, the *Wilmington Star* reported that on Feb. the 8th, *"a land transaction of larger proportions than usual has just been consummated in this county. The property is that known as The Oaks, in Town Creek Township, 20,500 acres, owned by I. T. Robbins and Isham D. Harrelson, both substantial and prominent citizens of Brunswick County. The purchasers of this land were R. J. Ramseur, Gorge W. Ramseur, and John J. Ramseur, all of Lincolnton, the consideration being about one dollar per acre. The new owners intend to cultivate rice, which was grown on part of the acres at one time. There is also some timber on the property. Robert W. Davis, Esq., represented the parties in the transfer in Southport."*

On October 28, 1925, the *Wilmington News-Dispatch* reported that *"On Monday, Scipio Clark, colored, 17 years of age, while making a trip in a small boat from the Oaks Planatation to Big Island in the Cape Fear, where he was going to cut wild rice on the island, had his boat upset and he drowned, being unable to swim."*

*The Oaks* was offered for sale on April 14, 1929: *"For Sale - a real old time Southern Plantation, comprising 2,70 (?) acres, situated in Brunswick County, about*

*10 miles from Wilmington, with about 2 miles of river front. Unlimited fresh water fishing. Woods well stocked with game. Colonial home and seven smaller houses. 150 acres planted in rice and 250 acres in wheat, cotton and staple crops. Barn and farm implements. This property must be seen to be appreciated. H. F. Wilder, Real Estate."*

In November of 1930 the death of Mrs. Margaret Dudley Catlett, 71, wife of Washington Catlett, was announced. She was born January 21, 1860 at the Oaks Plantation and was the daughter of Thomas C. and Margaret Dudley McIlhenny. She was the granddaughter of Governor Edward B. Dudley, of North Carolina.

**Old Town Plantation:** was located at the mouth of Old Town Creek which is now a development called *Old Town Plantation.* Judge Maurice Moore originally bought this from his brother, General James Moore in 1761, and sold it to John Ancrum (Anerum?) in 1768. By 1860, Tom Cowan owned it and lived there until the Civil War.

On December 24, 1869 it was offered for sale for delinquent taxes and owned by Thomas Cowan, Town Creek Township, who owed $178.74. The sale ad was placed on January 1, 1870 by the *Wilmington Star.*

Bad luck struck in 1898 when a barn *"containing 900 bushels of rice in the straw, belonging to Mr. W. H. Batson, was burned. The barn was some distance from the house and "Mr. Batson did not know the fire had occurred until he was notified yesterday morning. The loss is estimated at about $1,200 and there was about $1,000 worth of insurance. Mr. Batson had intended to thresh his rice today."* Wilmington Messenger, Jan. 11, 1898.

The *Old Town Plantation Mansion House Site*, on the north bank of Town Creek, at the Cape Fear River was listed on th North Carolina State Inventory of Historic Resources. Date unknown.

**Old Town Creek Plantation:** was located at the mouth of Town Creek, on the western bank about eight miles south of Wilmington. This is the location where Sir John Yeamans settled the first Charles-town colony about 1664-65. In 1761 Judge Maurice Moore, son of Col. Maurice Moore, bought this plantation from his brother, General James Moore. He later sold it in 1768 to John Ancrum who was a leading merchant.

**Orton Plantation:** was originally settled by Maurice Moore, a grandson of Sir John Yeoman. He later sold it to his brother, Roger Moore who became known as King Roger of *Orton.* Roger built the lower central part of the present mansion in 1725. It was one of the largest and most beautiful estates. His descendents remained there for three generations then sold it to Richard Quince who owned it for the next thirty years. Then, Governor Benjamin Smith bought it. It was the most southern rice plantation on the river located about seventeen miles from Wilmington. It is still a beautiful showplace today.

The Roger Moore plantation had a brick home located about two miles from Brunswick Town and about half a mile from the river, although there is a creek that comes "up close to the door between two beautiful meadows about three miles in length.

The home Moore built had walls three-feet thick and made of brick. It was one and a half stories, and "loop-holed for firearms" so the home could be used as a fortress if needed.

George Moore, Roger Moore's son, lived at Orton when he became one of the leaders in the resistance against the Stamp Act in 1766. He later sold it to his brother-in-law who sold it to Benjamin Smith, a Governor of North Carolina and an aide to George Washington.

In 1812, Frederick J. Hill and Anne I. Watters were married on the plantation according to the St. James Parish Register, 1811-1854.

In 1826, Dr. Frederick Hill bought the estate and improved the rice plantation by using the ponds to irrigate the fields. This method was efficient and productive only when a "large number of *slaves* were used to keep down *week* (?) competition." It became less productive than the other plantations further up the Cape Fear as they learned to utilize tidal swamps to water the fields, which was much easier to manage, and less labor intensive. Orton had to continue to rely on the ponds because the tidal waters near it were too saline (salty) which was deadly to the rice plants. This intensive labor required a rather large slave population that was estimated to be about *160*.

Dr. Hill also added another floor to the main home, an attic, and the four-fluted columns on the front porch. He died at 51 years of age on May 9, 1847. Dr. Hill was president of the Bank of Cape Fear and was buried at Orton.

On November 6, 1835, the *Peoples Press* reported that Kindred Saul, "An honest man", had died on the 30th at Orton at the age of 50.

Orton operated milling facilities for threshing and polishing the rice. In 1860 Brunswick County had ten rice mills averaging forty bushels per acre at Orton.. Miller owned it at that time. The rice value was $15,704. Other tidal swamp plantations averaged sixty bushel per acre.

"The *Orton Plantation* remained in Hill's possession (heirs?) until the fall of Fort Anderson and Fort Fisher during the Civil War. Following the Confederate defeat at Fort Fisher, Union soldiers confiscated Orton Plantation and used the home as a military hospital, thus sparing it from destruction. Orton Plantation was abandoned after the War and the house sat empty for 19 years." *Wikipedia.*

After the Civil War emancipation of the slaves, individuals were hired for wages. Owners arranged to trade a portion of the crop in exchange for labor. The plantation was finally sold at auction in 1872. The purchaser committed suicide soon after.

The purchaser.... In 1876 Currer Richardson Roundell, 24 years old, single, of England, committed suicide in a Wilmington hotel. He was the owner of Orton plantation after the war. He was buried in Oakdale Cemetery in Wilmington July 26, 1876. (In 1784-1873 Currer Danson Richardson Roundell was listed in the English Peerage. Could this have been his father?)

Eventually Col. Kenneth MacKenzie Murchison purchased it, in 1880 (1884?), and began the restoration. It cost him over $25,000 to repair the rice fields. The owners discontinued the rice production and turned their interest toward restoring the buildings and grounds. Turpentine, tobacco and cotton paid for the "saddle horses and London finery."

Local newspapers recorded several *Orton* deaths in the late 1800s. Mrs. Lizzie Pope, of Warsaw, NC died in February of 1888 and her body was brought back to be buried on *Orton Plantation* "at her father's place". *(Wilmington Messenger.)* In 1891, Samuel R. Chinnis, Superintendent of *Orton*, died of malarial fever. He was 62 years old and "sick for some time on the plantation and died at Phoenix, NC on the Carolina Central Railroad." *(Wilmington Messenger.)*

*Orton Plantation.*
*Photography by John Muuss, Photographic Artist.*

103

In 1897 a news account stated that "*A few days ago, Col. Murchison, Mr. F. S. Ellis and Mr. James Sprunt made some excavations in the ruins of Governor Tryon's palace, at Russellborough, on Orton, near Old Brunswick on the Cape Fear, which had been identified by Mr. Sprunt from records in the Brunswick County courthouse. The search for relics of colonial days was only partially rewarded by the recovery of some broken pieces of Dutch tiling from the fireplace and some ancient sack bottles of curious make.*"

Mr. Wesley Corbett was the plantation superintendent on April 21, 1897. He married Miss Maud Griffith of Wilmington and lived on the plantation grounds. Murchison died in 1904 and *Orton Plantation* was purchased by his son-in-law and daughter, Luola Sprunt.

James Sprunt and his wife Luola added wings to both sides of the home and began to design and plant the gardens. Luola's Chapel was added in 1916 after his wife's death from scarlet fever. The Chapel has four columns with a cupola on top of the roof.

In 1924, Sprunt's son, James L. Sprunt became the owner. He opened the old colonial road to Wilmington. Prior to this it was accessible only by water. He also expanded the garden area adding flowering peach trees and cedar trees. In 1998 the size of the plantation gardens grew to 20 acres. *Orton* is one of the most well preserved historical sites in eastern North Carolina with a magnificent display annually of azaleas, live oaks, pansies, and camellias. The formal gardens are decorated with stone sculptures and are also home to the local wildlife where over 250 species of birds reside in its six-mile long and half-mile wide lands.

*Orton Plantation* was named for the village of Orton near the town of Kendall in the Lake District of England, the ancestral home of the Moore's. The original grant was for over 8,000 acres and grew when the Moore's bought two adjoining plantations, *Kendall* and *Lilliput*.

The old mansion is not open to the public but the structure of the home is visible in the gardens, which are especially beautiful in early April when azaleas and camellias bloom under the shady oaks.

In April of 1941 approximately 50,000 acres of forest land was swept by a forest fire which ranged from Beaver Dam to *Orton Plantation*, about 13 miles. "The woods burned were the most valuable crop of timber in Brunswick County." (*Wilmington Star.*)

In August of 1950, two swords from the Revolutionary War era were unearthed near *Orton* by a grading crew working on River Road.

**Owen Plantation:** was owned by Gov. John Owen and located near Elizabethtown.

**Owen Hill Plantation:** was owned by Col. Thomas Owen, the son of Governor John Owen who lived there later. John married Elizabeth, daughter of General Thomas Brown. Gen. James Owen also owned it.

**Pleasant Garden Plantation:** was owned by Thomas and Barbara Fonte. Fredrick Jones owned another Pleasant Garden Plantation. It is unknown whether these were two different plantations or owned by both at different times.

**Pleasant Hall Plantation:** was located near *Mt. Gallant Plantation* and the home of William Davis, Esq., who also owned a place on Turkey Creek called *Bloom Hill* (1809).

**Pleasant Oaks Plantation:** was granted to the widow of John Moore (brother of Maurice and Roger) in 1728. The name Widow Moores Creek is derived from this plantation and its owner. (See also *Haw Fields Plantation and Sandy Bay Plantation*)

In 1948 the *Wilmington Star* newspaper announced that this spring, *Pleasant Oaks* would have 7,000 more azaleas. Joe Ramsauer and his father were co-managers of the plantation for the owner, F. B. Adams of New York.

**Point Pleasant Plantation:** At the sharp bend of the Northeast River west of Castle Haynes, Col. James Innes resided on *Point Pleasant*. He died in 1759 leaving no children. He left the bulk of his estate to help educate other children.

Janet Schaw, who wrote the *Lady of Quality*, said the "plate, linen, furniture, jewels and cloths of the house were very considerable." The home stood on a fine lawn but burned before 1782.

**Point Repose Plantation:** was located between Hood's Creek and the river. It was first owned by "*Point Repose*" and later bought by James Murray in 1735. General Robert Howe died on *Point Repose* in 1786. He was buried a few miles away on the Grange farm in an unmarked grave. John Howell owned the plantation next door to it at *Westmoreland*. Also nearby was the *Rowan Plantation*.

At one time Murray's nephew, General Thomas Clark, a Revolutionary War officer, owned this plantation.

**Poplar Grove Plantation:** was located near Wilmington and owned by Joseph Mumford Foy, the son of James Foy, Jr. Joseph is the one who designed and built the current manor house in 1850 in the Greek Revival Style. It has 4,284 square feet, 12 fireplaces, 2 pairs of corbelled interior chimneys and 12 rooms.

The Foy family originally bought the land in 1795 and kept it until the 1970s. James Foy, Jr. purchased 628 acres from Frances Clayton. It is one of the south's oldest peanut plantations. It also originally produced peas, corn and beans with *64 slaves* working the fields.

*Joseph M. and Henrietta Foy, Poplar Grove Plantation*

More recently, the *Wilmington Star* news reported in November of 2008, that "The Foy family walked these woods beside *Poplar Grove Plantation* for years. It's where their ancestors cut logs for lumber and dammed a pond for grinding corn. But about three years ago, they decided as a family to donate 67 acres of these woods, including the millpond, to the Coastal Land Trust. The Abbey Nature Preserve

was born. The Foys wanted to ensure their land did not succumb to development, but they also wanted a memorial for Margaret Abbey Foy Moore, a family member who died of breast cancer four years ago, said Betty Foy Taylor, Margaret's sister and site manager at Poplar Grove."

*Poplar Grove Plantation House.*
*Photos Courtesy of Poplar Grove*
*Plantation Archive.*

**Porter's Bluff Plantation:** was the property of John Porter in 1751. It was located near *Lillington Hall* on the Northeast River.

**Prospect Hall Plantation:** is part of a tract of 850 acres entered by Thomas Brown who died in New Hanover County in 1748/49, as stated in his Last Will and Testament. He left his wife, Fortune Brown, 500 acres on the sound. (Masonborough

107

Sound.) Earlier James Hasell had purchased 320 acres of this land (1743). *Prospect Hall Plantation* was located next to *Hassell's Place*, in Myrtle Grove.

After Brown's death, his wife married Robert Stanton. She gave the property to her son, Henry Irby, Jr. by a former husband, Henry Irby, Senior, and also deeded part to William Brown. In 1860 William Brown and his wife, Isabella, sold William Tuckey 200 acres of the 850 acres originally granted by patent to Hon. James Hasel(l). In 1760 William and Isabella Brown sold another 100 acres of his 300 to John Morris of New Hanover County. In 1761 Henry and Mary Irby sold James Moran 100 acres on Cabbage Inlet. Moran named his plantation *Prospect Hall*, and decreed in his will in 1773 that at his death, it was to be sold. Moran hailed from Ireland. His son, James Shirley Moran became the "entry taker" in New Hanover County by 1784.

In April 1800, John McDonnel sold it to Griffith J. McRee for $250. It was located near a small creek opposite Cabbage Inlet and runs up Cabbage Creek. On the south is the island of James Hasell. On the north is the island of John Morris/John Walker (100 acres).

Maj. John Walker (born 1741) later owned it. He was the nephew of the famous Major "Jack" Walker, of the Revolution. He was *uncultured and unrefined, a great fighter but considered good-natured.* Walker died in 1813 and left his estate to his namesake, his nephew, John Walker. Walker, II married the daughter of Colonel Thomas Davis of Fayetteville and died in 1862, leaving a large family.

In 1804 Richard Langdon purchased it for $300 and sold it in 1807 (100 acres). In 1805 Langdon bought another 100 acres for $400. By 1807 Langdon sold 100 acres to Thomas Cragg in Brunswick County for $360, including all buildings, etc.

In 1846 Thomas Green sold a small part of this land to Benj. Cragg for $50…near Benj. Cragg's house 150 yards to a stake, west to a post near the Cragg house, due west of Jumpin Run Branch. This tract consisted of 50 acres.

**Purviance Plantation:** was located on Purviance Creek next to *Prospect Hall*. It has also been called *Whiskey Creek*. Col. William Purviance owned it.

**Ramah Plantation:** was located on Carver's Creek in Bladen County and owned by the Andres family.

**Reaves Point:** was the residence of Joel Reeves and his family. In 1908 it was referenced in the obituary of William Martin, aged 85, whose home was in the vicinity of Reaves Point, near the fisheries.

**Red Banks Plantation**: was located in New Hanover County in August of 1769. Richard Quince sold Lewis Henry DeRossett 5 tracts of 2,805 acres on the Northeast branch of the Cape Fear River for 150 pounds of sterling, which included 640 acres known as *Red Banks*. The original patent was to William Gray in June of 1736 who sold it to his brother, Jn. Gray. Then his "heir-in-law" sold it to Wm. Lithgow in 1742. It was also known as *Gray & Carter's Plantation* when the patent was given to William Gray and William Carter in June of 1736.

Another track, 185 acres adjoined the *Gray and Carter Plantation*, which was originally a patent to Lewis Briant in June of 1736 and sold in February 1739 to William Gray, and eventually ended up with Lithgow. By 1779, 2,805 acres was in Henry DeRossett's hands.

***Rice's Plantation:*** Nathaniel Rice owned this plantation located on the south side of Old Town Creek.

***Roan Landing Plantation:*** was owned by Mr. J. C. Rowell in September of 1874. It had a fishpond on the premises, which contained large perch and trout. Mr. Rowell kept them as pets and fed them by hand where they frequently raised their heads an inch above the water to take food according to an article in the *Wilmington Star n*ews.

***Rock Hill Plantation:*** John Davis, Esq. was the owner of Rock Hill. He also owned the *Mulberry Plantation* on the Northwest River. It was the residence of Jehu Davis and later his son, Thomas J. Davis.

***Rocky Point Plantation:*** was originally granted to Col. Maurice Moore on the 6th of June 1725. However, by the 1st of January 1796, it was sold to Samuel Ashe upon the death of Frances Clayton. Ashe paid 4,111 pounds for 650 acres at Rocky Point on the Northeast branch of the Cape Fear River. This area was sometimes called *White Marsh.*

The True Republican or American Whig newspaper posted the following announcement in the 23rd of May 1809 and 20th of June 1809 editions: "Five Dollars reward. Ranaway from my Plantation at Rocky Point, some months since, a negro man known by the name of Demar. He is a stout, lusty and ill put together fellow, and walks clumsily, and is between thirty and forty years of age. He has been frequently seen in Wilmington, and is supposed (to be) lurking in and about there, as it has become an asylum for runaways. Whoever shall apprehend and deliver him to Messrs. Robert and William Mitchell, reasonable expenses paid. Samuel Ashe. May 23, 1809."

***Rocky Run Plantation:*** This estate was located next to *Rose Hill* and owned by Maurice Jones, Esq., and later his son-in-law, Dr. Nathaniel Hill.

***Rose Hill Plantation:***  A 1736 land grant to William Gray began the legacy of the *Rose Hill Plantation*.  In 1784 Lewis Henry DeRossett conveyed the land to Parker Quince who then sold it to Thomas Davis.  It contained about 400 acres.  The remainder (?) was given to Richard Quince by way of the Parker Quince Last Will and Testament (1785).  Rose Hill was then willed to Richard Quince by his father, Parker Quince.  The Quince family came from Ramsgate, England.

By 1797 Richard Quince sold George Moore a tract of 400 acres, which he received from his father, Parker in addition to 1530 acres, which were patented to Richard Quince on 15 December 1796.

A cemetery remains on this land with massive headstones, mostly in disrepair due to vandalism and decay.  It is located on the east side of the Northeast River.  Headstones recorded in 1963 included the following:  Nathaniel Hill Quince (Died Oct. 25, 1842, age 20 years old); Jane Quince (Died Aug 23, 1849, age 47 years); William Soranzo Hasell, a Native of Charleston, South Carolina, died Oct. 6, 1815, age 36 years).  Broken stones read:  Elizabeth Moore Davis (died March 24, ___, age 27); J. Q (nothing more); ____ "She who knew him best".

In 1842 Richard Quince and William Quince sold James F. McRee the Rose Hill Plantation for $4,000.  The plantation contained 2,287 acres.

By February 1845 James F. McRee sold Rose Hill to Levin Lane for $5,000.  This included 800 acres originally granted to Richard Quince for a total of 2,287 acres.

The *Wilmington Herald* published, on the 26th of March 1853, the following notice: *"Died near Wilmington on the 24th at the residence of her father, Parker Quince, Mrs. Elizabeth Davis, wife of Frederick Davis, age 27 years."*  The Parish records of St. James Church show that the funeral of Mrs. Jane Quince was on August 24, 1849.  She was the wife of Parker Quince and daughter of Dr. Nathaniel Hill.  Nathaniel Hill Quince was the son of Parker Quince and his wife, Jane.

In June of 1855, Parker Quince mentioned his granddaughter, Jane Hill Davis in  his will.  Jane Hill Davis was the daughter of Frederick S. Davis and "my deceased daughter Elizabeth M. Davis, *a slave.* He also mentioned his grandson, Thomas J. Davis.

In 2008, Mr. Jim Summey, of the General Electric Corporation, contacted members of the Brunswick Search and Rescue Team (including the author), along with Candace McGreevy of the Lower Cape Fear Historical Society, to request that Human Remains Detection dogs determine the extent of the cemetery located on the former Rose Hill Plantation. Christy Judah, K9 Bailey and K9 Gypsy, Jim Ware and K9 Storm, Shelley Wood and K9 Carlos, and two additional canine handlers from South Carolina, spent the day at the Rose Hill Cemetery determining and marking possible grave sites. The site was then cleaned up and preserved by the GE Corporation providing a white picket fence and plaque identifying the site for future generations.

The historical marker reads: "Rose Hill Plantation Cemetery. 1815-1867. This property was part of a 1736 land grant to William Gray. The cemetery served the communities of Rose Hill, Rock Hill and Rocky Run. Members of the Quince, Moore, Hasell, Hill and Davis families and their slaves were buried here."

***Rowan Plantation:*** was located near *Point Repose Plantation* and noted in a sale as land next to *Westmoreland Plantation* in 1798.

***Roxana Plantation***: The Cape Fear Rice Company operated the *Roxana Plantation*. They planned to build and maintain the roads, bridges, canals, operate mills, steamboats, dredge, tran rods (sic), and operate all kind of machinery to conduct a mercantile, brokerage, and commission business in October of 1902.

***Russ Plantation:*** was located on the north side of the road leading from Supply to Bolivia across from the *Galloway Plantation*.

***Russelborough Plantation:*** was located north of Brunswick Town and contained only 55 acres. Captain Russell, of the British Navy, purchased it from Roger Moore's estate. Capt. Russell sold it to Brice Dobb. Later, William Moore willed these 55 acres, as a part of *Orton Plantation* on 1 March 1758. It was later sold to Governor Arthur Dobbs for 300 pounds of sterling and then sold by Arthur Dobbs' son to Governor Tryon in 1767. While Tryon lived there it was referred to as *Tryon's Palace*. It was also referred to as *Sound Land* on the south side. Originally it was part of the Orton estate.

The Russelborough home was built after the West Indian style with "double galleries or piazzas" as they were called.

*Governor Arthur Dobbs*

This estate had avenues, gardens, outbuildings, all planned with elegant formality. It was the location of the first armed resistance to British rule.

Governor Dobbs is buried at the St. Philips Church at Brunswick Town.

**San Souci Plantation:** was located north of the *Hilton Plantation.* Caleb Grainger, Sr., son of Joshua Grainger, originally owned this plantation and was one of the founders of Wilmington. In addition, he bought some land located near Masonborough from George Moore. It was named "*Masonboro*" since he was a prominent mason of the time. Mr. Arthur Hill later owned this plantation.

**Sandy Bay Plantation:** joined the *Lilliput Plantation.* In 1733 the Rev. John LaPierre owned it. The same year, he sold it to Jonathan Skrine who later sold it to Roger Moore. Roger left it in his will in 1751 to his son, George Moore. In 1779 it was sold to John Nutt and remained in their family until 1834. Eventually it was sold to F. B. Adams in 1934 in Brunswick County and became a part of the *Pleasant Oaks Plantation.*

**Schawfields Plantation:** was owned by Robert Schaw. It was the 4th place up the Northwest River on the west side, next to *Prospect Hall.* Robert Schaw was a merchant in Wilmington. Schaw participated in Tryons expedition in 1771 as a Colonel of Artillery under General Hugh Waddell. (See also *Shawfields Plantation.*)

**Schonwald Plantation:** was owned by Dr. Schonwald.

**Sedgefield on the Sound:** was located in Wilmington and mentioned in the Will of General Thomas Brown in 1814.

**Sedgely Abbey Plantation:** was located on the east sound side of the lower river opposite of Brunswick. John Guerard who is buried at Brunswick Town owned it. He died in 1789. His widow married Peter Maxwell who died in 1812. This land had a private racetrack on it but was not really a *plantation* as the soil was very sandy and covered by pines and scrub oaks. It was most likely a summer residence

**Shawfields Plantation:** In July of 1847 H. W. Burgwin advertised "*two runaway slaves from Shawfields, Brunswick County*" in a Wilmington newspaper. This may have been the same as the "*Schawfields*" *Plantation* but spelled slightly differently.

**Shine Plantation:** On February 25, 1846, there was a For Sale ad posted by the *Wilmington Chronicle* stating, "*On Thursday, the 19th of March next, a large number of valuable slaves will be sold at the residence of James B. Shine, in Brunswick County. The said slaves will be sold for cash, for the purpose of paying sundry debts specified in a mortgage executed by James B. Shine, in favor of the subscriber.*" No other information is presently available.

***Sloop Point Plantation:*** was located in Hampstead, N. C. It was first built by John Baptista Ashe in 1725 and later passed on to his son Governor Samuel Ashe. The Sloop Point home has been authenticated as the oldest surviving structure in North Carolina.

Thomas T. Waterman dates the structure as circa 1728 and possibly built by John B. Ashe himself. (Later inherited by General John Ashe.) It was originally called *Ashe's Neck* but it is not known if any of the Ashe family actually lived there other than as a secondary residence.

The kitchen was brick and the home large for the period. This is generally accepted as one of the oldest buildings on the coast. The main house was utilitarian in scope and not exquisitely designed, as were some other plantation great houses.

The location of *Sloop Point* is about 25 miles from the Cape Fear River, the outer limits of settlement in the lower Cape Fear valley.

***Smith Plantation:*** was located near Whiteville and owned by James Smith.

***Smith, Thomas.*** Landgrave Thomas Smith was given 48,000 acres as early as 1713 but made no attempt to settle them. This included the present Bald Head Island. Most of the land was on the west side of the river below Wilmington and on the upper Northwest River. Some of the land included the Lockwood Folly River area.

The Northwest branch of the River was prime for crops, especially in the Rocky Point area on the northeast branch. The principal crops were rice, indigo, corn and tobacco, but wheat was grown also. However, it was cheaper to bring wheat into the area from Fayetteville that was grown in the backcountry than to grow it here. This was because of where the grinding mills were located and it was cheaper to bring the ground flour to Wilmington than to ship it from Wilmington and then return it in the form of flour.

***Smithfield Plantation:*** was located on both sides of the Northwest, between *Blue Banks* and *Drury Allen's*, and contained about 2200 acres of land. It was offered for sale in Wilmington on July 2, 1788. There are several former *slaves* who listed Smithfield as *their* plantation in the interviews section of this book.

***Snow's Plantation:*** The *Wilmington Chronicle* posted the following on March 5, 1847: *"REWARD: Some time since, the subscriber's house, at Snow's Plantation, Brunswick County, was burned; and a few days ago fire was again rekindles (d) on his premises and a task of turpentine trees ruined. I therefore have reason to believe there is a villain at work determined to injure me at all hazards; and I offer a good reward for proof sufficient to convict a law, the persons that perpetrated the above acts. Samuel Beery."*

***Spring Garden Plantation:*** *(formerly Groveley)* John Baptista Ashe sold this plantation to Maurice Moore on the 5th of December 1727. It included about 640 acres on the north side of Old Town Creek about five miles from ye Old Town, commonly known as *Spring Garden*. He paid 50 pounds for it.

Mr. Moore's ancestors changed the name to *Grovely*. Later Ann R. Quince bequeathed it in her Will to her cousin, A. D. Moore and it was later bought by Dr. John D. Bellamy (1850) and passed to his descendents.

The *Spring Garden Plantation* was also the home of Frederick Jones, Esq. It was located near *Swann Point*. This may be a different location than the Maurice Moore plantation.

***Springfield Plantation:*** was located near the Rocky Point settlement. It originally belonged to Col. Maurice Moore in 1725.

***Strawberry Plantation:*** was also located near the Rocky Point settlement and originally belonged to Col. Maurice Moore in 1725.

***Stag Park Plantation:*** was located on the west side of the Northeast River. Some of the first explorers to this site named it. Governor Burrington was issued this land in 1711. He was given 640 acres but altered the grant to include 5,000 acres. A Mr. Strudwick and the Hawfields of Orange County later owned it.

***Swann Point Plantation:*** was owned by lawyer John Swann. It was considered one of the finest residences in the area.

***Sturgeon Creek Plantation:*** was first settled by four brothers, Jehu, John, William, and Roger Davis who emigrated from Massachusetts to South Carolina and then moved into the Cape Fear region about 1723. Jehu Senior married Miss Jane Assup, an Irish lady and had four children: Jehu Jr., Thomas, Ann and Rebecca. In a deed from Thomas Davis to John Roots, dated March 22, 1773, there is a reference to a "burying ground" on the plantation.

The original patents were for 1580 acres. Jehu Senior received a patent on the 19th of September 1737 for 640 acres, granted by Governor Gabriel Johnston (e). The next 140 acres was granted in 1753 and a third patent of 400 acres in 1755. The 4th patent was for another 400 acres and described the land as "cross the branch" and *"Westfield"*.

In 1765, Jehu Davis Senior, in his Will, left his property to his son, Thomas. Thomas Davis married Mary Moore, granddaughter of Roger Moore of the *Orton Plantation* legacy. They had six children. Thomas sold his property to John Roots in 1773, and died a few years later in 1796. Roots increased the size of the plantation to 2680 acres by buying a tract at a time and receiving more grants. He died in the 1790s leaving all his land to his daughter, Mary. She married John Lock and they had one son who died young. His tombstone is currently located in an old cemetery, beyond Hala Wasi subdivision on Village Road in Leland.

'She then married a Mr. Berry from Bladen County and sold *Sturgeon Creek Plantation* to Benjamin Smith in 1803.

*Sturgeon Creek Plantation* was recorded in April of 1806 as being on the sales listings of Benjamin Smith. Mary Beery (daughter of John Roots) of Brunswick County, sold another portion of the home place for a sum of one thousand six hundred dollars, to Benjamin Smith in January of 1813 (incorrect date perhaps? or adding more acreage from Mary Berry after the initial purchase.) This sale included several tracts of land including a saw mill beginning "*at a large pine in the edge of the Long Savannah on the west side of a large bay said to (be at) the head of the western branch of said Sturgeon Creek; the center tree of a tract granted to Thomas Davis on the twelfth of April one-thousand seven-hundred and seventy-five for six-hundred and forty acres running thence with the line thereof south thirty degrees west forty four chains to a stake; then with another line thereof south eighty-four chains to a pine corner near the edge of a bay called the head of Alligator Creek; then south thirty west twenty-five chains to a pine by the north side of large bay across the main road at seven chains fifty links leading from Wilmington Fayetteville, then south forty-one east twenty-five chains through the bay to a stake; then east forty-one chains fifty links to a pine on the northern side of the rice field of Greate Branch of Sturgeon Creek, standing eight chains fifty links due south from the main road being the south east corner of said grant......down to the corner of the tract to John Davis.....to the line of the tract granted to Benjamin Smith....along the high land on the same side of the juniper to the Old Mount Misery Road.......back line of Bluff tract which was grante to Roger Moore, Esquire...from Welches Creek....tract granted to John Roots.....said tract containing two-thousand six-hundred acres....except the parts of the tract sold to Edmun Homes and all houses buildings, orchards ways, water courses, profits commodities....all appurtenances....*" *Signed by Mary Beery.*

By March 31, 1889, the late W. R. Penny owned this plantation and listed it for sale in *The Messenger*, in Wilmington. It consisted of 275 acres, a new house, good rice land and was six miles from town. It sold again on the 26th of August 1911 under foreclosure, listed as being on Penny or King Landing and containing an entire saw mill, equipment, and one pair of mules; one black mare called Rhody and one horse/mule called Red. It was sold to satisfy the mortgage of N. A. Franks and J. C. Robertson.

Suffice it to say this was an extremely large plantation.

**Summer Hill Plantation:** In 1834 William M. Green sold Governor Edward B. Dudley a part of *Summer Hill,* which was on Green's Creek, and another tract in 1844, which he deeded to his son, Christopher H. Dudley (1441.75 acres). (*See Greenfield and Green Hill Plantations.*)

**Swan Point - Turkey Creek:** was located in New Hanover County and Frederic J. Swann sold the 375 acres to Joseph A. Hill in November of 1834 for 2500 dollars. This tract known as *Swan Point,* began on Turkey Creek and ran along the main road and down the same to a road or avenue leading to Swann Point House, running adjacent to White Oak Field to Turkey Creek.

*Taylor Plantation:* was located in the Holden Beach area and once owned by Mary Hemingway. This later became part of the *Job Holden Plantation* as outlined in her Last Will and Testament from the 1840s. Mary Hewett Hemingway owned many slaves, some of which are outlined in her Will. She is buried on Kinston Street just off the Holden Beach Causeway.

**Thornbury Plantation:** was owned by John F. Burgwin, formerly of New York, on the 19th of April 1813. He bought it with George C. Clitherall for $7,147. It was located on the Northeast River and contained 25 acres of tidal swamp, 240 acres on the west side of the river and was formerly the property of Daniel Mallett who was deceased in 1813. They also bought another 26 acres of tide swamp from Thomas J. Davis. In 1809 the following advertisement was run in the local Wilmington, NC papers:

**May 30, 1809.** The True Republican or American Whig (Vol. 1, No. 23, 25, 27, 45 on 7 November 1809.)
Ten Dollars Reward.
"Ranaway from Mr. John Williams, in Wilmington, about the first of April, 1808, a negro woman named Jessa, about 23 years of age, 5 feet 5 inches high, slender made, and likely dresses very genteelly, and generally wears a blue handkerchief on her head, which comes down over her eyes, on account of their being very weak. She is light complected, was brought up in the family of Mr. Daniel Mallet, is a tolerable good seamstress, and is very well acquainted with housework. Having purchased the above negro wench some time ago from Mr. J. Williams, I will give the above reward for delivering her to me, or the jailor of this place, or any other in the state. If she is returned to me in the course of two or three months from this time, I will give her the liberty of procuring another master, provided she does not wish to live with me, or hiring her own time. Thomas Hunter, May 30, 1809."

***Trapland Plantation:*** was mentioned in the Will of Dr. Samuel Green as he left his young daughter, Hannah, this plantation which was 640 acres joining the *Greefields tract.*

***Trip Plantation:*** was located off of the current highway 179, turn onto Hale Swamp Road and take the first dirt road on the left to visit the *Trip Plantation* Cemetery. This old cemetery is said to be the final resting place of many of the slaves from the Trip Plantation according to 100-year old Harvey Robinson in March of 2009.

***Vats Plantation:*** was located near the Rocky Point settlement. It originally belonged to Col. Maurice Moore in 1725.

This is the location where the body of Colonel Moore and his two sons, Judge Maurice and Gen. James Moore (as well as other family members) were buried in a vault.

It was later bought by Ezekiel Lane and inherited by his son, Levin Lane.

***Walker's Run Plantation:*** was mentioned in the Will Abstract of General Thomas Brown in 1814.

***Walnut Grove Plantation:*** was owned by Col. Thomas Robeson and located in Bladen County.

***Wanet or Locke Plantation:*** was noted for sale in the Wilmington Chronicle on June 3, 1846. *"For Sale: 600-700 acres of land lying on the Cape Fear River and Hood's Creek in Brunswick County. It is well timbered with pine, oak, etc. Some few boxes are cur for turpentine. It is the tract on which Mrs. Anna Locke resides. For conditions apply to A. A. Wanet."*

***Waters Plantation:*** (or perhaps Watters Plantation?) There were several Watters family members who lived in the early 1700s to the mid 1700s that owned plantations, so this may simply be referring to their collective lands instead of the more proper plantation name. The *Wilmington Weekly Star* posted on the 12th of September 1879 that *"on Watter's Place in Brunswick County, the property of Col. S. L. Fremont, there are 108 acres in rice that is estimated to yield fifty bushes to the acre - a portion of it will yield more than this, probably sixty bushels to the acre."*

***Westmoreland Plantation:*** On the 19th of March 1798, there was an advertised public auction at the Court House in New Hanover County. The plantation where the late John Howell lived was being sold. It was listed as 400 acres on the Northwest River and Wood's Creek, running back to Indian Creek. It was located between *Point Repose* and *Rowan Plantation.*

**White Marsh Plantation:** was mentioned in an advertisement in the Wilmington Gazette (No. 646) on May 23, 1809. The ad said, "Ranaway, a likely negro fellow, named Tom, formerly owned by Mr. Lucas at the White Marsh. He is about 5 feet 8 or 9 inches high and well made. Having a wife here and a mother on Town Creek, he may probably be lurking about town. All masters of vessels and other persons are therefore cautioned at the peril of the law (which shall be strictly enforced against them) not to harbor or carry him away. Whoever shall deliver the said fellow to the subscriber, or lodge him in jail, shall receive 15 dollars. Henry Young. May 9, 1809."

**Williams Plantation:** was located 1/4 mile from DuPont Plat in the Summerville community of Brunswick County. A circa 1840 house was on the property. No other information is known.

**Winnabow Plantation:** was the birthplace of Governor Daniel Russell in 1845. It is located on the southwest side of state road 1521 along the edge of Rice's Creek. It was built during the 1730s and originally owned by Nathaniel Rice. It later became a part of Governor Russell's plantation that was located a few hundred feet further south.

### Notes on Rice's Creek:

Recently the NC Coastal Land Trust purchased portions of this magnificent shoreline. In a news release it was described as: *"Sweet gums, bays and tupelos dot the shoreline, but it's the bald cypresses that stand out." "Some of the towering specimens are believed to be 300 to 500 years old and were likely passed over by loggers generations ago because they were misshapen or subject to interior decay. Yesterday's "loss" is today's treasure, as many of these trees harbor a variety of birds and other wildlife. Some died long ago and lost their interiors to fire, but still they stand like stubborn smokestacks."*

Wildlife still seen along the banks of Rice's Creek includes kingfishers, ospreys, herons, turkey vultures and several species of songbirds. In addition, alligators, bald eagles, bears and white-tailed deer greet the bass and catfish. The Brunswick County Nature Park includes hundreds of acres along Town Creek, which accesses Rice's Creek.

A recent news release by the NC Coastal Land Trust provides a background on Rice's Creek:

*"Rice's Creek is named after Nathaniel Rice of Old Town Creek, according to historical texts. A 1733 map of the area shows the plantation of "N. Rice" roughly*

*at the confluence of Rice's Creek and Town Creek – a first-order tributary of the Cape Fear River. Rice was also listed as a homeowner at old Brunswick Town and considered a prominent planter in the Colonial and Revolutionary periods. In 1729, Rice was one of four justices of county court, along with Roger Moore, William Dry and Jehu Davis. Brunswick was part of New Hanover County in those days. Rice was also on the losing side of a fight to keep the seat of pre-Revolutionary government at Brunswick Town. It was moved to Newton, now known as Wilmington."*

Nathaniel Rice came to the area along with John Baptista Ashe and a number of other prominent men from Bathe, England about 1727. He was the Secretary of the Province in 1729 and became a Justice of the Peace for New Hanover County in 1734. He was later named a member of Governor Burrington's Council and a Vestryman in St. Philip's Parrish, then appointed to erect a fort in Southport, later called Fort Johnston.

This mansion is located on 220 acres and has nine fireplaces. It was built around 1840. The original name was reportedly "Winnebah" according to Helen Taylor, a Winnabow resident, and was most likely an Indian word. Ms. Taylor is a descendent of Governor Russell. Her father, Jackson Johnson once owned the plantation.

Nathaniel Rice lived on Governor's Road (where *Winnabow Plantation* is located) prior to 1730 after purchasing the 200 acres from Jeremiah Bigford. James Hassell also owned acreage on this road.

At the death of Governor Burrington in 1734, Nathaniel Rice became acting Governor until Gabriel Johnston could be sworn in later that year. Governor Daniel Russell also occupied this plantation. He used a great deal of the same details as the Rice house when he built his own mansion a few hundred yards away.

*Winnabow Plantation*

**Woodburn Plantation:** There is a *Woodburn Plantation* in Pendleton, South Carolina, which is in Anderson County. However, this one was located in the Leland area and owned by the Woodburn family. Two churches in the area are also named for the Woodburn family, Woodburn Presbyterian and Woodburn Baptist Church. Later this estate became part of the *Belvedere Plantation*. It had also been referred to as the *Westfield* area (1830). In 1830 it was valued at $10,000 and had *42 slaves* living there.

**York Plantation:** was owned by Nathaniel Moore, (c. 1699-1747) a brother of Col. Maurice Moore and "King" Roger Moore. Roger Moore did not reside at this location. Nathaniel married Sarah Grange in 1720, in South Carolina, and after her death married a Miss Webb. The *Nathanial Moore plantation* was located up the Northwest branch of the Cape Fear River about forty miles from Brunswick Town. It was located on a bluff about sixty feet high.

*Date Unknown*
*Group of Slaves. Library of Congress.*

# Chapter Four

# *The Revolutionary War Years*

*There are countless books detailing the American Revolutionary War. It is not the intent of this chapter to rehash those commentaries or expand upon them. This book simply provides a brief overview pointing the reader toward a few events which occurred on the southeastern coast of the Carolinas. One will also find multiple references to the war throughout this book. This chapter highlights some of the North Carolina participants and provides selected information for the reader.*

One of the best-known skirmishes of the Revolutionary War occurred in southeastern North Carolina at Fort Johnston. Governor Josiah Martin was sent on his way as the patriots,with 500 Minute Men, under Robert Howe, attacked and burned the fort. The Governor fled aboard the *Cruizer*, a British man-of-war ship, anchored in the harbor, just before the Patriots began their move to attack. This battle left the Cape Fear River unguarded throughout the remainder of the Revolutionary War.

*Fort Johnston Hospital. Southport, NC.*

Fort Johnston contained three hundred acres in 1768 according to the account of the value of property in the NC Court of Pleas and Quarter Sessions (April 5, 1768). It was valued at fifty pounds of Proclamation money. It also contained an old house and kitchen called "Walden's" valued at 15 pounds, a house and kitchen called Judah Swaine's valued at 100 pounds, a house called William Dry's valued at 10 pounds, and a house and kitchen called John Galloway's valued at 100 pounds. This order came back to court on the 23rd of June in 1768 and was registered and placed in the court minutes.

## The Battle of Waxhaws

A notable battle occurred on May 29, 1780 at the Battle of Waxhaws, on the North and South Carolina border near Union County.

The Battle of Waxhaws began further south just north of Charleston as Col. Abraham Buford clashed with Lt. Col. Banastre Tarleton. It began when General Isaac Huger ordered Colonel Buford to retreat to Hillsborough, N. C. on April 14th of 1780. This was called the *Battle of Monck's Corner*.

The next month, on May 27th, Lt. Col. Tarleton set out from Nelson's Ferry with 270 men after South Carolina's Governor John Rutledge, who was said to be with Col. Buford. His command included forty British regulars, 130 of the British Legion Infantry, 100 British Infantry Calvary, and one three-pound artillery piece. He caught up with him on May 29th but Col. Buford refused to surrender and a battle ensued. Col. Buford was defeated. Lt. Col. Tarleton was not known for his mercy.

At three o'clock in the afternoon on May 29, Lt. Col. Tarleton caught up with Col. Buford near the Waxhaws district on the border of North and South Carolina. Tarleton's guard slashed through Col. Buford's rear guard. "Col. Buford now formed his men up in a single line..." Tarleton attacked from the left flank, a charge through the center, and on the right flank. He formed his troops on a low hill opposite the American line and at 300 yards the Calvary began their charge.

With only fifty yards separating them, the Americans presented their muskets but were ordered to hold their fire until the British were closer. At ten yards they opened fire.

Lt. Col. Tarleton's horse was killed and Tarleton claimed he was pinned under the horse. His troops thought he was dead. They angrily attacked slashing at everyone, even those kneeling with their hands in the air surrendering.

The Patriots claimed that Tarleton himself ordered the attack, not wanting to bother with prisoners. He was known for his aggressiveness and brutality in other skirmishes. The slaughter lasted only fifteen minutes but resulted in 113 Continentals killed and 203 captured, 150 of those wounded. However, Col. Buford managed to escape. On the British side, only five were killed and twelve wounded. Lt. Col. Tarleton earned his nickname "Bloody Ban" and "Ban the Butcher."

Buford's Massacre became a rally cry for the Patriots and was sounded at the Battle of King's Mountain later that fall. Of note, Lt. General Charles Cornwallis occasionally reminded Lt. Col. Tarleton to "look after the behavior of his men".

Blood had run on both sides of the North and South Carolina border.

## *North Carolina Continental Regiments*

Military regiments were formed in North Carolina in 1775-76. Each consisted of three field officers, an adjutant, and ten companies as outlined in September of 1775.

By November, they reorganized into eight companies each with 728 men. Each company was to have a captain, two lieutenants, one ensign, four sergeants, four corporals, two drummers or fifers, and 76 privates. The Wilmington District included the counties of Bladen, Brunswick, Cumberland, Duplin, New Hanover, and Onslow. In 1776, John Ashe, of New Hanover County, 1720-1781, was appointed by the Provincial Congress to command the militia of the Wilmington District. The following is a brief overview of the composition of the major regiments.

**September 1, 1775**
*1st North Carolina Regiment*
This regiment was at the defense of Charleston, SC in June 1776.

*2nd North Carolina Regiment*
This regiment served in Virginia at the siege of Norfolk. It also had detachments in North Carolina, South Carolina, and Georgia. They were assigned to guard the coast from British invasion and help round up the local Tories. This regiment was at the defense of Charleston, SC in June 1776.
*"In May 1777, the 2nd NC Regiment, as part of the NC Brigade (which now consisted of nine regiments), was ordered north to join the troops under General Washington. The NC Brigade marched through Williamsburg and Richmond, Virginia and paused at Alexandria to undergo inoculations for smallpox. By July, the Brigade was in New Jersey. In July and August, the troops were marched northward into New Jersey and then again south to Wilmington, Delaware to help counter a British thrust toward Philadelphia from the south." Lewis, J. D., 2007.*
Colonel Robert Howe and Colonel Alexander Martin led the regiment in 1776. Colonel Alexander Martin and Colonel John Patton took over in 1777.

**January 16, 1776**
*3rd North Carolina Regiment*
This regiment was at the defense of Charleston, SC in June 1776.

**March 26, 1776**

*4th North Carolina Regiment*

This regiment was at the defense of Charleston, SC in June 1776.

*5th North Carolina Regiment*

Other accounts say the 5th North Carolina Regiment was organized March 26, 1775 at the Wilmington District. It included eight companies from New Bern, Edenton, and Hillsborough Districts and was led in 1776 and 1777 by Colonel Edward Buncombe.

**May 7, 1776**

In addition to the five regiments listed, the following were created:

*6th North Carolina Regiment*

This regiment was officially formed on the 13th of April 1776 with men from Wilmington and Hillsborough military districts, nearly one-half of the state. They were under the command of Colonel Alexander Lillington, the hero of the Battle of Moores Creek Bridge. He later stepped down due to ill health and was replaced by Colonel Gideon Lamb.

The 6th Regiment marched north in the spring and joined the main army, brigaded under General Francis Nash. They were in the battles of Brandywine and Germantown. They spent the winter at Valley Forge in General Lachlan MacIntosh's Brigade. The NC troops were noted by Washington to be the poorest supplied of all the destitute men there. Their desertion rate was ten percent, the lowest in an Army that averaged 18 percent. It was a long way home. (It should be noted that the North Carolina troops listed as deserters were often missing only temporarily as they traveled back home to plant the crops for their family, then returned to their units making sure their families were being provided necessities of life.)

The 6th Regiment ceased to exist officially in early 1781.

**September 16, 1776**

*7th North Carolina Regiment*

Colonel James Hogan led the regiment from 1776-1777.

*8th North Carolina Regiment*

It included eight companies from New Bern and Wilmington Districts and was led by Colonel James Armstrong from 1776-77.

*9th North Carolina Regiment*

Colonel Abraham Shephard led the regiment from 1776-77.

*10th North Carolina Regiment*

This regiment was organized on the 17th of April 1777 at Kinston, N. C. and included eight companies from the northeastern part of the state. Colonel John Williams was the leader during 1777.

In addition there were:
*Three Troops of Light Horse Company*
*Artillery Company*
*Five independent companies* of state troops (three of them with only sixty men each)

**May 3, 1777**

A *24-man company* was added to garrison a frontier fort.

**1778**

The NC troops participated at Valley Forge in 1778 and endured much suffering. Of 1,188 men, 323 were listed as sick with 249 unfit for duty for want of clothing. General Washington declared the "NC Brigade was sicklier, for want of clothing and provisions, than any other unit at Valley Forge." The nine NC Regiments were so under-strength they were consolidated into four regiments with those from the 4th Regiment reassigned to the 2nd.

In June 1778, the 2nd NC Regiment fought in the Battle of Monmouth, New Jersey as part of Scott's division in La Fayette's brigade.

In November of 1770, the NC Brigade was ordered south marching in bitter winter with snow as deep as three feet. They reached Charleston, SC on the 3rd of March 1780 and after two months with no hope of relief from their sieges, surrendered to General Benjamin Lincoln. The British took over 5,000 men prisoner.

## The Battle At Moores Creek

While the forces were still being organized, the fighting continued. The Battle at Moores Creek proved to be the one, which ended the British rule forever. As Loyalists charged over the partially dismantled Moores Creek Bridge, over 1,000 patriots waited with cannons and muskets on the 27th of February 1776.

The Scottish Highlanders, with broadswords in hand, expected only a small patriot force. As the patriot shots rang out dozens of Loyalists fell.

In confusion, the Loyalists surrendered with their wagons, weapons and British sterling. After the victory, the Fourth North Carolina Provincial Congress met in Halifax, N. C. and on the 12th of April, 1776 led North Carolina as it became the first colony to vote for independence. The Battle of Moores Creek Bridge and the Battle of Sullivans Island near Charleston, S. C., influenced thirteen colonies to declare independence on the 4th of July 1776.

By 1781 (October 19th), Cornwallis surrendered to Washington at Yorktown, Virginia. North Carolina Regiments diminished as enlistments expired. The war was coming to a close. By June 1783 the remaining troops were furloughed at James Island, South Carolina while awaiting the peace treaty with Great Britain. The 2nd North Carolina Regiment was officially disbanded on the 15th of November 1783.

## Loyalist Militia

One must not forget, there were certain North Carolinians who were Loyal to the King and fought against the Patriots throughout the Revolutionary War. Some of the known companies from North Carolina include:

> British Legion
> NC Highlanders
> NC Independent Dragoons
> NC Militia
> NC Provincials
> NC Volunteers
> Royal Highland Emigrants
> Royal North Carolina Regiment
> Volunteers of Ireland

Other Loyalist Companies include:

> Armed Batteau-men
> Armed Boatmen
> Arnold's American Legion
> Black Pioneers
> British Legion
> Buck's County Light Dragoons
> Callbeck's Company
> Carolina King's Rangers
> DeDiemar's Hussars
> DeLancey's Brigade
> Emmerick's Chasseurs & Dragoons
> Ferguson's Corps
> Georgia Light Dragoons
> Georgia Loyalists

Gov'r Wentworth's Volunteers
Hierlihy's Corps
Independent Troops of Cavalry
King's American Dragoons
King's American Regiment
King's Orange Rangers
Loyal American Rangers
Loyal American Regiment
Loyal Foresters
Loyal New Englanders
Loyal Nova Scotia Volunteers
Maryland Loyalists
Nassau Blues
New Jersey Volunteers
New York Volunteers
Pennsylvania Loyalists
Philadelphia Light Dragoons
Prince of Wales American Regt.
Provincial Light Infantry
Queens Rangers
Rogers' King's Rangers (1 Company)
Roman Catholic Volunteers
Royal American Reformees
Royal Fencible Americans
Royal Garrison Battalion
Royal Guides and Pioneers
Royal North Carolina Regt.
South Carolina Dragoons
South Carolina Rangers
South Carolina Royalists
Volunteers of Ireland
Volunteers of New England
West Florida Foresters
West Jersey Volunteers
Young Royal Highland Emigrants

Some of those commanders included:

1. King's Royal Regiment of New York (or Royal    Greens), two battalions, commanded by **Sir John Johnson,** raised in 1776 and 1777.
2. Butler's Rangers, raised in 1776 and 1777 and commanded by **Lieut. Col. John**

**Butler**.

3. Queens Loyal Rangers, raised early in 1777, and commanded by **Lieut. Col. John Peters**.

4. Royal Americans, organized early in 1777 by **Lieut. Col. Ebenezer Jessup.**

5. **Rogers Kings** Rangers, of which corps the larger part (raised in 1781-2) was enrolled in the Northern Division.

6. **Major McAlpine's** Royal Americans.

7. **Major Holland's** Loyal Yorkers.

8. **Mackay's** Loyal Volunteers.

9. **Capt. Robert Leake's** Independent Company.

10. The 1st Battalion of the 84th, or Royal Highland Emigrant Regiment, raised by **Colonel Allen Maclean** in 1775.

A Loyalist served in a military capacity for the British or provided services to the military. Some remained in America after the war, some left the country, and some were killed or died during the war. At the close of the war, Loyalists could choose to swear an oath to uphold the new Constitution of the state of North Carolina or face confiscation of all their property and be banished from the state. Even if they swore the oath, some had their lands taken anyway.

## Roll of Officers

### Major General
**Tryon, William** - Major General and Commander in Chief of the Provincial forces in America.

### Brigadier Generals
**Arnold, Benedict** -Commissioned about close of 1780.
**Browne, Montford** - Commanding Prince of Wales American Regiment, 1777.
**Cunningham, Robert** - In 1780 in command of a garrison in South Carolina.
**DeLancey, Oliver** - Commanding Delancey's Brigade 1776, Senior Brigadier.

### General
**Skinner, Cortlandt** - Commanding New Jersey Volunteers, Sept. 4, 1776.

### Colonels
**Wm. - Nassau Blues**, May 1st, 1779 (Corps disbanded Dec. 1779).
**Brewerton, George** - 2 Batt. DeLancey's Brigade, Aug. 1776. **Cathcart, Right** - British Legion, June 1778.
**H. Clinton**, Feb. 1779.
**Kemble, Stephen** - Deputy Adjt. General Provincial Troops, 1776.

**Fanning, Edmund** - King's American Regiment, Dec. 11, 1776.

**Innes, Alexander** - South Carolina Royalists, Feb. 1, 1779, Inspector General of Provincial Forces in 1777.

**Legge, Hon. Francis** - Loyal Nova Scotia Volunteers, October 1775.

**Ludlow, Gabriel G.** - 3 DeLancey Battalion, 4 Sept. 1776.

**Robinson, Beverley** - Loyal American Regiment, March 28th, 1777.

**Rawdon, Lord** - Volunteers of Ireland, Dec. 1778, Adjt. Gen. of Prov. Forces.


*Lieutenant Colonels*

**Allen, Isaac** - New Jersey Volunteers 6th Batt, afterwards 3rd Batt. and 2nd Batt., Dec. 3rd, 1776.

**Allen, William** - Pennsylvania Loyalists, October 14, 1777.

**Barton, Joseph** - New Jersey Volunteers, 5 Batt. and afterwards 1 Batt.; Nov. 27, 1776.

**Bayard, John** - King's Orange Rangers, Dec. 25, 1776.

**Browne, Thomas** - Carolina King's Rangers, June 1, 1776.

**Campbell, George** - King's American Regiment, Jan. 1777.

**Chalmers, James** - Maryland Loyalists, Oct. 14, 1777.

**Clifton, Alfred** - Roman Catholic Volunteers, Oct. 14, 1777.

**Connolly, John** - Loyal Foresters, April 1781.

**Cruger, John Harris** - 1st DeLancey Batt., Aug. 1776.

**DeLancey, Stephen**- 2nd DeLancey Batt., Aug. 1776, P. W. A. R. Sept. 1781, 1st. N. J. V. Feb. 1782.

**DeVeber, Gabriel** - Prince of Wales American Regiment, 1782.

**Dongan, Edward Vaughan** - 3 New Jersey Vol., Nov. 20 1776 - died of wounds received Aug. 22, 1777.

**Donkin, Robert** - Royal Garrison Battalion, October 25, 1779.

**Doyle, Welbore Ellis** - Volunteers of Ireland, August 1778.

**Emmerick, Andreas** - Chasseurs and Dragoons, April 11, 1778.

**Goreham, Joseph** - Royal Fencible Americans, December 1775.

**Hamilton, John** - Royal North Carolina Regiment, 1779.

**Hewlett, Richard** - 3 DeLancey Battalion, Aug. 1776.

**Hierlihy, Timothy** - Royal N. S. Volunteers, May 5, 1782; of Hierlihy's Brigade April, 1777.

**Lawrence, Elisha** - 1 Batt. New Jersey Volunteers, July 1, 1776.

**Morris, John** - 2 Batt. New Jersey Volunteers, Nov. 1776.

**Pattinson, Thomas** - Prince of Wales American Regiment, 1777. Retired 1781.

**Ritzema, Rudolphus** - Royal American Reformees, Ap. 24, 1778.

**Robinson, Beverley, Jr.** - Loyal American Regiment, Oct. 7, 1777.

**Robinson, Joseph** - South Carolina Royalists.

**Rogers, Robert** - King's Rangers, May 1779.

**Stewart, Allan** - North Carolina Highlanders, 1783.
**Simcoe, John Graves** - Queen's Rangers, December 1777
**Small, John** - Young Royal Highland Emigrants, 1783.
**Tarleton, Banistre** - British Legion, June 1778.
**Thompson, Benjamin** - King's American Dragoons, March 178
**Turnbull, George** - Loyal American Regiment 1777, and N. Vols. Oct. 7, 1777.
**Upham, Joshua** - Volunteers of New England, 1781.
**VanBuskirk, Abraham** - 4th New Jersey Volunteers, November 16, 1776.
**Vandiek, John** - West Jersey Volunteers, March 19, 1778.
**Watson,-** Bucks County Light Dragoons, 1778.
**Wightman, George** - Loyal New Englanders, 1777.
**Winslow, Edward** - Muster-Master-General of Provincial Troops, July 30, 1776.

## *Revolutionary War Leaders of Southeastern North Carolina*

The citizens of southeastern North Carolina banded together to fight the British during the war. The names of the leaders and their general tone of defiance can be felt in the following from the colonial records, specifically the: Minutes of the Bladen, Brunswick, Duplin, and Wilmington-New Hanover County Committees of Safety, which took place on the 20th and 21st of May in 1775.

*"At a general meeting of the several committees of the District of Wilmington held at the Court House in Wilmington, Tuesday the 20th of June, 1775."*

For the **County of New Hanover**—Present: Cornelius Harnett, Francis Clayton, George Moore, Sen., Jno. Ashe, Jno. Quince, Wm. Ewins, James Walker, James Blythe, John Devane, Wm. Jones, Long Creek, Wm. Jones, W. T., John Ancrum, James Moore, Rob't Hogg, Alexander Lillington, Wm. Robeson, Sam. Swann, Fred. Jones, Sr., Jno. Colvin, Jno. Hollingsworth, Sam. Ashe, Geo. Merrick, And'w Ronaldson, Arch'd Maclaine, James Wright, Jno. Marshall, Sampson Moseley, Tho. Devane.

For the **County of Brunswick**—Rich'd Quince, ser., Rob't Howe, Thos. Davis, Rob't Ellis, Rich'd Quince, Jr., Parker Quince, Wm. Lord, Wm. Cains, Tho. Allen, Step. Daniel, Wm. Davis, James Bell.

For **Bladen County**—Nath'l Richardson, Thos. Owens, Walter Gibson, Thos. Brown, Faithful Graham.

For **Duplin**—Charles Ward.

*The Committee having met agreeable to summons, they proceeded to choose a Chairman; accordingly Richard Quince, Sr. was unanimously chosen.*

*A letter from the Committee of Cross Creek was read, and an answer was ordered to be wrote by the Chairman to the said letter.*

*The Governor's Proclamation, dated at Fort Johnston, the 16th inst. was ordered to be read.*

*On motion, Ordered that a committee be appointed to answer the said Proclamation; and that Robt. Howe, Arch. McLaine, and Samuel Ashe, be a committee for that purpose.*

*On motion, for leave to —————— Elletson to import his house servants from Jamaica, not exceeding six in number.*

*It was carried against the motion, by a great majority.*

*The Committee then adjourned to 10 o'clock to-morrow.*

## Wednesday, 10 o'clock. May 21, 1775.

*The committee met according to adjournment.*

On motion, ordered, that Cornelius Harnett be appointed to write to the committee of Cumberland County, to secure the Gunpowder that may be in that county, for the use of the public:

*On motion, For the more effectually disarming and keeping the negroes in order, within the County of New Hanover,*

*It was, unanimously agreed, by the members of the committee, for said county, to appoint Patrols to search for, and take from Negroes, all kinds of arms whatsoever, and such guns or other arms found with the Negroes, shall be delivered to the Captain of the company of the District in which they are found—to be distributed by the said officers, to those of his company who may be in want of arms, and who are not able to purchase: and that the following persons be Patrols, as follows:*

From **Beauford's Ferry**, to the end of Geo. Moores District—Sam'l Swann, Thos. Mosely, Geo. Palmer, Henry Beauford, Wm. Robeson, Luke Woodward.

**Burgaw**—Sampson Moseley, William Moseley, Jno. Ashe, Jr.

**Black River**—Geo. Robeson, Thos. Devane, Jno. Colvin, Thos. Corbit, Jr., Benjamin Robeson, James Bloodworth.

**Welch Tract**—Barnaby Fuller, Geo. McGowan, Wm. Wright, Martin Wells, Morgan Swinney, David Jones.

**Beatty's Swamp, to Perry's Creek**—Elisha Atkinson, Bishop Swann, Aaron Erskins, Peter McClammy, Jno. Watkins, Edmond Moore, Jno. Lucas.

**Perry's Creek to Baldhead**—James Middleton, Charles Morris, Jno. Nichols, Samuel Marshall, Joseph Nichols, James Ewing, George Stundere, Jas. Jones.

**Long Creek**—Wm. Jones, James Ratcliff, John Kenner, Thos. Bloodworth, Wm. Hennepy, Jno. Marshall.

**Holly Shelter**—Thos. Jones, Edward Doty, Henry Williams, Thos. Simmons, Jno. Simmons, Joshua Sutton.

*Resolved, That the following Association, formerly agreed by the Committee of New Hanover County, stand as the Association of this Committee, and that it be recommended to the inhabitants of this District, to sign the same, as speedily as possible, and that the same, with this Resolution, be printed in the public Newspaper.*

*Unanimously agreed to, by the inhabitants of New Hanover County, in North Carolina, 19th June 1775.*

The actual commencement of Hostilities against this Continent by the British Troops, in the bloody scene, on the 19th April last, near Boston: The increase of arbitrary impositions from a wicked and despotic ministry; and the dread of instigated insurrections in the colonies, are causes sufficient to drive an oppressed people to the use of arms. We, therefore, the subscribers, inhabitants of New Hanover County, having ourselves bound by the most sacred of all obligations, the duty of good citizens towards an injured country; and, thoroughly convinced that, under our present distressed circumstances, we shall be justified, before God and Man, in resisting force by force: Do unite ourselves under every tie of religion and honor and associate as a band in her defense against every foe; hereby solemnly engaging that whenever our Continental or Provincial Councils shall decree it necessary we will go forth and be ready to sacrifice our lives and fortunes to secure her freedom and safety. This obligation to continue in full force until a reconciliation shall take place between Great Britain and America, upon constitutional principles, an event we most ardently desire and we will hold all those persons inimical to the liberties of the Colonies, who shall refuse to subscribe this Association. And we will in all things, follow the advice of our Committee, respecting the purposes aforesaid, the preservation of peace and good order, and the safety of individuals and private property.

The Committee appointed to answer the Governor's Proclamation, of the 16th inst., returned the following answer, which was read and ordered to be printed in the public papers and in hand bills.

At a General meeting of the several committees of the District of Wilmington, held at the Courthouse, in Wilmington, Tuesday, 20th June 1775.

Whereas, his Excellency, Josiah Martin, Esq., hath by Proclamation, dated at Fort Johnston, the 16th day of June 1775, and read this day in the committee, endeavored to persuade, seduce, and intimidate the good people of the province, from taking measures to preserve those rights, and that liberty, to which, as the subjects of a British King, they have the most undoubted claim, without which, life would be but futile considerations, and which therefore, it is a duty they owe to themselves, their Country, and posterity, by every effort, and at every risk, to maintain, support, and defend against any invasion or encroachment whatsoever.

And whereas, many unconstitutional and oppressive acts of Parliament, invasive of every right and privilege, and dangerous to the freedom of America, have laid the people of this colony under the fatal necessity of appointing committees for the several Districts, Towns, and Counties of this province, who were instructed, carefully to guard against every encroachment upon their invaluable rights, and steadily oppose the operation of those unconstitutional acts, framed by a wicked administration entirely to destroy the freedom of America: and as among other measures, those committees found it absolutely necessary, either by themselves, or by persons appointed under them, to visit the people and fully to explain to them the nature and dangerous tendency of those acts, which the tools of administration, were by every base art, endeavoring to prevail upon them to submit to: and as his Excellency has endeavored by his Proclamation, to weaken the influence, and prejudice the characters of those Committees, and the persons appointed under them, by wantonly, cruelly, and unjustly, representing them as ill-disposed people, propagating false and scandalous reports, derogatory to the honor and justice of the King; and also, by other illiberal and scandalous imputations expressed in the said Proclamation: We, then, the Committees of the counties of New Hanover, Brunswick, Bladen, Duplin and Onslow, in order to prevent the pernicious influence of the said Proclamation, do, unanimously, resolve, that in our opinion, his Excellency Josiah Martin, Esq, hath by the said Proclamation, and by the whole tenor of his conduct, since the unhappy disputes between Great Britain and the colonies, discovered himself to be an enemy to the happiness of this colony in particular, and to the freedom, rights and privileges of America in general.

Resolved, nem. con. That the said proclamation contains many things asserted to be facts, which are entirely without foundation; particularly the methods said to have been made use of, in order to compel the people to sign an Association against any invasion, intestine insurrection, or unjust encroachments upon their rights and privileges; no person having signed such Association but from the fullest conviction that it was essentially necessary to their freedom and safety; and that if his Excellency founded such assertions upon information, it must have been derived from persons too weak or wicked to have any claim to his credit or attention.

Resolved, nem. con. That it is the opinion of this Committee, that America owes much of its present sufferings to the information given by Governors and men in office, to administration, who having themselves adopted belief from improper informants, or, in order to sacrifice to the pleasure of the ministry, have falsely represented, that His Majesty's American subjects were not generally averse from the arbitrary proceedings of a wicked administration, but that the opposition, made to such unconstitutional measures, arose from the influence of a few individuals upon the minds of the people, whom they have not failed to represent as "false, seditious, and abandoned men;" by these means, inducing the ministry to believe, that the Americans would be easily brought to submit to the cruel impositions so wickedly intended for them; that his Excellency's proclamation is evidently calculated for this purpose, and is also replete with the most illiberal abuse and scandalous imputations, tending to defame the characters of many respectable persons, who zealously attached to the liberty of their country, were pursuing every laudable method to support it.

Resolved, nem. con. That the resolution respecting America, introduced by Lord North, into the British House of Parliament, which his Excellency, in his proclamation, alludes to, is such a glaring affront to the common sense of the Americans, that it added insult to the injury it intended them: That Lord North, himself, when he introduced it, declared to the House, that he did not believe America would accept of it, but that it might possibly tend to divide them, and if it broke one link in their chain of Union, it would render the enforcing his truly detestable acts the more easy; therefore,

Resolved, That this was a low, base, flagitious, wicked attempt to entrap America into Slavery, and which they ought to reject with the contempt it deserves; that the uncandid and insiduous manner in which his Excellency has mentioned the said resolution, is a poor artifice to seduce, mislead, and betray the ignorant and incautious into ruin and destruction, by inducing them to forfeit the inestimable blessings of freedom, with which nature and the British Constitution have so happily invested them; and also, indisputably proves, that his Excellency is ready to become an instrument in the hands of administration to rivet those chains so wickedly forged for America.

Resolved, nem. con. That at this alarming crisis, when the dearest rights, and privileges of America are at stake, no confidence ought to be reposed in those, whose interest is to carry into execution every measure of administration, however profligate and abandoned; and who though they are conscious those measures will not bear the test of enquiry and examination, will and endeavour to gloss over the most palpable violation of truth with plausibility, hoping, thereby, to blind, mislead and delude the people; that this Committee therefore, earnestly recommend it to the other committees of this province, and likewise to all our Brethren and suffering fellow subjects thereof, cautiously to guard against all those endeavours, which have been, or shall be made to deceive them, and to treat such attempts as wicked efforts of the Tools of Government calculated to throw this Country into confusion, and by dividing to enslave it.

The committee adjourned till a meeting occasionally.

Account of money received, at this committee:

|  | £ | s. | d. |
|---|---|---|---|
| From Bladen county, by the hands of Mr. Richardson, in good bills | 36 | 11 | 2 |
| One Bill counterfeit of | 2 | 0 | 0 |
| From Cornelius Harnett, for sundry subscriptions to purchase gunpowder | 49 | 15 | 6 |
| From Wm. Jones, L. C. by the hand of R. Hogg for do | 10 | 0 | 0 |
| do. Jno. Slingsby do | 5 | 0 | 0 |
| do. Doct. Cobham do | 2 | 10 | 0 |
| do. R'd Bradley do | 1 | 0 | 0 |
|  | 106 | 16 | 8 |

Money paid for Sundries:

| | £ | s. | d. |
|---|---|---|---|
| Paid 350 ☐s. Gunpowder in the hands of Burgwin, Humphrey & Co. pr. Rec't | 52 | 10 | 0 |
| P'd Jno. Slingsby for 50 ☐s. Gunpowder in his hands | 7 | 10 | 0 |
| P'd Wm. Grant to pay for cleaning out the court-house | 0 | 2 | 6 |

## Waccamaw Skirmishes

In a letter from John Alexander Lillington to James Kenan on March 27th, 1782, he noted that he had received a letter from Colonel Young which had been sent to Colonel Leonard, telling him that "the Tories to the number of five hundred embodied on the Waccamaw River and have sent parties into Brunswick County, stealing horses and threatening to plunder Wilmington and will not suffer cattle to be driven to General Greene's Camp. You will therefore lose no time in embodying one hundred and fifty men of your county, and when you have them collected you will send me an Express. You will see that they are well armed. I wish you to postpone your going to the Assembly for a few days, as there is no telling what assistance they may have from Charlestown. Colonel Brown informs me that the Tories are very bad in Bladen. They are frequently calling musters, etc. I wish to hear from you as soon as possible." Lillington was obviously most concerned about state of affairs in the region. Not long after the war finally ended.

## The End of the WAR

The Revolutionary War finally came to a close with the Commons voting to end the war in April of 1782 and the signing of the Treaty of Paris September 3, 1783. The last British troops disbanded on November 25, 1783.

The casualties included many deaths as a result of disease and conditions as well as deaths in battle. "*An estimated 25,000 American Revolutionaries died during active military service. About 8,000 of these deaths were in battle; the other 17,000 deaths were from disease, including about 8,000 - 12,000 who died while prisoners of war, most in rotting prison ships in New York. The number of Revolutionaries seriously wounded or disabled by the war has been estimated from 8,500 to 25,000. The total American military casualty figure was therefore as high as 50,000.*" (Wikipedia.)

"*About 171,000 seamen served for the British during the war; about 25 to 50 percent of them had been pressed into service. About 1,240 were killed in battle, while 18,500 died from disease. The greatest killer was scurvy, a disease known at the time to be easily preventable by issuing lemon juice to sailors. About 42,000 British sailors deserted during the war.*" (Wikipedia.)

*Old Burying Grounds in Southport, NC. Model, Katie Stewart with K9 Bailey.*
*Photographer, John Muuss, Photographic Artist.*

*"Approximately 1,200 Germans were killed in action and 6,354 died from illness or accident. About 16,000 of the remaining German troops returned home, but roughly 5,500 remained in the United States after the war for various reasons, many eventually becoming American citizens. No reliable statistics exist for the number of casualties among other groups, including Loyalists, British regulars, Native Americans, French, Spanish troops, and civilians."* (Wikipedia.)

137

# Chapter Five

# *Crime and the Law*

*Notice to all readers: This chapter is not for the light of heart. It contains true accounts of slave torture, murder, deplorable conditions, and man's inhumanity to man.*

In 1783 the punishment for constructing counterfeit bills was the loss of both ears and a fine, standing in the pillory for one hour, a disqualification to give testimony thereafter, and the infliction of thirty-nine lashes on a bare back.

Not keeping the Sabbath holy and profane swearing in court was punishable by a fine and the stocks. Less severe punishments included being placed in a dunking stool and plunged into water, not intending to drown the perpetrator.

## *Early 1800s*

Early in the 1800s, there was a Judge Taylor who pointed out many defects in the current penal code. In Edenton District Court, North Carolina, he said: *"In some cases the punishment ordained by law may appear to us disproportionately severe,"* and it may seem *"that the penalty of death is indiscriminately applied to acts of very different degrees of turpitude. It is believed that all persons...who calmly reflect on the legitimate ends of punishments...will unite in the opinion that this is a defect of our criminal jurisprudence."* (Raleigh Register, 1806).

Later that year the reigning Governor Nathaniel Alexander asked the Legislature to review the penal code as changes were being made in the court system at that time. Actually, just a few years prior (1800) there was a bill to abolish the death penalty except in cases of first degree murder, although it did not pass. However, by 1817, the code boasted only a few changes.

In 1806 the ordination of women in the clergy was allowed by law and expanded to slaves in 1816. In 1802 if one of the persons involved in a duel died, the shooter was subject to the death penalty. Slaves or free negroes "rebelling or conspiring to rebel" faced a possible death penalty. In 1801 and again in 1817 the Legislature sought (As it had been since 1791) to declare that the offense of killing a slave was to be a homicide. It continued to be rejected.

In 1817 the penal code sought the death penalty for at least twenty-eight offenses. These included:

arson, burglary (an actual breaking into a dwelling, outhouse, shop or warehouse with the intent to steal whether goods were or were not taken),
murder,
highway robbery, accessories before the fact,
treason,
housebreaking in the daytime and taking goods worth 20 shillings;
bestiality or sodomy,
dueling,
bigamy,
stealing slaves or aiding them to escape, stealing free negroes from the state and selling them, voluntary return of slaves transported from the State by sentence of the court;
rebellion of slaves or conspiracy to incite insurrection, free persons joining a conspiracy or rebellion of slaves,
concealing childbirth,
breach of prison by a person committed for a felony,
counterfeiting notes of the Bank of North America;
and the second offense of manslaughter, forgery, horse-stealing,
maiming by putting out eyes or disabling the tongue,
counterfeiting or knowingly passing counterfeited bills of credit, public certificates or lottery tickets;
robbery except in a dwelling house or near a highway;
larceny from a person to the amount of 12 pence or upwards;
too great duress of imprisonment on the part of a jailor;
embezzling or vacating records in a court of judicature;
and embezzlement by a servant more than eighteen years old of his master's goods to the value of $10 or upwards.

Even before 1816 a fine was a legal substitute for branding or whipping in the charge of manslaughter. On the other extreme some cruel and unusual punishment might include the castration of slaves who raped a white woman, amputating the hand of a serial felon, disemboweling and worse.

After the passage of the Constitution in 1776 there was still extreme and cruel punishments in some slave cases. In 1801 a slave was hanged for rape in Rutherford County and had his head separated *"from his body and stuck on a pole as a terror to Evil doers and all persons in like cases offending."* *(Raleigh Register, 1805).* In 1805 a negro woman was burned at the stake in Wayne County, North Carolina for poisoning four persons including her master and mistress. *(History of Crime and Punishment in North Carolina.)*

In 1812 a Wake County court ordered a negro to be hanged and his body publicly burned. A petition was circulated to stop this punishment protesting the inhumanity and the order was stopped. *(Raleigh Register, February 28, 1812.)* This was not the only instance of the public and/or individuals standing up for more humane punishment conditions. Frederick Nash of Hillsboro, in the state legislature, in 1817, who later became the Chief Justice of the Supreme Court, spoke against the harsh punishments for years afterwards. He said, *"I pledge myself, as long as I have a seat on this floor, this subject shall neither sleep nor slumber; I will continue to raise my voice in behalf of justice and humanity; I will not cease to display before gentlemen, the black catalogue of sanguinary punishments which disgrace our criminal code--to urge them to rescue our common country from the foul reproach of being the last of her sister States in laying aside that sanguinary code which we inherited from our mother country. . . For what cause are we at liberty to take the life of our fellow-creature? I contend, only for one--and that is murder."* Addressing those who declared prisons would be too expensive, he said, *"True it will be expensive --And is North Carolina too poor to be just? Must she hang her citizens as being not able to bear the expense of saving their lives?"*

In 1818 several crimes were changed from felonies to misdemeanors such as concealing the birth of an illegitimate child. However, if the child died the mother was still liable for murder. The next year counterfeiting was no longer punishable by death and in 1829 bigamy was "demoted" from a death sentence offense. But in 1823 the crime of rape against a white woman by a slave was still a capital case facing the death penalty.

## The Overseer

In 1830 the General Assembly passed an act requiring slave owners to keep an overseer if they had fifteen or more slaves at least 12 years of age. This law was applicable *only* to Brunswick and New Hanover Counties. The overseer assisted in the management of the negroes and the crops. As early as 1818 a group of planters in Brunswick County urged the state to make it compulsory for owners of as many as ten slaves to employ some white male person to superintend and oversee the negroes. The skillful management of the slaves affected the success of the plantation. *"Surly hands could defy an overseer, break a vast amount of equipment, and otherwise interrupt the plantation routine without seeming to do so."*

A good overseer was sometimes difficult to find as the work was hard and the pay low. To entice a worker, the plantation owner offered lodging and pay in one of three ways: money wage payable in notes which could be converted into cash at a discount, a smaller amount of money added to provisions and a share of the crop, or just money. In 1853 one of the local newspapers, *The Journal*, thought "*an overseer more likely to be an inexperienced young man, who was not stimulated to exertion either by his employer or the hands who might be found asleep in the corner of the fence and the negroes idling away their time.*" Gray Armstrong (who owned two farms near Rocky Mount in 1856) found his overseer at the "*grogshop and bowling alley*" during the daytime working hours and even found him playing cards at 10 am, "*excited with spirits but not drunk.*"

In Person County, Mr. Phillips Moore made the following agreement with his overseer, Nathaniel Smith, in 1819-20: "*Said Smith undertakes to perform the duties of Overseer for said Moore under his particular advise and direction, to take charge of the hands, to work with them diligently, to assist in feeding the stock of every kind with all care of the same that is requisite in all seasons of the year, to see that there is plenty of fire wood always provided at the door for the house fires, to take care of all the farming utensils of every description, and have them housed except when immediately in use to repair fences, take care to prevent any damage or loss of any kind whatever and to make up all loss time whatever and find himself. And said Moore for his part is to pay unto said Smith two hundred dollars or its value for the term of one year.*"

To this agreement Smith added a provision of his own to which the owner agreed: "*And we further agree that if any dispute does arise which cannot be mutually settled we bind ourselves to leave it to three persons to be chosen by ourselves.*" Mr. Moore supervised his overseer closely and monitored all store accounts. At the end of the year he charged him with having lost twenty-two and a third days from work. He even had each one listed and described such as "*Nathaniel Smith lost this day, his wife being sick. This day away about your pork...went away at a time I wanted you to work at tobacco...fattening hogs got out...you unconcerned, came and set down by fire. No care taken of tobacco strip the other night, at night a horse very sick, paid no attention to him. Went to the Court house...went to muster...went to mother-in-law's...went fishing...left the plow and horse and neglected the hands (corn very foul..ch'd you $1)..Thursday went to the election...went to sale...went to General Muster...Taking out $14 for lost time, and about $12 for provisions advanced, chiefly brandy, show repairing and a barrel of flour.*" Moore discharged his part of the agreement by giving the overseer three notes for $58 each and set about looking for another manager.

As the overseer represented the owner, it was in his duty to have the same authority over the slaves. He had the power to impose punishment although some planters preferred to do this themselves. However, if a slave injured an overseer, the negro was charged as if he had attacked the master.

There were never many overseers in North Carolina. Here it was more of a system of having a close relationship with the master. It is estimated that over 67%

of the masters worked side-by-side with their slaves. (*S. vs. David, 49 NC, p 354. - Johnson, Buion Griffis.*)

## *Dismemberment and Other Codes in 1831*

In 1831 the Legislature changed some of the code regarding dismemberment and now only allowed ears to be cut off in the case of perjury at trial during a capital offense. At the same time embezzling became a misdemeanor and was no longer a death penalty crime, as was inciting slaves by word of mouth. The following other crimes became a misdemeanor in 1831: retailing liquor by the small measure without a license, trading with slaves, teaching slaves to read and write, harboring runaway slaves, issuing a license for marriage between a white person and a person of color, and conducting a lottery, or selling lottery tickets. North Carolina was still known to have the "bloodiest" criminal code in the Union. (*Hillsborough Recorder, March 21, 1844*).

## *New Crimes in 1848*

By 1848 the code was revised and some of the new crimes included: removing and defacing tombstones over the dead; voting fraudulently at elections; constructing or operating faro banks; stealing, destroying, or concealing wills of living or dead persons; polluting well or spring water; maliciously injuring plank roads, turnpikes, canals, or railroads; destroying or defacing public buildings, churches, outhouses, or fences; willfully killing or injuring live stock running at large in the range; altering the marks on ton timber; extortion and blackmail by letter. However, the cruel and barbarous punishments like dismembering, the pillory, cutting off ears, slitting noses, branding, and public whipping remained.

In 1856, Edward Cantwell, in his *North Carolina Magistrate,* said, "*the extreme technicality and irregularity of the law, the unnecessary difficulties which attend the obtaining of justice, the expense or tedious length of litigation, the uncertainty of issue, and the delay of decision are well-known to all....*" By 1857 men like Reverend William Hooper, spoke out supporting the *"sacredness of human life."* He said, "*There is a growing feeling of distrust and insecurity as to the administration of the criminal law."* The complicated system of justice was about to change.

## *Typical Crimes*

In 1860 the most frequently committed crime in North Carolina was disturbing the peace. This included assault, battery, affray, riot, rout, and unlawful assembly. The next most common crime was against public morality and decency. Fornication, adultery and bastardy were the most committed offenses.

The next most committed crime was that of being a public nuisance. This included the drunkards, gamblers, prostitutes, common scolds and troublemakers, as well as, simple crimes of neglecting to repair bridges and the like. Larceny and trespass rounded out the most common misdemeanors. Based on 4,397 crimes from the legislative papers and court records from 1800 to 1860, the following table was constructed from Orange, Cumberland, Edgecombe and Rutherford County records:

| Offenses Heard in NC Courts Offense | Number | Per Cent |
|---|---|---|
| Assault and battery | 538 | 48.0 |
| Affray | 146 | 12.1 |
| Bastardy | 134 | 12.0 |
| Petit larceny | 55 | 5.0 |
| Disturbing the peace | 52 | 4.5 |
| Trespass | 29 | 3.0 |
| Retailing liquor without license | 26 | 2.3 |
| Fornication and adultery | 26 | 2.3 |
| Common nuisance | 24 | 2.1 |
| Misdemeanors, unnamed | 24 | 2.1 |
| Trading with slaves | 23 | 2.0 |
| Not stated | 19 | 1.8 |
| Miscellaneous | 11 | 1.0 |
| Slander | 10 | .9 |
| Unlawful fence | 10 | .9 |
| Total | 1,127 | 100.0 |

(The records used are as follows: 1801-1805, Orange and Rutherford county court minutes; 1831-1835, Cumberland and Rutherford county court minutes; 1851-1855, Orange, Cumberland, and Edgecombe County court minutes.)

| Offenses Heard in Sixty-four NC Courts, 1811-1815 Offense | Number | Per Cent |
|---|---|---|
| Common nuisance | 369 | 21.22 |

| | | |
|---|---|---|
| Petit larceny | 332 | 19.03 |
| Fornication and adultery | 178 | 10.21 |
| Riot | 152 | 8.84 |
| Miscellaneous misdemeanors | 114 | 6.60 |
| Murder | 89 | 5.13 |
| Perjury | 88 | 5.08 |
| Affray | 87 | 5.02 |
| Grand larceny | 45 | 2.60 |
| Conspiracy | 38 | 2.20 |
| Trespass | 36 | 2.10 |
| Forgery | 25 | 1.44 |
| Miscellaneous felonies | 24 | 1.40 |
| Disorderly house | 23 | 1.32 |
| Maiming | 21 | 1.21 |
| Burglary | 20 | 1.16 |
| Deceit | 20 | 1.16 |
| Rescue or escape | 20 | 1.16 |
| Malicious mischief | 19 | 1.10 |
| Retailing liquor without license | 15 | .88 |
| Forcible entry and detainer | 11 | .64 |
| Libel | 8 | .50 |
| Total | 1,734 | 100.00 |

\* Assault and battery, bastardy cases, and disturbing the peace not included.

## Prisons and the Death Penalty

One must remember that state prisons were nonexistent during this time period and so other punishments were implemented. By 1800 a bill to establish a penitentiary, originating in the Senate, had been defeated in the House according to the *House Journal.*

In 1801 and again in 1802 the penitentiary bills were introduced in the House by Absalom Tatom of Hillsboro who had already freed his slaves by will and left his estate in trust for their use. He also advocated the abolishment of punishment by death in all instances except first-degree murder. Other serious crimes such as rape, arson and burglary, which were punishable by death, he advocated to be punished by imprisonment of from three to twenty-one years.

Tatom's bill was eventually defeated in 1801 with a vote of 72 to 49 and again by 73 to 44 in 1802. A gentleman from Fayetteville, William Watts Jones, stated, *"I hold it to be my duty to oppose the passage of any bill which would be attended with so many evil consequences as this would be, and hope to strangle, in its infancy, this darling child of the Gentleman from Hillsborough."* The representatives from the eastern part of North Carolina overrode their counterparts from the west two years in a row. A few years later, in 1810, it lost again by one vote and again failed in 1818. The chief objection in the late 1820s was the cost.

Although death penalties remained for many crimes, the public was beginning to recognize that "public" executions were not in the best interests of the citizenry. At one public hanging in Raleigh in 1830, a crowd of over 3,000 watched; among them were women and children. Raleigh newspapers described the ceremony. Not long after this the public began an outcry against public executions. Private executions were promoted to avoid the spectacle of a public assembly.

Another hanging is remembered by a Brunswick County native, Ms. Mamie Hankins Frazier, who related the story of the hanging of Saul Hewett. He had been convicted of "looking at a white woman." The date is uncertain. The location: Conway, South Carolina where he was working. Saul Hewett had killed a white man.

Saul Hewett and his wife, Flora, had one son. Before his hanging, Saul was planning to kill his wife and son (Von Hewett) in order to not leave them alone after his death. He had beaten them so bad one day; they left and went to a friend's two-story house to hide. It was located just off of the present highway 211 on Macedonia Road. Saul went to the house looking for his wife and son but the lady of the house told him they were not there. In fact, they were hiding in the attic upstairs. Saul left and was soon captured for his "other crime."

Saul stuffed his pockets with "loadstone" to make himself too heavy to allow the hanging rope mechanism on the gallows to operate. Twice the hangmen tried to start the mechanism…it wouldn't work. Finally Saul was stripped of all clothes and the rocks removed. He began to cry, as he knew his time was short. The third time, with no loadstone, the mechanism worked.

Mrs. Mamie remembers "seeing" Aunt Flora…so this may put the date of her husbands execution sometime during the pre or post Civil War era. Aunt Flora still living in 1924; age unknown.

Note: In the Last Will and Testament of Mary Hemingway, dated 1842, a slave is mentioned by the name of Flora Jane who was bequeathed to her niece, Sarah Ch--oy. It also mentions other slaves who resided on the *Taylor Plantation* such as Slurry (male), and his wife, Nancy. Also mentioned are: Friday (male), Elcy (female) and her boys Cuff and Henry, Robert (male), English (male), Mary Ann

(Elcy's daughter), Rose (Charity's daughter), Whitfield (male), Charity and her son Fuller, Beck (female), and Sarah (Elcy's daughter). James Bell, Robert Woodside and Anthony Clemmons witnessed this will. (Her Last Will and Testament, in its entirety, can be found in *The Legends of Brunswick County* written by J. C. Judah. It enumerates to whom each was given. In this Last Will and Testament "Henry" was bequeathed to her niece Elizabeth Robinson who also received 1/2 of her household and kitchen furniture and Elcy, along with her boys Henry and Cuff.

There is another "hanging tree" still visible off of Big Macedonia Road in Brunswick County, NC, slowly rotting after having been damaged in a storm which split it in two. It certainly appears to be as big as the infamous George Washington tree located in the Ocean Isle area. It rivals any other tree in Brunswick County as one of the largest trees. The "hanging tree" is shown in the following photo in March of 2009. Locals looking for firewood are slowly ravaging pieces of the tree. It appears to have been a mighty oak, also known as an old time gum tree.

The last known man hanged in Brunswick County was said to be Jones Brooks (according to Harvey Robinson, long-time historian). Descendents of Mr. Brooks still reside in Brunswick County. He was hung for "*going about a white woman.*" Mr. Robinson relates that the story is that "*he was going with this woman in Southport. He usually knocked on her window where she slept and she would let him in. However, this particular night when he knocked, she went to screaming. The reason why was that she done had a white man in there with her. They chased down Brooks and sentenced him to hang. He was hung on a Friday. They always had hangings on Friday because that is when Christ was crucified, on a Friday.*" Year unknown.

Some say the crime of Jones Brooks was so heinous that residents would not allow him to be buried in the local black cemetery. Instead he was buried him in the woods somewhere outside of Southport.

Legislative papers of the Senate in December of 1850 documented that hanging its criminals from scaffolds erected on spots convenient for the assembling of multitudes was still the norm. The public gallows was slowly being phased out. The stocks and whipping posts had been removed to the county jail yards about 30 years earlier in several counties across North Carolina. And in 1846 a "Phil" wrote to the *Raleigh Register*, "*We have, this day, witnessed the most humiliating scene that has ever been exhibited before us. Two white men were, by order of the court, led to the public whipping post, there stripped and fastened, and lashed with nine and thirty, until their skin was rough with whelps and red with blood. We have never beheld a scene more degrading to the noble sentiments that should be nurtured and cultivated in the breast of every freeman. It makes us almost hate ourselves, to think that we are of their kind--yea, their fellow-citizens.*" He had hoped that just reading this description might reform some people. It must be noted though, that some preferred the public punishment to the worse conditions in the county jails in "irons."

It even took a law to require some jails to provide blankets to prisoners during the winter months. In 1822 in Wake County a white man had nothing to protect him from the weather, not even clothes, as winter approached. No bed was provided and no means of warmth such as a fire. He begged for provisions such as was provided to the negro prisoners.

Finally in the legislature of 1844-45, representatives put the question of the penitentiary to the voters calling for a state prison costing $100,000. Again it was overwhelmingly defeated. The *North Carolina Standard* of September 16, 1845, put its finger directly on the real issue: "*. . . the State is in debt on account of Rail Roads, etc. and numbers doubtless voted against it because they were opposed to any increase of the public taxes.*" Two years later, however, Dorothea L. Dix was able to push through the Legislature a bill establishing a State hospital for the insane which called for an expenditure of public money only slightly less than a penitentiary would have cost.

By 1848 most jail conditions locally had improved from the earlier poor conditions. Of those inspected, 35 were in good condition with only 13 in poor condition with the "*uncleanliness such as a dungeon*" as Dorthea Dix described them in her travels. The Surry County jail was "*miserably dilapidated; the Wilkes, "comfortless and old"; the Wayne, "an old dilapidated building"; the Duplin, "defective", the Northampton, "noisome, damp, and cold.*" Of course the jailers resided in another part of the building. The Burke and Orange County jails were noted to be well built and in good order. The Guilford jail was noted to be isolated but offered a large chapel room for religious services.

Edward J. Hale of the *Fayetteville Observer* echoed the public sentiment from another perspective when he said in the 25th of April 1859 issue: "*The people of North Carolina voted wisely, some years ago, against the establishment of a State penitentiary. Their principal objection to it was, we believe, the cost; but in our opinion the pernicious effects of the system upon society and upon convicts furnishes a stronger reason still. . . .*" "*When a man commits murder . . . hang him; when he swears to a lie, crop him; when he steals, whip him. . . . But do not put him in a penitentiary, with a crowd of the worst of mankind, that he may there, study villainy, and graduate proficient in every species of crime.*" "*It has not been found that crime is frequent or increasing in North Carolina--at least not increasing with rapid strides as in other States. And the reasons doubtless are, that criminals (not all, but many) are convicted and punished in North Carolina, and not either suffered to escape altogether or sent to a penitentiary to be educated in crime.*"

## *Punishment*

Crime continued and punishments were ordered. Listed below are some notable crimes which occurred in North Carolina, particularly the New Hanover, Brunswick, and southeastern coastal areas. You will no doubt recognize many names from earlier chapters.

According to the *Court Minutes of February 8, 1768, the Magistrates and Freeholders* held Court in Wilmington. On "tryal" was a negro man named Quamino belonging to the estate of John DuBois, Esq, deceased. Quamino was charged with robbing sundry persons. Present were Cornelius Harnett, John Burgwin, John Lyon, Frederick Gregg, William Campbell, John Walker, John Campbell, Anthony Ward and William Wilkinson. These gentlemen found him guilty of several robberies and sentenced him to be hanged by the neck until he is dead, tomorrow morning between the hours of ten and twelve o'clock; and his head to be affixed up upon the Point near Wilmington. The Court valued the said negro, Quamino, at eighty pounds proclamation money. Signed by Cornelius Harnett.

North Carolina General Assembly notes from November the 6th, 1769 allowed John Rowan, Esq., his claim of eighty pounds for a negro man named Gwyn who was executed for Felony in Brunswick County and valued to that sum as per his certificate. Among other accounts settled that day were:

-Christopher Robinson allotted eighty pounds for a negro man named Batt who was executed for a felony. Bute County.

-Osborn Jeffrys, Sheriff of Bute County, was allotted forty shillings for fees in the execution of "Batt."

-Benjamin McCulloh, Clerk of Bute County was allotted twenty shillings for his fees at the trial of "Batt."

-Daniel Little, public gaoler, of Salisbury District, was allowed his claim of seventy pounds and eight pence for prison fees and sundry guards summoned to Guard the Said Gaol when Henry Ferril, Hugh Berry, Govay Black and William Fields, Felons were confined therein as per their accounts. (Gaoler - jailer.)

-Andrew Allesson, Sheriff of Rowan County was allowed his claim of five pounds for executing and burying William Fields, a felon.

-Francis Clayton of New Hanover County was allowed his claim of one hundred and sixty pounds for two negroes named Jack and Toney who were executed for Felony in the same county.

-Thomas Polk was allowed his claim of nine pounds, four shillings for victualing Cherokees at the request of His Excellency, the Governor. (Victualing: providing food supplies.)

-John London was allowed his claim of seven pounds for fees incurred in the trial of seven negroes executed for Felonies. Clerk of New Hanover County.

-Humphrey Nichols of Craven County was allowed his claim of fifty shillings for conveying John Nanpelt, a felon, to Newbern Gaol. He was also allowed his claim of four pounds for executing two negroes for felonies.

In **1771**, November 17th, in the New Hanover Courts, Henry Young, Esq., and Coroner of the said county told, under oath, that "*on or about the beginning of August last, David Pollock, keeper of the prison of the same county for this deponent, came to him; this deponent wounded in a dreadful manner with part of his bowels* *out. That, understanding the wound was given by one or more of the criminals then in his custody, this deponent pursued and overtook them and found one of the prisoners whose name is Thomas Clarke with a knife in one hand and a razor in the other. That after some threats and attempt to escape, the said Thomas Clarke surrendered, and acknowledged that he had wounded the said David Pollock. This deponent further saith that the said Thomas Clarke was committed to prison by a Magistrate of Brunswick County for breaking a chest on board of a vessel and stealing thereout money cloaths and other effects on a considerable value."*

The Minutes of a Court of Magistrates and Freeholders in Brunswick County, North Carolina, on March 5, **1778**, describes a case of murder in the county.

These minutes describe the trial of a negro man slave charged with the murder of Henry Williams (of Lockwood Folly). The slave was the property of Mrs. Sarah Dupree. Justices of the Peace present: William Paine, John Bell and Thomas Sessions. Freeholders present: John Stanton, James Ludlow, Needham Gause and Aaron Roberts. The negro was valued at eighty pounds "Procklamation" money.

The court proceeded "*on said trial and the said fellow, James, confessed himself to be the one that had a hand in the murdering of said Henry Williams in concurrence with the evidence of four other malefactors that were executed for being concerned in said murder on the 18th day of March 1777.*"

Ordered that the Sheriff take the said Jimmy from hence to the place of execution where he shall be tyed to a stake and burnt alive. Given under my hands this 5th day of March 1778.

In **1840** there was a case of burglary charged against a slave in Wake County where "*prosecution was not pressed and the defendant was carried off.*" Sometimes the clerks were hesitant to convict due to the burdensome and extreme punishments for the crime. In a case of arson against a negro boy twelve years old, the jury returned a guilty verdict but "*the solicitor did not pray Judgement as supposed in consequenve of the severity of the punishment*" and the boy was permitted to be sent out of the state." In another case a slave was branded, whipped and sent out of the state for manslaughter. Juries were cautioned not to consider the punishment in their decisions of guilty vs. not guilty but history bears out that this sometimes became a weighty factor in their decisions. The result was that some crimes were never prosecuted or enforced because of the severity of the punishment. Two of those crimes noted were the murder of slaves and horse stealing. Judge Taylor stated, "*Among the accusations for capital crimes, none occurs more frequently in the courts than that for the murder of slaves. Convictions have, in a few instances, though rarely, taken place; but I believe not one execution has ever followed.... It is generally believed that the punishment of death is too severe for the crime of horse stealing.*"

In Elizabeth City, in **1840**, a white man pled guilty to forgery and begged for mercy. The courts ordered him to pay costs and leave the state. This was a great disparity in punishments for the same crime committed by the black slave.

Life continued. Sometimes.

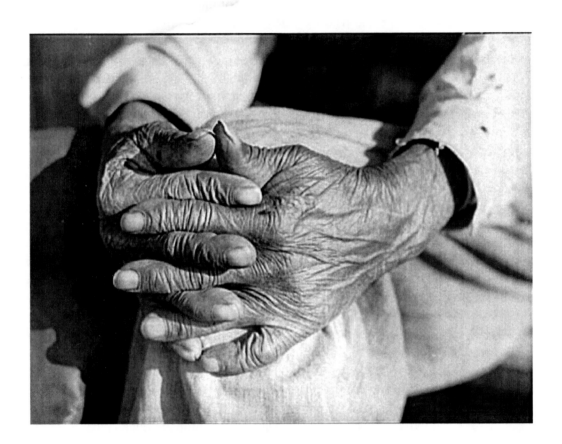

*Slave Hands*

*Slave Holding Pens*

*Plantation Slaves.*

# Chapter Six

# The Slaves of North Carolina

*Notice to all readers:  This chapter is not for the light of heart.  It contains true accounts of slave torture, deplorable conditions, and man's inhumanity to man.  This chapter is included as a testament to the lives of those living in the 1700 - early 1800s.  But through education, an understanding, and acceptance of the past can we progress to a better future. --The Author*

## Indian Slaves

The first slaves in America were Indians who were brought from the West Indies by the Spaniards.  Indians taken prisoner in war were also enslaved, as was the custom of the Europeans in the English colonies.

John Lawson attempted to plant a colony of settlers at the mouth of the Cape Fear about 1660, but the colonists were driven off by the Indians….some of whom had had their children captured by the colonists on the pretext of educating them…more likely to use them as slave labor.  The Indians became suspicious and soon drove the whites from the area.

## White Slaves

Whites were actually the first laborers that were brought to the New World from Europe.  In the white servitude plan individuals were obliged to work as indentured servants and often served seven years to pay for travel to America. These were either individuals with no means to pay for passage to America, transported felons, or kidnapped persons; sometimes children.

There is further documentation of white slaves owned by Indian masters described by Strachev in his *Travayle into Virginia*.  He tells the story of an Indian Chief named Evanoco, who lived at Ritanoe (south Virginia), who kept seven whites who escaped from the massacre at Roanoke, and these whites were *made to beat copper.* This particular tribe is said to have taken in whites who were shipwrecked off the coast.

*(Documented according to the preamble of an act of the Assembly about 1707. "Whereas it hath pleased Allmighty God so to bless and prosper the English plantations on the maine Land of America that all the Sea Coast from the most Easterne parts of New England to the Southermost part of Carrolina with all the Ports and Harbours thereon are possest by English under the dominion of our most gracious Soverreign Lady Ann by the Grace of God of England Scotland France and Ireland Queen Defender of the faith save only one Tract of land lying in this Government which lying waste the Comunication of her Majties Subjects by land is not only interupted but the Enemy in time of Warr and Pyrates in time of Peace have hitherto made use of the Harbours therein to careen and fitt their vessells as also to Wood and Water to the great annoyance of her Majties Subjects trading along the Coast and the Place being inhabited (as has been lately discovered) only by some fugitive Indians under no manner of Government and living chiefly by Rapine who do murder or hold in Slavery all persons that either by Shipwrack or passing in small vessells so unhappily fall under their Power And whereas the Inhabitants of this Government by reason of their fewness are subject to the dayly Insults of the Heathen owing their Lives and safety's to the courtesy of the Heathen rather then their own strength, therefore for the more speedy peopling the said Tract of Land and for the uniteing her Majts Empire in America and preventing the Enemy from Harbouring in those parts for the subdueing the Inhabitants and security of her Majties Subjects trading along the sea coast as also of the Inhabitants settled in this Government we pray that it may be enacted and it is hereby enacted by his Excell: the Palatine & the rest of the true and absolute Lords Proprs by and with the consent & advice of this present grand assembly and the authority thereof."*

"North Carolina has so many inlets, harbors, and barrier islands along its coast that enemy ships and pirates could easily hide there. During Queen Anne's War (1702–1713), French and Spanish ships harrassed the coast of North Carolina, and in 1706 they attacked Charleston. That attack was fresh in Carolinians' minds when they passed this law a year later." *(NC Colonial Records Comments.)*

## *Negro Slaves*

Bartolome Las Casas, an explorer in the 1600s, was eventually successful in substituting the negroes for the Indian slave labor. (Las Casas was a Spanish priest who lived in the 16th century. As a settler in the New World he witnessed, and was driven to oppose, the torture and genocide of the Native Americans by the Spanish colonists.)

The use of the negro as slaves was less expensive than keeping the white servants and the idea of using negroes as slaves soon replaced the former practice.

156

The negroes, because of the black man's superior endurance, docility and labor capacity, replaced Indian slavery and white servitude. The negroes were considered fitter than the white slaves and they remained the field masters even in the situations where Indians, whites and negroes all served a common master.

In 1703 Ludwig Michel, who was looking for a suitable tract of land in America on which to settle a group of Swiss, wrote of the planting regime in North Carolina: *"One employs slaves, and though they seem to be expensive they are always considered to be much better than the servants in Europe, being more submissive and more robust for work and one feeds and clothes them as one finds proper."* The cost was the same in the years of plenty and in years of lean. Planters had to care for the slaves in sickness and in health, as well as old age. An indulgent master might run into debt to care for them. The other end of the scale brought about half-starved negroes in rags.

*The Southern States of America*, in Chapter III - North Carolina 1775 - 1861, attempted to explain the thought processes of slavery at that time. It said, *"Toward the slavery question and the agitation which resulted in secession, North Carolina's attitude was conservative. For this there were various reasons. The small farm and the middle class planter being the dominant factors in industry, the milder type of slavery prevailed and the slave system never secured so strong a hold on the life of the people as in most other Southern states. Moreover, in the middle and western counties, there was a strong anti-slavery sentiment. Scotch-Irish, Germans and Quakers had settled these counties. Slavery had far less hold than in the east. Illustrative of this sentiment were Hinton Rowan Helper, Benjamin S. Hedrick, Daniel R. Goodloe, men who opposed slavery in the interest of the whites rather than the negroes. Indeed, in spite of the intense political controversy over slavery, there seems to have been a steady undercurrent of feeling among thinking people that sooner or later the institution must end."*

*"Therefore, sympathy with other states and the logic of events, rather than personal grievances, led North Carolina into the Confederacy."* Although secession had been advocated by political leaders, notably Thomas L. Clingman and William W. Holden, the principle made no headway among the people until 1857. Then the publication of *Helper's Impending Crisis* and John Brown's raid aroused public sentiment. Possession of Helper's book at once became a political crime, and sympathy for Virginia was expressed. (Hinton Helper was the author of *The Impending Crisis*, a bitterly controversial book that denounced slavery. *"Helper went further, denouncing slave owners as robbers, thieves, ruffians, and murderers, and advocating that slaves should gain freedom by violence if necessary."*

*"In the South, and North Carolina in particular, Helper became a villain of the highest order. His book was outlawed, and anyone found owning a copy could be sentenced to prison time. Daniel Worth, Methodist preacher and cousin of Governor Jonathan Worth, found with several copies, received a one-year jail sentence, but*

*fled the South while out on bond. In 1858, a public burning of Helper's book took place in High Point."*

*The Impeding Crisis* further polarized American politics, and helped get Abraham Lincoln elected in 1860. In 1857, *New York Herald* editor James G. Bennett handed President James Buchanan a copy saying, *"There is gunpowder enough in that book to blow the Union to the devil."* Three years later, Bennett wrote, *"Lincoln's election was due to the very work of Mr. Helper, and kindred speeches and documents."*

In 1868, Helper returned to the United States, and settled in Asheville. Despite the hatred most Southerners formerly held for him, Helper met with no problems. He subsequently moved to New York, St. Louis, and Washington, D. C. He wrote five other books, three of which were extremely racist and openly denounced the Negro race. Again changing his stance on slavery and African-Americans, Helper blamed blacks for the Civil War, and for the lack of Southern industry.

*"After 1890, Helper spent the majority of his time in Washington, D. C. His writings became more and more delusional, and his wife and son soon returned to Argentina."*

*"Increasingly despondent and mentally unstable, Helper killed himself on March 9, 1909, in a Washington hotel room. He is buried in an unmarked grave, the burial expenses paid by the Authors Society of New York."*

The Council of State adopted resolutions threatening a new form of government unless slave property was protected.

Public meetings were held in various counties that expressed defiance to the North and to abolition.

In one year secession sentiment had grown more than in all the preceding ones, and a secession party, small but active, had come into existence." *(North Carolina Department of Cultural Resources Markers web page.)*

In 1860 African Americans made up about one-third of North Carolina's population. Of the 361,522 negroes in N. C. on the eve of the Civil War, 30,463 were already free. Slaves or free, all lived in a society of strict legal codes. Regardless of their status, many played an active role in the coming days of war, 1861-1865.

North Carolina seceded from the Union-May 20, 1861. Many of the plantation owners went with their slaves to join N. C. Regiments. Many returned home in a wooden box.

It continues to be difficult to understand or appreciate the toils or lifestyles of the colonial slaves. Their hard work built the foundations of the plantations in the early 1700s. Their journey from Africa alone claimed an estimated 10-20% of all, passengers and crew alike. Upon arrival to the New World they faced an uncertain future sealed in a public auction where they were bound to the highest bidder.

In 1754 only 19 negroes entered the new world at Bath, N. C. Charleston, S.C welcomed 3,648. North Carolina looked to South Carolina and Virginia for their slaves. Governor Burrington noted in 1733 that most of the slaves in North Carolina were brought here from other governments (Barbados, etc.) and not directly from Africa. These negroes were described as "distemper'd." This would mean that they would need to "tame" them. This process of "taming" was done with the negroes coming directly from Africa and sometimes took several years. Therefore a seasoned negro was more valuable than one newly arrived from Africa.

Negroes entered North Carolina free of duty until 1787. After that there was a tax of 5 shillings on slaves between the ages of seven and twelve, and ages thirty to forty. There was a tax of 10 shillings on those between the ages of twelve and thirty; and a tax of 50 shillings on those under seven years old or over forty years old. They also taxed each slave from *Africa* at a rate of 5 shillings. By 1790 this tax was repealed...until 1795. At that time the General Assembly made the importation of slaves "by land or water" liable to a fine of 100 pounds. They did not want slaves coming in from the West Indian or Bahama Islands or South America. The spread of disease was taking a toll on the planters and this was, in part, an attempt to curb the spread of disease in 1795.

The largest percent of increase in slave populations in North Carolina occurred after the American Revolution from 1790-1800. The population increased by almost a third. At that time there was a grace period which Congress gave states before closing the African slave trade.

The *Wilmington Journal*, on October 14, 1859, published advertisements for five negro traders. Three were in Clinton, one at Warsaw and one at Six Runs in Sampson County. All offered high pRice's for plantation negroes. Sometimes the plantation owners chose to sell a slave if their financial situation warranted the action. Others were very reluctant to ever sell their slaves. Many owners left wills which indicated that upon the sale of their slaves, no slave family would be separated. However, the Supreme Court held that "it was the duty of an administrator to get as much as he could from the sale of slaves even if it required that families be separated." *(Cannon v. Jenkins, 16 N. C. 426.1)*

In 1803 a young African usually sold for about $300. In the Norcom Papers *(John Norcom, Jr., February 6, 1840)* the price of slaves is noted and climbing. In Fayetteville, in February 1859, the *"negroes ranging in age from four to fifty belonging to the estate of Andrew Gordon sold at an average of more than $1000. The men, field hands, brought from $1500 to $1700 and the women sold for from $1300 to $1500."* The negroes were sold on twelve-months credit with interest. About the same time, John P. Brown sold the slave groups in families of up to twenty negroes ranging in age from one to forty-five. They sold at a private sale for $17,900. In 1859 a blacksmith alone sold for $2,100.

Notices of the auctions were posted to announce the events to the wealthy plantation owners. The price of a slave......from fifteen to twenty-six pounds of silver, dependent upon age, health and disposition.

Slave auctions must have been frightening as families were separated and any individuality disappeared. The slave was forevermore known by a name assigned by the "master" and most often took the last name of the new owner. This made it difficult to find a family member once they were sold multiple times, each time changing last names.

A poster advertising the sale of negroes read: *To be sold on board the ship Bance Yland, on Tuesday the 6th of May, at Ashley Ferry a choice cargo of about 250 fine healthy Negroes, just arrived from the Windward & Rice Coast. The utmost care has been taken, and shall be continued, to keep them free from the least danger of being infected with the SMALL-POX, no boat having been on board, and all other communication with people from Charles-Town prevented. Austin, Laurens, & Appleby.*

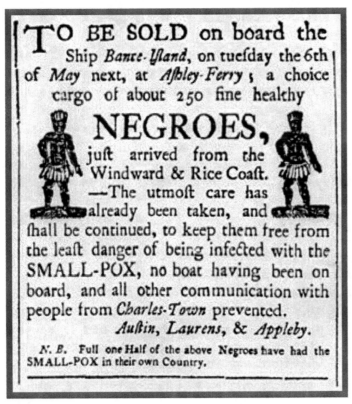

*N. B. Full one Half of the Negroes have had the SMALL POX in their own Country.*

Individuals such as John Spencer Bassett documented the life and times of slaves in 1896 in his book *Slavery and Servitude in the Colony of North Carolina.* John Bassett was born in 1867, just at the end of the slave period and died in 1927. He was a professor of political history and science at Trinity College in North Carolina. He began his documentation by acknowledging that the reconstruction of the Negro and slavery in North Carolina is done with unsatisfactory materials. He continues to say, *"At best it can give but a partial picture of the real life of the slaves, yet it can give all there is to give."* With that same premise, I acknowledge the snapshot described in this book is but that, a snapshot of their lives and in no way meant to be a comprehensive view of slavery in America or North Carolina.

*Slave Auction*

The negro was brought to the New World for economic reasons. An abundant supply of undeveloped land, and subsequent wealth, was coupled with a scant supply of labor. Colonists readily accepted thousands of acres of land with little more than their immediate families and fortitude. This situation led to the purchase of labor in the slave trade. It is generally accepted that the Spaniards from the West Indies birthed the idea of importing African people and placing them into slavery. The ideology spread to Jamestown and eventually across the coast of North America.

The Dutch traders brought the first slaves to the coast of Maryland and Virginia in the early 1700s. The earliest plantation owners purchased the African slave but did so with much trepidation. They were unsure if this arrangement would in fact profit them in the end. The Africans were uneducated, uncultured in the European traditions, and even spoke varying languages.

The Indian populations in the coastal regions were sparse by the end of the 1700s. However, remaining Indian populations were also captured and placed in slave quarters with the Negroes. In addition, there were white indentured servants who were bound for the colonies in the mix working to pay off their voyages to America.

Josephine Smith, at the age of 94 remembered her family history; being bought on the block at Richmond. She and her mother brought a thousand dollars. A preacher named Maynard who took them to Franklinton bought them. She remembered seeing a "heap" of slave sales, with (negroes) in chains and the "*speculators*" buying and selling. Some of the slaves had on nothing but a rag between their legs. She said, "S*lavery wasn't so good, cause it divided families and done a heap of other things that was bad, but the work was good for everybody. It's a pity that these younguns nowadays don't know the value of work like we did. Why, when I was ten years old, I could do any kind of housework and spin and weave to boot." "All my white folkses was good to me, and I reckon that I ain't got no cause for complaint. I ain't had much clothes and I ain't had so much to eat, and a-many a whupping, but nobody ain't never been real bad to me.*"

The Spaniard plan was to establish colonies of slaves, driven to the farmland fields and back to the barracks not unlike the slaves of the Romans. The Virginia farm owner, much like the Carolina farmer, planned a more personal approach and being the country gentleman expected to live on his own estate with his group of slaves around him. He would subsequently feed, house, give in marriage, and train them to fulfill his needs.

When North Carolina was first being settled, the Virginia planters had experimented with the use of Africans as slaves and the North Carolina colonists were satisfied that it would be profitable for them to use slaves in the fields.

The danger of the Indian attacks was subsiding by about 1712. By this time the Tuscarora were almost exterminated. The plantation owners began to take the chance of inevitable Negro uprisings should they employ a large number of slaves. They recognized that to attempt to settle a new plantation without a few slaves was certain failure. The additional labor was required to successfully settle and profit. Slavery was born in the Carolinas.

"*The lords, proprietors of Carolina recognized the value of slaves to the settlers from the first. In the Concessions of 1665, their earliest announcement of terms of settlement in Albemarle, they offered to give every master or mistress who should bring slaves into the province fifty acres of land for each slave above fourteen years of age so imported.*" (*Slavery and Servitude in the Colony of North Carolina, p. 17*). This basic principle continued in the early settlements of southeastern North Carolina established in the 1700s.

(*It is embodied in the instructions to Governor Burrington in 1730 (Col. Recs., III. 101-102); in those to Governor Dobbs in 1754 (ibid, V., 1133); and in those to Governor Tryon in 1765 (ibid. VII, 127).*

It is unknown if it was in that of Governor Martin in 1771. It is well to note, however, that Gov. Johnston in 1735 said he knew of no such instruction. The leaders of the colonists declared that such had been the custom. It was decided not to follow the custom, but how long this was enforced does not appear.

Governor Burrington, in 1730, encouraged the immigrants to seek the rich lands around Brunswick and Wilmington. Planters gradually settled in these areas as well as Bladen, Cumberland and Anson Counties. With the harbor at the Cape Fear, the slave trade expanded.

Burrington was the first Royal Governor of North Carolina, 1724 to 1725. He was reappointed from 1731 to 1734 and according to him there were about 30,000 white and about 6,000 negroes in North Carolina in 1730.

By 1761, Governor Arthur Dobbs reported there were about 12,000 negroes within North Carolina, increasing numbers due to births since few slaves were imported after the French and Indian Wars. By 1764 the numbers were estimated to be 10,000. By 1766, estimates were reported to be 21,281 negro taxables. In 1767 estimates in Brunswick County were 224 whites and 1085 negroes.

Reverend John McDowell, the Pastor of the Brunswick Town Parish, said, in 1762: *"We have but few families in this parish, but of the best in the province, viz., His Excellency the Governor, His Honor the President, some of the honorable Council, Col. Dry, the Collector, and about 20 other good families, who have each of them great gangs of slaves. We have in all about 900 whites and 1800 blacks."*

## Slave Laws

(The law and crime in North Carolina have already been described in the preceeding chapter. This section shall deal with laws regarding to the slave and his position providing examples of penal code and criminal proceedings.)

The North Carolina politicians spoke to the legality of slavery in the Fundamental Constitution stating, "Every freeman of Carolina shall have absolute power and authority over negro slaves of what opinion and religion so ever." Slaves were treated as property, much like a horse or land.

Slaves were also treated differently in court. They were tried before any three justices of the peace and three additional freeholders who were slaveholders, or the majority of them were slave owners, all of whom lived in the precinct where the crime was committed. This group had the power to try the case according to its best judgment and to decree a punishment, including life, death, or other corporal punishment. The regular officers of the law would implement the punishment. This type of trial was quick in order to avoid inconveniencing the owner of his labor in the field.

In 1740, two of the Justices of the Peace were removed from their positions for refusing to participate in the trial of a negro. John Swann and John Davis were removed from the roles of Justices. (*Col. recs., IV., 460*).

If the slave was to be executed, or was killed while resisting arrest, a certificate was issued to the owner providing a value. This entitled the owner to a poll tax from the government in order to reimburse him for his loss. This was in force until about 1741 when a new act concerning servants and slaves was passed. At that time the provisions were slightly changed with the slave being committed to jail by any Justice of the Peace (for good reason). The sheriff would summon two justices and four slave-owners/freeholders to meet at the county courthouse to hear all charges. This tribunal could accept the confession of the slave, hear witnesses of anyone, including negroes, mulattoes, or Indians, bond or free. They could then pass any judgment including execution. The master of the slave could speak on behalf of the slave. This process remained in place throughout the colonial period.

In Southern Slavery, it must be noted that a slave could not testify against a white person in the courts. Tobias Knight, charged in 1719 with complicity with the pirate, Teach, tried to get his defense to introduce evidence of the testimony of four negro slaves. It was forbidden as a negro was not allowed to testify except against another negro. Tobias was white.

"*Not satisfied with denying them the right to testify against the whites, the Assembly, in the law of 1741 (sect. 50), enacted that if any negro, mulatto, or Indian, bond or free, be found to have testified falsely, he should without further trial be ordered by the court to have one ear nailed to the pillory and there to stand one hour, at the end of which time that ear should be cut off; then the other ear should be nailed to the pillory, and at the end of another hour be cut off as the former. Finally the luckless fellow received thirty-nine lashes on his bare back, well laid on. This, it must be confessed, was vigorous enough to reach the conscience of even a pagan.*" (*Slavery and Servitude in the Colony of North Carolina, p. 31*).

"*In 1758 the Assembly decided to try an experiment. They were dissatisfied with existing conditions. Paying for executed slaves they considered a hardship, and they thought that they had come upon a plan that would save the lives of the slaves and still act as a deterrent from further crimes. They enacted that except for rape or murder no male slave who had committed a crime which was ordinarily punished by death should suffer death for the first offence; but that on due conviction such an offender should be castrated, the sheriff to be allowed for the operation twenty shillings to be paid by the public. The court must fix the value of the slave before the execution of this sentence, so that if it should be the cause of his death there might be no dispute as to the value to be paid his master. Three pounds were allowed by the public for the curing of the slave's wounds.*"

*"For the second offence death might be the penalty. At the same time it was ordered that no owner should recover more than sixty pounds for a slave executed or killed in outlawry." (Laws of 1758, Ch. 7, p. 31).* This was repealed in 1764, at least in regards to castration, and raised to an eighty-pound limit per slave value. *(Laws of 1764, Chap. 8)*

## Runaway Slaves

One of the common infractions for slaves was a runaway charge. Few freemen would help the runaways, as the laws against the practice were severe. The act of 1715 provided that someone who harbored a runaway more than one night should pay the slave owner ten shillings for each twenty-four hours kept in excess of the first night. It stated that no master should allow any slave to leave his plantation, except he be with the livery, master, mistress or other white servant. He must also have a ticket stating the place from which and to where he was traveling. The penalty was five shillings for violating this part of the law. All persons were to arrest slaves found off their master's plantation without the appropriate ticket. They were to deliver them back to the master if known or the provost marshal (high sheriff) of the colony. He would then receive pay for his trouble from either the one or the other at a specified rate.

Unknown slaves captured would be advertised for several months. John Poisson, of Wilmington, advertised his runaway slave on the 15th of April in 1806 offering a ten-dollar reward for his return. He was described as a negro fellow by the name of John, about 5 foot 10 or 11 inches high, likely and well made, and a carpenter by trade. It is unknown whether he was found and returned or not.

A person who killed an escaped slave (who had escaped from the provost marshal) would not be held accountable for the death if the slave had been escaped for at least two months and if the person swore that he killed the slave in self-defense. Stealing slaves was likewise prohibited and specific punishments set forth.

The negroes of the early 1700s were basically made up of two groups: those recently brought from Guinea and those reared in the New World. The latter were more manageable. The more recently imported slaves were more prone to run away. Those reared in the colonies were more polished and refined in their behavior according to Brickell in the *Natural History of North Carolina*.

Slaves who decided to run away into the swamps of southeastern North Carolina found primarily one foe, the native Indian. While hiding in the swamps, the runaways would commit damages on the property of the whites. They made themselves feared and dreaded because of their treacherous dispositions. The Indians, on the other hand, had a natural and irreconcilable hatred for the negroes and delighted in torturing them. When they came upon a runaway, they attacked them and either killed them or drove them back onto the plantation.

According to *Tales From Old Carolina* (by F. Roy Johnson, printed in 1965), in 1801, the Dismal Swamp offered shelter to the runaway negroes. Sanctuaries were located on the sand ridges, which lay behind the deep and dark primeval black gum forests. A slave had to get through tangled juniper forests, cane and vine jungles, paths of wild animals and it was this, which led to their safe location. They left the swamp to rob and commit other crimes against neighboring farms. "*Pompey Little, was heavy-set, full-faced, six-foot-tall negro fellow who had worked upon W. P. Little's, Littleton Plantation, in Hertford County's Maney's Neck area.*" One day in 1815, Pompey ran away, took off for the Chowan River area into Gates County, headed for safety. Within seven years he became a notorious outlaw in the Dismal Swamp area. In 1822 he was 36-37 years old, well fed and remarkably fat in the face. He robbed James W. Langley as he traveled the nearby road. Langley told him that he intended to publish this whole account upon returning to Suffolk. Pompey replied he was "*welcomed to do so and could add his name, Pomp.*" Langley ended up killing Pompey during that robbery. It is interesting to note that in a slave cemetery in Brunswick County, there was a negro named Pompey (Pompii) buried in the "old slave cemetery" on Stone Chimney Road. He was reported to be the last person buried in that particular cemetery...about the 1920s. A distant ancestor perhaps?

Many slaves did escape and appeared in publications like the following ad: "*Notice! $500 Reward. Ran away from the subscriber on the night of June 18th, my negro man, Simon. He may be making his way to the Dismal Swamp...*"

The tangled vines, snakes, and distant bay of the bloodhounds did not deter the runaways from seeking their freedom...sometimes for as long as their freed wives could earn enough to purchase their freedom.

During the slave times, according to Harvey Robinson, Brunswick County native, the slaves liked to go visiting. "If they stayed too late, they would put the dogs on em. The dogs were specially trained to run down the slaves and would bite em." "Them slaves cost something." "We ain't having no hard times now is we? When you go back and look at slave times, what got the slaves through was the man upstairs--if you don't believe in God, you are lost." Harvey Robinson.

The following are some examples of local slave runaway advertisements that were published in out- of-state newspapers; there are very few early copies of NC newspapers still remaining.

**April 24, 1746**   Virginia Gazette
"RAN away from the Subscriber, living in Fredericksburg, a Negro Man, named Tom; he formerly belonged to [illegible] Mark Morgan, of Bladen County, in North Carolina, and was brought to Virginia by the George [illegible], a Stay-maker, who purchased him of the said Morgan. He is a middle siz'd Fellow, about 46 Years of Age, [illegible] and Beard very grey. Had on a blue broad Cloth Vest, a Pair of black Everlasting Breeches, and a Chex Shirt; plays on the Violin, and is a Sawyer.

Whoever will secure the said Negroe, and convey him back to me, will have Four Pistoles Reward."
John Thurston

**February 28, 1751**   Virginia Gazette
Williamsburg, Feb. 21, 1750.
"NOW in the Public Goal of this City, Five Negroes, viz. Mingo, Phillis, Peter, Judy, and Fanney a Girl, supposed to be run-away Slaves, and to belong to Thomas Willes, in North Carolina. The Owner may have them on proving his Property, and paying Charges."
John Lane, K. P. G.

**January 23, 1753**   Edinburgh Evening Courant
"The captain is since arrived at New York, and says, that at Cape Fare there was an insurrection of the Negroes, which greatly alarmed the inhabitants, but it was quelled before any great damage was done:"

**January 18, 1770**   Virginia Gazette (Purdie & Dixon) Bute    county,    North Carolina.
"To all sheriffs, constables, and other his Majesty's liege people.  WHEREAS Astons [torn] jun. of the [torn] Esq; one of his majesty's justices of the Peace in and for the said county of Bute, that Joseph Duncan, late of the said county, blacksmith, did confess to him that he, Joseph, with a false key, and with force and arms did feloniously break open the jail of the said county some time in August last, and stole from the aforesaid jail a Negro fellow, who called himself TOM, a runaway, the property, as he said, of John Mayo, of Cumberland County, Virginia; and him the said Negro Tom the said Joseph Duncan did take and carry away, and sold to one Richard Sears for a consideration of five pounds proclamation money, and a horse of the value of eight pounds Virginia money, against the peace of our Sovereign Lord the King, his crown and dignity: These are therefore, in his Majesty's name, to command you forthwith to make diligent pursuit after the said felon, and hue and cry him from town to town, and from county to county, as well by horsemen as footmen, in order to apprehend the said felon, and when taken that you carry him forthwith before some one of his Majesty's Justices of the Peace in and for the said county where he shall be apprehended, to be by such Justice examined and dealt with according to law; and hereof fail you not respectively, upon the peril that shall ensue thereon."
GIVEN under my hand and seal, the 7th day of December 1769.
JETHRO SUMNER.
N. B. The said Joseph Duncan resides, it is said, in Fauquier County, Virginia

**January 2, 1772**   Virginia Gazette (Purdie & Dixon)

"COMMITTED to Dinwiddie Jail, on the 15th of October last, a short yellow Virginia born Negro, who says he belongs to William Watt of North Carolina; he had on a Sheeting Shirt, a spotted lapelled Jacket, a green Cotton One, Buckskin Breeches, an old Pair of Boots, and a Half worn bound Hat. The Owner is desired to take him away, and pay Charges."

EDWARD PEGRAM, Junior, Jailer

**June 24, 1773** *Virginia Gazette*
TEN POUNDS REWARD.
"RUN away from the Subscriber, about January last, a NEGRO MAN about forty Years of Age, a short thick Fellow, very black, both Ears cropped, has a Brand on his Forehead, though hardly perceivable, and a large Hole in one of his Legs, occasioned by a Bite from a Dog; he can read and write tolerably, and is a very good Hewer, Sawer, and Fiddler. I expect he is somewhere about Norfolk, or the Great Bridge, in Virginia, and will endeavour to pass for a Freeman.
Hertford County, North Carolina, June 9, 1773."

JOHN HARE.

**June 23, 1779** *Pennsylvania Gazette*
Two Hundred Pounds Reward.
"RUN away from the subscribers, two NEGROE MEN, viz. DICK, a likely fellow, about 24 years old, low and well set, has three remarkable scars on each side of his face, being his country mark, and speaks very little English; had on, and took with him, two country linen shirts, a superfine red broad cloth double breasted jacket, blue coat, country linen trowsers, and sundry other clothes, also a large old bed rug. TOM, about 30 years of age, a likely fellow, and taller than Dick, has lost his two upper fore teeth, and has a number of flourishes or artificial cuts on one of his arms, being his country mark; had on a blue jacket, brown surtout coat, blue stockings, and old shoes. They are old offenders, and know the country well, and did belong to Dr. William Mills, of North Carolina, from whom they ran away about three years ago, and were taken up in Pennsylvania, and committed to Lancaster goal, and on their return were purchased of an agent appointed by Dr. Mills to sell them. Whoever apprehends and secures the said Negroes, so that we get them again, shall receive One Hundred Pounds, of Fifty Pounds for either of them, and if delivered at Alexandria the above reward, or One Hundred Pounds for either of them."
MICHAEL GRETTER,
ROBERT GAMBLE.

*Slave o f Dismal Swamp by Porte Crayon*

**August 15, 1792** *The Pennsylvania Gazette*
Extract from a letter from Newburn, N. C. July 26.
"The negroes in this town and neighbourhood have stirred a rumour of their having in contemplation to rise against their masters, and to procure themselves their liberty, the inhabitants have been alarmed and they keep a strict watch to prevent their gathering by numbers, and to prevent their procuring arms; should it become serious, which I don't think, the worst that could befal us would be if they should set the

town on fire.—It is very absurd of the blacks, to suppose they could accomplish their views; and from the precautions that are taken to guard against a .....

**July 29, 1795**   *The Pennsylvania Gazette*
NORFOLK, July 18.
Extract of a letter from Wilmington, NC. dated July 5.
"For some weeks past a number of run away Negroes, who, in the day time secrete themselves in the swamps and woods in the vicinity of this town, have at night committed various depredations on the neighbouring plantations; not contented with these predatory excursions, they have added to their other enormities the murder of Mr. Jacob Lewis, overseer to A.D. Moore, Esq; and have also wounded Mr. Wm. Steely.—These continued outrages induced the Magistracy to outlaw the whole of the banditti, in consequence of which a number of them have been shot at different times and places; among the number killed is their chieftain, who stiled himself the General of the Swamps. And yesterday the following, who murdered Mr. Lewis, expiated his crimes by a public execution at Gallows Green. He confessed the crime, and acknowledged the justice of his sentence.  These well-timed severities, together with the necessary measures now pursuing, will, it is hoped, speedily and totally break up this nest of miscreants."

**February 28, 1809**   *The True Republican or American Whig* (Vol. 1, No. 9)
Wilmington, NC.
"Five dollars reward.  Ran away from the subscriber, About three weeks ago, a negro man, Named Jack;  well-known in and about Wilmington - any person that will deliver the above negro to me in Brunswick County or to Owen Kenan, in Wilmington, shall receive the above reward.  Thomas Smith."

Also in the same paper:

"STOP the SWINDLERS!  1000 dollars reward.  Will be paid for the apprehending and delivery of JOHN THOMAS AND HONORE MONPOEY, WHO ABSCONDED FROM THIS CITY ON Tuesday or Wednesday last having swindled several persons to a considerable amount.  John Thomas is a small thick set well made man, about 5 feet 4 inches high, 34 or 35 years of age, dark complexion, short black hair, and a very black beard; speaks fast, and usually with a smile in his countenance; has a remarkable scar on the side of his face; much inclined to dress; pretends to have someknowledge of horses, and frequently rides on a good one.  Said Thomas resided for many years in Union Street, where he kept a boarding house and grocery store.  Honore Monpoey is about 5 feet 9 or 10 inches high, a Creole of St. Domingo, speaks broken English, of slender make, is lame in one foot, has a dark swarthy complexion, with short coarse curly hair, so much so that many would not take him for a white man, but from his residence in th city for many years past, he has generally been considered as such, pitted with the small pox, speaks fast tho' he stammers while he speaks usually very slovenly in his dress, pretends to have a knowledge of horses, having latterly been in the habit of trafficking in the above species of property, as well as letting public hairs. Monpoey resided at the corner of Wentworth and King Streets, where he kept a grocery store. From their connections, it is highly probably they have traveled the same road, and may make for St. Mary's, Georgia or New Orleans. Five Hundred dollars reward will be paid for apprehending and delivering each, or one thousand dollars for both. Signed: William Porter, Washington Potter, Daniel Latham, Philip Cohen, Joshua Brown, committee in behalf of the creditors, Charleston, SC. February 20."

**February 21, 1809.** The Wilmington Gazette (Number 636, 13th Year)
Five Dollars Reward. Wilmington, NC.
"RAN AWAY from the subscriber living in Wilmington a negro woman named Lucy of a yellowish complexion about 23 years of age, remarkable for her loquacity. Any person delivering said negro to the subscriber or securing her in Wilmington jail shall be entitled to the above reward. Alice Heron."

**April 18, 1809.** The True Republican or American Whig (Vol. 1, No. 16), Wilmington, NC.
"Ran Away from the subscriber, in Wilmington, two negro men, Jack & Peter. Jack is a Cooper, and formerly belonged to Joseph Scott, deceased, of Sampson County; he is about 38 years of age, 5 feet, 8 inches high, stout made and looks well; he has a scar on the side of his nose, and the lower part of an ear bit off in fighting. It is probable he will be lurking about the North-east River, between the Big and Little Bridges, or at Mr. T. Larkins on Long Creek, as he has a wife there. Peter is between 30 and 40 years of age, about 5 feet, 9 inches high, very stout made, and quite black. I expect he will lurk about town, or perhaps, may endeavor to get to Fayetteville, as he was once owned by James Beggs, and waggoned for him, or to Raleigh where he was owned by James Meares. A reward of five dollars for each, if taken with the County, or double, if taken without it, will be paid to any person, who will lodge them in the Wilmington jail. I do hereby forbid all persons from harbouring or employing in any way whatever, the said negroes, Jack and Peter and particularly caution master of vessels against carrying them away, or suffering their crews to conceal them, as the law will be rigidly enforced against such offenders. Samuel Noble. April 12. 1809."

**May 10, 1809.** The True Republican or American Whig, Vol. 1, No. 20.
Runaway Negro. Wilmington, NC.

"A reward of fifty dollars will be given to any person who will apprehend and bring to the subscriber, or confine in any jail within the state so that I get him, a certain negro man by the name of John. He is about forty years of age, upwards of 6 feet high, speaks broken English, and is considerably ruptured, which may be plainly perceived. He was born and raised in the island of St. Croix; is a tolerable good sailor, and I expect he will endeavor to get on board of a vessel, by calling himself a free man. It is probable he is lurking about Wilmington or Newbern, or in the neighborhood of Mr. Edward Hatch, Jun. on Trent River, in Jones County, as he has a wife there. All captains of vessels, or other persons, are forewarned from concealing or harboring of the said negro, under penalty of the law. Edward Ward, Jun. Onslow County, May 10, 1809."

**May 16, 1809.** The True Republican or American Whig. Vol. 1, No. 21, 21, 23, 25, until 10 June 1809.) Wilmington, NC.
Twenty Dollars Reward.
Runaway from the subscriber about the 20th of April last, an apprentice boy, about 18 years of age, named Thomas Bell. I will give the above reward to any person who will deliver the said boy to me in Wilmington. Benjamin Jacob.

**May 23, 1809.** The True Republican or American Whig. Vol. 1, No 21.), Wilmington, NC.
One Hundred Cents reward.
"Absconded from the subscriber an apprentice boy named Larkins Rowe, about 19 years of age, (as may be seen by his indentures.) All persons are forbid harboring or employing said runaway. John Maccoll, May 23, 1809."

**May 23, 1809.** The True Republican or American Whig. Vol. 1, No 21, 21). Wilmington, NC
Ten dollars reward.
"Runaway from the subscriber on the night of the first of this month, a negro woman named Flora, she is of a yellow complexion and between twenty and twenty-five years of age. I expect she is lurking about Mr. James Price's, on th Sound, or about Mr. William Jones's, near Wilmington. I will give the above reward to any peron who will deliver her to me. Captains of vessels and all other persons are cautioned against harboring or concealing said negro, under the penalty of the law. Andrew Thally. Duplin County, May 19, 1809." Posted in Vol 21, 23, 25, 27 through 4 uly 1809.

**May 23, 1809**. The Wilmington Gazette. No. 646. Wilmington, NC. No. 646.
Run-away.

"A mulatto boy named George, belonging to the subscriber. As it is probably that he is gone to Wilmington, all masters of vessels and other persons are cautioned, at the peril of law, which shall be strictly enforced against them, not to harbor or carry him away. Any person who shall deliver the said boy to Messrs. John Mitchell, at Wilmington, or Duncan McRae of Fayetteville, shall be entitled to a handsome reward. William Duffy."

**May 23, 1809**. The Wilmington Gazette. No. 646. Wilmington, NC.
30 Dollars Reward.
"Run-away from the subscriber on the eleventh instant three negro men, belonging to the estate of Capt. John Green, named Moses, Harry, and Carolina. Moses is a stout, able, and likely fellow, about five feet ten inches high, very large eyes, about 22 years of age and speaks very distinct, not very dark; had on blue dyed homespun pantaloons, blue negro cloth jacket. Harry is a very likely fellow, about 21 years of age, five feet 8 inches high, very dark skin, pleasing countenance, had on a glossed servant's hat, dressed in blue negro cloth, and wears his hair platted before and behind. Carolina is about 28 years old, slender made, narrow long face, swings himself very much when he walks, about five feet seven inches high and homely. Thirty dollars will be paid for apprehending said negros and securing them in any goal, or ten dollars for each and if delivered to the subscriber in addition all necessary expenses paid. All persons forwarned from harboring said negroes or masters of vessels from carrying them off under the penalty of the law. John Grange. Brunswick County, NC. Town Creek, May 13, 1809."

**May 30, 1809.** The True Republican or American Whig (Vol. 1, No. 23, 25, 27, 45 on 7 November 1809.) Wilmington, NC.
Ten Dollars Reward.
"Ranaway from Mr. John Williams, in Wilmington, about the first of April, 1808, a negro woman named Jessa, about 23 years of age, 5 feet 5 inches high, slender made, and likely dresses very genteelly, and generally wears a blue handkerchief on her head, which comes down over her eyes, on account of their being very weak. She is light complected, was brought up in the family of Mr. Daniel Mallet, is a tolerable good seamstress, and is very well acquainted with housework. Having purchased the above negro wench some time ago from Mr. J. Williams, I will give the above reward for delivering her to me, or the jailor of this place, or any other in the state. If she is returned to me in the course of two or three months from this time, I will give her the liberty of procuring another master, provided she does not wish to live with me, or hiring her own time. Thomas Hunter, May 30, 1809."

**June 6, 1809.** The True Republican, Vol, 1, No. 23, 25, 27), Wilmington, NC.
Sixty Dollars Reward.

"Ran Away from the subscriber, living on Bay River, Craven County, NC, two negro fellows, named Bob and Luke. Bob, who sometimes call himself Jack, is about 5 feet 3 or 6 inches high, is of a yellow complexion, stoops a little when walking and speaks tolerable good English; had on when he went off, a thick grey cloth jacket, without any buttons, but probly he may have shifted his dress. Luke is rather taller than Bob, alias Jack, and of a deeper black, has thick lips, and had on a thick gray cloth jacket, but as they had all their clothes with them, nothing is more likely than they may have shifted their outside dress, and perhaps they may endeavor to pass for free men. Whever will secure them in any jail and give the owner notice, so that he may get them again, shall have the above reward of 60 dollars, or 30 dollars for either of them. It is not unlikely they may make for some seaport town, and endeavor to get on board some vessel bound to sea, masters of vessels, therefore,and all other persons, are hereby forbidden to take them on board, harbor or in any wise conceal them, under the penalty of the law. Richard Crutch. April 8, 1809."

**June 4, 1809.** The True Republican or American Whig (vol. 1, No. 25), Sloop Point, New-Hanover, Wilmington, NC.
Twenty Dollars.
"Will be given by the subscriber, for taking up and confining in jail, or delivering to him, the following runaways, or ten dollars for either of them - viz. Yorkshire, a likely young fellow, about five feet, nine or ten inches high, rather, slim, straight, and well made; wears his hair queued and platted. He formerly belonged to Mr. George Merrick, deceased; is well known in Wilmington, on the Sound, and Rocky Point; and has a wife belonging to Miss Howe, near Wilmington, by whom he is no doubt harboured. Jupiter or Jube, a very small fellow, about five feet high, twenty-one or twenty-two years old; has thick lips and small eyes. He runaway on the night of the 22d ultimo, and stole a horse, a double barrel gun, and a pair of boots. The horse was found the next morinng on the side of New River. Jupitor formerly belonged to Mr. Richard Roberts, on White-Oak, and lately to Mr. William Hadnot of Onslow County. He has a wife belonging to Mr. Cooper Huggins, on the north-east branch of New River; his mother is owned by Mr. Frederick Foy, near Newbern, and he has a sister at Mr. Daniel Newton's, at the mouth of Wallace's Creek, in Onslow County. It is supposed he will harbor at some one or all of the above mentioned places, or on French's Neck, where he is well known. Allmand Hall. Sloop Point, New-Hanover, June 4, 1809."

**June 27, 1809.** The True Republican or American Whig. Vol. 1, No 27.), Wilmington, NC.
Ten Dollars Reward.
"Ran away from the subcriber, on the 7th instant, a negro fellow by the name of Caesar, about thirty years of age, speaks slow, and one of his hands has been burnt

when he was small, which had deformed it; he has also a hole in the crown of his hat. He was formerly the property of M. M'Clammy, deceased. I expect he will lurk about Wilmington or the Fort in Brunswick County, as he has acquaintances in both places; he may perhaps, on particularly occasions, lurk about Mr. William Hansley's as he has a wife there. Whoever will deliver the said negro to the subscriber, on Topsail-Sound, or lodge him in the Wilmington jail, shall receive the above reward. N. B. Masters of vessels, and all othe persons are hereby forbid harboring, employing or carrying away said negro, under penalty of the law. Stockley Sidbury, Jun. June 27, 1809."

**November 7, 1809.** the True Republican or American Whig (Vol. 1, No 45). Wilmington, NC.
"Ranaway from the subscriber, on the 15th of September last, a negro fellow named Harry, about five feet eight inches high, stout built, coarse complexion, large teeth in the fore part of his mouth, and plausible in his conversation. A liberal reward will be given to whoever will deliver the said negro to the subscriber in Wilmington, or lodge him in some jail where he may be got. James Usher. October 31, 1809."

## *Slaves and Hunting Rights*

No doubt the prohibition of hunting rights for slaves was wrought in not allowing slaves to be in possession of weapons that might be used in a rebellion. They were allowed, however, to hunt on the master's land except in the company of a white man. The penalty for hunting off the master's land was fixed at twenty shillings that was to be paid by the master. The slave also received twenty lashes. An additional requirement made the slave carry a certificate giving him permission to carry a weapon. Future laws required slave owners to search the quarters of the slaves at least four times per year to confiscate any weapons. The laws intended to prevent slaves from shooting hogs or cows.

In addition, slaves were not allowed to hunt with dogs. In 1766 the law also included provisions to prevent hunting deer at night. Violators would pay a five-pound fine. Slaves found hunting deer at night or by firelight had their guns confiscated and received fifty lashes on a bare back, "well laid on". By 1738 it was unlawful for any person to kill deer from January 15 to July 15.

## A Slave's Right to Travel and Own Property

A negro found in a white person's kitchen at night would receive up to forty lashes according to the law. Any negroes found in other negro homes would receive twenty lashes.

*"In 1741 the Assembly took up the matter of the stealing of stock by slaves. Thievish by nature, the African in America became especially expert in petty larcenies. He was the more impelled to it because he felt that he had worked to raise the stock and ought to have a full share. At the time of which we are now speaking it was enacted that if any negro, Indian, or mulatto slave should kill any horse, cattle, or hogs without the owner's consent, or should steal, misbrand or mismark any horse, cattle, or hogs, he should have his ears cut off and be publicly whipped, at the discretion of the court trying the offence. For the second offence he should suffer death (sect. 10)."*

A typical Negro Cabin of the South.    *See page 9?.*

*Typical Negro Cabin*

The law of the same year was more severe still. It provided that no slave should on any pretext raise hogs, horses, or cattle, and that all such stock as was found in the possession of slaves six months after the passage of this act was to be seized and sold by the churchwardens, one-half to go to the informer and the other half to go to the parish. *(Slavery and Servitude in North Carolina, p. 41.)*

176

The planters sometimes gave slaves small patches of land upon which they were allowed to raise tobacco for themselves. They often sold the crop for extra funds. In addition, many Last Will and Testaments left freedom and sometimes land. In addition, some slave owners left provisions for the slaves to be taken care of without the expectation of labor until the end of their natural lives as a thank you for a lifetime of service.

*Slave-like Quarters still standing in Clarkton, NC.*

## Religion and Slaves

Most African slaves were considered to be pagan. Little information is available on the slave religious practices but the white attitude seemed to be that it would have been unfit to hold Christian persons, so they were content to allow the slaves to remain pagan, although no laws prohibited any slave from worshipping as they chose. *"This guarantee might have been successfully used to protect the planters should a case have arisen over the point in question, and yet it left the matter with an element of risk in it that made the planters unwilling to allow the conversion of the negroes."*

*"The condition that followed these circumstances is well seen from a statement of James Adams, a clergyman of the Established Church who was in the colony in 1709. He complained because the masters would 'by no means permit [their slaves]*

*to be baptized, having a false notion that a Christian slave is by law free.' A few of the negroes, he said, were instructed in the principles of religion, but he says plainly that they were not baptized."* (Colonial Records, 720.).

The missionaries of the *Society for the Propagation of the Gospel in Foreign Parts* preached vigorously against this notion. Giles Rainsford, one of these missionaries, writing from Chowan in 1712, tells how he had much trouble to induce one Martin to allow three slaves to be baptized. By 1715, he had baptized over forty negroes.

Clergy by 1735 readily reported baptized slaves and a Rev. Marsden noted that during his stay at Cape Fear he baptized about 1300 men, women and children and some negro slaves. In another account in 1762, another missionary reported that there were 1000 whites and 2000 slaves in New Hanover County, NC. This missionary had baptized 307 whites and 9 slaves on that particular visit. Most often slave owners did not take the time or effort to convert their slaves. The information gained by the slaves was usually through individual effort.

By 1754 Governor Dobbs decreed there must be some method to instruct their negroes in Christianity. Several governors had already discussed this but nothing much became of this decree.

The laws of 1715 related that: *"Although the negroes were allowed to join any church they might fancy, they were not allowed to have a church organization among themselves. To have one was at once against the policy of the English Church and against the sentiments of the planters. At that time, as well as now, the negro knew but little distinction between church and secular organizations. The planters feared that negro churches might become centers of negro conspiracies. It was in this spirit that there was incorporated in* The Law Concerning Servants and Slaves, *revision of 1715, the following remarkable section: "Be it further enacted, That if any master, or owner of negroes, or slaves, or any other person or persons whatsoever in the government shall permit or suffer any negro or negroes to build on their or either of their lands or any part thereof any house under pretense of a meeting house upon account of worship or upon any pretense whatsoever, and shall not suppress and hinder them, he, she, or they so offending shall for every default forfeit and pay fifty pounds, one-half towards defraying the contingent charges of the government, the other to him or them that shall sue for the same."* This section was subsequently left out of the laws enacted in 1741.

Elias Thomas, a slave on the Baxter Thomas plantation near Moncure, in February 1853, said they *"had prayer meetings on the plantation about once or twice a week."* They were allowed to attend the white churches on Sunday and went to the Methodist and Presbyterian Churches. The preacher often instructed them to obey their masters. Many slaves were baptized in the Shattucks Creek and Haw River. When the war ended, Thomas remained with his master for another eight years.

After that he went to the North Carolina State Hospital for the insane where he remained for twenty-eight years and reportedly *"learned to talk like a white man"*.

## Slave Marriage

Slave marriages were of little ceremony. Masters had to consent to the marriage before the man sought his bride and offered her some toy such as a brass ring. If she accepted, she was then married to him. This was the custom according to some accounts.

Other accounts of slave marriage include a wedding feast with the colored people furnishing coon, possum, and sweet potatoes. Sometimes the master would lead the ceremony and other times he allowed a leader of the slave group or old negro preacher to conduct the ceremony. It was sometimes held in the yard, master's home, or the slave quarters. If the couple was young, the young ladies held a broomstick knee high. If the couple was older, the older ladies held it. At the end of the ceremony, the preacher invited the marrying couple to jump the broomstick and then were pronounced married. A simple celebration may have included singing and dancing after which the couple went to their newly assigned cabin to begin their married life.

Marriages were between negroes. In 1715 intermarriages were prohibited with a penalty of fifty pounds. (It is noted that at this time period many white men suffered from a malignant venereal disease that they obtained from the slaves who came to the New World already infected.)

Marriage did not guarantee a life together. Even after years living as man and wife, and fruitful with children, wives or their spouses might be sold to another owner in a neighboring community or state. In some cases each remained faithful to the separated/sold spouse but it was acceptable to remarry if they so desired. Since slave marriages were not sanctioned by law, there was no avenue to dissolve one either. (Slaves were not allowed to enter into a contract.) The law did, however, recognize that marriage between slaves was acknowledged in that if a wife kills a husband who is caught in the act of adultery, it is a charge of manslaughter because of the provocation, somewhat of a contradiction of legalities.

If the couple separated, the ring was returned. This sometimes occurred against the will of the spouses. Fruitful women were much sought after and if, after a couple of years, there were no babies, the women were encouraged to seek out other husbands as the planters needed to keep their supply of labor.

A slave man would became just as enraged as a white man if he found his marital rights were violated. For example, Jacob, the property of William Lightfoot of Raleigh, suspected that Trueman Goode, a free negro, was consorting with his wife. Court records of Alvaney v. Powell from the 54 N. C. Court Documents stated, *"Upon returning home unexpectedly one day, he found Goode there and immediately attacked him with a stick."* In a similar situation, *The Star* documented on the 5th of May, 1826, that *"A slave named John, a house painter by trade, frequently quarreled with his wife Flora because he suspected her of adultery with a slave named Ben. John and Flora frequently separated and came together again. One day, complaining that his dinner was not properly prepared, John became angry, whipped Flora and turned her out of his house, telling her not to return. Flora pretended that she was going to her mother, but actually went to Ben's house. When John learned of Flora's whereabouts, he declared that "he would have his wife out of Ben's house," and killed Ben in the scuffle that followed."*

After the war ended, one former slave described her own wedding dress as

*"cream silk, made princess with pink and cream bows."* She wore a pair of morocco store-bought shoes. Her husband dressed in a store-bought suit with a coat made pigeon-tail. He wore a velvet vest and a white collar and tie. Hannah related *"someone stole the vest after the wedding."* *(Hannah Crasson Story and Photograph).*

## Naming Slaves

Slaves usually took the last name of their masters. Others resumed the names of origin from Africa after freedom. Still others selected a name of desire. Regardless, it was difficult to track or find relatives who were sold or moved with various surnames. Sometimes, after the Civil War, families who were able to reunite got together to select a name for uniformity, each assuming a familial identity.

## Family Life

The Master gave each slave family group a place to live, rations to subside, encouraged marriages, and respected their grief when a family member died. Some families built a strong sense of loyalty to each other, master to slave and vice versa. This is evident in many Last Wills and Testaments admonishing the descendents to keep slave families together and sometimes bequeathing their freedom.

The slave cabins were usually built for the woman as she was recognized to be the leader in a matriarchal family. Slave children were considered as belonging to the mother and referred to as such in conversation and plantation records. The man might be referred to as Mary's Toby. When the man was listed, it was usually as Jumper and his family, viz. Amey and her children, Sam Frank, Hester, Valentine, Molly and Joe.

One former slave described her home as a *"nice house." "Grandma had a large room to live in and we had one to live in. Daddy stayed at home with Mother. They worked their patches by moonlight, and worked for the white folks in the daytime."* (Hannah Crasson.) Jacob Manson, a former slave, described his cabin as *"built of poles"*, with stick and dirt chimney, one door, one window and dirt floor. Slave homes were called *quarters*. The plantation owners' home was called the *great house*.

It was the mother who went to the storehouse for the weekly rations, cooked, made clothing when the master issued some fabric, and hoarded some savings to make the cabin more comfortable. Some slaves had masters who provided for "plenty" while others lived on meager rations. Special meals allowed butter with the biscuits, a fine fare for the holidays. Another former slave, Isaac Johnson who served on a farm in Lillington, N. C. He was owned by Jack Johnson and his wife, Nancy. Jack remembers his food was *"fixed up fine." "It was fixed by a regular cook, who didn't do anything but cook. We had gardens, a-plenty of meat, a-plenty, and more biscuit than a lot of white folks had. I can remember the biscuit."*

The slaves wove the fabric for their clothes, called homespun, and even made the shoes they wore. Sometimes Christmas brought a new pair of shoes from the master as well as a week respite from the chores. Jacob Manson, a former slave remembers that many of the slaves went bareheaded and bare-footed. Some of the shoes actually had wooden bottoms. Some slaves wore rags around their heads and some wore bonnets. He grew up in Warren County on a plantation having about fifty slaves owed by Colonel Bun Eden.

By 1860 some of the annual costs that slave owners bore to keep slaves on their plantations included $7 per hand for slave clothing and medical charges of about $1.00 per year per slave. This expense came out of the plantation owners profits. Another expense of the planter was the overseer's salary, which was estimated to be about $100 to a $1,000 per year. In addition, the owner provided housing, and an allowance of corn and pork.

Isaac Johnson, a former slave, remembers the herbs and "things" used when a slave was sick. Sassafras tea and mullein tea were common. In addition, sheep pill tea was given for measles. He claims it cured the measles. An undetermined informant described *sheep pill tea* in the following: *"It was common to make a tea from sheep manure and give it to patients suffering from the measles." "They put something with it, and didn't tell the people what it was they used."* Another said, *"I know what they give me for measles, it was from sheep; this old woman was there and she made the tea. My father went out and got it from the sheep pen. They told me it was 'Siphon Tea' but it was boiled sheep dung."* But most patients didn't know what they were drinking, *"My brother was awful sick ... and my sister fixed sheep manure tea and he got better, but when he found out what it was, he got so mad he wouldn't even look at her!"*

Another informant recalled, *"One time the family was down with measles. I put sheep manure in boiling water, strained it, and added two ounces of moonshine. It wasn't long before those measles started popping out! When I told them after what I used, some went outside and vomited."* The sheep manure tea was used to help bring out the measles and shorten the length of the sickness. Pills were also made of the sheep dung and taken orally. *(According to the Pennsylvania Germans living in the Shenandoah Valley, Virginia.)*

On the Sam Brodie plantation, near Raleigh, there were about 162 slaves. Every Sunday morning the children were bathed, dressed and had their hair combed. They were to be presented to the Master and Missus for breakfast where they were observed for their health. Any child not eating properly was given medical care. The food was presented on a large tray where each child used a mussel shell as a spoon to dip into the food. Ailing children who refused to eat were taken to the great house for meals and medicine until they were well. Everyone got biscuits on Sunday, the best day of the week for slaves.

## *Education*

The master usually determined the amount of education afforded a slave. Many slaves did know how to count or "cipher". The primary education needed was to understand the plantation routine and instructions. Most learned a craft under a master craftsman. They were bound to a carpenter or bricklayer to learn the trade.

The slaves who did learn to read and write were most often taught this in Sunday school. Jehu Whithed of Orange County was the exception when in his will he gave instruction that his mulatto slave, Fanny, was to be sent to school for six months with those expenses paid for by his executors. His daughter perhaps?

Hannah Crasson, a former slave, said, *"The white folks did not allow us to have nothing to do with books. You better not be found trying to learn to read. Our marster was harder down on that than anything else. You better not be catched with a book. They read the bible and told us to obey our marster, for the Bible said obey your marster."*

After 1830, teaching slaves to read and write was an indictable offense. Owners did not want slaves reading abolitionist literature and forbade slaves to even teach each other, give books, or to sell printed materials to each other. This offense was punishable by a fine from $100 to $200. Much disagreement occurred on this topic within North Carolina

The white people did not teach the negroes to read or write but many of them could not read or write either. Very few of the poor whites could read and most farmers were poor, not at all like the wealthy plantation owners.

## *Recreation*

Slave families did have time for some leisure activities. Most of this was spent on their own plantation for the slave mobility was watched closely and regulated by law. A slave must have a certificate with permission from his master to leave the plantation as per an act of 1715. A slave in good standing could generally get this pass whenever he asked. As most slaves were unwilling to risk the displeasure of the master, they generally remained on the plantation when required and did not abuse the privilege of "sneaking away" from the plantation at night. If one happened to forge a pass, the punishment was thirty-nine lashes.

Saturday afternoons, Sundays and general holidays brought considerable freedom. Christmas brought three to four days without laboring, sometimes through the New Year. This is when it was possible to visit neighboring plantations or towns to see relatives and friends. Masters gave small presents to slaves, sometimes a brightly colored head cloth for the women and a "hand of tobacco" for the men. In addition they might receive some barbecued pork, molasses or weak liquor. At the end of the holiday season, they were generally "done up" with plenty of beef and whiskey.

On Christmas Day the slaves in Wilmington would have a "John Kunering" day. (In Edenton, this was called "John Canoeing" day.) *"With liquor on their breaths and money in their pockets they spent the day in one long jubilee."* In 1824, Dr. James Norcom described this custom as practiced in Edenton as "dancing and entertainments among themselves, celebrating the season."

The Wilmington News-Dispatch described the custom of *John Kunering* in 1925 as *"with the rattling of bones, the blowing of cows horns, and the tinkling of tambourines, the singing slaves, grotesque in their "Kuner" costumes.......Strips of bright colored cloth, which had been sewn to their usual garments, fluttered gaily as the Kuners danced. They wore masks, some with horns, beards, staring eyes, enormous noses and grinning mouths. All were men, but some were disguised as women. After a few songs, one of the dancers would approach the spectators with his hat extended and collect the pennies, which were the Kuners' reward. Shouting again their chant, they were off again in search of another crowd and more pennies. This custom seems to have died out in North Carolina in the eighties, but it is still a part of the Christmas celebration of the negroes of the Bahamas and Jamaica."*

Corn huskings sponsored by the masters were another opportunity for the slaves to dance and frolic. This was a reward for the hard work and job well done. After the corn was shucked, a bounty of barbecue, whiskey and brandy was provided to celebrate. The dancing would begin and the fiddle and banjos brought out.

While dancing, drinking, and picnics were encouraged, gambling of any sort was prohibited. (1829 Supreme Court decision.) Drinking alcohol was common and many white men were said to make their fortunes selling the three-cent drinks to the negroes; but it is unlikely that a poor slave drank heavily and this was probably only the case during the holidays. One slave described the "dram" made by the barrel by the master and sold to the slaves for ten cents a quart. This brandy provided the drink for the Fourth of July, Christmas and other holiday socials.

*Attendees of Old Slave Day, Southern Pines, 1937.*

## Slave Discipline and Punishment

The planters continued to fear the rebellion of the slave communities. They were very severe in dealing with uprisings or noncompliant slaves frequently whipping them until large pieces of skin were hanging down their backs. With this much pain inflicted upon them, they seldom shed a tear.

Slaves hitting back in violence toward the master could be hanged. Other planters brought their slave communities to observe the hanging as a lesson to be learned.

Not all punishments were through hanging; one slave in Granville County was burned alive after murdering a white man. In 1778 another was burned alive in Brunswick County for the same crime. Around 1741 a law was considered to include the clause that any slave conspiring with three or more others could be guilty of a felony and sentenced to death. The same held true for a conspiracy to murder a white man. It never passed.

REV. W. H. ROBINSON, AUTHOR.

*Rev. W. H. Robinson*

By 1741, the laws provided that a disobedient servant should be tried before a justice of the peace and, if convicted, suffer corporal punishment not to exceed twenty lashes, as the court might deem. It joined a 1715 law that required all masters to provide a competent diet, clothing and lodging for all servants. It exerted that no master should exceed the bounds of moderation in correcting their demerits (behaviors or deeds against the master's rules). It also gave the servant the option to file a complaint against the master through the next precinct court. The 1741 law reaffirmed these rights and added that no master should whip his servant naked without an order by the Justice of the Peace. The penalty for violation was forty shillings. If the master did not agree, the servant could be sold at public auction for the balance of his servitude. The Reverend W. H. Robinson recorded his memories of slavery and life in the 1800s in his book *From Log Cabin to the Pulpit or Fifteen Years in Slavery.*

His words alone describe his intent in writing this book and sharing these thoughts and are worth repeating in this era: *"My friends, it is not the purpose of the writer to place before the public something to bias the minds of the people or instill a spirit of hatred. My book reveals in every chapter either the pathetic moan of slaves*

"FROM LOG CABIN TO THE PULPIT" OR "FIFTEEN YEARS IN SLAVERY"

*in almost utter despair, yet panting, groaning, bitterly wailing and still hoping for freedom, or of slaves with their hearts, lifted to God, praying for deliverance from the cruel bonds, the auction block, and years of unrequited grinding toil for those who had no right to their labor."*

*"Realizing, as I do, the injunction of the Lord Jesus, when he said, in Matthew VII, 12: "Therefore, all things whatsoever ye would that men should do to you, do ye so to them, for this is the law and the prophets" my deliberations have been many and constant that God would take out of my heart all the spirit of retaliation or revenge. This is why my book has not been before the public years ago. I wanted to be assured of the fact that I could give to the world at least some thoughts that would not only be a remembrance, but would prove beneficial to all in whose hands this book may chance to fall. I would not have this all important fact pass from the mind and memory of men, that they should not give their consent, nor cast their ballot for the enslavement of any human being."* Hopefully we have risen above the past and can appreciate his heart and words.

Although born in Wilmington in 1848, both of the parents of W. H. Robinson hailed from the Madagascar tribe in Africa, noted for their mechanical skill. A wealthy man owned his parents, Peter and Rosy. The master had two farms and over five hundred slaves. Rosy, his mother, was a cook in the main house and paid three dollars per month.

"Peter towed vessels in and out of Wilmington harbor into the Atlantic ocean. He pursued this occupation for over fifteen years and received many tips by being courteous and always on the alert for ships heaving in sight. While the master received pay for the towage, my father by constant contact with white men, received money in many other ways."

Slaves were hired to sack the ground-peas (peanuts), and paid one cent and a half per sack. Other sources of income for slaves included working in the hogsheads of molasses, unloading them from the docks. The hot sun caused the molasses to ferment and run out through the containers. The negro women would catch the molasses by running their hands over the hogshead and wiping the molasses from their hands into a pail. (A *hogshead* is a large cask of liquid - of a food commodity).

More specifically, it refers to a specified volume, measured in Imperial units, primarily applied to alcoholic beverages such as wine, ale, or cider. - *Wikipedia.)*

Peter Robinson would tow Mr. Sam Fuller and Mr. Elliott in and out each day. They were two Quaker gentlemen that sometimes assisted the slaves in obtaining their freedom. Together they devised a plan for Peter to escape to Canada. The system would use an underground railroad dividing the country into sections. At every fifteen or twenty miles was a station. The runaway would switch wagons that often had double linings, with corn or wheat visible while the cavity of the wagon filled with women and children. The Quakers planned to help Peter purchase his own freedom (with the eleven hundred dollars he had so meticulously saved over the years) with his family following in the Underground Railroad.

(Note this account on file with the NC Department of Archives:
December 6, 1797          The Pennsylvania Gazette
To the Senate and House of Representatives of the United States in Congress assembled.

The Memorial and Address of the people called Quakers, from their yearly meeting held in Philadelphia by adjournments, from the 25th of the 9th month, to the 29th of the same inclusive, 1797, Respectfully sheweth, That being convened at this, our annual solemnity, for the promotion of the cause of truth and righteousness, we have been favoured to experience religious weight to attend our minds, and an anxious desire to follow after those things which make for peace; among other investigations, the oppressed state of our brethren of the African race has been brought into view, and particularly the circumstances of 134 in North Carolina, and many others, whose cases have not so fully come to our knowledge, who were set free by members of our religious society, and again reduced into cruel bondage, under the authority of existing or retrospective laws; husbands and wives and children, separated one from another; which we apprehend to be an abominable tragedy, and with other acts of a similar nature practised in other states, has a tendency to bring down the judgment of a righteous God upon our land.)

W. H. Robinson, Peter's son, related the story of meeting Mr. Fuller, long after the historic escape plan. "Allow me to state here that in 1875, while on the train going to Wilmington, North Carolina, in search of a sister and brother, I met a white man having the appearance of a lawyer. He talked very freely with me and I soon learned that he was from Boston, Massachusetts, and that he was a merchant instead of a lawyer. His continued conversation with me attracted the attention of nearly all the passengers in the car, and they were not careful or considerate in their criticism, for they were heard to say several times, "he is a Northern negro lover," or, "one of Lincoln's hirelings," and such like expressions. We were truly glad when we reached Wilmington and could get away from the scrutinizing eyes and listening ears of the passengers in the car. He asked me if Wilmington was my home. I told him it was, but that I did not love a grain of sand of that soil. He assured me that this was the case with him, for said he, "my father lost his life here trying to help a colored man to liberty." I asked him who his father was. He said, "Sam Fuller." When he learned that I had known his father from my childhood days it seemed to draw him closer to me, and we were both dumbfounded for a moment when it was made known that his father had lost his life because he had tried to help my father secure his freedom. We both broke down and wept for a few moments, but I recognized the danger we were in, even in 1875, in a southern state. So we parted with the understanding that we keep in touch with each other until we got to Indianapolis, Indiana. As there was danger of both being murdered, we passed each other almost as strangers on the streets of Wilmington for over a week, and finally we both left on the same train. We spent a week together in the city of Indianapolis, Indiana. From the way he spent money on me it seemed that he thought he owed me some gratitude instead of my owing it to him."

"He now told me the story of the death of his father and how it came about. My (father's) master became suspicious, or mistrusted from surrounding circumstances, (and suspected) that Mr. Fuller was the deviser of (Peter's) attempt to buy his freedom. A few nights after father was sold from Wilmington, a posse of men notified Mr. Fuller to leave the state at once, and they left a crossbone and skull on a stick in front of his door. He left his wife and four children, Samuel, Jr., the man I met on the train being the oldest, with the understanding that he would send for them in a few days. He has never been heard from since. The supposition is that he was murdered. The family remained there until the rebellion, when they left for Indiana, afterward going from there to Massachusetts."

Sam Fuller's business in Wilmington was to look after a small homestead of about forty acres of land. I (W. Robinson) was not successful in finding my brother or sister but felt *"amply paid by meeting an old friend to the negro race and one who helped my father in many different ways."*

The escape plan of my father was put into effect in 1858 when my father, Peter, went to his master to find out what he might have to pay to become free. The first question asked of him was "what white man has put you up to this?" Suspicion fell upon the two Quakers, Mr. Sam Fuller and Mr. Elliott. My father denied their involvement. The next question…"how much money do you have?" Peter told him $450 and the master agreed to take $1,150 for his freedom. The master doubted that Peter would ever be able to save this amount. Peter was to pay for himself on the installment plan paying the $450. down and monthly payments. This was with the understanding that Peter was to teach another man how to run the tug for six months, and then he could work wherever he pleased. He was to continue payments until the total was paid off, with interest.

In 1859 Peter went as far as California working with a surveying company, returning and paying another $350 toward his ultimate freedom. He returned to California but about three months later news arrived that he would be returning to us "in chains". That surely meant that he would be sold away from us and surely lose all the money already paid. This news arrived to us through the slave network with one relaying to the next, even across the country as the opportunity presented.

Peter arrived back to Wilmington about two months later, bound in chains. He had been in handcuffs for fourteen days and his ankles were "raw as a piece of beef." They took him to the negro pen (jail). "When we left him they were trying to unlock his handcuffs as his hands had swollen and it was difficult to unlock them."

The negro trader ordered Rosy and the children to return home telling them they could see him in the morning. Rosy prayed all night, sometimes on her knees and sometimes prostrate upon her face on the floor, begging God to use his power to intervene and keep her husband from being sold. By midnight that night Rosy went to the great house, risking the law that if any negro was caught out after nine o'clock at night they would receive forty-nine lashes.

She awoke Master Tom and asked "Master Tom, have you forgotten your religion? Have you the heart to sell my husband from me and my children after he has served you all these days and made you a fortune?" He said, "No, Rosy, I've nothing to do with that. Your husband is in the hands of the state of California, but I'll see that he is not taken out of this state."

Rosy was ignorant of the law and didn't realize that any offense would have to be tried in the state that it was committed. Master Tom told her, "Peter had become intimate with a white lady." "Then he wrote us a pass to return back home." (Rosy)

By three in the morning, Rosy concluded she had better return to the jail, so she headed back there, her children in tow. She and the children saw Peter standing at the window and called to him, but he waved his hand to tell them to go back home.

THE LATE MRS. W. H. ROBINSON

Rosy cooked a good breakfast for her husband and returned to the trader's pen but heard voices singing and rejoicing along the way. She knew this meant that some were sold and hoping to fall into better hands than the ones they left; others singing as they hoped to meet their mother, father or child at the new home. Rosy knew the group was about to travel to Richmond. Three hundred men, women and children lined up. They hastily scanned the line for Peter but he was not to be seen.

There was one other vehicle that could convey passengers with heavy oak boards with staples driven into them. Men who were valuable and not to be whipped were handcuffed to the staples. Peter was among them. His son, William, saw him first. He gave his son a piece of advice that day. Peter said, "William, never pull off your shirt to be whipped. I want you to die in defense of your mother; for once I lay in the woods eleven months for trying to prevent your mother from being whipped." He shook his son's hand and kissed him goodbye through the iron bars. Then three daughters and two more sons climbed about the wheel and told him goodbye. Rosy climbed upon the wheel and Peter told her, "I'm bound for Richmond, Virginia, and from there to some southern market, I don't know where. We may never meet again this side of the shores of time, but Rosy, keep the faith in God, and meet me in heaven. I want this one assurance from you before we part: I want to know if you believe the charge brought against me, for which they are robbing me of my liberty?" Rosy assured him she did not believe it. Peter kissed her goodbye as the trader ordered her down. With a mutual agreement that they would never marry another, forty years passed and then Rosy died, in 1898.

Three weeks after Peter was taken away, his children were all separated from their mom, Rosy, and sent to other farms. Peter's son William was taken into the great house to wait on tables.

William remembered an incident when the master asked him to light his pipe. Then he ordered him to bring him a glass of water. When William returned with the water, the master did not answer when spoken to and his complexion had turned sallow. William called the mistress (his wife). She came and spoke to him but there was no answer. He had died while sitting in his chair.

The custom was for the older slaves to come and view the remains of the masters or mistresses while they lay in state. If he was a good master, there were genuine tears shed. In this situation, however, Master Tom was not well liked as he had sold Peter. This did not set well with the others.

Peter was very well respected among his people because he shared all the news that he heard from his Quaker friends. The other slaves came to the wake as was the custom but stopped just prior to entering the door of the house to wet their fingers with saliva to create the expected tears. As they passed by him they pretended to cry lamenting, "Poor Massa Tom is gone." Of course they didn't mention where he had gone. Had they not demonstrated this custom, they would have been in danger.

Three weeks later at the reading of the will, the mother (of William) and the three children were given to Scott Cowens, the meanest of all the Cowens family. He was known to be a drunkard and a gambler and even gambled away three sons (ages 12-14) of different women leaving the families in anguish. *(Not my words but those of Robinsons.)* Rosa went to his home as a cook.

He was angry at Rosy who was accused of saying that "God had sent swift judgment upon his father." Rosy denied it. Master Cowen threatened her but did not strike her.

Cowen returned home drunk one morning and sat down at the breakfast table demanding a glass of cool water right from the spring. As soon as she brought it to him he threw the water in her face saying, "I will show you how to bring me dirty water to drink."

A few days later Cowen found fault with the biscuits. He called for Rosy and knocked her from the porch to the ground. This was too much for her son, William, to endure as he watched Cowen curse and kick her. William reached for an ax handle and knocked Cowen down. His only option at that point was to run away. William ran to the three-mile farm and found sympathy from an old woman who gave him a chunk of fat meat and half of a corndodger while directing him to a hiding place. She put her hands on him and prayed for slavery to end. (A corn-dodger was a small oval cake made of corn bread and baked or fried hard in a skillet. It also may refer to a boiled dumpling made of corn meal.)

Later that night William found his hiding place amidst the thick canes in a low swampy place. That area was thick with bears and more than once he saw a bear come out of the cornfield carrying corn. Hazards included the water moccasins and rattlesnakes. About three in the morning he came out of the canes and began to enter the cave he had heard about. The voice of a man asked him "who is dat?" William answered, "dis is me." The voice knew whom to expect and knew who "me" was. He questioned him about his name and parents' names being very cautious about who was to be admitted into the cave. White men were known to have disguised themselves as a slave trying to determine who was helping the runaways.

William passed muster and was finally admitted. Several other men soon joined them with food stolen from the farm. The cook joined them and wrapped chicken in cabbage leaves and then placed it on a bed of ashes. Then he made dodgers, rolling them in cabbage leaves and baking them in the ashes. These were called *ashcakes*. Fifteen men total joined them for breakfast with the two hunters, the old man who admitted him, and William making nineteen in all; all runaways.

Frank Anderson, one of the hiders, ran away from his father, a white man of Wilmington, and had a reward of one hundred dollars on his head. He had been with the group for the past eleven months and had "stripes on his back like the ridges of a washboard," put there by his father's overseer.

The watchman of the group was called Uncle Amos. He took William as his companion because he was the only boy among the men. William slept during the day and helped him stand guard at night. William had been at the hiding place about three weeks when Uncle Amos told the group that it was time to move on "as within three days the negro hunters would be among them." The group then moved fourteen miles away.

The runaways secured a mowing scythe, removed the crooked handle and put on straight ones to protect themselves from the bloodhounds. Robinson describes one particular morning when "at breakfast, negro hunters appeared with shot guns and revolvers drawn and demanded us to wade over to them through the waters." "We did." One of the hunters threatened Frank Anderson and told him "if you run I'll blow your brains out." Frank ran like a deer, only to be cut down by a bullet. His crime was not consenting to be tied up and whipped when he was late returning from a Saturday night dance. For thirteen miles his blood seeped through the cracks in the cart.

Eventually the hunters surrendered the group of slaves to the jailers or keeper of the negro pen. If the negro transgressed, he paid the penalty with a lacerated back, from fifty to three hundred lashes. The captors received three dollars per head as their reward and an additional two hundred for Frank Anderson. Each of the prisoners was struck with thirty-nine lashes and then returned to their masters. For some reason William was exempted from the lashes and just turned over to his master.

William was eventually sent to Richmond to be sold again. He hoped for a better placement this time.

Miss Marguerite Robinson.

*Miss Marguerite Robinson, daughter of William Robinson.*

All of Williams's brothers and sisters except two had been sold and removed from Wilmington. He suspected they were in Georgia.

A poor man from East Virginia bought William. A William Scott paid four hundred and fifty dollars cash and gave a mortgage of sixty acres of land, including one colored girl he had bought four years before, as payment for William Robinson. In the three days that Robinson remained in the pen he witnessed many women and children separated, heard the wail of the children and the mother for her child. He saw husband and wife bid each other farewell, as well as, brothers and sisters saying goodbye. William said, "There could not have been any darker days to them than these; it was with them as it was with Job." Over three million lived to see freedom.

## Slave Funerals

Families mourned their losses and funerals were full of emotion. Church members were sometimes buried in the church cemeteries. Planters also set aside a burial ground for the use of their slaves. The master or the slave family sometimes erected a tombstone if they had a little money. Such is the case in the slave cemeteries in Brunswick County on Stone Chimney Road and Highway 87 in the Winnabow areas. Another not yet located as of this date, is reported to be directly behind the Western Auto/Jones/Belks Stores in Shallotte, NC. Harvey Robinson, presently 100-years old, stated in March 2009 that his brother, Donnie, knows exactly where it was located.  Graves were marked with fat-lighter stakes, some carved with the names of the deceased.  It was said to be a large cemetery, sporting more than fifty gravesites.  Among those graves is the final resting place of his great-grandmother, Charity.  It was unclear if her last name was Gore or Ward, but he felt "Ward" was her correct maiden name.

Funerals included a feast and a "play for the dead" or celebration of sorts, which lasted till dawn.  The play included leaping, jumping and dancing.  They assumed the deceased had gone to heaven regardless of the manner of living in life.  The *Carolina Watchman* describes a slave funeral on June 6 that occurred in 1850 in Salisbury.  A Negro woman belonging to Hamilton C. Jones died.  The master asked the Reverend M. Ricaud to preach a sermon at the plantation Sunday afternoon, and sent out a notice to that effect.  "*At the appointed hour,*" said the *Watchman, "the slaves of this Town were seen moving*

*out--not on foot, like beasts of Burden, or like friendless, unrespected human wretches, but like genteel and able folk, in carriages, barouches, buggies, carryalls, on horse back, etc. It is estimated that there were some five hundred in attendance at the funeral. The masters and mistresses of these slaves had lent their horses and vehicles for the occasion.*"

Most slaves were buried so that when they rose up from the dead they would be facing toward the east; home toward Africa. While few headstones remain, there are local groups planning to preserve the known graveyards as they are fast disappearing into the landscape.

### The Headman and Other Job Duties

The key slaves on the plantation were the "headmen".  This would have been the slave who sold for the highest price.  Overseers came and went on a farm but the "headman" remained.  He organized the men who did the actual work providing the routine.  He was the "foreman or driver."  He took his orders directly from the overseer or the plantation owner then assigned each man his task and saw to it that it was completed before the day's end.  On larger plantations he sometimes kept the keys to the corncrib and assisted in distributing rations.  He monitored the quarters at night and was responsible for seeing that the quarters were kept clean.

In the scope of hierarchy, next came the house servants and the mechanics.  This might include a cook, maid, and butler who could also be the coachman or gardener.  There may also be a seamstress on a larger plantation.  Others would be blacksmiths, carpenters, bricklayers or jacks-of-all-trades.  The rest would be field hands.

Everyone received a job...including the young and the old who were given lighter jobs.  The "trash gang" might pull weeds, nurse the black children, sweep yards, clear brush, pick cotton or worm the tobacco.  Children did not usually go into the field until they were twelve to fourteen.  After the assigned tasks were completed, the slave had the remainder of the day off during the slack seasons. "*Our slaves*" declared the *North Carolina Standard* in 1850, "*are...as a general rule by no means overworked.*" During the summer it was not uncommon for the owner to give the slave two hours of break at lunchtime during the hottest time of the day. Even during the busy season all work on the plantation stopped at noon on Saturday. It resumed on Monday morning. A planter could be arrested if he violated the Sabbath.

Plantation work began at daybreak and during the busy season lasted until dark. Overtime wages were offered for extra hours worked, or traded for holidays or delicacies such as molasses, tobacco or a barbecue.

## *Free Negroes before the Civil War*

An interesting case occurred in 1857. Miles, a slave, married another slave. After he was freed, he purchased his wife. They had one child, then his wife was set free, and they had several more children. After his wife died, Miles married another negro woman and had three more children. When Miles died, in 1857, the two sets of children filed counterclaims. The Supreme Court decided that the children of the first court had no claim. They said: "*A slave cannot make a contract; therefore, he cannot marry legally. Marriage is based upon contract. Consequently, the relation of man and wife cannot exist among slaves. Neither the first nor the others of the children by the first wife were legitimate. The parties after being freed ought to have married according to law; it is the misfortune of their children that they neglected or refused to so do, for no court can avert the consequences.*"

"*The possession of slaves by free negroes was the only type of personal property that was ever questioned during the ante-bellum period.*" (*The Free Negro in North Carolina.*) There was little objection to "owning" one's own family by a free negro, but acquiring slaves was frowned upon by the whites. In 1833 another Supreme Court decision tackled this issue: "*By the laws of this State, a free man of color may own land and hold lands and personal property including slaves. Without therefore stopping to inquire into the extent of the political rights and privileges of a free man of color, I am very well satisfied from the words of the act of the General Assembly that the Legislature meant to protect the slave property of every person who by the laws of the state are entitled to hold such property. I am, therefore, of the opinion that the owner is a citizen within the meaning of the act of Assembly, and it appearing he was a mulatto is not a reason to grant a new trial to the person who concealed his slave.*"

By 1860-61 additional acts stated that "*no free negro, or free person of color shall be permitted or allowed to buy, purchase, or hire for any length of time any slave or slaves, or to have any slave or slaves bound as apprentice or apprentices to him, her, or them, or in any other wise to have the control, management or services of any slave or slaves, under the penalty of one hundred dollars for each offence, and shall further be guilty of a misdemeanor, and liable to indictment for the same."* Free slaves who already possessed slave property were not affected by this enactment.

In some cases the slaves were granted their freedom by the master's Will and sometimes left considerable financial means as in the life of Julius Melbourn from Raleigh who was raised as a gentleman and made sole heir to an estate worth $20,000. He later sailed for England after amassing over $50,000 through careful management and financial savvy.

In 1860, the NC census lists fifty-three free negroes who possessed more than $2,500 worth of property. Among these was Jesse Freeman of Richmond County, James D. Sampson, a carpenter in New Hanover County, Hardy Bell, a farmer and merchant of Robeson County, and Lydia Mangum of Wake County. Others listed in southeastern North Carolina included: Solomon Webb (Brunswick), James Erwin, David Lansington, Jr., Jas. Sampson, and E. Hites (New Hanover); and Wiley Locklier, Nelson Smith, Hardy Bell, Geo. Dial, Jas. Oxendine (Robeson).

Free negroes who owned slaves themselves in southeastern North Carolina in 1790 included: *New Hanover*: Pages (2), Hannah (1), Hesse (3); Robeson: James Lowry (3), Gibert Cox (8), Cannon Cumbo (1); *Bladen*: Gooden Bowen (44), Eliza Spendlove (1), Molsy Spendlove (3), Michael Blanks (1), Samuel Allen (4), Ann Spendlove (1), Catherine Smith (1); *Brunswick*: John A. Potter (3), Jimboy McKenzie (2); *New Hanover*: Geo. Ware (1), Wanely Mosely (1), Mary Cruise (3), Simon Larington (1), Phillis Bagaeir (1), Wm. Buffo (1), Leuris Pajay (4), John Walker (44), Roger Hazell (5), Jas. Campbell (2), Henry Sampson (5); *Onslow*: Caesar Loomiss (2), Genj. Jarman (5), Rose Winslow (3), Luke White (5), Sampson Lawrence (7).

However, the bulk of the free negros had small parcels and only about 3,659, or 10% owned any property. New Hanover County was ranked first in free negro real property worth over $37,000. But many of the free negroes were lucky to own farm tools and thousands were landless.

At no time during the ante-bellum period were free negroes in North Carolina without some slaves. Many free negroes possessed slaves for the same reasons the white planter had them, for their own economic well-being. Thomas Day owned a carpentry shop and owned slaves for thirty years. In 1830 he had two; by 1860 he had three.

Other free negroes owned slaves for benevolent reasons. Their purchases were friends, neighbors and family members. Slave Richard Gaston ran away from his master and hid in the woods until his free negro wife could save the necessary funds to purchase him. In 1790, twenty-five free negroes in eleven counties in North Carolina owned a total of seventy-three slaves. In 1830, 191 free negroes owned 620 slaves in 37 counties. By 1860, only eight free negro owners had 25 slaves.

Although most free negroes owned just a few slaves, several owned an appreciable number. Gooden Bowen of Bladen County owned 44 slaves. John Walker in New Hanover County owned 44 slaves in 1830. In North Carolina, in 1830, over 600 slaves were owned by free negroes. There are also documented cases of Indians who were slave owners.

In 1860, Brunswick County listed 17 slave apprentices to free slaves, New Hanover listed 7, Bladen County listed 29, Columbus listed 9, Cumberland listed 55, Duplin listed 16, Onslow listed 14 and Robeson listed 12.

At the same time there was a movement in the 1830s by several groups to re-colonize all free negroes in North Carolina. A group of Quakers supported the proposal to the General Assembly to establish a fund for the removal of free negroes from the state of North Carolina. Apparently they had already helped upwards of "40 taken to Liberia, 119 to *Hayti*; 11 to Philadelphia; and the remainder to Ohio and Indiana." There was little hope that they would have the cooperation of the Assembly at any time in the future.

Other groups in Fayetteville endorsed sending the free slaves back to Africa. This was considered the civil, moral and religious thing to do. The idea was to help the freed slaves to return to their homes in Africa. Newspaper accounts documented ships leaving for Liberia, Haiti, and Trinidad (1840). Between 1825 and 1860, the American Colonization Society sent 1,363 negroes from North Carolina to Liberia. In forty-two sailings, the Society sent negroes from North Carolina ranging from one to hundreds at a time, many of the negroes looking forward to their new lives back on the continent of Africa. Others preferred to go to other states and some requested to remain with their former owners such as Emily Hooper, a negro and citizen of Liberia who posted: " be an she is hereby permitted, voluntarily, to return into a state of slavery, as the slave of her former owner, Miss Sally Mallet of Chapel Hill."

The *Western Democrat* of Charlotte remarked that "this free negro woman was the daughter of an official of the Liberian government, and although she ranked among the big fish of the free negro colony, is sick of freedom and prefers living with her mistress in the Old North State than to being fleeced by abolition friends in Liberia." (1858) These requests were sometimes approved and at other times left to stand on the table with no action taken.

## *Freedom*

Negro slaves became free in North Carolina by will, by deed or by legislative enactment. A law passed in 1715 allowed the owners to free their slaves as a reward for honest and faithful service. Those persons were expected to leave the colony within six months. Later, the courts or Assembly could free slaves. Children took the status of their mothers so could become free in that manner. Mulatto children born to slave women were slaves but were often freed by their white fathers.

Mulatto children born to white or Indian women were free. In some cases freed negroes purchased other negro slaves, particularly family members. Negro slaves who were runaways came to North Carolina and passed as free.

Mary Anderson, a former slave, recalls the war years. Mary and her family, along with 162 others slaves, lived on the *Sam Brodie Plantation* near Franklinton in Wake County, North Carolina. He and his wife Evaline, were noted to be kind and fair to their slaves. This slave owner forbad *whuppings* on his plantation.

The war had begun and many stories circulated among the slaves. Miss Anderson remembers hearing thunder in the background for several days, "boom, boom, boom," but she did not understand the implication. For several days the Master and Missus were very "disturbed." They finally ordered all slaves to come to the great house at nine o'clock where they stood on the porch to deliver the news. Through tears they told us all, "*Men, women and children, you are free. You are no longer my slaves. The Yankees will soon be here.*" Within an hour the Yankees arrived. They announced our freedom then promptly broke into the smokehouse and took all the hams. They went to the icehouse and got several barrels of brandy and soon the slaves and Yankees were cooking and eating together. They never bothered the Master or Misses.

Many of the slaves went with the Yankees when they left. Others wandered around for a year or so. By the second year, the master and missus looked for their old slaves and many went back home with them, voluntarily. Some were so glad to get back they cried, "cause fare had been mighty bad part of the time they were rambling around, and they were hungry." When they returned to the plantation, the master said, "Well, you have come back home, have you?" The former slaves continued to refer to them as Marster and Missus and felt that returning home was the "greatest pleasure of all." Mary went on to say that "*I think slavery was a might good thing for Mother, Father, me, and the other members of the family, and I cannot say anything but good for my old Marster and Missus, but I can only speak for those who conditions I have known during slavery and since. For myself and them, I will say again, slavery was a might good thing.*"

Another former slave, Betty Cofer, heard the soldiers coming. Fellow slaves turned the horses out into the woods but had to go retrieve them after the Yankees arrived. A few of the colored folks left with the Yankees but most remained on the plantation with the Marster and Missus. They knew they were free but had no place to go. They continued to work on the home place. By the time two years of freedom had passed, some estimate that two out of three slaves wished they were back with their masters. Many masters were kind and loved their slaves like family.

According to Harvey Robinson, 100-year old resident of Supply, NC, "after freedom some had nothing. A lot of em when supposed to be free slaves were held by the owners right on and they made em work for nothing. In South Carolina, one owner, when found holding on to his slaves, was grabbed and beat on. His slaves were told not to work for nothing and if caught working for nothing again we would get them." Mr. Robinson is unsure who was behind this "enforcement activity" but this story has been passed down and presumed true.

Slaves prayed for their freedom; then didn't know what to do with it once they received it. They had no experience to provide for themselves and no resources to do it with. The first winter was tough, many almost starved to death. Most never said anything about the forty acres of land and a mule promised by the Yankees. Many returned to the plantation seeking food. The adjustment took many years before opportunity allowed the negro to become educated and prosper.

## Statistics

North Carolina was not known to be one of the larger slave states. In 1860 there were an estimated 331,059 slaves to Virginia's 490,865. South Carolina had 402,406. Georgia had 462,198. Louisiana had only about 4,000. In 1830 the slave population in North Carolina was about one-third of the total state population.

In 1850 there were 52 slaves in North Carolina for every 100 whites. Comparatively there were 53 in Virginia, 140 in South Carolina, 91 in Georgia and 105 in Mississippi according to the U. S. Census Office, Century of Population Growth. Only 28,303 families in N.C. were slaveholders...about 27% in 1850. In VA 33% were slaveowners. In that same year, in South Carolina, 48% had slaves and nearly 70% had them in Georgia.

In North Carolina slave owners were more concentrated on the coastal plain and the piedmont. The greatest numbers were along the Virginia border. More than half of the families in North Carolina had slaves in 1850; roughly 67% had less than ten slaves. By 1860, 72% of the families in North Carolina owned NO slaves.

# Chapter Seven

# Slave Narratives:

## In Their Own Words

In 1936-38 over 2,300 slaves were interviewed in a project called the *Federal Writers Project*. Over 500 black-and-white photographs of former slaves were taken and their words recorded. The following list contains the names of over 200 persons interviewed in North Carolina with the first portion of the introductory sentence for each and sometimes more of their commentary. The remaining interviews are available at the Library of Congress. *.Born in Slavery: Slave Narratives from the Federal Writers' Project, 1936-1938* were collected, assembled and microfilmed in 1941 as the seventeen-volume *Slave Narratives: A Folk History of Slavery in the United States from Interviews with Former Slaves.*

Additional slaves of southeastern North Carolina are listed as referenced by family records of present residents. All known sources are listed if not one of the original interviews with the Federal Writers Project. These listings are second-hand accounts of slaves and their lives. Other slaves are identified in the Last Wills and Testaments in the appendix of this book. These slaves are not listed in this alphabetical listing.

The last names of many slaves were the ones of the slave owner. When a slave was sold, he/she often took a new last name of the new owner. This chapter listing is alphabetized by first name. The town listed is the location of the residence at the time of the interview in 1936-38, not the location of their former plantation or owner. Several of these interviews were included in the preceding chapter. A few South Carolina narratives are included and identified as being from South Carolina. Each is a part of our history.

## Abner Jordan.

"I wus bawn about 1832 an' I wus bawn at Staggsville, Marse Paul Cameron's place. I belonged to Marse Paul. My pappy's name wus Obed an' my mammy wus Ella Jordan an' dey wus thirteen chillun on our family."

"I wus de same age of Young Marse Benehan, I played wid him an' wus his body guard. Yes, suh, where ever young Marse Benehan went I went too. I waited on him. Young Marse Benny run away an' 'listed in de war, but Marse Paul done went an' brung him back kaze he wus too young to go and fight de Yankees."

"Marse Paul had heap if (negroes); he had five thousan'. When he meet dem in de road he wouldn' know dem an' when he ased dem who dey wus an' who dey belonged to, dey' tell him dey belonged to Marse Paul Cameron an' den he would say dat wus all right for dem to go right on."

"My pappy wus de blacksmith an' foreman for Marse Paul, an' he blew de horn for de other (negroes) to come in from de fiel' at night. Dey couldn' leave de plantation without Marse say dey could."

"When de war come de Yankees come to de house an' axed my mammy whare de folks done hid de silver an' gol', an' dey say dey gwine to kill mammy if she didn' tell dem. But mammy say she didn' know whare dey put it, an' dey would jus' have to kill her for she didn' know an' wouldn' lie to keep dem from hurting her."

"De sojers stole seven or eight of de ho'ses an' foun' de meat an' stole dat, but dey didn' burn none off de buildin's nor hurt any of us slaves. My pappy an' his family stayed wid Marse Paul five years after de surrender den we moved to Hillsboro an' I's always lived 'roun' dese parts. I ain' never been out of North Carolina eighteen months in my life. North Carolina is good enough for me." Durham."

**Abraham Thomas.**  came from Georgia to the Brunswick County area according to Harvey Robinson, resident of Brunswick County, NC. Mr. Robinson used to listen to Abraham tell his slave stories about when Sherman marched from Georgia to Virginia. "Everyone was walking and when one of the slaves gave out, they left him and the rest kept on walking. When they came across a cow, they slaughtered the cow, cooked him, ate, then continued to march. On the march, old man Abraham gave out right along the present highway 130 very near the current Brunswick Electric building, near the school (West Brunswick High School). He layed there for two days. Mr. Ruark sent someone to check on him and git him. Abraham stayed with the Ruarks for the remainder of his life, a long one as he recovered and went on to work on the Ruark farm.

Abraham is buried at the Rasher Bay Cemetery, off highway 179, down a dirt road on the left off of Hale Swamp Road, just around the curve. There is a gate up now because of people discarding their trash in the area. This was the location of the old *Trip Plantation*.

According to Robinson, "everyone followed Sherman. More men were killed at Gettysburg and when the south gave up you could walk on dead men. The same was true for Fort Fisher...old man Gause told me that you could walk on dead men there too." These stories from Abraham and John Faulk, former slaves.

**Addy Gill**; "I am seventy four years of age..." Raleigh.

**Adeline Crump;** "My name is Adeline Crump, and I am 73 years old... " Raleigh.

**Adora Rienshaw, Age 92.** "I wuz borned at Beulah, down hyar whar Garner am now, an' my parents wuz Cameron an' Sally Perry..." Raleigh.

*Adora Rienshaw, Age 92.*

**Alex Huggins.** "I was born in New Bern on July 9, 1850..." Wilmington.

**Alex Woods.** "My name is Alex Woods..." Raleigh.

**Alice Baugh.** "My mammy Ferbie, an' her brother Darson belonged ter Mr. David Hinnant in Edgecombe County till young Marster Charlie got married..." Raleigh.

**Alonzo Haywood.** The blacksmith. "On East Cabarrus Street is a blacksmith shop which is a survival of horse and buggy days, and the smiling blacksmith, a Negro, although he was hazel eyes, recounts the story of his father's life and his own..." Raleigh.

**Amy Penny.** "I do not know my age..." Raleigh.

**Analiza Foster.** "I wuz borned in Person County ter Tom Line an' Harriet Cash..." Raleigh.

**Anderson Scales, 82.** " Three fourths of a mile from his master's mansion in Madison on Hunter Street, with his large plug tobacco factory across the street on the corner (where in 1937 stands the residence of Dr. Wesley McAnally,) in some "quarters" which Nat Pitcher Scales had near Beaver Island Creek, Anderson was born to slave mother, Martha Scales of a father, "man name uh Edwards..." Madison.

**Andrew Boone.** "I been living in dese backer barns fifteen years...." Wake County.

**Anna Mitchel.** "I wus borned in Vance County an' I 'longed ter Mr. Joseph Hargrove, de same man what owned Emily an' Rufus Hargrove, my mammy an' pappy..." Raleigh.

**Ann Parker.** "I reckon dat I is a hundert an' three or a hundert an' four years old... Miss Parker related her story at a hundred and three years old at a rest home in Raleigh. She was an adult at the end of the Civil War. She described her mother, Junny, as a Queen back in Africa and stories of how queens don't marry, so she did not know her father. Her mother *commanded* as a result of her background, especially when the master was not around."

Ann belonged to Mr. Abner Parker, who lived near Raleigh with a large estate and holdings of a hundred slaves. She did not like Mr. Parker who did not allow a lot of fun and rationed food to the workers. However they sometimes went to neighboring plantations, like Mr. Liles's place, for singing and dancing. If they were caught, they got a "whupping," but in her own words, she "got several whupping for this, that, and t'other; but I 'spects that I needed them." She related that she was raised "right", not allowed to sass nobody, and "we old ones still knows that we is got to be polite to you white ladies." She said she got along well after the war until lately, as she had gotten too old to work, so sits on the post office steps and begs. She accumulated adequate money but someone has stolen it and now she is in the county home after falling and breaking her arm some time ago. She notes that others "don't have the manners they ought to have and aren't raised like she was...." Raleigh.

**Anna Wright.** "I wus borned de year de war ende so I can't tell nothin' dat I seed, only what my mammy tol' me..." Wendell.

**Annie Stephenson.** "I wus born in Hillsboro, N. C. I 'longed to Charles Holman and my missus wus named Rachel.... " Raleigh.

**Annie Tate.** "I wuz a year old when de war wuz ober but of course I ain't knowin' nothin' 'bout slavery 'cept what my mammy said, an' dat ain't so much... " Raleigh.

**Anthony Ransome.** "I reckon dat I is eighty years old, an' I wus borned in Murfreesboro in Hertford County..." Raleigh.

**Barbara Haywood.** "Anything dat I tells you will near 'bout all be 'bout Frank Haywood, my husban'..." Raleigh.

*Ben Horry*

**Ben Horry.** Age 87. Interviewed in Murrells Inlet, S.C. in August of 1937. "I the oldest liver left on Waccamaw Neck, that belong to Brookgreen, Prospect, Longwood, Alderly plantations. I been here! I seen thing! I tell you. That woods you see been Colonel Jos Ward's taters patch. Right to Brookgreen Plantation where I born."

"They say Colonel Ward the biggest rice man been on Waccamaw. He start that big gold rice in the country. He the head rice captain in them time. My father, the head man, he tote the barn key. Rice been money, them day and time."

"My father love he liquor. That take money. He ain't have money, but he have the rice barn key and rice been money. So my father gone in woods, take a old stump, have 'em hollow out. Now he same as mortar (used for separating seed from husk) to the barnyard. And my father keep a pestle hide handy. Hide two pestle! Them pestle make outer heart pine. When that pestle been missed, I wasn't know nothing."

"The way I knows my age, when the slavery-time war come, I been old enough to go in the woods with my father and hold a lightwood torch for him to see to pestle off that golden rice he been tote out the barn and hide. That rice he been take to town Saturday when the colonel and my father go to get provision, like sugar, coffee, pepper, and salt. With the money he get when he sell that rice, he buy liquor. He been hide that sack of rice before day clean, in the prow of the boat, and cover with a thing like an old coat."

"I remembers one day when he come back from town he make a miss when he unloading and fell and broke he jug. The big boss see; he smell; and he see why my father make that miss step. He already sample that liquor. But the boss ain't say too much."

Saturday time come to ration off. Every head on the plantation to Brookgreen line up at smokehouse to draw he share of meat, rice, grits, and meal. (This was before my father been appointed head man. This when they had a tight colored man in that place by name Fraser. They say Fraser come straight from Africa.)

"Well, Saturday, when time come to give my father he share of rations, the head man reach down in the corner and pull out a piece of that broke whiskey jug and put on top my father rations where all could see. Colonel Ward cause that to be done to broke him off from that whiskey jug. My father was a steady liquor man till then, and the boss broke him off."

"Slavery going in. I remembers Marster Josh and Miss Bess had come from French Broad where they summered it. They brought a great deal of this cloth they call blue drilling to make a suit for every boy big enough to wear a suit of clothes and a pair of shoes for every one. I thought that the happiest setup I had in boyhood. Blue drilling pants and coat and shoe. And Sunday come, we have to go to the big house for Marster Josh to see how the clothes fit. And him and Miss Bess make us run races to see who run the fastest. That the happiest time I remembers when I was a boy to Brookgreen."

"Two Yankee gunboats come up Waccamaw River. Come by us plantation. One stop to Sandy Island, Montarena landing. One gone Wachesaw Landing. Old marster Josh and all the white buckra (*Gullah dialect for white person*) gone to Marlboro County to hide from Yankee. Gone up Waccamaw River and up Pee Dee River, to Marlboro County, in a boat by name *Pilot Boy*. Take Colonel Ward and all the Captain to hide from gunboat till peace declared. I think *Pilot Boy* been a rear-wheeler. Most boats like the *Old Planter* been side-wheeler."

\*\*\*\*\*\*\*\*\*\*\*\*\*\*\*\*\*\*\*\*\*\*\*\*\*\*\*\*\*\*\*\*\*\*\*\*\*\*\*\*\*\*\*\*\*\*\*\*\*\*\*\*\*\*\*\*\*\*\*\*\*\*\*\*\*\*\*\*\*

## *Notes on the Gullah/Geechee Culture*

According to published information by the *Heritage Corridor*:

"The Gullah/Geechee people survived the Middle Passage to America as enslaved Africans who were captured from the rice producing regions of West Africa. In the United States, they lived in isolation on the sea island communities while working on vast plantations in semi-tropical conditions. Because of their isolation, they were able to maintain the Gullah language, traditions, arts, crafts, and resources. Today, much of this heritage remains in the community."

The Heritage Corridor was created in 2006 to recognize the important contributions made to American culture and history by Africans and African Americans known as Gullah/Geechee who settled in the coastal regions of the four states. Legislation designated the barrier islands and coastal regions along the Atlantic Ocean as the *Heritage Corridor*. The emerging National Heritage area spans a geographical area encompassing over 12,000 square miles along the coast through four states: South Carolina, Georgia, North Carolina, and Florida.

North Carolina, serves as the Vice Chairman on the Executive Committee for the *Heritage Corridor* Committee, which was established in 2006. Mayor Willis describes the Gullah people, "Almost all of the major plantations along the Cape Fear River participated in some form or the other with rice production. Rice production requires a lot of water for irrigation, and, marshy land; both of which are plentiful along the Cape Fear. West African slaves who were experts at this production from their homelands brought the skill associated with growing rice to the southern U.S. Most of these slaves (about 80% of them) entered the U. S. through the port of Charleston (SC) and were sold to plantation owners all over the south. These West Africans were the fore-parents of the Gullah/Geechee society."

*The Mayor of Navassa, Eulis Willis, (shown in photo, 2009.)*

"The Gullah/Geechee culture developed here in America among the previously enslaved West Africans. Because of the rice production, which took place on the southeastern coast of North Carolina, and the preponderance of formerly enslaved west Africans at the plantations in Brunswick and New Hanover Counties, both of these counties were added to the Gullah/Geechee Heritage Corridor. The Corridor runs from northern Florida to the two most southern counties in NC."

\*\*\*\*\*\*\*\*\*\*\*\*\*\*\*\*\*\*\*\*\*\*\*\*\*\*\*\*\*\*\*\*\*\*\*\*\*\*\*\*\*\*\*\*\*\*\*\*\*\*\*\*\*\*\*\*\*\*\*\*\*\*\*\*\*\*\*\*\*\*\*\*\*\*\*\*

"They say the Yankee broke in all the rice barn on Sandy Island and share the rice out to colored people. The big mill to Laurel Hill been burn right then. That the biggest rice mill on Waccamaw River. Twasn't the Yankee burn them mill. These white mens have a idea the Yankee mean to burn these mill so they set 'em afire before the Yankee come. Nothing left to Laurel Hill today but the rice mill tower. That old brick tower going to be there. Fire can't harm 'em."

### Notes on the Waccamw River:
Recently the Waccamaw River was described by scientists *"to be one of the most pristine and unusual of Southeastern blackwater rivers. It originates in a Carolina bay that encompasses Lake Waccamaw in North Carolina, forms part of*

*the border between Brunswick and Columbus counties and flows through Horry and Georgetown counties before emptying into Winyah Bay. "* The NC Coastal Land Trust recently purchased a four mile section which will preserve mature cypress-gum swamp, bottomland and hardwood forest that lie near it.

*"The river and its floodplain forests are home to black bear, deer and wild turkey as well as to rare and endemic species such as the Waccamaw killifish, the Waccamaw fatmucket and the Waccamaw lance pearlymussel. The latter three are found nowhere else in the world."*

"The worst thing I remembers was the colored overseer. He was the one straight from Africa. He the boss over all the mens and womens, and if womans don't do all he say, he lay task on 'em they ain't able to do. My mother wn't do all he say. When he say, "You go barn and stay till I come," she ain't do 'em. So, he have it in for my mother and lay task on 'em she ain't able for do."

"Then, for punishment, my mother is take to barn and strapped down on thing called The Pony. Hands spread like this and strapped to the floor and all two both she feet been tied like this. And she been give twenty-five to fifty lashes till the blood flow. And my father and me stand right there and look and ain't able to life a hand! Blood on floor in that rice barn where barn tear down by Huntington."

"If Marster Josh been know about that overseer, the overseer can't do em, but just the house servant get Marster Josh and Miss Bess ear. Them things different when my father been make the head man. What I tell you happen before Freedom, when I just can remember."

"Father dead just before my mother. They stayed right to Brookgreen Plantation and dead there after they free. And all they chillun do the same, till the old colonel sell the plantation out. Where we going to? Ain't we got house and rations there?"

"After Freedom, from my behavior with my former owner, I was appointed head man on *Brookgreen Plantation.* When canal been dug out from the *Oaks Plantation* to Dr. Wardie C. Flagg house, I was appointed head man. Canal cut 1877. Near as I can, I must task it on the canal and turn in every man's work to Big Boss. That canal bigger than one Mr. Huntington dig right now with machine."

"After Flagg storm (1893), Colonel Ward take me and Peter Carr, us two and a horse, take that shore to Little River. Search for all them what been drowned. Find a trunk to Myrtle Beach. Have all kinder thing in 'em: comb for you hair, thing you put on you wrist. Find dead horse, cow, ox, turkey, fowl--everything. Gracious God! Don't want to see no more thing like that!"

"Find two of them chillun way down to Dick Pond what drownded to Magnolia Beach, find them in a distance apart from here to that house. All that family drown out, because they wouldn't go to this lady house on higher ground. Wouldn't let none of the rest go. Servant all drown. Betsy, Kit, Mom Adele. Couldn't identify who lost from who save till next morning. Find old Doctor body by he vest stick out of the mud. Fetch Doctor body to shore and he watch still a-ticking. Dr. Wardie Flagg been save hanging to a bech cedar. When that tornado come, my house wash down off he blocks. Didn't broke up."

"Religion? Reckon Stella (his wife) got the morest of that. I sometimes a little quick. Stella, she holds one course. I like good song." " Once I like best,

Try us, Oh, Lord
And search the ground
Of every sinful heart!
Whate'er of sin
In us be found,
Oh, bid it all depart!"

"Make my living with the oyster. Before time, I get seventy-five cents a bushel; now I satisfy with fifty cents. Tide going out, I go out in a boat with the tide. Tide bring me in with sometimes ten, sometimes fifteen to twenty bushels. I make white folks a roast. White folks come to Uncle Ben from all over the country--Florence, Dillon, Mullins--every kind of place. Same price roast or raw, fifty cents a bushel."

**Benjamin Gore.** was the great-grandfather of Mamie Hankins Frazier (born 17 Sept. 1924) and married Betsy, listed next. Benjamin was a slave, according to Ms. Mamie. Ben and his brother were able to eventually buy the same plantation where they worked as slaves because the Fullwood's needed the money. (i.e. *Fullwood Plantation.*)

**Betsy ___ Gore.** Betsy was the great-grandmother of Mamie Hankins Frazier (born 17 Sept. 1924) and married Benjamin Gore. She used to live in an old log cabin on "old 17" near Gilbert Road. Her people are buried in the Francis Galloway Cemetery near a two-story house. Betsy was a slave, according to Ms. Mamie. Brunswick County.

**Betty Cofer.** "I was lucky. Miss Ella (daughter of the first Beverly Jones) was a little girl when I was borned and she claimed me. We played together an' grew up together. I waited on her an' most times slept on the floor in her room. Muh was cook an' when I done got big enough I helped to set the table in the big dinin' room. Then I'd put on a clean white apron an carry in the victuals an' stand behind Miss Ella's chair. She'd fix me a piece of somethin' from her plate an' hand it back over her shoulder to me (eloquent hands illustrate Miss Ella's making of a sandwich.) I'd take it an run outside to eat it. Then I'd wipe my mouth an' go back to stand behind Miss Ella again an' maybe get another snack."

"Yasm there was a crowd of hands on the plantation. I mind 'em all an' I can call most of their names. Mac, Curley, William, Sanford, Lewis, Henry, Ed, Sylvester, Hamp, an' Luke was the men folks. The women was Nellie, two Lucys, Martha, Hervie, Jane, Laura, Fannie, Lizzie, Cassie, Tensie, Lindy, and MaryJane. The women mostly worked in the house. There was always two washwomen, a cook, some hands to help her two sewin' women, a house girl, an' some who did all the weavin' an' spinnin'. The men worked in the fields an' yard. One was stable boss an' looked after all the horses an' mules. We raised our own flax an cotton an' wool, spun the thread, wove the cloth, made all the clothes. Yasm, we made the mens' shirts and pants an' coats. One woman knitted all the stockin's for the white folks an' colored folks too. I mind she had one finger all twisted an' stiff from holdin' her knittin' needles. We wove the cotton an' linen for sheets an' pillow-slips an' table covers. We wove the wool blankets too. I used to wait on the girl who did the weavin'. 'When she took the cloth off the loom she done give me the 'thrums (ends of thread left on the loom.) I tied 'em all together with teensy little knots an' got me some scraps from the sewin' room and I made me some quilt tops. Some of 'em was real pretty too!'

"All our spinnin' wheels and flax wheels and looms was handmade by a wheel wright, Marse Noah Westmoreland. He lived over yonder. (A thumb indicates north.) Those old wheels are still in the family'. I got one of the flax wheels. Miss Ella done give it to me as a present. Leather was tanned an' shoes was made on the place. 'Course the hands mostly went barefoot in warm weather, white chillen too. We had our own mill to grind the wheat an' corn an' we raised all our meat. We made our own candles from tallow and beeswax. I 'spect some of the old candle moulds are over to 'the house' now. We wove our own candlewicks too. I never saw a match 'till I was a grown woman. We made our fire with flint an' punk (rotten wood). Yes'm, I was trained to cook an' clean an' sew. I learned to make mans' pants an' coats. First coat I made, Miss Julia told me to rip the collar off, an' by the time I picked out all the teensy stitches an' sewed it together again I could set a collar right! I can do it today, too!"

"Miss Julia cut out all the clothes for men and women too. I 'spect her big shears an' patterns an' old cuttin' table are over at the house now. Miss Julia cut out all the clothes an' then the colored girls sewed 'em up but she looked 'em all over and they better be sewed right! Miss Julia bossed the whole plantation. She looked after the sick folks and sent the doctor (Dr. Jones) to dose 'em and she carried the keys to the store-rooms and pantries. Yes'm, I'm some educated. Muh showed me my 'a-b-abs and my numbers and when I was fifteen I went to school in the log church built by the Moravians. They give it to the colored folks to use for their own school and church. (This log house is still standing near Bethania). Our teacher was a white man, Marse Fulk. He had one eye, done lost the other in the war. We didn't have no

208

colored teachers then. They wasn't educated. We 'tended school four months a year. I went through the fifth reader, the 'North Carolina Reader'. I can figure a little an' read some but I can't write much 'cause my fingers 're all stiffened up. Miss Julia use to read the bible to us an' tell us right an' wrong, and Muh showed me all she could an' so did the other colored folks. Mostly they was kind to each other."

"No'm, I don't know much about spells and charms. 'Course most of the old folks believed in 'em. One colored man used to make charms, little bags filled with queer things. He called 'em 'jacks' an' sold 'em to the colored folks an' some white folks too."

"Yes'm, I saw some slaves sold away from the plantation, four men and two women, both of 'em with little babies. The traders got 'em. Sold 'em down to Mobile, Alabama. One was my pappy's sister. We never heard from her again. I saw a likely young feller sold for $1500. That was my Uncle Ike. Marse Jonathan Spease bought him and kep' him the rest of his life."

"Yes'm, we saw Yankee soldiers. (Stoneman's Calvary in 1865) They come marchin' by and stopped at 'the house. I wasn't scared 'cause they was all talkin' and laughin' and friendly but they sure was hongry. They dumped the wet clothes out of the big wash-pot in the yard and filled it with water. Then they broke into the smoke-house and got a lot of hams and biled 'em in the pot and ate 'em right there in the yard. The women cooked up a lot of corn pone for 'em and coffee too. Marster had a barrel of 'likker' put by an' the Yankees knocked the head in an' filled their canteens. There wasn't ary drop left. When we heard the soldiers comin' our boys turned the horses loose in the woods. The Yankees said they had to have 'em an' would burn the house down if we didn't get 'em. So our boys whistled up the horses an' the soldiers carried 'em all off. They carried off ol' Jennie mule too but let little jack mule go. When the soldiers was gone the stable boss said, "if ol' Jennie mule once gits loose nobody on earth can catch her unless she wants. She'll be back!" Sure enough, in a couple of days she come home by herself an' we worked the farm jus' with her an' little jack."

"Some of the colored folks followed the Yankees away. Five or six of our boys went. Two of 'em travelled as far as Yadkinville but come back. The rest of 'em kep' goin' an' we never heard tell of 'em again."

"Yes'm, when we was freed Pappy come to get Muh and me. We stayed around here. Where could we go? These was our folks and I couldn't go far away from Miss Ella. We moved out near Rural Hall (some five miles from Bethania) an' Pappy farmed, but I worked at the home place a lot. When I was about twenty-four Marse H. J. Reynolds come from Virginia an' set up a tobacco factory. He fetched some hands with 'im. One was a likely young feller, named Cofer, from Patrick County, Virginia. I liked 'im an' we got married an' moved back here to my folks. (The Jones Family). We started to buy our little place an' raise a family. I done had four chillen but two's dead. I got grandchillen and great-grandchillen close by. This is home to us. When we talk about the old home place (the Jones residence, now some hundred years old) we just say 'the house' 'cause there's only one house to us. The rest of the family was all fine folks and good to me but I loved Miss Ella bettern any one or anythin'. I just asked her an she give it to me or got it for me somehow. Once when Cofer was in his last sickness his sister come from East Liverpool, Ohio, to see 'im. I went to Miss Ella to borrow a little money. She didn't have no change but she just took a ten dollar bill from her purse an' says 'Here you are, Betty, use what you need and bring me what's left'."

"I always did what I could for her too an' stood by her - but one time. That was when we was little girls goin' together to fetch the mail. It was hot an' dusty an' we stopped to cool off an' wade in the 'branch'. We heard a horse trottin' an' looked up an' there was Marster switchin' his ridin' whip an' lookin' at us. 'Git for home you two, and I'll tend to you,' he says an' we got! But this time I let Miss Ella go to 'the house' alone an' I sneaked aroun' to Granny's cabin an' hid. I was afraid I'd get whupped! 'Nother time, Miss Ella went to town an 'told me to keep up her fire whilst she was away. I fell asleep on the hearth and the fire done burnt out so's when Miss Ella come home the room was cold. She was mad as hops. Said she never had hit me but she sure felt like doin it then."

"Yes'm, I been here a right smart while. I done lived to see three generations of my white folks come an' go, an' they're the finest folks on earth. There used to be a reglar buryin' ground for the plantation hands. The colored chillen used to play there but I always played with the white chillen. (This accounts for Aunt Betty's gentle manner and speech) Three of the old log cabins (slave cabins) is there yet. One of 'em was the 'boys cabin' (house for boys and unmarried men). They've got walls a foot thick an' are used for store-rooms now. After freedom we buried out around our little churches but some of th' old grounds are plowed under an' turned into pasture cause the colored folks didn't get no deeds to 'em. I won't be long 'fore I go too but I'm gwine lie near my old home an' my folks."

"Yes'm, I remember Marse Israel Lash, my Pappy's Marster, he was a low, thick-set man, very jolly an' friendly. He was real smart an' good too, 'cause his colored folks all loved 'im. He worked in the bank an' when the Yankees come, 'stead of shuttin' the door gainst 'em like the others did, he bid 'em welcome. (Betty's nodding head, expansive smile and wide-spread hands eloquently pantomine the banker's greeting.) So the Yankees done took the bank but give it back to 'im for his very own an' he kep' it but there was lots of bad feelin' 'cause he never give folks the money they put in the old bank."

"I saw General Robert E. Lee, too. After the war he come with some friends to a meeting at Five Forks Baptist Church. All the white folks gathered 'round an' shook his hand an' I peeked 'tween their legs an' got a good look at 'im. But he didn't have no whiskers, he was smooth-face!"

"Miss Ella died two years ago. I was sick in the hospital but the doctor come to tell me. I couldn't go to her bury'n'. I sure missed her. (Poignant grief moistens Betty's eyes and thickens her voice). There wasn't ever no one like her. Miss Kate an' young Miss Julia still live at 'the house' with their brother, Marse Lucian (all children of the first Beverly Jones and 'old Miss Julia',) but it don't seem right with Miss Ella gone. Life seems dif'rent, some how, 'though there' lots of my young white folks an' my own kin livin' round an' they're real good to me. But Miss Ella's gone!"

"Goodday, Ma'am. Come anytime. You're welcome to. I'm right glad to have visitors 'cause I can't get out much." (A bobbing little curtsy accompanied Betty's cordial farewell.)  ( Writers notes: Although a freed woman for 71 years, property owner for half of them, and now revered head of a clan of self respecting, self-supporting colored citizens, she is still at heart a "Jones negro," and all the distinguished descendents of her beloved Marse Beverly and Miss Julia will be her "own folks" as long as she lives.)

**Bill Crump, Age 82.** "I reckon dat I wus borned in Davidson County on de plantation of Mr. Whitman Smith, my mammy's marster..."

*Bill Crump, Age 82.*

**Blount Baker.** "Yes'um, I 'longed ter Marse Henry Allen of Wilson County an' we always raise terbacker..."

**Bob Jones.** Warren County. "I wus borned in Warren County on de plantation 'longin' ter Mister Logie Rudd..." (Mr. Jones was born in Warren County on the Bogie Rudd Plantation to Harry and Frankie Jones.) His father and his older brother, Burton belonged to a Mister Jones. Bob and his mother belonged to "Marster Bogie and young Marster Joe". Both of them were considered nice but Miss Betsy was "crabbed and hard to get along with." "She fussed so bad that she mighty nigh run all us crazy. It was her what sold my Aunt Sissy Ann." Among the six slaves there, each was quick to stay out of the way of Miss Betsy."

"The young Master Joe went off to fight the war and was only seen twice after that; once when he came home to visit and lastly in a casket. He had been dead so long when returned to his home that his body was "turned dark". A young slave told Bob that "I thought that I'd turn white when I went to heaven, but it appears to me like the white folkses (sic) am going to turn black."

Bob stayed on the Rudd Plantation for two years after being freed and eventually moved to Method where he met his future wife, Edna Crowder. They had five children but only one lived to be a month old; then he too died. In 1984 he was hoping that he might be able to leave the County Home and move in with his niece who lived on Person Street. If he could get the pension then she can afford to let me stay there.

**Burnett, Midge.** "I wus borned in Georgia eighty years ago, de son of Jim an' Henretta Burnett an' de slave of Marse William Joyner..." Raleigh.

**C**aroline Richardson. "I reckin dat I is somers 'bout sixty year old..." Selma.

**Catherine Scales.** " About ten years old at the "Srenduh", now quite feeble, but aristocratic in her black dress, white apron and small sailor hat made of black taffeta silk with a milliner's fold around the edge, Aunt Catherine is small, intensely black with finely cut features and thin lip..."

**Catharine Williams.** "My name is Catharine Williams..." Raleigh.

**Celia Robinson.** "My name, full name, is Celia Robinson... I can't rest, I has nuritus so bad; de doctor says it's nuritus. I do not know my age, I wus eight or ten years old at de close o' de war. De ole family book got burned up, house an' all. I wuz borned a slave. Dat's what my father and mother tole me. My father, he 'longed to Dr. Wiley Perry of Louisburg, N. C., Franklin County, an' my mother 'longed to McKnight on an adjoining plantation. I do not know McKnight's given name. My father wus named Henderson Perry. He wuz marster's shop man (blacksmith). My mother wus named Peggy Perry. McKnight's wife wus named Penny. I member her name."

"I member when de Yankees came ter my mother's house on de McKnight Plantation near Louisburg an' dey went inter her things. When de Yankees came down my brother Buck Perry drug me under de bed and tole me to lie still or de Yankees would ketch me. I member de sweet music dey planed an' de way dey beat de drum. De came right inter de house. Dey went inter her chist; they broke it open. Dey took mother's jewelry. But she got it back. Missus went to de Captain an' de give it back de jewelry. My Missus was de cause of her gittin' it back."

"I wuz old enough to go up ter where my brother kept de cows when de war ended. I member where he kept de calves. My brother would carry me up dere ter hold de calves off when dey wuz milking de cows. My marater would take me by de hand and say, "Now, Celia, you must be smart or I will let de bull hook you." He often carried me up to de great house an' fed me. He give me good things ter eat. Yes, I am partly white. It won't on my mother's side tho', but let's not say anything about dat, jist let dat go. Don't say anything about dat. Marster thought a lot o' me. Marster and missus thought there wuz nothin' like me. Missus let me tote her basket, and marster let me play wid his keys."

"I cannot read an' write. I have never been ter school but one month in my life. When I wus a little girl I had plenty ter eat, war, an' a good time. I 'member when my father would come ter see mother. De patterollers tole him if he didn't stop coming home so much dey wuz goin' ter whip him. He had a certain knock on de door, den mother would let him in. I 'member how mother tole me the overseer would come ter her when she had a young child an' tell her ter go home and suckle dat thing, and she better be back in de field at work in 15 minutes. Mother said she knowed she could not go home and suckle dat child and git back in 15 minutes. So she would go somewhere an' sit down an' pray de child would die."

"We lived at Dr. Wiley Perry's one year atter de war, then we moved ter de plantation of Seth Ward, a white man who was not married, but he had a lot of mulatto children by a slave woman o' his. We stayed dere four years, den we moved ter de Charles Perry Plantation."

"Father stayed dere and raised 15 children an' bought him a place near de town o' Franklinton. I got along during my early childhood better dan I do now. Yes, dat I did. I plowed, grubbed an' rolled logs right atter de war, I worked right wid de men."

"I married Henry Robinson. We married on de Perry Plantation.We had two children born ter us, Ada an' Ella. De are both dead. I wish I had had two dozen children. I have no children now. If I had had two dozen maybe some would be wid me now. I am lonesome and unable to work. I have been trying to wah and iron for a livin', but now I am sick, unable to work. I live with my grandson an' I have nothing."

**Chana Littlejohn.** "I remember when de Yankees come..."

**Chaney Hews.** "My age, best of my recollection, is about eighty years... " Raleigh.

**Chaney Spell.** "I really doan know who my first marster wus, case I has been sold an' hired so much since den..." Wilson.

**Charity Austin.** "I wus borned in the year 1852, July 27..." Raleigh.

**Charity McAllister.** "My name is Charity McAllister..."

**Charity Riddick.** "I am 80 years old, you know after 79 comes 80, dats how old I am... " Raleigh.

**Charity Ward.** Served as a slave in Brunswick County for the Ward family. She was the great-grandmother of Harvey Robinson, current 100-year old resident of Supply, North Carolina who stated that she was buried in the Slave Cemetery located directly behind the current Belks Shopping Center in Shallotte, North Carolina. Her name was carved on a wooden grave marker before being burned when a fire swept through the cemetery sometime in the past. Harvey Robinson remembers visiting the gravesite each Sunday as a child.

*Charles Dickens, former slave.*

**Charles Lee Dalton, 93.** In July, 1934, the census taker went to the home of Unka Challilee Dalton and found that soft talking old darky on the porch of his several roomed house, a few hundred feet south of the dirt road locally called the Ayersville Road because it branches from the hard surfaced highway to Mayodan at Anderson Scales' store, a short distance from Unka Challilie's... " Madison.

**Charles W. Dickens.** "My name is Charles W. Dickens. I lives at 1115 East Lenoir Street, Raleigh, North Carolina..." Wake County.

**Charlie Barbour.** "I belonged ter Mr. Bob Lumsford hyar in Smithfield from de time of my birth..." Smithfield.

**Charlie H. Hunter.** "My full name is Charlie H. Hunter..." West Raleigh.

**Clara Jones.** "I doan know how old I is but I wus borned long time ago case I wus a married 'oman way 'fore de war... " Raleigh.

**Clara Cotton Mc-Coy.** "Yes'm, I was bawn eighty-two years ago... " Durham.

**Clara Jones.** "I been unable ter work fer 10 years; I am blind..."

**Charlie Crump.** "I wuz borned at Evan's Ferry in Lee or Chatham County, an' I belonged ter Mr. Davis Abernathy an' his wife Mis' Vick..." Cary.

*Charlie Crump and Granddaughter.*

**Clay Bobbit.** "I wuz borned May 2, 1837 in Warren County to Washington an' Delisia Bobbit... " Raleigh.

*Clay Bobbit*

**Cornelia Andrews.** "De fust marster dat I 'members wuz Mr. Cute Williams an' he was a good marster, but me an' my mammy an' some of de rest of 'em wuz sold to Doctor McKay Vaden who wuz not good ter us..." Smithfield.

**Cy Hart. 78 yrs.** Ephram Hart was my pappy and my mammy's name was Nellie..." Durham.

**D**ave Lawson. "Yes, suh, de wus' I knows 'bout slavery times is what dey tole me 'bout how come dey hung my gran' mammy an' gran' pappy... " Blue Wing.

**David Blount.** As told By Uncle David Blount, formerly of Beaufort County, who did not know his age..." Raleigh.

**Dilly Yelladay.** "Yes sir, I 'members 'bout what my mammy tole me 'bout Abraham Lincoln, Grant, an' a lot of dem Yankees comin' down ere 'fore de surrender..."

**Doc Edwards**. I was bawn at Staggville, N. C., in 1853..." Staggville.

**Dorcas Griffeth.** "You know me every time you see me don't you?"

**E**dwin...Raleigh.

**Elbert Hunter, Age 93.** "I wuz borned eight miles from Raleigh on de plantation of Mr. Jacob Hunter in 1844..." Method.

*Elbert Hunter, Age 92*

**Elias Thomas.** "I was her when the Civil war was goin' on an' I am 84 years old...It took a smart (negro) to know who his father was in slavery time. I don't know my father's name, but my mother was named Phillis Thomas. I was born in Chatham County on a plantation near Moncure, February 1853. My marster was named Baxter Thomas and Missus was named Katie.......My marster's plantation was the first the Thomas place. There was about two hundred acres in it, with about one hundred acres cleared land. He had six slaves on it..........." Raleigh.

**Ellen Trell.** "Needham Price owned about fifty slaves, and mother an' I were among that number... " Raleigh.

**Emeline Moore.** "I don' exac'ly know how ole I is, but dey say I mus' be eighty. No mam, I ain't got nothin' in no fam'ly Bible. My mammy (with a chuckle) had too many chillum to look after to be puttin' em down in no Bible, she did'n have time, an' she did't have no learnin' nohow. But I reckon I is eighty because I 'members so much I's jes' about forgotten it all. My folks belong to Mr. Taylor. He and Mis' Kitty lived in that big place on Market Street where the soldiers lives now (The W. L. I. Armory), but we wus on the plantation across the river mos' of the time. Of co'se I was born in slavery, but I don' remember nothing much excep' feedin' chickens. And up on Market Street Mis' Kitty had chickens an' things an a cow. The house had more lan around it than it got now. I do remember when they thought that eve'ybody 'roun here was goin' to die, an' I got skeered. No'm t'want no war it was the yaller fever. We was kept on the plantation but we knowd folks just died an' died an' died. We thought t'would'nt be nobody left. I don't remember nothin' about Lincoln travelin' aroun'. I always heard he was President of the Lunited States an' lived in Washington, an' gave us freedom, an' got shot. Of co'se I knows all about Booker Washington, a lot of our folks went to his school, an' he been here in Wilmington. I'd know a lot about slave times only I was so little. I have heard my mammy say she had a heap easier time in slavery than after she was turn' loose with a pa'cl of chillun to feed. I married as soon as I could an' that's how I got this house. but I can't work and I disremembers so much. The Welfare gives me regerlar pay, an' now an' then my friends give me a nickel or a dime."

"I lives alone now until I can git a descent oo'man to live with me. I tells you

Missus these womens an young girls today are sumpin' else. After you had 'em aroun' awhile you wish you never knowed 'em."

"Sometimes when I jes sets alone an rocks I wonder if my mammy didn't had it lots easier than I does. ... " Wilmington.

**Emma Blalock.** "I shore do 'member de Yankees wid dere blue uniforms wid brass buttons on 'em... " Raleigh.

**Emma Stone.** "My mammy wuz a Free Issue an' my pappy belonged ter de Bells in Chatham County..." Durham.

**Essex Henry, Age 83.** "I was borned five miles north of Raleigh on de Wendell Road, 83 years ago..." Raleigh.

*Essex Henry, Age 83.*

**Eustace Hodges.** "I doan know when I wus borned, ner where but at fust my mammy an' me 'longed ter a McGee here in Wake County..." Raleigh.

**F**anny Cannaday. "I don' 'member much 'bout de sojers an' de fightin 'in de war kaze I wuzn' much more den six years ole at de surrender, but I do 'member how Marse Jordan Moss shot Leonard Allen, one of his slaves..." Durham.

**Fanny Dunn.** "I don't 'zakly know my age, but I know and 'members when de Yankees come through Wake County..." Raleigh. (Note: Unconfirmed information: There was a parcel of land offered for sale in the True Republican, vol. 1., No 7,

Wilmington, NC) which was formerly owned by James Clark, lying on Goshen, In Duplin County. It contained about 328 acres and was located near the premises of Wm. Dunn in the (then) Newbern area on February 10th, 1809.)

**Fannie Moore**, Age 88.  "Nowadays when I heah folks a 'growlin an' a' grumblin bout not habbin this an' that I jes think what would they done effen they be brought up on de **Moore Plantation**...De Moore Plantation to Marse Jim Moore, in Moore, South Carolina. De Moores had own the same plantation and the same (negroes) and de children for yeahs back. When Marse Jim's pappy die he leave the whole thing to Marse Jim, effen he take care of his mammy. She shore was a rip-jack. She say (negroes) didn't need nothin' to eat. De just like animals, not like other folks. She whip me many times wif a cow hide, till I was black and blue. Marse Jim's wife was Mary Anderson. She wore the sweetest woman I ebber saw. She was allus good to evah (negro) on de plantation. Her mother was Harriet Anderson, and she visit the Missus for a long time on de farm. She nebber talk mean. Jes smile that sweet smile and talk in de soffes' tone. And when she laugh she soun' just like the little stream back ob de spring house gurglin' past de rocks. An her hair all white and curly, I can 'member her always."

"Marse Jim own de biggest plantation in de whole country. Jes thousands acres ob lan'. An de old Tigger Ribber a running right through de middle ob de plantation. On one side ob de ribber stood de big house, whar de white folks lib and on the other side stood de quarters. De big house was a purty thing all painted white. a standin' in a patch o' oak trees. I can't remember how many rooms in dat house but powerful many. O'corse it was built when de Moores had sech large families. Marse Jim he only hab five children, not twelve like his mammy hab. De was Andrew and Tom, den Harriet, Nan, and Nettie Sue. Harriet was jus like her granny Anderson. She was good to ebberbody. She git de little (negroes) down an' em de Sunday School lesson. Effen old Marse Jim's mammy ketch her she sho' raise torment. She make life jes as hard for de (negroes) as she can."

"De quarters jus long rows o' cabins daubed with dirt. Ever one in the family lib in one big room. In one end was a big fireplace. Dis had to heat the cabin and do the cookin' too. We cooked in a big pot hung on a rod over de fire and bake de co'n pone in de ashes or else put it in de skillet and cover the lid wif coals. We allus hab plenty wood to keep us warm. Dat is ef we hab time to get it outen de woods."

"My granny she cook for us chilluns while our mammy away in de fiel. De wasn't much cooking to do. Jes make co'n pone and bring in de milk. She hab big wooden bowl wif enough wooden spoons to go 'roun'. She put de milk in de bowl and break it up. Den she put de bowl in the middle of de 'flo an all de chillum grab a spoon."

"My mammy she work in de fiel' all day and piece and quilt all night. Den she had to spin enough thread to make four cuts for the white fo'ks ebber night. Why sometimes I nebber go to bed. Hab to hold de light for her to see by. She hab to piece quilts for de white fo'ks too. Why der is a scar on my arm where my brother let the pine drip on me. Rich pine war all the light we ebber hab. My brother was a'holdin' the pine so's I can help mammy tack de quilt and he go to sleep and let it drop."

"I never see how many stan' sech ha'd work. She stan' up fo' her chillum tho'. De ole overseeah he hate my mammy, case she fight him for beatin' her chillum. She hab twelve chillum. I member I see de three oldes' stan in de snow up to dey knees to split rails, while de overseeah stan's off and grin."

"My mammy she trouble in her heart, bout de way de treated. Ever night she pray for de Lawd to git her and her chillum out ob de place. One day she plowin' in de cotton fiel. All sudden like she let out big yell. Den she sta't singin' an' a-shoutin', an' a whoopin' and a-hollowin'. Den it seem she plow all de harder. When she came home, Marse Jim's mammy say, "What all dat goin on in de fiel'? Yo' think we sen' you ou there jes to whoop and yell? No siree, we put you out there to work and you sho' bettah work, else we git de overseeah to cowhide yo old black back." My mammy jes grin all over her black wrinkled face and say: "I's saved. De Lawd done tells me I's saved. Now I know de Lawd will show me de way, I ain't gwine a grieve no more. No matter how much yo' all done beat me an' my chillum de Lawd will show me de way. An' some day we nevah be slaves." Ole granny Moore she grab de cowhide and slash mammy cross de back but mammy nebber yell. She jes go back to de fiel' a'singin'."

"My mammy grieve lots over brothah George, who die wif de fever. Granny she doctah him as bes' she could, evah time she git way from de white folks kitchen. My mammy nevah git chance to see him, 'cept when she git home in de evenin'. George he jus lie. One day I look at him an' he had sech a peaceful look on his face, I think he sleep an' jes let him lone. Long in de evenin' I think I try to wake him. I touch him on de face, but he was dead. Mammy nebber know till she come at night. Poor mammy kneel by de bed and cry her heart out. Ol' Uncle Allen he make pine box for him an' carry him to de graveyard over on de hill. My mammy just plow and cry as she watch 'em put George in de groun'."

"My pappy he was a blacksmith. He shoe all de horses on de plantation. He wo'k so hard he hab no time to go to de fiel'. His name war Stephen Moore. Mars Jim call him Stephen Andrew. He was sold to de Moores, and his mammy too. She war brought over from Africa. She never could speak plain. All her life she been a slave. White folks never recognize 'em any more than effen dey was a dog."

"It was a tubble sight to see de speculators to de plantation. De would go through de fiel's and buy de slaves de wanted. Marse Jim nebber sell pappy or mammy or any ob dey chillum. He allus like pappy. When de speculator come all de slaves start a shakin'. No one know who is a goin'. Den sometime dey take 'em and sell 'em on de block. De 'breed women' always bring mo money den de res', ebben de men. When dey put her on de put all her chillun aroun her to show folks how fas she can hab chillun. Sometime she hab colored children and sometime white. Taint no use to say anything case effen she do she jes git whipped. Why on de Moore Planatation, Aunt Cheney, everybody call her Aunt Cheney, have two chillum by de overseeah. De overseeah name war Hill. He war as mean as de devil. When Aunt Cheney not do as he ask he tell granny Moore. Ole Granny call Aunt Cheney to de kitchen and make her take her clothes off den she beat her till she jest black an' blue. Many boys and girls marry dey own brothers and sisters an' nebber know de difference lest they git to talkin' bout dey parents and where dey uster lib."

"De (negroes) allus hab to get pass to go anywhere offen de plantation. Dey git de pass from de massa or de missus. Den when de paddyrollers come dey had to show de pass to dem, if you had no pass dey strip you an' beat you."

"I remember one day one time dey was a dance at one ob de houses in de quarters. All de (negroes) was a laughin' an' a pattin' dey feet an' a singin', but dey was a few dat didn't. De paddyrollers shove de do' open and sta't grabbin' us. Uncle Joe's son he decide dey was one time to die and he sta't to fight. He say he tired standin' so many beatin's, he jes can stan' no mo. De paddyrollers start beatin' him an' he sta't fightin'. Oh, Lawdy it war tubble. De whip him wif a cowhide for a long time den one of dem take a stick an' hit him over de head, and jes bus his head wide open. De pore boy fell on de flo' jes a moanin' an' a groanin'. De paddyrollers jes whip bout half dozen other (negroes) an' sen' em home an' leve us wif de dead boy."

"None o' the (negroes) have any learnin', warn't never 'lowed to as much as pick up a piece o' paper. My daddy slip an' git a Webster book and den he take it outen de fiel and he larn to read. De white folks 'fraid to let de children learn anythin'. De 'fraid de get too sma't and be harder to manage. De nebber let em know anythin' about anythin'. Never have any church. Effen you go you set in de back of de white folks chu'ch. But de (negroes) slip off an' pray an' hold prayer-meetin' in de woods den dey tu'n a big wash pot and prop it up wif a stick to drown out de soun' ob de singin'. I 'member some of de songs we uster sing. One of dem went somethin' like dis'...."

"Hark from de tomb a doleful soun'
My ears hear a tender cry.
A livin' man came through the groun'
Whar we may shortly lie.
Heah in dis clay may be you bed

220

In spite ob all you toil
Let all de wise bow revrant head
Mus' lie as low as ours."

"Den de sing one I can hardly remember but dis is some of de words:"

"Jesus can make you die in bed
He sof' as downs in pillow there
On my bres' I'll lean my head
Grieve my life sweetly there.
In dis life of heaby load
Let us share de weary traveler
Along de heabenly road."

"Back in dose time dey wasn't no way to put away fruit and things fo' winter like dey is today. In de fall of de yeah it certainly was a busy time. We peel bushels of apples and peaches to dry. Dey put up lots o' brandied peaches too. De way de done dey peel de peaches and cut them up. Den dey put a layer ob peaches in a crock den a layer of sugar den another layer of peaches until de crock was full. Den dey seel de jar by puttin' a cloth over de top den a layer o' paste then another cloth den another layer ob paste. Dey keep dey meat bout de same way foks do today 'cept de had to smoke it since salt was so sca'ce back in dat day. Dey can mos' ob de other fruit and put it in de same kin' o' jars dat dey put de peaches in. Dey string up long strings o' beans an' let 'em dry and cook em wif fat back in de winter."

"Folks back den never heah tell of all de ailments de folks hab now. Dey war no doctahs. Jes use roots and bark for teas of all kinds. My ole granny uster to make tea out 'o dogwood an' give it to us chillum when we have a cold, else she make a tea outen wild cherry bark, pennyroil, or hoarhound. My goodness but dey was bitter. We do mos' anything to git out a takin' de tea, but twarnt no use granny jes git you by de collar hol' yo nose an' you just swallow it or get strangled. When de baby hab de colic she gets rats vein and make a syrup an' put a little sugar in it an' boil it. Den soon as it cold she give it to de baby. For stomach ache she give us snake root. Sometime she make tea, other time she jes cut it up in little pieces an' make you eat one or two ob dem. When you hab fever she wrap you up in cabbage leaves or ginsang leaves, dis made de fever go. When de fever got too bad she take de hoofs offen de hog dat had been killed and parch 'em in de ashes and den she beat 'em up and make a tea. Dis was de mos tubble of all."

"De yeah fore de war started Marse Jim died. He war out in de pasture pickin' up cow loads a thrownin' em in de garden an' he jes drop over. I hate to see Mars Jim go, he not sech a bad man. After he die his boys, Tom an' Andrew take cha'ge of de plantation. Dey think de runs things diffe'nt from dey daddy but dey jes git sta'ted

221

when de war come. Marse Tom and Marse Andrew both hab to go. My pappy he go long wif dem to do der cookin. My pappy he say dat some day he ran four or five miles wif de Yankees ahind him afore he can stop to do any cookin. Den when he stops he cooks wif de bullets afallin all roun de kettles. He say he walk on ded men jes like he was walkin on de groun'. Some of de men be ded, some moanin' an' some a groanin', but nobody paid no tention, cause de Yankees keep a comin. One day de Yankees came awfully close Marse Andrew hab de Confed'rate flag in de han'. He raise it high in de air. Pappy say he yell for him to put de flag down case de Yankees was a' comin' closer an' was agoin' to capture him anyway. But Marse Andrew jes hol' de flag up an run 'hind a tree. De Yankee sojers jes take one shot at him an' dat was de las' of him. My pappy bring him home. De fambly put him in alcohol. One day I went to see him and there he was a swimmin round in de water. Mos' ob his hair done come off tho. He buried at Nazereth. I could go right back to de graveyard effen I was there. Den my pappy go back to stay with Marse Tom. Marse Tom was jes wounded. Effen he hadn't had a Bible in his pocket de bullet go clear through his heart. But yo' all kno' no bullet ain't goin' through de Bible. No, you can't shoot through God's word. Pappy he bring Marse Tom home an' take care of him til he was well. Marse Tom give pappy a horse an' wagon case he say he saved his life."

"Many time de sojers come through de plantation an' dey load up dey wagons wif ebberthin' dey fin', lasses, ham, chickens. Sometime dey gib part of it to de "negroes" but de white folks take it way when dey git gone. De white folks hide all de silverware from de soldiers. Dey fraid dey take it when dey come. Sometime dey make us tell effen dey think we know."

"After de war pappy go back to work on de plantation. He make his own crop on de planation. But de money was no good den. I played with many a Confed'rate dollar. He sho was happy dat he was free. Mammy she shoult fo' joy an' say her prayer war answered. Pappy git pretty feeble, but he work til jes fore he die. He made patch of cotton wif a hoe. Dey was enough cotton in de patch to make a bale. Pappy die when he was 104 years old. Mammy she live to be 105."

"After de war de Klu Klux broke out. Oh, miss, dey was mean. In dey long white robes dey scare de (negroes) to death. Dey keep close watch on dem afeared de try to do somethin'. Dey have long horns an' big eyes an' mouth. Dey never go roun' much in dey day. Jes night. Dey take de pore (negroes) away in de woods and beat em' and hang em'. De (negroes) were afraid to move, much less try to do anything. Dey never kno' what to do, dey hab no larnin. Hab no money. All dey can do was stay on de same plantation til dey can do better. We lib on de same plantation till de chillum all grown an' mammy and pappy both die then we leave. I don't know where any of my people are now. I know I was bo'n om 1849. I was 88 years old de furst of September." Asheville---1937.

**Frank Freeman.** "I was born near Rolesville, in Wake County, Christmas Eve, 24 December 1857. "My wife's name is Mary Freeman. I belonged to Jim Wiggins in Roseville...." Wiggins owned 3 1/4 plantations. The one in Roseville was 3,000 acres. Raleigh.

**Frank Magwood.** "I was born in Fairfield County, South Carolina, near the town of Ridgeway..." Raleigh.

**G**eorge Eatman. "I belonged ter Mr. Gus Eastman who lived at de ole Templeton place on de Durham highway back as far as I can 'member..." Cary.

*George Eatman, Age 93.*

**George W. Harris.** "Hey, don't go 'roun' dat post gitting it "tween you and me, it's bad luck..." Raleigh.

**George Rogers.** "George Rogers is the name..." Raleigh.

**Georgianna Foster.** "I wus born in 1861.." .Raleigh.

**H**annah Crasson. Miss Crasson was born on John William Walton's plantation about four miles from Garner, N. C. She was the daughter of Frank and Flora Walton. Her grandmother died at 104 years old on the plantation. Her great-grandmother was Granny Flora who was stolen from Africa with a "red pocket handkerchief" according to Miss Crasson. She was initially taken to New England but they were afraid of the Africans and soon shipped her down south.

John Walton was not known to sell off his slaves but instead gave them to his children as they married and left home. Miss Crasson described John as "He didn't whup us and he said he didn't want nobody else to whup us. It is just like I tell you; he was never cruel to us." Garner.

**Handy H. Williams, Reverend.** "My name is Handy H. Williams..." Dunn.

**Hannah Plummer.** "My name is Hannah Plummer...I was born near Auburn in Wake County, January 7, 1856. My father was Allen Lane and my mother was named Bertcha Lane. We belonged to Governor Charles Manley, that is mother and myself, father belonged to some maiden ladies Susan and Emma White. The

Governor had large plantations, but mother and myself lived with them on their lot right where the Rex Hospital now stands on South and Fayetteville Streets. Governor Manly owned the block down to the railroad, and we chillun went into grove, to pick up walnuts and hickory nuts."

"My father was a stonecutter and he hired his time and gave it to his Missus and lived with us. Mother was at Governor Manly's. He said father was a high-headed fellow and said he was livin' on his lot and in his house and that he didn't do anything for him, and that he ought to keep up his family. Missus Manly, the Governor's wife, I forget her first name, did not take any particular interest in her servants. She had slave servants for everything: a washer and ironer, a cook, waiting men, waitresses and a maid who did nothing but wait on her."

"Governor Manly was a might rich man, and he had several plantations, an' a lot o' slaves. I don't remember how many slaves he owned. Mother was given meal and meat and had to cook it just the same as she would not. They didn't allow her food from the great house. Mother had ten children, and at times we did not have enough to eat. The boys were named Fred, David, Matthew, Allen and Thomas. Girls Cinderilla, Corinna, Hannah, Victoria and Mary. All were born slaves but two.

Thomas and Mary. David and myself are all that are left alive."

"I remember that we lived in a plank house, with three rooms and a shed porch. Mother washed clothes under the porch. The house had two rooms downstairs and one upstairs. (Oh! I have thought of the Governor's wife's name, Missus name, it was Charity.) We used trundle beds of wood. Mother made our bedclothes at night. She also made bonnets and dresses. Sometimes she made bonnets and sold them. The child that set up with her she gave some kind o' sweets. I set up with her a lot because I like to eat. Mother was allowed the little money she made makin' bonnets and dresses at night."

**Hattie Rogers.** "I was born a slave in New Bern, N. C., Craven County, the 2nd day of March 1859..." Raleigh.

*Harriet Ann Daves, Age 81.*

**Henry James Trentham.** "I wus born de second day of December 1845 on a plantation near Camden. I belonged to Dr. Trentham and my missus was named Elizabeth. My father was named James Trentham and Mother was named Lorie. Marster's plantation was a awful big plantation with about four hundred slaves on it. It was a short distance from the Wateree River." ......Raleigh.

**Henry Roundtree.** "I wus borned an' bred in Wilson County on de plantation of Mr. Dock Rountree..." Wilson County.

**Harriet Ann Daves.** Age 81. "My full name is Harriet Ann Daves, I liked to be called Harriet Ann...."

**Hector Hamilton.** "Dey wuz two General Lee's in de 'Federate War..." Raleigh.

**Henrietta McCullers.** "I wus borned roun' eighty-seben years ago in Wake County..." Raleigh.

**Henry Bobbit.** "I wuz borned at Warrenton in Warren County in 1850..." Raleigh.

**Henry Bell.** was born into slavery and married Lucy Fullwood at the Zion Hill Church in the Sunset Harbor area of Brunswick County, NC.

*Henry Bobbit, Age 87.*

**Herndon Bogan.** "I wus bawned in Union County, South Carolina on de plantation o' Doctor Bogan, who owned both my mammy Issia, an' my pap...."

**Hilliard Yellerday.** "My mother and father told me many interesting stories of slavery and of its joys and sorrows..." Raleigh.

# I

**da Adkins.** Age 70. "I was born befo' de war..." Durham.

**Isaac Johnson.** "I am feelin' very well this mornin', while I don't feel like I used to......I belonged to Jack Johnson. My missus' name was Nancy. My father was Bunch Matthews; he belonged to old man Drew Matthews, a slave owner. My mother was named Tilla Johnson. She belonged to Jack Johnson, my marster. The plantation was near Lillington, on the north side of the Cape Fear River, and ran down to near the Lillington Crossroads, one mile from the river. ......" Lillington.

**Isabell Henderson.** "I'll be 84 years old come August 9..." Wilmington.

**J**acob Fullwood. was sold to the Green Family by the Fullwoods. He worked on the *Fullwood Plantation* which was located in the Zion Hill area of Sunset Harbor, in Brunswick County, NC.

*Jennylin Dunn, Age 87*

**Jacob Thomas.** "I wus borned in Elberton County, Georgia, on de plantation of Marse Tom Bell..." Raleigh.

**James Turner McLean.** "My name is James Turner McLean..." Lillington.

**Jane Anne Privette Upperman.** "I wusn't livin in Raleigh when my mother wus freed from slavery..."

**Jane Arrington.** "I ort to be able to tell sumpin cause I wus twelve years old when dey had de surrender right up here in Raleigh..."

**Jane Lassiter.** "I am 'bout 80 years old..." Raleigh.

**Jane Lee.** "I wus borned de slave of Marse Henry McCullers down here at Clayton on de Wake an' Johnston line..." Selma.

226

**Jennylin Dunn.** "I wuz borned hyar in Wake County eighty-seben years ago..." Raleigh.

**Jerry Davis.** "I wus borned in Warren County ter Mataldia an' Jordan Davis..." Raleigh.

**Jerry Hinton.** "My full name is Jerry Hinton..." Raleigh.

**Jim Bryant.** Date unknown, married Rachel Bryant. They had a son, Harry Bryant who married his cousin Annie Bryant. Annie's father was Sam Bryant. Jim is presumed to have been a slave. Brunswick County, NC.

**Job Manson.** "It has been a long time since I wus born- -bout all my people am dead 'cept my wife an one son an two daughters...I belonged to Colonel Bun Eden. His plantation was in Warren County, and he owned about fifty slaves or more. there was so many of them there he did not know all his own slaves......." Raleigh.

**Joe High.** Age 80. "My name is Joe High..." Raleigh.

*Joe High, Age 80.*

**Joe Robinson.** Joe was born into slavery during the Civil War. He was the father of Harvey Robinson, currently 100-years old and a resident of Supply, NC. Joe married Nancy Gore and had three children; Harvey (born 1908), Donnie (born 1912), and Gatlin (born 1910.) According to his son, Harvey, Joe was born in Boones Neck, the slave of Sam Robinson. He also had a granddaughter, born into slavery, also owned by Sam Robinson. After the Civil War, Joe moved from that area and relocated his family to the Cox's Landing area near Sunset Harbor, Brunswick County, NC. Joe had one sister, Mary Robinson who marrie dAaron Fullwood. They were married at Zion Hill Church. Aaron died on a ship.

**Joseph Fullwood.** Joseph was inducted into the army at the age of 15 in 1862. He later changed his name to Joseph Monroe…either while enlisting in the army or later when sold to the Monroe family in Shallotte, NC. He worked for the Fullwood family at the *Fullwood Plantation* in Zion Hill, near Sunset Harbor, in Brunswick County, NC.

**John Beckwith.** "I reckon dat I wuz 'bout nine years old at de surrender, but we warn't happy an' we stayed on dar till my parents died..." Cary.

*John Beckwith, Age 80.*

**John C. Bectom.** "My name is John C. Bectom..." Raleigh.

**John Coggin.** Age 85. When the interviewer first visited Uncle John he was busy cutting hay for a white family nearby, swinging the sythe with the vigor of a young man..." Method.

**John Daniels.** "I"se named fer my pappy's ole massa down in Spartanburg, South Carolina, course I doan know nothin' 'bout no war, case I warn't borned..."

**John Evans**. Age 80. I was born August 15th, 1859..."

*John Coggin, Age 85.*

**John Faulk**. was "an old slave" according to Harvey Robinson, current resident of Supply, NC. Robinson used to visit Mr. Faulk on Sundays where he talked about his slave experiences. He was Mr. Robinson's great uncle.

According to Mr. Robinson, John told the story of "boiling salt at Bricklanding." "John was boiling salt (boiling down sea water to obtain the sea salt) when the Yankees tried to come ashore. The shooting took place between the two armies above the head of John as he continued to boil his salt. Eventually the shooting became too much and John took off running. The north came ashore. When the battle was over, there was a lot of dead men. all that war over old black slaves. They wanted them bad."

John Faulk was married to Lenora Joyner who was William Joyners sister. Both were born right after slavery. Another individual born just after slavery was Albert Joyner, born 1865-66. (Source: Don Joyner.)

*John Evans, Age 80*

**John H. Jackson.** "I was born in 1851, in the yard where my owner lived next door to the City Hall..." Wilmington.

**John Jack Bryant.** Oral history and scattered documents show that the Bryant family first came ot Brunswick County as the slaves of Jesse Lancaster. These first Bryants, John Jack Bryant and Holland Lancaster were from Pitt or Craven County. It is difficult to determine who their ancestors were. John Jack Bryant died November 19, 1887 at the age of 76. This would put his birth date prior to November 19, 1811. Holland Lancaster Bryant died July 1, 1889 at the age of 63 which places her birth about 1826.

Jack and Holland began living together as man and wife in May 1842. The laws of that time prevented them from being formerly married. After the abolishment of slavery in 1865, they were issued a "Certificate of Cohabitation." This certificate was issued by Swift Galloway, Clerk of the Court of Pleas and Quarter Sessions of Brunswick County on August 31, 1866.

It is thought that maybe three of their children were born before they moved to Brunswick County. Some of these early children were told that they were named in honor of the brothers of John Jack Bryant. They were sold into slavery.

During the time that Jack and Holland Bryant lived on the Lancaster Plantation, they farmed cotton, potatoes, corn, tar, and turpentine. It was the custom after the abolishment of slavery for a generous master to give faithful slaves a tract of land and provisions to start their life of freedom. Jesse Lancaster gave John Jack Bryant and Holland Lancaster Bryant the tract of land that is still owned by the Bryants today which borders Stone Chimney Road and the Lockwood Folly River.

Jack Bryant's home was located on the Charlie Bryant estate. Slavery "broke" five days before the Bryant name would have traditionally changed to Lancaster. As a result, the BRYANT name remains today. *(Bryant history courtesy of Bertha Bell, descendent.)*

**John Smith.** Age 108. "My mother was named Charlotte Smith and father was named Richmond Sanders...Raleigh.

*John Smith, Age 108*

**John Smith.** "John Smith is my name, an I wuz borned at Knightdale, right at my marster's house..." Raleigh.

**John Thomas Williams.** "I don't know who I am nor what my true name is..." Raleigh.

**Joseph Anderson.** "Yes'm I was born a slave..." Wilmington.

**Joseph Monroe.** fought in the the Civil War according to Don Joyner, local historian. He was 15 years old when he joined the army, according to one family story at Fort Monroe in Virginia changing his name from Joseph Fullwood to Joseph Monroe to protect his family back home from any retaliation. Other sources report that he enlisted in 1865 at the Faison Station in Wilmington, NC. Yet other probabilities include being sold to the Monroe family in Shallotte, NC. He later became a deacon at the Zion Hill Church in Brunswick County, NC and drove a "big ole black mule cart" according to Harvey Robinson. He was five foot seven inches tall. He died in 1922. His grandson was Tommy Wescott whose mother was Greer."

**Josephine Smith.** Age 94. "I wuz borned in Norfolk, Virginia an' I doan know who we belonged to, but I 'members de day we wuz put on de block at Richmond.." .Raleigh.

*Josephine Smith,*
*Age 94.*

**Julia Crenshaw.** "My mammy wuz named Jane an' my pappy wuz named Richard..."

**Julius Nelson.** Age 77. "I doan 'member no slavery, of course, so 'taint no use ter ax me no questions..."

*Julius Nelson, Age 77.*

**K**itty Hill. "I tole you yesterday dat my age wus 76 years old, but my daughter come home, I axed her 'bout it an' she say I is 77 years old..." Raleigh.

**L**ancy Harris. 84 years old. Born in Edgecombe County, NC about July 1852. I dunno my father nor my mudda. Jessup Powell always went o' Richmond to buy good breeders. Perry Powell (an ex-slave), who died here last month was one o dem da Jessup Powell bought o Richmond. Jessup Powell drawd my father and moudda, den Lewis drawd my father and he took the name o Lewis. Dey neber hab

231

no no chillen. I didn' t no my father. One day my mudda showd me a man driving his missus to town and said dat wus my father."

"I remember when he throwd me ma first dress from the hoot of the marriage. I remember whut it look like. Yeah, jes a red dress wid black flowers in it.
Ma bed had fo' posts and a cord running from pos' to pos' to make spring. We sleep in a room wid pot racks near the fire place, a barrel of soap up in a corner, but the floors wus white like a bread tray. Everything wus in one room. We used to call granpa William Joiner cause he wus a blacksmith and carpenter. He joined so many things togeder. Ha, ha! my mem'ry goes and comes. Billie was my grandpa's name. My sight is better now than den, wood you blive it?"

"I didn't work. I used to stay wid Aunt Kate. I done all the cooking for Aunt Kate -- ash cake, ho-cake. William Joiner used to fetch possums, coon and sometimes raccoon and rabbit and I used to do the cooking. My husban' and I used to pick cotton every day. When fodder time come I work Sunday. Some Sunday I worked my own garden."

"So many chillen didn't wear clothes. But the missus owned the loom and de servants weave. When de chillen are big enough to work dey gib 'em some cloth from the loom. When I got my issue and my clothes wus good I wud make my cloth into dresses and gib to da chillen."

"Old man Jessup Powell married the Doctor' s wife after the doctor was dead. The doctor had lots o land. All went to his wife so Jessup didn't know how much land he had fo his new missus had plenty o' land and slaves. I reckon dey had well ni 500 or 600 slaves."

"Dick Harrison was another slave owner. He was never married, never had no chillen wid the slave girls. He was good to his (negroes). He never allowed anybody to whip his slaves. "I neber would for anyone to whip (negroes)," he wud say. But when Dick need money tho he wud send the nicest looking one to Richmond jail fo sale. " (They evidently had no jail on the plantation. The only jail existed was the one in Richmond.)

"Old man Henry Downing , (negro)-driver, he wud eat you alive-- L-o-r-d he wus so mean. Yo'ud better not let him see you wid a book let alone learning to read.
We used to go over to the plantation of ole man Stanley White. Sometimes we used to call him 'Stamper.' He wud come and preach to us. We wud go up stairs and dey (white folks) downstairs. We had another preacher we used to call Preacher Gold.
I remember Fred Douglass, Perry Coston from Virginia, and a man by the name of Mason. I shook hands with Booker T. Washington."

"I joined the church the year Garfield was shot in the 6th depot near the old Center Market."

"I have two grandsons living somewhere. Their names are George Barnes and Joseph Dellworth."

**Laura Bell.** "Being informed that Laura Bell was an old slavery Negro, I went immediately to the little two-room shack with its fallen roof and shaky steps..."

**Laura Sorrell.** "My mammy, Virginia Burns, wus borned in Fayetteville, Cumberland County..."

*Lila Nichols, Age 89.*

**Lila Nichols.** Age 89. "We belonged ter Mr. Nat Whitaker atter his marriage..." Raleigh.

**Lily Perry.** "I wus borned on de plantation of Mister Jerry Perry near Louisburg, about eighty-four ago..." Raleigh.

**Lindsey Faucett.** " Yes, Mis', I wuz bawn in 1851, de 16th of November, on de Occoneachee Plantation, owned by Marse John Norwood an' his good wife, Mis' Annie..." Durham.

**Lizzie Baker.** "I was born de las' year o' de surrender an 'course I don't remember seein' any Yankee soldiers, but I knows a plenty my mother and father tole me..." Raleigh.

**Lizzie Williams.** "I's bo'n in Selma, Alabam' I can't mind how long ago, but jes bout ninety yeahs..." Asheville.

**Louisa Adams.** "My name is Louisa Adams..." Raleigh.

*Louisa Adams*

**Louise Evans.** Raleigh.

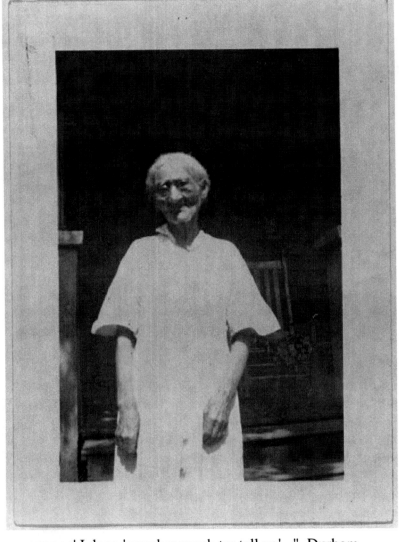

*Louise Evans*

**Lucy Fullwood.** married Henry Bell who was born into slavery. They were married at Zion Hill Church near the Sunset Harbor area of Brunswick County, NC.

**Lucy Ann Dunn.** "My pappy, Dempsey, my mammy, Rachel an' my brothers an' sisters an' me all belonged ter Marse Peterson Dunn of Neuse, here in Wake County..."

**Lucy Brown.** "I wuz jist a little thing when de war wuz over an' I doan 'member much ter tell yo'..." Durham.

**M**aggie Mials. "I'll never forgit de day when de Yankees come through Johnston County." Raleigh.

**Mandy Coverson.** "I wuz borned in Union County to Sarah an' Henderson Tomberlin..." Raleigh.

**Margaret E. Dickens**. Age 76. "My name is Margaret E. Dickens and I was born on the 5th of June 1861..." Raleigh.

*Margaret E. Dickens. Age 76.*

**Margaret Thornton**. I wus borned an' raised on de plantation of Jake Thornton of Harnett County..." Four Oaks.

**Martha Adeline Hinton**. "I was born May 3, 1861 at Willis Thompson's plantation in Wake County about fifteen miles from Raleigh..."

**Martha Allen.** "I wuz borned in Craven County seventy eight years ago..." Raleigh.

**Martha Organ.** "I doan know nothin' 'bout slavery 'cept what I hyard my mother tell, an' dat ain't so much..." Cary.

**Mary Anderson.** "My name is Mary Anderson. I was born on a plantation near Franklinton, Wake County, on May 10, 1851. I was a slave belonging to Sam Brodie, who owned the plantation. My missus' name was Evaline. My father was Alfred Brodie, and my mother was Bertha Brodie. I think slavery was a might good thing for Mother, Father, me and the other members of the family..." Raleigh.

**Mary Barbour.** "I reckon dat I wuz borned in McDowell County, case dat's whar my mammy, Edith, lived......She belonged to Mr. Jefferson Mitchel there, and my pappy belonged to a Mr. Jordan in Avery County, so he said......." Raleigh.

**Mary Wallace Bow.** "My name is Mary Wallace Bowe..." Durham.

**Mattie Curtis.** "I wus borned on de plantation of Mr. John Mayes in Orange County ninety-eight years ago...Several of the chilluns had been sold before the speculator come and buyed Mammy, Pappy and we three chilluns. The speculator was named Bebus, and he lived in Henderson, but he meant to sell us in the tobacco country....." aleigh.

**Melissa Williamson.** "Dis June fifteenth sebenty-eight years ago I wuz borned in Franklin County near Louisburg..." aleigh.

**Melvin Hill.** was born in 1842 and died in 1922. He wa born in to slavery and was the great-grandfather of Don Joyner, current resident of Brunswick County, NC. According to Mr. Joyner, "the story is that he sold all his land for two kegs of rum; but the story is not yet verified." .

**Millie Markham.** "I was never a slave..." Raleigh.

**Milly Henry.** "I wus borned a slave ter Mr. Buck Boylan in Yazoo City, Mississippi..." Raleigh.

*Millie Henry, Age 82.*

**Nancy Gore.** was the mother of Harvey Robinson, local Brunswick County native who at 100-years old sharing information about his mother. Nancy was born into slavery and married Joe Robinson. Nancy told Harvey, her son, that "slaves didn't have much. Sometimes we had no shoes and our feet were wrapped in rags. When the ground froze, slave feet cracked so bad, that they would be driving the cows, and you could track the slaves by the blood on the ground." Harvey says, "slavery times, there was some better than others, like today and that's the way its going to continue."

**Nellie Smith.** "My name is Nellie Smith... " Dunn.

**Ophelia Whitley.** "I wuz borned at Wakefield in 1841, here in Wake County..." Zebulon.

**Ora M. Flagg.** "My name is Ora M. Flagg..." Raleigh.

**Parker Pool.** "Good Morning, how is yer?" Raleigh.

**Patience ___ Price.** Patience was the great-grandmother of Mamie Hankins Frazier (born 17 Sept 1924.) and reported to be a slave in Brunswick County. She reports the plantation may have been located in the Mulberry Road Cart path on the northern side of Shallotte. Patience married William Henry Price.

**Patsy Mitchner.** "Come right in, honey, I been expectin' some of you white folks a long time from what I dreampt an' I wants to tell you my story..." Raleigh.

**Penny Williams.** "I wus borned at de Hinton place 'bout three miles south of Raleigh an course we 'longed ter Mr. Lawrence Hinton..." Raleigh.

**Plaz Williams.** "Margaret Thornton sez dat she has got de world record beat on nussin' but dat's whar she's wrong..."

**Porter Scales.** Monday, December 19, 1933, the faithful colored friends of Uncle Porter Scales transported his body from St. Stephen's African Methodist Episcopal Church located on the Madison-Mayodan highway to a plantation grave yard several miles east of town, along roads slippery with sleet....Madison.

**Princess Quango Hennadonah Perceriah.** "I was eighteen years old in 1875 but I wanted to get married so I gave my age as nineteen..." Raleigh.

**R**ansom Sidney Taylor. R. S. Taylor. "My name is Ransom Sidney Taylor..." Raleigh.

**Rena Raines.** "I wus three years ole when de Yankees come through..." Raleigh.

**Ria Sorrell.** "I jist lak three years of bein' one hundred years old...Raleigh.
**Richard C. Moring**. "My mammy wus Cherry, an ' my pappy wus Jacob..." Raleigh.

**Robert Glenn.** "I was a slave before and during the Civil War..." Raleigh.

**Robert Hinton.** "My name is Robert Hinton ..." Raleigh.

**Roberta Manson**. "I wus borned de second year of de war an' de mos' I know 'bout slavery wus tole to me by other colored folks..." Raleigh.

**S**am T. Stewart. Age 84. "My name is Sam T. Stewart...Raleigh.

*Sam T. Stewart, Age 84.*

**Sarah Anne Green**. 78 years old. "My mammy an' pappy wuz Anderson an' Hannah Watson..." Raleigh.

**Sarah Ann Smith.** "I wus borned January 22, 1858 ter Martha an' Green Womble in Chatham County, near Lockville..." Raleigh.

**Sarah Debro.** "I was born in Orange County way back some time in the fifties. Miz Polly White Cain and Marse Dr. Cain was my white folks. Marse Cain's plantation joined Mr. Paul Cameron's land. Mares Cain owned so many (negroes) that he didn't know his own slaves when he met them on the road. Sometimes he would stop them and say: "Whose (negro) are you?" They'd say, "We's Marse Cain's (negroes)." Then he would say, "I's Marse Cain," and drive on."

"Marse Cain was good to his (negroes). He didn't whip them like some owners did, but if they done mean, he sold them. They knew this so they minded him. One day Grandpappy sassed Miss Polly White, and she told him that if he didn't behave hisself that she would put him in her pocket.

Grandpappy was a big man, and I ask him how Miss Polly could do that. He said she meant that she would sell him, then put the money in her pocket. He never did sass Miss Polly no more."

"I starched the aprons stiff. I had a clean apron every day. We had white sheets on de beds an' we (negroes) had plenty to eat too, even ham. When Mis' Polly went to ride she took me in de carriage wid her. De driver set way up high an' me an' Mis' Polly set way down low. Dey was two hosses with shiney harness. I toted Mis' Polly's bag an' bundles, an' if she dropped her hank'chief I picked it up. I loved Mis' Polly an' loved stayin' at de big house."

"I was 'bout wais' high when de sojers mustered. I went wid Mis' Polly down to de musterin' fiel whare day was marchin'. I can see de feets now when de flung dem up an' down, sayin', hep, hep. When dey was all ready to go an' fight, de women folks fixed a big dinner. Aunt Charity an' Pete cooked two or three days for Mis' Polly. De table was piled wid chicken, ham, ___, barbecue, young lam', an' all sorts of pies, cakes an' things, but nobody eat nothing much. Mis' Polly an' de ladies got to cryin.' De vittles got cold. I was so sad dat I got over in de corner an' cried too. De men folks all had on dey new sojer clothes, an' dey didn' eat nothing neither. Young Marse Jim went up an' put his arm 'round Mis' Polly, his mammy, but dat made her cry harder. Marse Jim was a cavalry. He rode a big hoss, an' my Uncle Dave went wid him to de fiel' as his body guard. He had a hoss too so if Marse Jim's hoss got shot dare would be another one for him to ride. Mis' Polly had another son but he was too drunk to hold a gun. He stayed drunk."

"De first cannon I heard skeered me near 'bout to death. We could hear dem goin' boom, boom. I thought it was thunder, den Mis Polly say, "Lissen, Sarah, hear dem cannons? Dey's killin' our mens." Den she 'gun to cry."

"I ran in de kitchen whare Aunt Charity was cookin an' tole her Mis' Polly was cryin. She said: "She ain't cryin' kaze de Yankees killin' de mens; she's doin' all dat cryin' kaze she skeered we's goin' to be set free." Den I got mad an' tole her Mis' Polly wazn' like dat."

"I 'members when Wheelers Cavalry coms through. Dey was "Federates but dey was mean as de Yankees. Dey stold everything dey could find an' killed a pile of (negroes). Dey come 'roun' checkin'. Dey ax de (negroes) if dey wanted to be free. If dey say yes, den dey shot dem down, but if dey said no, dey let dem alone. Dey took three of my uncles out in de woods an' shot dey faces off."

"I 'members de first time de Yankees come. Dey come gallupin' down de road, jumpin over de palin's, tromplin down de rose buses an' messin' up de flower beds. Dey stomped all over de house, in der kitchen, pantries, smoke houke, an' everywhere, but dey didn' find much, kaze near "bout everything done been hid. I was settin' on de steps when a big Yankee come up. He had on a cap an' his eyes was mean. "Whare did dey hide do gol' an silver, (negro)?" he yelled at me. I was skeered an my hands was ashy, but I told him I didn' nothin' 'bout nothing; dat if anybody done hid things dey hid it while I was sleep."

"Go ax dat ole white headed devil," he said to me. I got mad den kaze he wuz tawkin' 'bout Mis' Polly, so I didn't say nothin'. I jus' set. Den he pushed me off de step an' say if I didn' dance he gwine shoot my toes off. Sheered as I was, I sho done some shuffling. Den he give me five dollars an' tole me to go buy jim cracks, but dat piece of paper won't no good. "Twuzn nothin' but a shin plaster like all dat war money, you couldn' spend it."

"Dat Yankee kept callin' Mis' Polly a white headed devil an' said she done ran-snacked 'till dey wuzn' nothin' left, but he made his mens tote off meat, flour, pigs, an' chickens. After dat Mis' Polly got mighty stingy wid de vittles an' de didn' have no more ham."

"When de war was over de Yankees was all 'roun' de place tellin' de (negroes) what to do. Dey tole dem dey was free, dat dey didn' have to slave for de white folks no more. My folks all left Marses Cain an' went to live in houses dat de Yankees built. Dey wuz like poor white folks houses, little shacks made out of sticks an' mud wid stick an' mud chimneys. Day wuzn' like Marse Cain's cabins, planked up an' warm, dey was full of cracks, an' dey wuzn' no lamps an' oil. All de light come from de lightwood knots burnin' in de fireplace."

"One day my mammy come to de big house after me. I didn't want to go, I wanted to stay wid Mis' Polly. I 'gun to cry an' Mammy caught hold of me. I grabbed Mis' Polly an' held on so tight dat I tore her skirt bindin' loose an' her skirt fell down 'bout her feet. "Let her stay wid me," Mis' Polly said to Mammy. But Mammy shook her head. You took her away from me an' didn' pay no mind to my cryin', an now I'se talkin' her back home. We's free now, Mis' Polly, we ain't gwine be slaves no more to nobody." She dragged me away. I can see how Mis' Polly looked now. She didn' say nothin' but she looked hard at Mammy an' her face was white."

"Mammy took me to de stick an' mud house de Yankees done give her. It was smoky an' dark kaze day wuzn' no windows. We didn' have no sheets an' no towels, so when I cried an' said I didn' want to live on no Yankee house, Mammy beat me an' made me go to bed."

"I laid on de straw tick lookin' up through de cracks in de roof. I could see de stars, an' de sky shinin' through de cracks looked like long blue splinters stretched 'cross de rafters. I lay dare an' cried kaze I wanted to go back to Mis' Polly."

"I was never hungry till we waz free an' de Yankees fed us. We didn' have nothing to eat 'cept hard tack an' middlin' meat. I never saw such meat. It was thin an' tough wid a thick skin. You could boil it all day an' all night an' it wouldn' cook done, I wouldn' eat it. I thought 'twuz mule meat; mules dat done been shot on de battle field, den dried." "I still believe "twuz mule meat."

"One day me an' my brother was lookin' for acorns in de woods. We foun' sumpin' like a grave in de woods. I tole Dave dey wuz sumpin' buried in dat moun'. We got de grubbin hoe an' dug. Dey wuz a box wid eleven hams in dat grave."

**Sarah Gudger.** Age 121. Investigation of the almost incredible claim of Aunt Sarah Gudger, ex-slave living in Asheville, that she was born on Sept. 15, 1816, discloses some factual information corroborating her statements. Asheville.

*Sarah Gudger. Age 121*

"I 'membahs de time when mah mammy wah alive, I wah a small chile, afoah dey tuck huh t' Rims Crick. All us chillens wah playin' in de ya'd one night. Jes' arunnin' an' aplayin' lak chillun will. All a sudden mammy cum to de do' all a'sited. "Cum in heah dis minnit," she say. "Jes look up at what is ahappenin'," and bless yo' life, honey, da sta's wah fallin' jes' lak rain.* Mammy wah tebble skeered, but we chillen wa'nt afeard, no, we wa'nt afeard. But mammy she say evah time a sta' fall, somebuddy gonna die. Look lak lotta folks gonna die f'om de looks ob dem sta's. Ebbathin' wah jes' as bright as day. Yo' cudda pick a pin up. Yo' know de sta's don' shine as bright as dey did back den. I wondah wy dey don'. Dey jes' don' shine as bright. Wa'nt long afoah dey took mah mammy away, and I wah lef' alone."

*(One of the most spectacular meteoric showers on record, visible all over North America, occurred in 1833.)

**Sarah Harris.** "Sarah Harris is my name..."

241

**Sarah Louise Augustus**. "I was born on a plantation near Fayetteville, and I belonged to J. B. Smith. His wife was named Henrietta. He owned about thirty slaves. My father was named Romeo Harden, and my mother was named Alice Smith. The little cabin where I was born is still standing. "

"My first days of slavery was hard. I slept on a pallet on the floor of the cabin, and just as soon as I was able to work any at all I was put to milking cows."

"Mr. George Lander had the first tombstone marble yard in Fayetteville, on Hay Street on the point of Flat Iron Place. I waited on the Landers part of the time…"

"Grandfather was named Isaac Fuller. Mrs. Mary Ann Fuller, Kate Fuller, Mr. Will Fuller, who was a lawyer in Wall Street, New York, is some of their white folks. The Fullers were born in Fayetteville."

"When a slave was no good, he was put on the auction block in Fayetteville and sold. The slave block stood in the center of the street, Fayetteville Street, where Ramsey and Gillespie streets came in near Cool Springs Street. The silk mill stood just below the slave market. I saw the silkworms that made the silk and saw them gather the cocoons and spin the silk."

"They hung people in the middle of Ramsey Street. They put up a gallows and hung the men exactly at twelve o'clock. I ran away from the plantation once to go with some white children to see a man hung."

"The Yankees came through Fayetteville wearing large blue coats with capes on them. Lots of them were mounted, and there were thousands of foot soldiers. I took them several days to get through town. The southern soldiers retreated, and then in a few hours the Yankees covered the town. They busted into the smokehouse at Marster's, took the meat, meal, and other provisions. Grandmother pled with the Yankees, but it did not good. They took all they wanted. They said if they had to come again they would take the babies from the cradles. They told us we were all free. The Negroes begun visiting each other in the cabins and became so excited they began to shout and pray. I thought they were all crazy."

"We stayed right on with Marster. He had a town house and a big house on the plantation. I went to the town house to work, but Mother and Grandmother stayed on the plantation. My mother died there, and the white folks buried her. Father stayed right on and helped run the farm until he died."

"I was thirty yars old when I married. I was married in my missus' graduating dress. I was married in the white folks' church, to James Henry Harris. The white folks carried me there and gave me away. Miss Mary Smith gave me away. The wedding was attended mostly by white folks."

"My husband was a fireman on the Cape Fear river--boats and a white man's Negro too. My husband was finally offered a job with a shipping concern in Delaware, and we moved there. After his death I married David Augustus and immediately came back to North Carolina and my white folks, and we have been here ever since."

**Sharp Gore.** was the grandfather of Harvey Robinson, current resident of Supply, NC. He married Catherine Ward. They had a daughter named, Nancy who married Joe Robinson. Joe was born into slavery in Brunswick County during the Civil War. Joe and nancy had three boys, Harvey, Donnie and Gatlin Robinson.

**Simuel Riddick.** "My name is Simuel Riddick." Mr. Riddick belonged to Elisha and Sarah Riddick and was born in Perquimans County, N. C. He lived on a plantation of about two hundred cleared acres with about twenty-five other slaves. He felt that they had good food and lived in the "quarters." He had "mighty fine white people, yes, might fine white people." "The old man never whupped anybody. He was a rangtang who loved his liquor and he loved colored women." "There were no half-white children on Marster's plantation, and no mixups that ever came out to be a disgrace in any way. My white folks were fine people." "I haven't anything to say against slavery. My old folks put my clothes on me when I was a boy. They gave me shoes and stockings and put them on me when I was a little boy. I loved them, and I can't go against them in anything. There were things I did not like about slavery on some plantations, whupping and selling parents and children from each other, but I haven't much to say. I was treated good...."Raleigh.

**Squire Dowd.** Age 82. "My name is Squire Dowd, and I was born April 3, 1855... " Dunn.

*Rev. Squire Dowd. Age 82.*

**Susan High.** "My name is Susan High..." Raleigh.

**T**anner Spikes. "My mammy had fifteen chilluns which wus all borned on Doctor Fab Haywood's Plantation here in Wake County..." Raleigh.

**Tempe Herndon Durham.** Age 103. "I was thirty- one years ole when de surrender come. Dat makes me sho nuff ole. Near bout a hundred an' three years done passed over dis here white head of mine. I'se been here, I mean

I'se been here. 'Spects I'se de oldest (negro) in Durham. I'se been here so long dat I done forgot near 'bout as much as dese here new generation knows or ever gwine know."

"My white fo'ks lived in Chatham County. Dey was Marse George an' Mis' Betsy Herndon. Mis Betsy was a Snipes befo' she married Marse George. Dey had a big plantation an' raised cawn, wheat, cotton an' 'bacca. I don't know how many field (negroes)s Marse George had, but he had a mess of dem, an' he had hosses too, an' cows, hogs an' sheeps. He raised sheeps an' sold de wool, an' dey used de wool at de big house too. Dey was a big weavin' room whare de blankets was wove, an' dey wove de cloth for de winter clothes too. Linda Hernton an' Milla Edwards was de head weavers, dey looked after de weavin' of da fancy blankets. Mis' Betsy was a good weaver too. She weave de same as de (negroes). She say she love de clackin' soun' of de loom an' de way de shuttles run in an' out carryin' a long tail of bright colored thread. Some days she set at de loom all de mawnin' peddlin' wid her feets an' her white han's flittin' over de bobbins."

*Tempe Herndon Durham.*
*Age 103.*

"De cardin' an' spinnin' room was full of (negroes). I can hear dem spinnin' wheels now turnin' roun' an' sayin' hum-m-m-m, hum-m-m-m, an' hear de slaves singin' while dey spin. Mammy Rachel stayed in de dyein' room. Dey wuzn' nothin' she didn' know 'bout dyein'. She knew every kind of root, bark, leaf an' berry dat made red, blue, green, or whatever color she wanted. Dey had a big shelter whare de dye pots set over de coals. Mammy Rachel would fill de pots wid water, den she put in de roots, bank an' stuff an' boil de juice out, den she strain it an' put in de salt an' vinegar to set de color. After de wool an' cotton done been carded an' spun to thread, Mammy take de hanks an' drap dem in de pot of boilin' dye. She stir dem 'roun' an' lif' dem up an' down wid a stick, an' when she hang

244

dem up on de line in de sun, dey was every color of de rainbow. When dey dripped dry dey was sent to de weavin' room whare dey was wove in blankets an' things."

"When I growed up I married Exter Durham. He belonged to Marse Snipes Durham who had de plantation 'cross de county line in Orange County. We had a big weddin'. We was married on de front po'ch of de big house. Marse George killed a shoat an' Mis' Betsy had Georgianna, de cook, to bake a big weddin' cake all iced up white as snow wid a bride an' groom standin' in de middle holdin' han's. De table was set out in de yard under de trees, an' you ain't never seed de like of eats. All de (negroes) come to de feas' an' Marse George had a for everybody. Dat was some weddin'. I had on a white dress, white shoes an' long while gloves dat come to my elbow, an' Mis' Betsy done made me a weddin' veil out of a white net window curtain. When she played de weddin' ma'ch on de piano, me an' Exter ma'ched down de walk an' up on de po'ch to de altar Mis' Betsy done fixed. Dat de pretties' altar I ever seed. Back 'gainst de rose vine dat was full or red roses, Mis' Betsy done put tables filled wid flowers an' white candles. She spread down a bed sheet, a sho nuff linen sheet, for us to stan' on, an' dey was a white pillow to kneel down on. Exter done made me a weddin' ring. He made it out of a big red button wid his pocket knife. He done cut it so roun' an' polished it so smooth dat it looked like a red satin ribbon tide 'roun' my finger. Dat sho was a pretty ring. I wore it 'bout fifty years, den it got so thin dat I lost it one day in de wash tub when I was washin' clothes".

"Uncle Edmond Kirby married us. He was de (negro) preacher dat preached at de plantation church. After Uncle Edmond said de las' words over me an' Exter, Marse George got to have his little fun: He say, 'Come on, Exter, you an' Tempie got to jump over de broom stick backwards; you got to do dat to see which one gwine be boss of your househol'.' Everybody come stan' 'roun to watch. Marse George hold de broom 'bout a foot high off de floor. De one dat jump over it backwards an' never touch de handle, gwine boss de house, an' if bof of dem jump over widout touchin' it, dey won't gwine be no bossin', dey jus' gwine be 'genial. I jumped fus', an' you ought to seed me. I sailed right over dat broom stick same as a cricket, but when Exter jump he done had a big dram an' his feets was so big an' clumsy dat dey got all tangled up in dat broom an' he fell head long. Marse George he laugh an' laugh, an' tole Exter he gwine be bossed 'twell he skeered to speak less'n I tole him to speak. After de weddin' we went down to de cabin Mis' Betsy done all dressed up, but Exter couldn' stay no longer den dat night kaze he belonged to Marse Snipes Durham an' he had to go back home. He lef' de nex day for his plantation, but he come back every Saturday night an' stay 'twell Sunday night. We had eleven chillun. Nine was bawn befo' surrender an' two after we was set free. So I had two chillun dat wuzn' bawn in bondage. I was worth a heap to Marse George kaze I had so many chillun. De more chillun a slave had de more dey was worth. Lucy Carter was de only(negro) on de plantation dat had more chillun den I had. She had twelve, but her chillun was sickly an' mine was muley strong an' healthy. Dey never was sick."

"When de war come Marse George was too ole to go, but young Marse Bill went. He went an' took my brother Sim wid him. Marse Bill took Sim along to look after his hoss an' everything. Dey didn' neither one get shot, but Mis' Betsy was skeered near 'bout to death all de time, skeered dey was gwine be brung home shot all to pieces like some of de sojers was."

"(De Yankees wuzn' so bad. De mos' dey wanted was sumpin' to eat. Dey was all de time hungry, de fus' thing dey ax for when dey come was sumpin' to put in dey stomach. An' chicken! I ain' never seed even a preacher eat chicken like dem Yankees. I believes to my soul dey ain' never seed no chicken 'twell dey come down here. An' hot biscuit too. I seed a passel of dem eat up a whole sack of flour one night for supper. Georgianna sif' flour 'twell she look white an' dusty as a miller. Dem sojers didn' turn down no ham neither. Dat de onlies' thing dey took from Marse George. Dey went in de smoke house an' toted off de hams an' shoulders. Marse George say he come off mighty light if dat all dey want, 'sides he got plenty of shoats anyhow."

"We had all de eats we wanted while de war was shootin' dem guns, kaze Marse George was home an' he kep' de (negroes) workin'. We had chicken, gooses, meat, peas, flour, meal, potatoes an' things like dat all de time, an' milk an' butter too, but we didn' have no sugar an' coffee. We used groun' pa'ched cawn for coffee an' cane 'lasses for sweetnin'. Dat wuzn' so bad wid a heap of thick cream. Anyhow, we had enough to eat to 'vide wid de neighbors dat didn' have none when surrender come."

"I was glad when de was stopped kaze den me an' Exter could be together all de time 'stead of Saturday an' Sunday. After we was free we lived right on at Marse George's plantation a long time. We rented de lan' for a fo'th of what we made, den after while we bought a farm. We paid three hundred dollars we done saved. We had a hoss, a steer, a cow an' two pigs, 'sides some chickens an' fo' geese. Mis' Betsy went up in de attic an' give us enough goose feathers to make two pillows, den she give us a table an' some chairs. She give us some dishes too. Marse George give Exter a bushel of seed cawn and some seed wheat, den he tole him to go down to de barn an' get a bag of cotton seed. We got all dis den we hitched up de wagon an' th'owed in de passel of chillun an' moved to our new farm, an' de chillun was put to work in de fiel'; dey growed up in de fiel' kaze dey was put to work time dey could walk good."

"Freedom is all right, but de (negroes) was better off befo' surrender, kaze den dey was looked after an' dey didn' get in no trouble fightin' an' killin' like dey do dese days. If a (negro) cut up an' got sassy in slavery times, his Ole Marse give him a good whippin' an' he went way back an' set down an' 'haved hese'f. If he was sick, Marse an' Mistis looked after him, an' if he needed store medicine, it was bought an' give to him; he didn' have to pay nothin'. Dey didn' even have to think 'bout clothes nor nothin' like dat, dey was wove an' made an' give to dem. Maybe everybody's

Marse and Mistis wuzn' good as Marse George and Mis' Betsy, but dey was de same as a mammy an' pappy to us negroes." Durham.

**Tempe Pitts.** Age 91. "I wuz borned in Halifax County ninety-one years ago..." Wilmington.

*Tempe Pitts, Age 91*

**Thomas Hall.** "My name is Thomas Hall and I was born in Orange County, N. C. on a plantation belonging to Jim Woods whose wife, our Missus, was named Polly. My father, Daniel Hall, and my mother Becke Hall and me all belonged to the same man, but it was often th case that this was not true as one man, perhaps a Johnson, would own a husband and a Smith own his wife, each slave going by the name of the slave owner's family. In such cases, the children went by the name of the family to which the mother belonged…....." Raleigh.

**Tillie Caretaker.** Daughter of a Slave. "La, Miss Fannie, what you mean askin' me what I knows about slavery! Why I was bawn yeah's after freedom!" Wilmington.

**Tina Johnson.** Age 75. "I wuz bawned in Richmon', Georgia 'round eighty-five years ago..." Raleigh.

**Tiney Shaw**. Age 76. "My papa wuz a free (negro), case he wuz de son of de master who was named Medlin..." Wake County.

**Tom Wilcox.** "I wuz borned on March 18th, 1856 durin' de biggest snow dat eber hit Eastern Carolina; dey says dat hit wuz up ter de roof..." Method.

**V**alley Perry. "Course bein' no older dan I is I can't recollect 'bout de war, but I'se heard my Mammy tell a little an' my gran'mama, tell a right smart 'bout dem slavery times yo's talkin' 'bout..." Cary.

**Viney Baker.** Age 75. "My mammy wuz Hannah Murry an' so fur as I know I ain't got no father , do' I reckon dat he wuz de plantation stock (negro)..." Raleigh.

**W. L. Bost.** Age 88. "My massa's name was Jonas Bost. He had a hotel in Newton. My mother and grandmother both belonged to the Bost family. My old massa had two large plantations, one about three miles from Newton and another four miles away. It took a lot of (negroes) to keep the work a-going on them both. The women folks had to work in the hotel and in the big house in town. Old Missus, she was a good woman. She never allowed the massa to buy or sell any slaves. There never was an overseer on the whole plantation. The oldest colored man always looked after the (negroes). We (negroes) lived better than the (negroes) on the other plantations…..." Asheville.

*W. L. Bost, Age 88.*

**W. S. Debnam.** "Yes, I remember the Yankees coming to Raleigh..." Raleigh.

**William George Hinton.** "I wus born in Wake County in de year 1859, August 28th..." Raleigh.

*William Moore.*

**William Moore.** "Some Sundays we went to church some place. We allus liked to go any place. A white preacher allus told us to 'bey our masters and work hard and sing and when we die we go to Heaven. Marse Tom didn't mind us singin' in our cabins at night, but we better not let him cotch us prayin."

"Seems like (negroes) jus' got to pray. Half they life am in prayin'. Some (negro) take turn 'bout to watch and see if Marse Tom anyways 'bout, then they circle theyselves on the floor in the cabin and pray. They git to moanin' low and gentle, 'Some day, some day, some day, this yoke gwine be lifted offen our shoulders'."

"Marse Tom been dead long time now. I 'lieve he's in hell. Seem like that where he 'long. He was

248

a terrible mean man and had a indiff'ent, mean wife. But he had the fines', sweetes' chillun the Lawd ever let live and breathe on this earth. They's so kind and sorrowin' over us slaves."

"Some them chillun used to read us li'l things out of papers and books. We'd look at them papers and books like they somethin' mighty curious, but we better not let Marse Tom or his wife know it!"

**William Henry Price.** The author interviewed the granddaughter of William Henry Price on March 6, 2009 who was living on Big Macedonia Road in Supply, NC. Ms. Mamie Hankins Frazier (born September 17, 1924 and 84 years old), and her son, John A. Hankins, relayed the story of her grandfather who had died in 1921. Mr. Price had been a slave on the plantation that they referred to as "Potters Hole" which was located off the present Royal Oak Road. Mrs. Frazier stated that she had visited *Potters Hole* and used to "walk across Monster Bucks, two to three miles, to Uncle Sammy Price who was still living there" (when she was a girl). "You could go through the woods and come out at Mulberry, in Shallotte, using the cart road which used to go by the old Joes Barbeque Restaurant." (This was located near Main Street on the north end of Shallotte.)

"Grandaddy (William) visited his girlfriend, Patience, at the Mulberry location on Sundays. Granddaddy was a slave and the Marsah told him not to leave the plantation to go a'callin. 'If you leave the plantation, I'm gonna whip you every step of the way back.' Later that day the Marsah came home. He checked the quarters and William Henry was gone. The Marsah got on his horse and went to find him. When he found him both granddaddy and Patience were sitting on her front porch barefooted on Mulberry Street. They were "a 'callin'....which was the term for courting."

"The Marsah said, 'I told you not to leave the plantation and I'm gonna whip you every step of the way back.' Granddaddy daid, 'But Marsah, you are on four feet and I only have two. You could give me a headstart.' The Marsah said, 'I will let you get to the bend and when you get to the curve hold up your hand.' Well, William took off running and when he went 'round the bend, he threw up his hand. Every bend he threw up his hand. I don't know how far that was back. Henry eventually married Miss Patience."

"He outrun the horse and was sitting on the porch when the Marsah got there. Grandpa Henry said, 'What took you so long?' And he didn't get no whipping."

"My daddy could race the same way. Back when I was young I could get up and run too. On May Day we would go to Southport and I ran one-two-three by the girls and we got the trophy. I went to the Royal Oak Elementary School and then to the Training School in Southport."

Ms. Frazier was working on a beautiful children's quilt as the author visited her in her home. She makes and sells them for $150 each, all hand sewn. She recalled a day when her momma was quilting and Mamie wanted to stay home from school to learn how to quilt. Momma said ok and we quilted all day long. "I cried and cried when I was tired. Up until now, I have made over 90 quilts of all sizes. I have made a queen size and two baby quilts since this past Christmas." (Two months ago.)

She is shown her consulting with the family Bible. When she was 12 or 13 years old she worked in tobacco "handing" tobacco. "I handed the tobacco to someone else who loops it on the stick. I had earned $25 or $30 for six weeks worth of work. A man had come by selling Bibles and when I went to go pick up my money, my momma said "where is your money" and she took that money and bought the Bible."

In that Bible, very torn and tattered as of this date, but it still listed her ancestors. It shows her father, Henry Alva Price who was born on June 25, 1886, the son of William Henry Price, the slave. Henry Alva price died in 1953. He was married on the 7 April 1910 to my momma, Melvina Hemmingway, who was born June 30, 1890 and died August 14, 1982 at 92 years of age. Melvina's father was Samuel Hemingway, who was born on 23 December 1863, married Rachel Gore on the 20th of 1890. They had a son named Samuel, who was Mamie Hankins Frazier's other great-grandfather.

Patience and Henry Price were both slaves. They had four sons: Elijah, Henry, Frozen Bill and Lempus (spelling?). Mamie's other set of great-grandparents, Betsy and Benjamin Gore were also slaves. Betsy used to live in an old log cabin off of highway 17 where Louis Louis now lives.

*Ms. Mamie Hankins Frazier is shown consulting her family Bible in the following photo:*

**William Scott.** Age 77. "My name is William Scott. I live at 401 Church Street, Raleigh, North Carolina..." Raleigh.

**William Smith.** My full name is William Smith..." Raleigh.

**William Sykes.** Age 78. "My mammy Martha an' me we 'longed ter Mister Joshua Long in Martin County, an' my paw, Henry 'longed ter Squire Ben Sykes in Tyrell County..." Raleigh.

*William Sykes, Age 78.*

**Willie Cozart.** "No mam, Mistress, I doan want ter ride in no automobile, thank you, I'se done walked dese three miles frum Zebulon an' walkin' is what has kept me goin' all dese years...I was borned on June 11, 1845, in Person County. Mr. Starling Oakley of Person County, near Roxboro, was my master, and as long as him and Old Mistress lived, I went back to see them. He was right good to the good (negroes) and kinda strict with the bad ones……. " Zebulon.

**Willie McCullough.** "I was born in Darlington County, South Carolina, the 14th of June 1869..".

**Willis Williams.** Willis Williams, from Loris, South Carolina, belonged to John A. Williams, born on the Cape Fear. This plantation boasted four hundred slaves who sometimes hired out to work the turpentine boxes; sometimes for a year at a time. He then collected their wages.

Willis remembers working as a houseboy for the Marster. Every Saturday he would drive his master to Fayetteville. He remembers the Yankees arrival and watched them steal all the valuables, stock, and food available. He left with the Yanks, riding atop the carriage full of corn. "It was mighty cold up there."

When he left the Yankees, they gave him thirty-five dollars in cash. He spent it on crackers and peanuts and a pair of brogan shoes. Before his freedom, Willis said he had "a good enough time." After gaining his freedom, "had to get out and work, it most kill me." "After freedom, my mother wash for family to Beaver Creek and my father went to working on shares."

**Z**eb Crowder. "I wont nuthin' in slavery time and I aint nuthin' now..." Cary.

## *Slaves of Columbus County, NC*

According to Harvey Robinson, of Supply, North Carolina, in an interview on Sunday afternoon, March 15, 2009, Mr. Henry Candle Smith was the biggest slave owner on the coast. His plantation grew rice and cotton. He owned all the land where the present Home Depot Shopping Center in Shallotte, NC is now located. This is the plantation where a slave cemetery is described in the fields directly behind the Belks store in the same location. Several individuals are trying to locate this Slave Cemetery as of this date but have not yet located it. It is said to contain more than fifty burials, among them Charity Ward, great-grandmother of Mr. Robinson.

*Mr. Harvey Robinson, age 100. March 15, 2009. Supply, North Carolina.*

Mr. Smith sold this land to Rufus Hewett. Henry Hewett, his son, inherited it, and eventually lost this large farm. It was then bought by Fred Mintz who later sold it to Home Depot.

Mr. Henry Candle Smith, after selling his farm, moved to Columbus County, NC. He ran a "big business" according to Mr. Robinson. Mr. Smith was "good to his slaves." "Some were mean to slaves," according to Mr. Robinson. "My momma and her daddy were owned by Cobb Gore and he was mean to his slaves. He made them work barefooted on cold ground. After my granddaddy was freed, he stayed with us in Shallotte. Once one of the slaves of Cobb Gore talked back to him and Gore, he hit him and thought he had killed him. He hit him with a grubbin' hoe. Later he went back to bury him but the man was alive. He was bleeding, but alive. They doctored him and the slave lived out his life with Gore. He lived to be old." Robinson went on to reiterate that "Candle was the best man to slaves that you know about."

Mr. Robinson's grandfather's name was Sharp Gore. His grandmother was Catherine Ward Gore. They had a daughter named Nancy would married Joe Robinson. Joe was born into slavery in Brunswick County during the Civil War. Along with Harvey, born in 1908, Donnie, born in 1912 and Gatlin, born in 1910 and decreased about 15 years ago, all lived in Brunswick County.

252

**The Robinson Family**

From Left to Right: Walter Harvey Robinson , Dolly Bryant (a cousin),Mrs. Nancy Gore Robinson, Donnie L Robinson (sitting in Mrs. Robinson's lap), Mr. Joseph Robinson, and Arnie Gadling Robinson (sitting in Mr. Robinson's lap) Photo taken about 1914.

Photo above: L. Walter Harvey Robinson (born 1908), cousin Dolly Bryant (who married a Frink), Mrs. Nancy Gore Robinson holding boy Donnie L. Robinson (b. 1912), and Mr. Joseph Robinson holding little brother, Arnie Gadling Robinson (born 1910). (Mother is Nancy Gore Robinson who married Joseph Gore). The original photo is in the possession of Mr. Harvey Robinson of Supply, NC. The bright spot in the middle of the photo represents defects in the photo. The baby in the mother's lap was dressed in a long white gown, perhaps a Christening gown? All seemed to be dressed for a special occasion. Date unknown, however photo estimated to be taken about 1914 based upon Gadling's age.

Joe Robinson's brother went into south Georgia and the family never heard from him again. According to Mrs. Eva Robinson, "it is like selling pigs, we don't know who we were kin to." And family histories sometimes "leave out some information cuz we don't want someone getting mad."

Mr. Robinson ended his interview with his comments about how he never expected to see a black man elected President of the United States of America. His pride was evident with a poster of the newly elected president hanging on the living room wall of his living room while another newly purchased posted sat on the floor

253

ready for hanging. His advice for a long life: "Believe in the father above. It is in his hands."

Mr. Harvey Robinson was married to Ms. Eva Robinson in 1990. On the day in March 2009 when the author interviewed Mr. Robinson, his wife, Eva, watched Evangelism on TV, sometimes adding her comments about our historical discussions.

Eva Robinson.

*Slave Pen in Virginia*
*Note the two figures behind bars.*

# Chapter Eight

# The Civil War

The Civil War was the most prominent event for the Carolina's during the 1800s. The War Between the States was to divide even loyal families. By 1861 a great earthen-work fort was established. Fort Anderson was erected on the site of the St. Phillips Parish Church. It was bombarded but escaped total destruction and portions remain today.

*St. Philip's Church. John Muuss, Photographic Artist. Kate Stewart, model.*

Women also served in the war as nurses, *vivandieres,* sutlers, and as Union and Confederate soldiers, and even spies. A *vivandiere* is a French army term applied to women who provided food, provisions, and liqueurs to soldiers. Sutlers were peddlers who sold goods to military units in the field. Other women dressed as men and served side-by-side along with their brothers, fathers and cousins.

The Civil War lasted from 1861 to 1865 and is also known as the War Between the States. Eleven southern states declared their secession from the United States and formed the Confederate States of America. The Confederates were led by

Jefferson Davis and fought against the U. S. federal government (the Union led by President Abraham Lincoln), which included the free states and five border slave states. Violence began April 12, 1861 when Confederates attacked Fort Sumter in South Carolina. The conflict continued through many battles on land and sea sometimes brother against brother.

(See photo showing an unknown female soldier dressed in uniform.)

## Rose O'Neal Greenhow - Civil War Spy

Miss Rose O'Neal was born in 1817 and died on the 1st of October 1864 and was known as a Confederate spy. She had traveled in important political circles prior to the Civil War and had met many of the ranking politicians in these social activities. She used these contacts to pass along information to the confederacy at the beginning of the war.

Her father, John O'Neal was killed by one of his slaves in 1817. She, her three sisters, and mother were left in a cash-poor situation to fend for themselves. Rose later went to live with a wealthier aunt in Washington, D. C. where she had the opportunity to socialize with the elite. Her companion, John C. Calhoun, convinced

her to support pro-Southern interests. About 1830 she met Dr. Robert Greenhow and they married in 1835. They had eight children.

Dr. Greenhow died and Rose's sympathy for the Confederates grew and she was soon recruited as a spy. In 1861, she passed messages to Confederate General P. G. T. Beauregard about the First Battle of Bull Run and the plans of Union General Irvin McDowell.

Greenhow was captured on the 23rd of August 1861 and placed on house arrest by the newly formed Secret Service, under Allan Pinkerton. On the 18th of January 1862 she was transferred to Old Capitol. The colonists fought for their freedom just a little less than one hundred years before the Yankees and Rebels clashed so violently in the Civil War.

She continued to pass along information while in prison through ingenious methods such as securing information into the bun of a visitor's hair or positioning her blinds and candles in certain formations. She was released from prison on May

31, 1862 and deported to Richmond, Virginia. From 1863 to 1864 she traveled through France and Britain on diplomatic missions for the Confederacy. She wrote her memoirs titled *My Imprisonment and the First Year of Abolition Rule at Washington.*

"In September 1864, Greenhow left Europe to return to the Confederate States, carrying dispatches. She traveled on the *Condor,* a British blockade runner. On October 1, 1864, the *Condor* ran aground at the mouth of the Cape Fear River near Wilmington, North Carolina. A Union gunboat, USS *Niphon*, had been pursuing the ship. Fearing capture and reimprisonment, Greenhow fled the grounded *Condor* by rowboat. The rowboat was capsized by a wave, and Greenhow, weighed down with $2,000 worth of gold from her memoir royalties intended for the Confederate treasury, drowned.

"When Rose was pulled from her watery grave near Wilmington, North Carolina, searchers found a copy of her book "Imprisonment" hidden on her person. There was a note inside the book, which was meant for her daughter, Little Rose. The note read as follows:

London, Nov 1st 1863? You have shared the hardships and indignity of my prison life, my darling; And suffered all that evil which a vulgar despotism could inflict. Let the memory of that period never pass from your mind; Else you may be inclined to forget how merciful Providence has been in seizing us from such a people. Rose O'N. Greenhow."

"In October 1864, Greenhow received a full military burial in Oakdale Cemetery, Wilmington, North Carolina. Her coffin was wrapped in the Confederate flag; her epitaph reads, "Mrs. Rose O'N. Greenhow, a bearer of dispatches to the Confederate Government." To this day annual ceremonies are held graveside to honour Rose and her contributions to the confederate cause." (Wikipedia.)

## *Fort Johnston - 1861*

On January 20, 1861, James Dardin Keller invaded the Garrison at Fort Johnston, in Southport. An Ordinance Sargeant, James Riley, handed over the key and asked for a receipt. Governor Ellis requested that the keys be returned. Then on April 14th of that same year, the keys were demanded again. Riley mailed them into headquarters, resigned and became a Captain in the Confederate Army.

Fort Johnston was the first fort in the Province of North Carolina, built under the Act of Assembly of 1745 and completed in 1764. It was named in honor of Governor Gabriel Johnston. The fort was a refuge of Governor Josian Martin after his flight.

Fort Johnston was seized again after Fort Sumter fell with the Confederates maintaining this fort until the fall of Fort Fisher in 1865. All that remains are the officers quarters on E. Bay Street in Southport. The original building has been restored and bricked. It was not originally a brick building according to pictures taken in the early 1900s. The fort was officially closed in 1881.

The Fort Johnston Hospital which treated those injured during the Civil War is located just down the street from the Garrison Building.

*The Front Lawn of the Garrison at Fort Johnston, Southport, NC.*
*John Muuss, Photographic Artist. Kate Stewart, model. 2009.*

## *Battle at Fort Fisher*

Fort Fisher was the port open to blockade runners supplying necessary goods to the Confederate armies inland. By 1865 it was the last remaining supply line through to Wilmington.

It was also the largest fortification in the south. Over 500 slaves built the massive earth and sand protection. It was equipped with 22 guns on 12-foot high batteries with two larger ones on the south ranging from 45 to 60 feet high. Interior rooms in the mounds served for communications, hospitals and command planning. They were connected by underground passages and surrounded by a nine-foot high palasade fence.

*The Battle at Fort Fisher*

Wilmington, North Carolina, was the last of the ports used by blockade-runners carrying supplies to the Confederacy; the reduction of Fort Fisher, commanding the entrance to Wilmington, was therefore an objective of the greatest importance. Toward the end of October of 1864, Butler conceived the idea that Fort Fisher could be breached by a gunpowder explosion and that therafter the troops could easily take possession of the works. He had heard that the explosion of powder magazines at Erith on the Thames had blasted houses within a wide radius and broken window panes fifty miles away in the suburbs of London. When Lincoln sent him to New York to keep order at the November elections, a task for which he was eminently fitted. Butler thought that a boat loaded with three hundred tons of powder, if exploded close to the fort, would make a break in the walls through which the troops could enter.

"General Richard Delafield presented a summary of past powder explosions to demonstrrte that the plan was not practicable.....but the officers voted to try the plan. The old steamer, *Louisiana*, worth about a thousand dollars, was obtained at Newbern and loaded with powder." Butler, himself accompanied about six thousand troops to accompany the breach. All were assembled about twenty miles off shore on the 18th of December. Butler anchored about two hundred yards off shore of Fort Fisher, then boarded a tug to go 12 miles off shore. At 1:40 am on the 24th of December, the powder explosion was detonated. Confederate lookouts though a boiler of a Union ship had exploded. It burned like a Roman candle.

Butler did not arrive at Fort Fisher until the 25th. It was a fiasco and was described to Lincoln as "proven a gross and culpable failure."

*Unknown Soldier*

On the 13th of January, General A. H. Terry landed his troops in front of Fort Fisher and on the 15th the stronghold fell.

In summary, two major battles occurred at this site; the first on December 24, 1864 with two days of fighting. On January 12th they returned with a stronger assault and Fort Fisher fell on the 15th of January 1865. Federal ships had bombarded it from land and sea. On the 15th more than 3,300 Union forces including the 27th U. S. Colored Troops, attacked by land. Federal troops captured the fort after several hours of face-to-face battle. The remaining Confederate Army left their remaining forts and within weeks the Union Army marched through Wilmington. Soon after the War was over.

General Newton Martin Curtis (1835-1910) was one of the Union leaders at Fort Fisher. Born in New York the year before the war, he was a farmer. He participated in both battles: December 1864 and January 1865. He was wounded four times in the second attack and was promoted to Brigadier General and awarded the Medal of Honor for that battle. He remained in the army less than a year after the Fort Fisher attack.

Colonel William Lamb was an officer who is remembered for his role in the first battle of Fort Fisher commanding the Confederate garrison. He successfully led the defense of the fort against the Union attack by Benjamin Butler in December of 1864 but Alfred Terry was able to

*Col. William Lamb   (Photo courtesy of Richard Triebe.)*

defeat him in the second attack in January of 1865. Lamb was seriously wounded and eventually recovered. He later became the Mayor of Norfolk, Virginia. He died in 1909.

*Fort Fisher Battle Renactment.*
*(Photo Courtesy of Richard Triebe.)*

Another noted hero of the Battle of Fort Fisher was the Confederate officer, Major General W. H. C. Whiting .

*Maj. General W. H. C Whiting*

Courageous men and women on both sides of the war fought for their beliefs and convictions, but only one side was to succeed. General Robert E. Lee surrendered to Ulysses S. Grant at th Appomattox Courthouse on the 9th of April 1865.

Casualties during the Civil War included 620,000 soldier deaths plus an undetermined number of civilian casualties. The Union had 110,000 killed in action. The

Confederates had 93,000 killed in action. A final count listed (accidents, disease, etc.) 360,000 Union dead and 260,000 Confederates dead as a result of the war. The Union had 275,000 wounded; the confederates - 137,000 plus. Slaves were free and reconstruction had begun.

*Fort Fisher Reactment. (Photo Courtesy of Richard Triebe.)*

*Fort Fisher Bunkers and Hospital.*

*1864. The Army of the James. (June 1864-April 1865). Seven "Contrabands" dressed in Old Union uniforms standing in front of wagon and shack. Library of Congress.*

*Colored Troops. Arlington, VA; Band of 107th U. S. Colored Infantry at Fort Corcoran.*

### Psalms 89:16
*In thy name shall they rejoice--all the day and in thy righteousness shall they be exhausted.*

### Ecclesiastes 3:1-8

To every thing there is a season, and a time to every purpose under the heaven: A time to be born, and a time to die; a time to plant, and a time to pluck up that which is planted; A time to kill, and a time to heal; a time to break down, and a time to build up; A time to weep, and a time to laugh; a time to mourn, and a time to dance; A time to cast away stones, and a time to gather stones together; a time to embrace, and a time to refrain from embracing; A time to get, and a time to lose; a time to keep, and a time to cast away; A time to rend, and a time to sew; a time to keep silence, and a time to speak; A time to love, and a time to hate; a time of war, and a time of peace.

*The Bible*

*Colored Troops with White Officers*

# APPENDIX

## North Carolina Wills & Abstracts from the
## 1600s - 1700s

(Note: All of the Wills are indexed. However, not all of the names appearing in each will or appendix document are included in the index, but the names are highlighted to make for easier scanning. Note that wording and spelling are as read in the wills and do not represent typographical errors or improper grammar…they are as was recorded.)

### Albemarle County -**Bird, Capt. Vallentine** August 2, 1680

We the Subscribers being Ordered by the Grand Councell for the appraismt of ye Estate of **Capt. Vallentine Bird** Deceased wee doe In order hereunto appraise the sd Goods and Chattles as is brought before us to the best of our Skill and Judgment:

Imprimis 3 pr fine holland Sheets

| | |
|---|---|
| at 50 Shillings per paire | 07-10-00 |
| 3 Pr of Course Ditto att 30 s pr | 04-10-00 |
| 1 Ditto Course at | 01-05-00 |
| 2 Prs halfe worne Ditto 15 s Pr | 01-10-00 |
| 3 browne Orsenbrigg Sheets at 5 s | 00-15-00 |
| 1 Pr worne Sheets. | 00-08-00 |
| 11 pillows at 2s 6p | 01-07-06 |
| 6 Ditto at 2s 6p | 00-15-00 |
| 4 Cubboard Cloathes | 00-16-00 |
| 1 fine Holland Cubboard Cloth | 00-08-00 |
| 1 Dozn Daipr Napkins & Table Cloth | 01-10-00 |
| 1 Dozn and 9 Diaper napkins | 01-18-00 |
| 3 Table Clothes | 00-18-00 |
| 6 course Table Cloths | 01-10-00 |
| 2 dozn & 4 Course Napkins | 01-10-00 |
| 16 Course Towells | 01-10-00 |
| 1 fine holland Towell | 00-05-00 |
| 1 Tankard and 1 Dozen Silver Spoons | 13-07-04 |
| 1 Sett Curtains vallens & Counterpans | 01-10-00 |
| 1 Sett of old Curtains and Vallens | 00-10-00 |
| 1 fringed Shoulder belt | 00-10-00 |
| 1 gray Shagd Rugg | 00-10-00 |
| 1 green Shagd Rugg | 01-00-00 |
| 1 Shagd Rugg | 01-05-00 |
| 1 Ditto att | 01-02-00 |
| 1 Dark Cullowed Rugg Shagd | 01-00-00 |
| 1 Large Black Trunck | 00-15-00 |
| 1 Smaller Ditto with Drawers | 00-15-00 |
| 1 small Chest | 00-10-00 |

| | |
|---|---|
| 1 Iron bound Chest | 01-00-00 |
| 1 Iron bound Ditto | 01-00-00 |
| 1 New ffeather and boulster | 06-00-00 |
| 1 ffeather Bed and Boulster | 04-00-00 |
| 1 Hammacker | 00-18-00 |
| 1 bed boulster and pilloe | 05-10-00 |
| 1 bed boulster Coverlet & pillow | 04-10-00 |
| 1 Looking glass | 00-05-00 |
| 1 Glass Case | 00-10-00 |
| 1 dressing box | 01-00-00 |
| 1 Warming Pann | 00-10-00 |
| 1 Bed Stead | 00-08-00 |
| One Pcell of books | 06-00-00 |
| 2 hair Brushes | 00-01-06 |
| 23 Round and Square Bottles | 00-12-00 |
| 15 yd of Keirsey | 01-17-06 |
| 11 Prs plain Shoes at 3s Pr | 01-13-00 |
| 1 Black walnut Table & frame | 01-00-00 |
| 10 Chairs | 02-10-00 |
| 1 Couch at | 01-00-00 |
| 1 Table and frame . | 00-13-04 |
| 1 Table Cloth | 00-06-08 |
| 1 Striped Carpet | 00-05-00 |
| 1 Whip saw | 01-00-00 |
| 1 bed stead and Cradle | 00-10-00 |
| 1 fowling piece | 01-10-00 |
| 1 musket and fowling piece | 01-15-00 |
| 2 Smoothing Irons att | 00-10-00 |
| 1 pair of Stilliards and pea | 00-08-00 |
| 1 Dozen pewter plates | 01-10-00 |
| 1 Dozn Ditto | 01-04-00 |
| 19 pewter poringr at | 01-08-06 |
| 6 Small Salts | 00-06-00 |
| 2 Large Ditto at . | 00-06-00 |
| 2 pewter Candlesticks | 00-05-00 |
| 3 Sawsers at 1s 3p per lb | 00-04-06 |
| 51 Pewter Dishes at | 03-03-09 |
| 4 pewter Basons | 01-12-00 |
| 3 old pewter plates | 00-05-00 |
| 2 Large brass Candlesticks | 01-10-00 |
| A parcel of Tining ware | 02-00-00 |
| 2 pewter Chamber potts | 00-08-00 |
| 1 pewter Tankard | 00-03-00 |
| 1 paire Tongues & Fire Shovell | 00-05-00 |
| 1 brass Kittle: 32 pound at | 02-00-00 |
| 3 skillets at 18 shillings | 00-18-00 |
| 6 bell mettle mortor & pearsell | 00-10-00 |
| 1 posnet at | 00-04-00 |
| 1 brass (?) and Ladle | 00-05-00 |
| 1 frying pann at | 00-06-00 |

| | |
|---|---|
| 3 spitts | 00-10-00 |
| 1 paire andirons | 00-15-00 |
| 3 paire pothooks | 00-06-00 |
| 1: paire racks | 00-03-00 |
| 1 iron pott wt 50 lb at 4p pr lb | 00-16-08 |
| 1 ditto wt 36 lb at 4p pr lb | 00-12-00 |
| 2 dittoes wt 33 lb at 4p per lb | 00-11-00 |
| 1 Lignum vitee punch bowl | 00-15-00 |
| 1 Lignum vitee mortor | 00-02-06 |
| 1 flesh forke | 00-01-00 |
| 1 Cradle | 00-05-00 |
| **Negro men; (vizt: Mingo at** | **40-00-00** |
| **Andrew and Thom: at 35 lb** | |
|     **Sterling pr each** | **70-00-00** |
| **women: negroes Hanna; Betty; Betty; &** | |
|     **Bess at 30 lb Sterling each** | **120-00-00** |
| **Mary ye Indian** | **20-00-00** |
| **Negro boy mustapha** | **20-00-00** |
| **1 Small Ditto named Robin at** | **15-00-00** |
| **1 small negro Girl named Jane** | **15-00-00** |
| **1 Negro Child George** | **10-00-00** |
| **1 Woman Servant named Ann ffarmer of** | |
|     **4 years to serve** | **08-00-00** |
| 1 hand Mill | 06-00-00 |
| 1 sett of wedges . | 00-10-00 |
| 7 weeing howes at 1s: 6p: | 00-10-06 |
| 8 hilling howes at | 00-07-00 |
| 2 old Axes at | 00-02-00 |
| 1 spaid att | 00-06-00 |
| 1 Trowell at 2s: 6p: | 00-02-06 |
| 1 broad ax at | 00-04-00 |
| 1 hand saw at | 00-02-00 |
| 1 Lathing hamer at | 00-01-06 |
| 1 coopers adze & rift | 00-03-00 |
| 22 sheep at 10s: | 11-00-00 |
| **plantation and housen** | **80-00-00** |
| 12: old Sowes | 09-00-00 |
| 30 Shotes | 07-10-00 |
| 6 barrows and board | 05-05-00 |
| 12 cowes and calves at 30s | 18-00-00 |
| 6: 2 year old beasts | 06-00-00 |

| | |
|---|---|
| Total is | 583 lb-01s-03p |
| | **Samuell Daviss** |
| | **Wm. Nevell** |
| | **Jno. Die** |
| | **Signum** |

Tobacco lb

    By 2000 pounds of tobacco Due from **Capt Zacha Gilliam** &c 2000 I the Subscriber Doe present In humble Manner this as A True Inventory of the Estate of Capt Bird of this County Late

Deceased I being his Executrix The Debts of ye Estate being drawne up; I forgott to Bring them; which I humbly Crave Leave to the Next Session of ye Grand Councell; for presentmt of them and that to this Inventory Credits they may bee annexed; November 8th 1680

**Margaret Bird**

The pettionar is Lt Allowed for ye Bringing in of the Debts
**Robt Johnson Holden, Secrata**

++++++++++++++++++++++++++++++++++++++++++++++++++++++++++++++++++++++++++++

### Alexander Lillington's Will - 1697

IN THE NAME OF GOD AMEN. The ninth Day of September, Anno. Dom., 1697. I, **Alexander Lillington**, of Prcint of Peque-mons, being Sick & Weak in Body, But of Good & perfect mind and memory, praysed be God, Doe make and ordayne this my Last Will and Testament in forme following: First and principally, I surrender my Soul to Jesus Christ my only Saviour and redeemer trustin his Merritts & Precious ? Death to have full pardon of all my Sinns; and my Body I remitt to the Earth from whence it came to be decently interred accord-ing to the Discretion of my Executor hereafter named; and for my wordly Estate, after my Debts and funerall Expenses are paid, I give as followeth:

Imprimis, I give and bequeath unto my Son, **John Lillington**, and his heirs forever, my plantation whereon I now live, and the plantation which was formerly **Stephen Hancocks** over agt. mine, and all the Land to each of them belonging, to-gether with my Still & the Implements to them belonging, also my Silver hilted Sword and Belt, the Mills, and my Long Gunn. I give to my Son **John** my ffely'. Gunn and Backsword.

Item, I give to my Son, **George Lillington**, and to his heirs forever, my plantation att Yawpins River, called my Quarter, and my plantation att Little River whereon Francis Penrine lived, w'th all the Land to Each of them belonging. And if in Case that either of my Sons Dyes before they come to age, I give the part of him Soe dying to the Surviver and his heirs, and if both of them Dyes before they come to age then I give my plantation I now live on to my Daughter, **Ann Walker** & her heirs; and my plantation att Little River to my Daughter, **Elizabeth Fendall**, and her heirs; and my plantation called my Quarter, to my Daughter, **Mary Lillington,** & her heirs; andmy plantation which was **Stephen Hancocks** to **Sarah Lillington**, and her heirs.

Item, I give and bequeath to my Children, **Mary Lillington**, **John Lillington**, **Sarah Lillington** **& George Lillington**, & to Each of them thirty pounds apeece, to be paid them by my executors hereafter named, when they shall Severally come to age or Marriage. I having advanced Soe much already to my Eldest Daughters in Marriage.

Item, I doe Will that my wife, **Ann Lillington**, have a Decent livelihood out of my Estate Soe long as Shee keeps her self a Widow; and that She Shall have the management of my plantation in buying and Selling, Soe as that my Said Wife shall dispose of nothing but of the ground of the Said planta-tion, and that for and towards the maintenance of her Self and my Children, and to noe other use.

Item, I will that my wife shall have the disposal' of fifty pounds att her Decease to be paid to whom Shee shall give it to, by my Executors hereafter named.

Item, I will that my children Shall likewise have their maintenance out of the produce of my Stock and plantation, Soe long as they live together on the Same.

Item, I will that all the rest and residue of my Estate, be Equally divided among all my Children, to Say, **Ann, Eliz., Mary**, **John, Sarah, and George**, and to the survivors of them.

Item, it is my Desire that what I have given to my Daughter, **Sarah,** be laid out to buy her a *negro*, to be delivered to her att age or Marriage.

Item, I will that if any of my children dyes before they come to Enjoy the Thirty pound I have given them, the same Shall fall to the rest of my Children or the Survivors of them.

Item, I will that my Executors carry on my Son, **John**, in his learnings as I have begun, and that All my Children be brought up in Learning as conveniently can bee. I doe appoint my Son in Law, **Henderson Walker**, ex'tor to **John Fendall**, dect.

Item, I doe appoint **Coll. Willm. Wilkerson** & my said Son, **Henderson Walker**, Executors of this my last Will and Testament and if Either of them dyes before this my will is Executed, I appoint my Son, John, ex'tor in his Roome.

Item, I doe Will that my Executor have the management of my other plantations till my Children comes to age. And I revoake all other Wills by me made, as Wittness my hand & Seal this Day and year above Written.

**ALEX LILLINGTON** (Seal)
(Impression of Coat of Arms on Seal)
Sealed and Delivered in pres-
ence of.    **CALEB CALLOWAY.**
**JOHN BARRON**,
**ROBERT HARMAN**, Sen.

Att a Genrall Court held S'ber the 8th, 1697, this will was proved by the Evidences Subscribed thereunto By the hono'ble, the Palatin of Court.

**N. GLOVER**, C. Cor.

NORTH CAROLINA.

Whereas, Major Alexander Lillington is deceased, having made by his Last Will & Testament, a true Coppy whereof is hereunto Annexed, **Coll. William Wilkeson** and **Captn. Henderson Walker**, his Executors. These are to impower the Said Wm. Wilkison & Hen. Walker, to Enter in & upon all & Singular the Goods & Chattles, Rights & Credits of the Sd. Alex. Lillington, de. And a true Inventory thereof to returne w'thin one year after the Date hereof, and the Same to dispose of as by the Sd. Will. Dated the 9th. day of October, 1697.

++++++++++++++++++++++++++++++++++++++++++++++++++++++++++++++++++++++++++++

### Thomas Harvey's Will - 1699

IN THE NAME OF GOD AMEN. I, **Thomas Harvey**, of ye County of Albemarle, in ye Province of North Carolina, Esqr., being of sound and perfect memory, but considering ye un-certainty of this life, Doe make and Publish this my Last Will and Testament as followeth, Viz: I Humbly render my Soul unto Almighty God my Creator whensoever he shall in his Mercy call me out of this transitory life, Stedfastly beleeving ye free remission of my Sins through ye pr'tious Meritts of Jesus Christ my Lord and my Redeemer; And my Body I give to ye Ground from whence it was taken, decently to be buried at ye discretion of my Executrix hereafter named. And I doe hereby appoint and make my beloved Wife, **Sarah Harvey**, Executrix of this my last will and testament. Willing that all my just Debts be paid as soon as possibly may be after my death; And ye rest of any Personal Estate, I give one third part to my Sd. Wife, and ye rest to be devided between my Son, **Thomas Harvey**, and my Daughter, **Mary Harvey**; And if it shall happen that my Sd. Wife, shall after my decease bear to me a Child, my Will is that Such my poshume Child shall have equal share of ye two thirds of my p'sonel estate w'th my son and Daughter above named; and my will is that ye parts or portion above bequeathed to my Children, shall be paid to them respectively, viz: to my Son or Sons at ye age of twenty one yeares, and to my daughter or daughters at ye day of their Marriage or age of twenty one yeares, w'ch shall first happen; and if it shall hapen that one or any of my Children shall depart this life before ye time hereby appointed for the receiving of his or their part or portion above mentioned then I Will that the Survivor or Survivors Shall have ye Whole; and if all my Children die as aforesaid, then I Give all my p'sonel Estate to my said loving Wife, **Sarah Harvey.**

Ite. I give, Devise and Bequeath my Land and plantation which I purchased of **Roger Snell,** and my land called *Faulks Point,* containing in all five hundred acres of land, w'th ye appurtenance, lying upon Pequimons River, in ye County aforesaid, unto my Daughter, **Mary Harvey,** and to ye heirs of her Body for ever, and for want of Such heirs to my Son, **Thomas Harvey,** and ye Heirs of his Body for ever, and for want of Such heirs to such issue as is hereby appointed.

Item. I give, Devise and Bequeath my plantation whereon I live w'th five hundred acres of Land thereunto adjoying, w'th all and Singular, ye appurtinances unto my Loving Wife, **Sarah Harvey** abovenamed, for and During the Terme of her naturall life, and I will that the houses and fences thereupon be Kept in good and Sufficient repair.

Item. I Give, Devise and Bequeath my Plantation Called ye Quarter, w'th all my land not Bequeathed and the Remainder of ye Plantacon and land whereon I Live, to my Son, Thomas Harvey, & to ye Heirs of his Body for ever, and for want of Such Heirs to my Daughter, **Mary,** and the heirs of her body for ever. And if it shall happen that there remain none heires of ye body of my said son or Daughter then I give, Devise and Bequeath all my lands and tenements above said (reserving to my Wife her estate for life as is above mentioned), unto ye next heirs of my own body if any Such Shall be, And for want thereof to my Nephew, Thomas Harvey, Son of my Brother, **Richard Harvey,** late of London, Currior, and to ye Heires Male of his Body for ever; and for want of such heires to his Brother, **John Harvey,** and ye Heires Male of his body for ever; and for Want of Such heires to ye Eldest Son of my Brother **Robert Harvey,** of ye Heath in Sinter field Parish, in Warwick Shire, and to ye Heires male of his Body for Ever; and for Want of Such heires to his next eldest Brother and the Heires male of his brother; and for want of Such heirs to ye next Brother in like manner, and if noe Brother remain to ye next heir Male of my Sd. Brother, **Robert Harvey,** forever. (and)And it is my Will that if I shall have more Children than my Son and Daughter w'thin mentioned, then my personal estate to be devided equally between my Wife and Children. And I doe Give to my Sd. Loveing Wife, **Sarah,** my Silver Tankerd over and above her part of my personal estate. And I Doe hereby make void all wills by me formerly made.In testimony Whereof, I have hereunto Sett my hand and Seale, ye 31 day of March, Ano. Domi., 1696.

**THOMAS HARVEY**, (Coat of Arms on Seal)

Signed, Sealed and Published in presence of:
Signum
**HENRY HA NORMAN**
**ROBERT FENDALL.**
**JOHN PIERT,**
**W. GLOVER.**

Item. A Codicil. I do make & appoint Coll. **William Wilkinson**, Executor in my room as I am an Executor unto the Estate of John Harvey, Esqr., deceased, and this I do ordain to be my last will to be joyned to the above, written March 23d. Ano Dom., 1698/9.

**THOMAS HARVEY** (Coat of Arms on Seal)
Signed and published in the presence: **RICHD. FRENCH.**     **RUTH LUKER**. November, y't 2d, 1699.

++++++++++++++++++++++++++++++++++++++++++++++++++++++++++++++++++++++++++++

## John Fendall's Will

IN THE NAME OF GOD AMEN. I, **John Fendall**, of Pequimons Prcinct, being very Sick and weake in body tut of perfect mind and memory, God be praysed, doe make and Ordeyne this my last Will and Testament in forme following:

First, I surrender my Soul into the hands of Almighty God my maker & unto Jesus Christ my only Saviour & redeemer trusting in his merritts and prcious Death to have pardon of all my Sins; & my Body to the Earth from whence it came to be decently Interred according to the Discretion of my Executor; And for the Worldly Estate God bath given me, I bequeath as followeth:

Imprimis. I give unto my Brother, **Robert Fendall**, all my wearing Cloathes; And all the rest of my Estate whatsoever, be it real or personall, in any kind whatsoever, I give to my loving Wife **Elizabeth Fendall**, and to her heyrs forever.

And I make & Ordayne my loving Father in Law, **Alexander Lillington**, Executor of this my last will and Testament. And I revoake all former Wills by me in any wise made.

In wittness whereof, I have hereunto sett my hand & Seal, the Seventeenth Day of December, 1695.

### JOHN X FENDALL

Whereas, Captn. John Fendall, of Pequimons, is Deceased having made by his Last Will and Testament, **Major Alexander Lillington,** his Executor, a true Coppy whereof is hereunto annexed, These are to impower the said **Alexander Lillington**, to Enter in and upon all and Singular the Goods & Chattles, Rights and Creditts of the sd. **John Fendall**, and a True Inventory thereof to return, & within one year after the Date hereof, and the Same to dispose of as by the sd. Will.

Dated the Eighth Day of April, 1696.
**THOS. HARVEY,
DANIEL ABELHURST.
FRANCIS TOMES
SAM'L SWANN.**

++++++++++++++++++++++++++++++++++++++++++++++++++++++++++++++++++++++++++++

## George Durant's Will

IN THE NAME OF GOD AMEN, the ninth day of October, 1688. I, **George Durant**, of the Countie of Albemarle, in the Prov-ince of Carolina, Marriner, being in perfect health and memory, hanks bee to Al'mighty God for the same, and calling to mind the uncertain state of this transitory life and that all flesh must yeld unto Death when it shall please to call and being desirous to Settle things in order, Doe make this my last Will and Testament in Manner and forme following. Revoking and Absolutly Un willing by these presents, all and every testament and testaments, will and wills, heretofore by me made and declared, either by word or by wrighting, notwith-standing any promise to the contrary or clause derogatory in the same, and this to bee taken only for my last will and testament and non other.

First, I bequeath my soule to God my maker and to Jesus Christ my Redeemer and to the Holy Ghost my sanctifier; and my bodie to the Earth from which it came, to bee buried in such decent and Christian manner as to my Executor shall bee fitt and convenient, there to rest untill my body and Soul shall meete again at the Joyfull Resurection; and for my worldly estate I give and bequeath as followeth:

1st. I bequeath to my son John Durant my plantation wheron I now live with the eaquall part of on half of the tract of land belonging thereto to him and his Heiyrs male, lawfully begotten of his own bodie for ever, and the other half of the said tract of land I give to my son **Thomas Durant**, and to his Heiyres male, of his bodie lawfully begotten, forever, and in case of failing of Heiyrs as Aforesaid, that then the of * * either of them is * * (Illegible). My will is that my Nephew **George Durant**, the son of my brother **John Durant**, of London, Shall enjoy the whole tract of land, to him and his Heiyrs male, of his own body begotten, for ever and for want of such Heyers as aforesaid, that then the said plantation and land to fall to **Henry Durant**, the son of my Brother **John Durant** aforesaid, and for want of Heyre male as aforesaid in him, then my other Nephew **John Durant**, the sone of my Brother **John Durant** aforesaid, and his Heyres male as aforesaid, to have hold and enjoy for ever. and for want of Heyers in him I doe give and bequeath my said plantation and tract of land thereto belonging * * * (Illegible). Rights and priveledge for ever.

2ly. I doe give and grant to my loving wife, An Durant, my Said plantation, with all benefitts and profitts during hir naturall life, without controule or any molestation what-soever, and that all the remainder of my estate be equally divided between my loving wife, **An Durant**, and my Daughters **Sarah, Matytya, Pertyenia** and **Ann Durant**, and like-wise I doe here make my loving wife, **Ann Durant**, to bee my whole and Sole Executrix to see this my last will performed, leaving her the trust of my Children untill they shall come to age or marled.

In Witness whereof I have hereunto sett my hand and seale the day and year first above written.

**GEO. DURANT** (Seal)

Signed sealed and delivered in presence of

**JOHN PHILPOTT.**

The marke of

**FRANCIS X HOSSTEN.**

The Marke of

**JOHN C CULLY**

Proved in Court by the oath of Mr **John Philpott** and Mr **Francis Hossten**, ye 6th day of Feby 1693-4  Attested **EDWARD MAYO** Cler  Recorded ye 26th day of Feby, Anno Do: 1693-4, **EDWARD MAYO** Cler.

++++++++++++++++++++++++++++++++++++++++++++++++++++++++++++++++++++++++++

### James Blount's Will

IN YE NAME OF GOD AMEN. I **James Blount**, of Chowan precinct, in ye County of Albemarle, in ye Province of Carolina, Esqr., well knowing the uncertainty of this life, Do make, Ordain & appoint this to be my Last Will & Testament, hereby Revoking & Adnulling all former Wills by me Made, and this Only to be taken & reputed as my Last Will. Imp. I Bequest my Soule to God who gave it; & my body to ye Earth to be Decently Interrd; & as for that Worldly Estate wch it hath pleased God to bestow upon me in this Life; My Just Debts, funeral Expenses & Legaties being first payd, i give & bequeath as followeth:

Item. I give unto my son, **James Blounte**, one Shilling in Countrey Commodities to be pd him by my Executrix hereafter named, w'thin one year after my Discease.

Item. I give unto my son, **Thomas Blounte**, & to my two Daughters, **Ann Slocom & Eliz. Hawkins**, Each of them twelve penc a peice in Country Comodities to be paid them within one year after my Dissease.

Item. I give & bequeath unto my Grand Children, **James & Sarah Blounte**, the Children of my Son **Thomas Blount**, & to **Ann Slocum** ye Child of my Daughter **Ann Slocom**, & to **John Hawkins** ye Son of my Daughter **Eliz Hawkins**, Each of them a Cow & Calfe to be paid to their several parents w'thin three years after my Discease in some sort of Stock to run for ye use and behoofe of ye Sd Children, till they Severally Com of age or by Mariage Capacitated to receive ye Same.

Item. I give & bequeath all ye Remainder part of my Effects Reale & personall whither it Consist in Lands, houses, **negroes, Servants**, Stock, household goods, or any other Kind of Specie w'tSoever, unto my Loving wife **Ann Blounte** for her to have, hold, Occupie & enjoy, During her Naturall Life w'thout Lett or Controule, and att her Death to Dispose out of ye Same to ye Value of Sixti pounds in Countrey Comodities to Whoever She Shall think fitt. And after her, my D Wifes Disease, I give ye whole remainder of my Estate to my Son, **John Blount**, and his heirs for ever; And I do hereby appoint and ordaine that my said son **John** Shall be Decently Maintained out of ye Estate During his Minority. And in Case my said Wife, Ann Should Live till after my Said Son **John** Should come of Age, then if he Should Happen to Marry, or to go to Live in some Other place from my Sd Wife, then Shee to pay him thirty or forty pounds wch Shee please, in Country Comodities.

Lastly, I appoint my Loving Wife, **Ann Blounte**, my whole & Sole Executrix of this my last Will & testament, Desiring her to be carefull in every Article & Clause thereof; & for Confirmation of ye Same I have hereunto sett my hand & Seale, this 9th day of July, In ye year of our Lord God, 1685. March ye 10th &c. Before signing sealing or Publishing I do hereby Appoint yt, in Case My Son Jno Should Dye w'thout heirs Male, then I give & bequeath all my lands & houses to ye Heirs Male, of My son Thomas Blounte & so successively do Entaile the Same on their Heirs Male of my Son **Thomas** forever; But in Case the heirs Male, of my Said Sons **John & Thomas** should both fayle, then I Intayle ye Same on ye heirs genall of my Son **Jno**. first, then of my Son **Thomas**, & if both Should fayl, then of the heirs of My Daughter **Ann Slocum & Eliz Hawkins**.

JAMES: BLOUNTE (Seale)

Signed, Sealed & Published as his Last Will & Testam't in presence of her mark
JANE X MILLER
JNO BAILY
WILLIAM DOBSON
JNO WETTINHALL

This Will Proved by **Jno Hall** and **Jane Miller** on ye 17 Day of July, 1686, And by **Will'm Dobson** on the 11th of July, 1686, who upon their Oaths before me Duely administerd did Attest that they See ye Testator above named, **James Blounte**, Signe & Seale And heard him Declare the Above written to he his last Will and Testament.

SETH SOTHELL

++++++++++++++++++++++++++++++++++++++++++++++++++++++++++++++++++++++++++++

### John Lear's Will

IN THE NAME OF GOD AMEN, The twenty first day of November in ye year of our Lord, one thousand, six hundred, ninty and five. I, **John Lear**, of ye county of Nancemond in Virga. being weak in body and in good and perfect memory, thanks be to God, Doe make this my last will & Testament in manner and forme following, That is to Say, first I bequeath my Soul and Spirit unto ye hands of God, my heavenly father, by whome of his mercy and only grace I trust to be saved and received unto eternal rest through ye death of my Saviour & Redeemer Jesus Christ, in whose precious blood I sett ye hope of my salvation; and my body, in hope of a joyfull resurrection I committ to ye earth to be buried decently as my deare relation shall think fitt. And touching ye disposition of my worldly goods, I dispose of ye same as followeth: First, I will that all such debts as I owe shall be truely paid.

Imprimis, I give to ye widow **Pitt,** my Sister, besides what she owes me, five pounds.

Item, I give ye poor widow **Perdue** of ye Isle of Wight county, five hundred pounds of tobaco a yeare, so long as she lives.

Item, Ye bottles of all sorts, Silk, Silver & gold fringes, as all dresses fitted and made ___ now in ye house w'th belonging to my widow and daughter, as also New wearing linen, I Give to be Equally devided betwixt my daughter _____ **Burwell** and my daughter, **Elisabeth Lear**, widow of my deceased son, **Thomas Lear**.

Item, I give and bequeath my Grandaughter, **Elizabeth Lear**, all that tract & devidend of Land w'ch I leased to Coll. **James Jewell** and is now in possession of Capt. **Robert Randall**, for her life, and after her death to ye heirs of her body lawfully begotten, and for default of such heirs, I give ye said tract of land, being aboute two hundred & fifty acres, lying in Narrowsquick bay to **John George**, and ye heirs of his body; & in default of such heirs I give ye same to my grand Son, **John Lear**, to him and his heirs lawfully begotten for ever.

Item, I give unto **Charles Goremge**, all my lands in Surry County w'th I was about selling to **William Brown**, as per pattent about three hundred & thirty acres, to him & his heirs for ever. and I also give ye said **Charles Goremge**, ye **negro boy Charles** at Kerotan, and **ye negro girle Fanny** there also, & Six Cows and A bull.

Item, I give unto **John George**, ye **negroes Jack & Fido** & to use & plant, if he see good, only, point land whereon ye said negroes are till his own land, given by Coll. **George**, shall come into his hands, & I also give him what cattle is on ye said point belonging to me.

Item, I give my buff suit with fringe jacket & Silk hose unto **James Mountgomery**, in full compensation of his trouble from first to last. All other my wearing clothes linen & woolen I desire may be devided between **John George & Charles Goremge**.

Item, I give & bequeath unto my grand son, **John Lear**, all other my landes, tenements & hereditements _____ nature, quality, together with what leased & for tearme of years, to him & his heirs of his body lawfully begotten. As to all other my accompts, estate, whether merchantable goods, household goods, plate, money, bills, lands and accompts, or any other goods, wares, or merchandizes, of what nature soever, either here or in England, Carolina or elsewhere,my will and desire is, that it be equally shared after a true accompt taken in three parts. The first parte, I give to my grand son, **John Lear**, for ever. ye second third part thereof to my two grandaughters, **Elizabeth & Martha**, children of my only son, **Thomas Lear**, deceased, and in case of mortality ye survivors to enjoy ye deceased or deceases's parte; & ye third and last parte I give betwixt my daughter **Martha Burwell** & her children she had by **Col. Cole** & to ye survivors of them.And ye land I bought of **George Powell** and adding ye plantation whereon **John Mack Williams** did live, containing aboute three hundred & fifty acres, with all houses, orchards, tenements, hereditaments to ye Same belonging, to her, her heirs for ever, anything to ye contrary notwithstanding.

And Lastly, I doe appoint my son in law, **Maj. Lenoard Burwell**, & my good friend Capt. **Thomas Godwin**, my absolute, whole & Sole Executo'rs of this my last will & Testament, & every parte & Clause therein contained, making null & Void all other wills & Testam'ts whatsoever, & this only to be my last will & Testament and no other.

In witness whereof, I have hereunto sett my hand & fixed my Seale ye day & year above written.

**JNO. LEAR** (Come Sigilli)

Signed, Sealed & delivered in ye presence of:
Signum
**WILLIAM W.COFFEILD**
**JOHN LOWE.**
**ELIZABETH BRIDGERS.**
signum
**ANN A COFFEILD**

+++++++++++++++++++++++++++++++++++++++++++++++++++++++++++++++++++++++++++

# N. C. Wills and Abstracts - 1700s

### Henry Irby's Will - 1733

January 30, 1733. February 12. 1733-1734. Sons: **WILLIAM, HENRY** ("plantation up North West and House and Lott in Cape Fair to hold in common with **ELIZABETH,** his sister, and **FORTUNE HOLEDERLEY** their mother"). Daughters: **ANN and ELIZABETH IRBY.** Executrix: **FORTUNE HOLBDERLEY.** Witnesses: **JAMES ESPY, RORT. EATON, WILLIAM POWER.** Will proven before **GEP. BURRINGTON.**
*(Source: Abstracts of North Carolina Wills, By: J. Bryan Grimes, Secretary of State, 1910, Page 179)*

### John Johnson's Will - 1752

March 1, 1750. February Court, 1752. St. Andrews Parish in Brunswick County. Son and Executor: **WILLIAM** ("my land and plantation"). Daughters: **AMEY MITCHELL** and **ANN JELKS.** Granddaughters: **MARTHA** and **ANNE** (daughters of **WILLIAM).** Witnesses: **JOHN CARRELL, WILLIAM HOLLOWAY** and **WILLIAM MOSELEY.** Clerk of Edgecombe Court: **BENJ'N WYNNS.**

### Christian Kince's Will - 1761

December 24, 1761. January 19, 1762. Sons: **JOHN, EDWARD, WILLIAM.** Daughter: **ELIZABETH.** Executors: **JOHN** and **JOSEPH KINCE** and **EDWARD WILLIAMS.** WIFE: mentioned, but not named. Witnesses: **JOHN FILLYAW, SAMUEL KINCE, JOHN HOWARD.** Proven before **ARTHUR DOBBS.**

+++++++++++++++++++++++++++++++++++++++++++++++++++++++++++++++++++++++++

### John McDowell's Will - 1735

March 27, 1735. April 19, 1735. "Master of the scooner called the Jolly Batchelor, now riding at anchor in Cape Fear River, But of Brunswick * * *." Ten pounds is bequeathed to the Presbyterian Church at Dover, Delaware, and five pounds to the Episcopal Church at the same place. Brother: **JAMES MCDOWELL.** Sister: **ELEANOR NISBETT.** Friend: Executors: **HUGH CAMPBELL** and **JAMES ESPY LYDIA JONES.,** of Brunswick. Witnesses: **STEPHEN MOTT, A. DELABASTIE, ANDW. BLYTH, MAGDALEN CAMPBELL.** Proven before **GAB. JOHNSTON.** Provision in will that "a small brick wall be put around my grave wt two marble stones sett up, one att the head and the other att the foot, as is commonly us'd in such cases att Philadelphia."

+++++++++++++++++++++++++++++++++++++++++++++++++++++++++++++++++++++++++

### Richard Eagles' Will

IN THE NAME OF GOD AMEN. I, **Richard Eagles,** of the County of Brunswick and Province of North Carolina, Gen-tleman, being weak in body but of sound mind & memory, and Considering the uncertainty of this Life, do make this my Last Will and Testament in manner and form following, that is to say.

Imprimis: It is my will and desire that all my just Debts be paid out of the Profits of my Estate, by my Executors hereafter named.

I Give and Bequeath to my son, **Joseph Eagles**, son of **Margaret Henrietta Eagles**, my wife, formerly Call'd **Marg't Henrietta Bugnion**, his heirs and Assigns forever, the House, Plantation, Saw & Grist mills, where I now Live, together with all the lands I am now possessed of, Except such as is hereafter given to my Daughter, **Susannah Eagles**, or otherwise; Also I give to my Son **Joseph**, son to my wife **Marg't Henrietta Eagles**, formerly Called **Marg't Henrietta Bugnion**, fifteen **Negroes**, Big and little, as their families shall be; also, his Choice of four Lotts of Land in the Town of Wilmington, together with two thirds of all the stock I am Possessed of, Cattle, Horses, mares, hogs, sheep, &c.Item. I Give and Bequeath to my Daughter, **Susannah Elizabeth Eagles**, Daughter to my late wife, **Marg't Henrietta Eagles**, formerly Called **Marg't Henrietta Bugnion**, Six hundred and forty Acres of Land Adjoin'g the Bank'd piece now Intend for a rice field & Bought of **Hugh Blenning**. Also, one third part of all the Land I now owne on the Island Commonly Call'd Eagles's Island, together with one half the number of Lotts in Wilmington, that I am possessed of Except such as are already given to my Son, **Joseph**; Also, one third part of all the stock I am possessed of Viz: Cattle, Horses, Mares, Hogs, Sheep, &c.

Item. I Give and Bequeath to my Two Cousins, **Jean & Elizabeth Davis**, **one young Negro each**, about their owne Age, to them & their Heirs for ever.

Item. I give and Bequeath to my Sister, **Elizabeth Davis**, the House she now lives on the no. side of the mill Pond, with the field that is fenced in, as long as she Lives, after her Death, to return to my son, **Joseph Eagles**Item. I Give and Bequeath to **Jeanet McFarling**, for and in Consideration of her faithfull and Diligent Care & Attendance in Mrs. Eagles's life time as well as since; **two Negroes**, Vizt: a **wench Called Caelia**, and a **Boy** Call'd **Peter**, to her & her heirs forever; And it is my Desire that she, the sd. **Jeanet McFarling**, be and remaine in the house I now live, to have the Care of the Stock, Poultry, &c., and that my Execut'rs pay her the sum of Thirty five pounds, procl., Yearly until she is married or my son, **Joseph**, Come to the Years of Eighteen; Afterward as long as he shall think proper & no longer.

Item. I Give and Bequeath to **John Eagleson, my Negro boy Jack**, also, I do hereby Assign over to him the Mortgage of Price's Land, Commonly Call'd Judy's Branch, & four Mares & Colts.
It is my Desire that my **two Molatto Boys, Natt & George**, both have their freedom, when they arrive to the Age of thirty five Years. And Also that my **Negro fellow, old Larry** have his freedom, as soon as my son, **Joseph,** Comes of age, 'till which time to be and remaine on the plantation as usual, without being turn'd into the feild or other hard Duty.

Item. It is my will & Desire that **all my Negroes,** Except those already Bequeathed away, together with all my household Furniture, Plate, Beds, Bedding &cs., be Equally Divided between my Son, **Joseph & Susanna Elizabeth Eagles**, Son & Daughter of my late wife **Marg't Henrietta Eagles**, formerly **Marg't Henrietta Bugnion,** and that the remaining half of the Lotts of Land in Wilmington be the property of my Son, **Joseph**.

Lastly, I do hereby Nominate & Appoint, **John Gibbs, Robt' Shaw, John Ancrum, & Thos. Owen**, Executors of this my last will & testament, revoking all other former wills by me made, ratifying & Confirming this, & no other.

In witness whereof, I have hereunto set my hand & seal,
this Twenty third day of March, in the year of our Lordone
thousand, seven hundred & Sixty Nine.

**RICH'D. EAGLES**

Sign'd, Seal'd & Publish'd & Declared to be the last will and
Testament of Rich'd Eagles, In Presence of: (The Date alter'd before Sign'd.)
**JOHN, WALKER.**

Codicil of the Last will & Testament of Rich'd Eagles.

'Tis my will and Desire that Mr. Wm. Dry, has a Title for a Certaine piece of Land Bo't of my Father, Rich'd Eagles & never yet Confirm'd lying and being on the Island near the sd. Wm. Dry's Brick house, he making my Heirs a Title for one Square acre out of the same, on the Side next Wilmington.

**RICH'D EAGLES**

Sign'd Seal'd, Publish'd & Declar'd in the Presence of us, this 23d March 1769.

**MARY WALKER,**
**JOHN WALKER.**
**JNO. FERGUS.**

The within last Will and Testament of **Richard Eagles**, with the Codicil Annexed was proved before me this thirty first day of March, 1769, by the Oaths of **John Walker** and **John Fergus**, two of the subscribing Witnesses thereto, who swore they say the Testator sign, seal, publish and declare the same to be and contain His last Will and Testament; and that at the Time thereof, He was of sound and disposing Mind & Memory. **John Gibbs** and **Robert Shaw** two of the Executors therein named took the Oaths appointed for their Qualification. Ordered that Letters Testamentary issue thereon accordingly.

**WM. TRYON**

+++++++++++++++++++++++++++++++++++++++++++++++++++++++++++++++++++++++++++

### Miles Potter's Will

In the name of God AMEN! **Miles Potter** of the state of North Caolina and of the County of Brunswick Being weak of Body But perfect in memory and having my understanding do make ordain constitute and appoint this my Last Will and Testament and I do hearby disanul all former Will or Wills and declare this alone to be my Last Will and Testament.

First I comend my soul to Almighty God from whence it came and my body to the grave to be buryed in Desent Christian burial at the Discretion of my Executors.

Item I desire that my **negro woman Cloe** may serve my son **Miles Potter** the space, of two years from the day of my death and also **her child Janey**, and then to be freed if agreeable to the laws of the Country; if not consistent with the Law then to be sold at Vendue to the higest bidder, the money to be equally divided between my four sons **Miles, James, John & Robert Potter**, My son in law **Abraham Skipper** my daughter in law **Margaret McMurray.**

Item, I desire **Margaret McMurray** may have my cow named Martha two years.

Item, I desire **Miles Potter** may have my other cattle two years at the expiration of said two years the aforesaid cattle to be sold and the money equaly divided as before mentioned.

Item, I desire **James Potter** may have my two red sows and one Barrow.

Item, I desire **Abraham Skipper** may have one burrow & one sow.

Item, I desire **Miles Potter** may have one burrow.

Item, I desire **my negro woman** may have the two sows called hers.

Item, I desire **John Potter** may have my gun. Item, I desire my Executors raise six Dollars at or before the expiration of two years to pay my debts it being a just estimate of what I owe.

Item, I desire **Miles Potter** may discharge my note of hand of Eight Pounds fifteen shillings due **Thomas Leonard** I having paid him for a discharge of the same, and I do solemnly hereby appoint **Miles Potter** and **John Potter** Executors to this my Will and Testament for the faithfull fulfilling thereof. Signd sealed and acknowledged this tenth of October 1798.

Wittness **Miles Potter** {Seal}

**Nathan Christie** (His Mark)     **Abraham  Skipper** ( Mark)

Additional Comments:
It is probable that son-in law **Abraham Skipper** and daughter-in-law **Margaret McMurray** are stepchildren of **Miles Potter.**

+++++++++++++++++++++++++++++++++++++++++++++++++++++++++++++++++++++++++++++++++

## Robert Potter's Will

In the Name of God Amen

   I **Robert Potter** of the County of New Hanover in the province of North Carolina Joyner, being sick and weak of body, but of perfect mind and memory, thanks be to God for the same, & calling to mind the uncertainty of this mortal life, and it is appointed for all men once to die, do make & ordain this to be my last will & testament. That is to say, principly & first of all, I recommend my soul into the hands of God that gave it, And my body to the earth to be buried in a decent and Christian like manner at the discretion of my executors hereafter named. And as touching such worldly estate as it hath Pleased God to endow me with I give & dispose of, In manner and form following. Imprimus

   I give and bequeath unto **Mary** my beloved wife, all my cattle, horses, & hogs, together with all my household furniture, & my negroe fellow London.

   ITEM- I give & bequeath unto my son **John**, his heirs and assigns forever, four hundred acres of land lying on **Rock Fish Creek on the North East River of Cape Fear.**

   ITEM- I give & bequeath unto my son **John** his heirs & assigns forever, one hundred & seventy five acres of land on **Old Town Creek,** joyning the Plantation that formerly belonged to **Josiah Bell.**
ITEM- I give & bequeath unto my son **Miles** his heirs & assigns forever, two hundred acres of land on Old Town Creek lying on a branch called Russell's Branch.

   ITEM- I give & bequeath unto my son **Robert** his heirs and assigns forever the Plantation whereon I now live, at the decease of my beloved wife.

   ITEM- I will that my tract of land on Rattlesnake containing three hundred & forty five acres, may be sold, & the money equally divided between my three daughters, Viz: **Mary, Margarit, & Elizabeth.**

   And I do hereby constitute & appoint **Mary** my beloved wife executrix, and **John & Robert** my sons executors to this my last will & testament.In witness whereof I have hereunto set my hand and seal this 17th day of June Anno -Domini one thousand Seven hundred & Fifty six.

**Robert Potter** (Seal)
Signed & Sealed -in the presence of
**John A. Grume**
Febry Court 1757
**John Grume**, Junr.

**Keziah K Grume**

above will was proved in open court of **Keziah  Grume**
++++++++++++++++++++++++++++++++++++++++++++++++++++++++++++++++++++++++++++++++

## Jacob Simmond's Will

   In the name of God Amen, twentie fourth day of February in the year of our Lord 1735/6.
   I **Jacob Simmonds** of **Shallotte** in New Hanover Precinct in North Carolina Planter being very sick and weak in body but of Perfect Mind and memory thanks be given to God therefore calling into mind the mortality of my body knowing it is appointed for all men once to dye do make and ordain this my Last Will and testament that is to say Principally and first of all I give and recommend my soul to God that gave it and my body to the Earth to be buried at the discretion of my Executors and

as touching such worldly estate wherewith it hath pleased God to bless me in this Life. I give and dispose of the same in form and manner following.

In Primis. I give to my son **John Simmonds** two hundred and fifty acres of land lieng and being near Little River Butting upon the Sound allso I give to him one Large Chest and one large iron pot and one small iron Pot and a potrack & spit.

Item. I give to **Jacob Simmonds** my youngest son two hundred & fifty acres of **land lieng in the fork of Shallotte** and also one young mair and her increase allso one featherbed and furniture & two iron Pots and the Pewter allso one Red Kow & calf & their increas.

Item. I give to my daughter **Mary** thirty Pounds North Carolina Currency.

Item. I give to my well-beloved wife **Mary Simmonds** whom I likewise constitute, make and ordain my sole Executrix of this my last will and testament all and singular the remainder of my lands goods and chattels to be Possessed and Enjoyed during her life the Legicies not to be Commanded from her before her deceas and then the Plantation whereon I now dwell I doordain to be inherited by my youngest son **Jacob Simmonds** to be possessed and enjoyed by him & his heirs forever & I do constitute & appoint my trusty & well beloved friend **Jonathan Swain** of Lockwoodfolly trustee & assistant to my son Jacob in his minority & I do hereby Revoke & disallow all other Wills ratifieng & confirming this & no other to be my last will & Testament.

In witness whereof I have hereunto set my hand and seal the day and year above written in the presence of:

**Pheebe X Miller**
**Jacob (J) Simmonds**

his mark
**Thomas X Hopcraft**
mark
**Johosphephat Hallands**

NORTH CAROLINA

His Excellency Gabriel Johnston, Esqr. His Majts. Govr. In Chief of North Carolina Before Me Appeared Jehosaphat Hallands one the the Witnesses to the Within Last Will & Testament of Jacob Symonds who being duly Sworn Says that He was present and saw the said Will signed Sealed and Published and that the said Symons was then in Sound and disposing Mind and Memory to the best of the Depts. Memory and belief. Given at Newtown and my Hand 16 June 1736.

Before me appeared **Mary Symons** Widow Executrix to the Deceased and took the oath of Executrix according to Law. Given at Newton 16th June 1736.

**Gab. Johnston**
16TH JUNE 1736.

++++++++++++++++++++++++++++++++++++++++++++++++++++++++++++++++++++++++++++++

**John Sullavind's Will**

In the Name of God Amen, I **John Sullavind** of North Carolina Brunswick County being very Sick and Weak in Body, but of perfect Mind and Memory, Thanks be given unto God Calling unto Mind the Mortality of my Body and knowing that it is appointed for all men once to die, do makeand ordain this my Last Will and Testament that is to Say, Principally and first of all, I Give and Recommend my Soul into the Hand of Almighty God that gave it and my body I Recommend to the Earth, to be buried in decent Christian Burial, at the Discretion of my executor: nothing doubting but at the General Resurrection I Shall receive the Same again, by the Mighty Power of God, and as touching Such Worldly Estate Wharewith it has pleased God to bless me in this Life I Give divise and dispose of the Same in the following Manner and form:

First I Give and bequeath to **Agga** my beloved wife one mare Cauled Fan and bridle and Saddle allso I Give to my well beloved son Hamton Sullavind one Shilling Sterling also I give to my beloved son **John Sullavind** one Shilling Sterling allso I give to my beloved son **William Sullavind** one Shilling Sterling also I give to my beloved daughter **Nanny Sullavind** and my son **Calib**, and my son **Robbin**, and my son **Archer**, and my son **Elcany,** and my Daughter **Paully,** all my stock of Cattle and what Cattle'some of them had before to be Equally devided with my stock and for every child to have a part not one to have more than the other - also I give to my son **Mical Campeal** one Hundred acres of land joining **Bengamin Outlaw** old_ part of the land that I bought of **John Sullavind** and for him to pay to the Estate five hard dollars on the account _____ **Sullavind** and my son _____**n** and my Son **Archer** and my son **Elcany** and my daughter **Paully** all my _____ that the said lands may be sold and the money to be Equally divided among them and all the Dets thats Dew to me, I will that fore horses may be sold for the Use of the family, I will that three Guns may be devided amung the four youngest Boys, and all my houshold furniture to be the the property of my Loving wife **Agga Sullavind** to make yuse of and dispose of it at her own descretion further I will that if Either of the five youngest Children above mentioned should die, what Estate thay have shall be Equally devided amung the Rest of the Same Youngest Children, in Witness Whareof I halve hereunto put my name and Seal this twentieth day of September one thousand seven Hundred Eightty Two

**John Sulavint** seal

Request (**Abraham N (ott? Miller?)** [ **William Sullav-Executors**]

**Will'am Sullavint** Exetor

Signed Sealed and Delivered in the Presence of his mark

**Richard(i) Harriss**

**Peter Hanseli** his mark

**Ann(I)Harriss**

+++++++++++++++++++++++++++++++++++++++++++++++++++++++++++++++++++++++++++++++++

## Abraham Adams Will

IN THE NAME OF GOD, AMAN. The Last will & Testament of **Abraham Adams,** Seiner, being very Sick & weak of body, but of Sound & perfect memory, and Calling To mind ye uncertainty of This Transitory Life, hoping Through ye merits of Death & passion of my Saviour Jesus Christ to Inter in to Eternal Life, do, for avoiding Controversies after my Decease, make, publish & Declare This to be my Last will & Testamt. Revoking and Denying all other former wills by me made & recommending my Soul into ye hands of almighty God who gave it, and my body I commit to ye Earth to be Decently buried at ye Discression of my Exrs., hereafter mantioned, after all my Debts & funeral Charges are paid & Disbursed.

Item. I give & bequeath unto my Son, **Abraham Adams,** part of my Land lying on pamlico River, Beginning at ye fork of ye branch up ye Gut That parts me from Mr. Thomas Icevels, and running up noth Gut to a place Called ye Gum Going, and up along ye branch to ye back Line. Then beginning again at ye aforesd. for and running up ye Eastermost branch to a branch Called ye ISland branch: Thence up ye branch Till It Leaves ye Island, and So Still up ye branch to ye Going Over to make my Tarkiln; Thence aCross ye ridge to ye Savannah to ye back Line, Containing by Estomation Seventy Six acres of Land. which Said Land I give To my Son **Abraham**, and To ye male heirs Lawfully begotten of his own body, whose said Land I will not have to be Sold, Let or mortgaged, but from one brother To ye other.

283

Item. I give unto my Son, **Richd. Adams,** a part of ye Land I Live on in Pamlico River, Joyning upon my Son **Abraham** and Mr. **Thomas Icevel,** being ye upper part of my Land, being Seventy Six acres more or Less to ye male heirs Lawfully begotten of his owne body, wch said Land is not to be sold, Let or mortgaged, but from brother to brother.

Item. I give to my Son, **William,** all of my Tools, my horse, Gun & new Coat.

Item. I, give to my Son, Willoby, a Certain Cow yearling aforsd brown, white faced & her Increase.

Item. I give to my Daughter, **Abbia,** a Certain Two year old Heifer, black pied & her Increase. one Trundled bead Stead & bed & furniture belonging to it. I give to my Loving wife, Barthia, ye use of my plantation, Whereon I now Live, wth all ye rest of my Goods, Chattles & Estate, During her widowhood,

and in Case of Death or marriage, Then my said plantation I give To my son **Willoby** and his male heirs Lawfully begotten of his body, not to be Sold, Let or mortgaged, but from brother to brother, and my movebles, goods & Chattles to be Equally Divided between my Son **William & Willoby & Abia**, my Daughter. and I do hereby nominate & appoint my Loving Wife to be my hole & Sole Executrix of This my Last will & Testament, Revoking all other wills by me heretofore made.

In Witness whereof I have hereunto Set my hand and Seal. This Twenty-Third day of octobr., In the year of our Lord, one Thousand, Seven hundred and Thirty Three.

his

**ABRAHAM A ADAMS** (Seal)

mark

Signed, Sealed, published and Declared In the presence of us:

**PHILLIPS SHUTE.**

her

**MARY X SHUTE.**

mark

**JNO. COLLISON**

At a Court begun & held at bath Town, ye 13 day of march, 1734. Present, **Wm. Owen, Robert Peyton, Henery Croston, Edward Hadley, Wm. Dunbar**, Esqr.

The within Last will & Testament of **Abraham Adams**, Deed. was proved In open Court by ye oath of **John Collison** one of ye Subscribing EvidenceS Thereto. Ordered That ye Secretary have notice Thereof, ye Executrix having Taken Oath by Law appointed. Test. **JNO COLLISON**, Cler. Cur.

(Endorsement) **Abr. Adams** Will. L'res

Issd, March 27, 1734. RFDS.

++++++++++++++++++++++++++++++++++++++++++++++++++++++++++++++++++++++++++++

### Eleazar Allen's Will

IN THE NAME OF GOD, AMEN. I, **Eleazar Allen,** of New Hanover County, in the province of North Carolina, being in perfect health and of sound mind & memory do make and ordainthis my last will and Testament.

I most humbly bequeath my soul into the hands of Almighty God my Creator, the Infinite Father of Mercies, trusting in the alone Merits of his Son our blessed Lord & Saviour, for pardon of my Sins, and through his Mediation & Intercession hoping to be found acceptable at the last day. My Body I comit to the grave to be decently interred, attending a joyful resurrection: For such worldly goods as it has pleased God to bless me with I give and dispose of them as follows:

Imps. I will that all my just Debts & funeral Charges be first, fully paid, dischargd and Satisfyed out of my Estate.

Item. I give devise & bequeath unto my dear & well beloved wife **Sarah Allen**, all the rest & residue of my Estate both real & personal, wheresoever lying & being which I am now possessed of or shall be possessed of at the time of my decease. And to her Executr:, Administrs, Assignes forever, to be disposed by her as she shall think proper. Nevertheless, It is my desire & request unto my sd Wife that she will by her last will & testamt. give devise & bequeath, unto my two Nephews, & Neice, **William Daniel** & **Catherine Willard**, Children of **Josiah Willard**, Esqr., of Boston, by my Sister **Catherine Willard**, All that part of my Estate by me accquired, (& exclusive of what she shall be possessed, by Will, deed, or any writing whatsoever, from her Mother **Sarah Trott** of South Carolina) which she shall dye possessed of, or the value thereof; first deducting my debts, and funeral Charges out of the same, to be equally divided between my said Nephews and Neice or the survivers of them, not doubting but she will fulfill this my request.

Item. I do hereby constitute & appoint my sd loving wife Sarah Allen sole Executrix of this my last will & testament, desiring my good friends, Mr. **James Hassell** & **Nathan Rice** Esqrs., to assist her in the settlement of my affairs to the utmost of their Power. And Lastly I do hereby revoke and annul! all former Wills by me made.

In Witness whereof I have hereunto set my hand & Seal this first day of Janu in the year of our Lord 1742.

ELEAZR. ALLEN (Seal).

Signd, Seal'd, published & declar'd in the presence of us,

SUSANN HASELL,
JAS. HASELL,
E. MOSELEY.

These may Certifie that **James Hasel**, Esqr., one of the subscribing Evidences to the within will, appeared in open Court and made oath on the holy Evangelists that he was present and saw **Eleazer Allen** Sign, Seal & declare the within to be & contain his last will & Testament, and that the said **Eleazer Allen** then at that time of Sound & Disposing memory; and that allso he saw **Susanah Hasel** & **Edward Mosely** the other Sub- scribing Evidences, Sign their names thereto. **ISAAC: FARIES,** C. C.

++++++++++++++++++++++++++++++++++++++++++++++++++++++++++++++++++++++++++++++

### Sarah Allen's Will

IN THE NAME OF GOD, AMEN. I, **Sarah Allen**, Widow, relict of the late **Eleazer Allen**, Esquire, deceased, being weak in Body but of a sound Mind and Memory (thanks be to God.) Do make this my last Will and Testament, hereby revoking all my former Wills.

First, I Commit my Soul to God, in humble hopes of his Mercy through Jesus Christ, and of a joyfull Resurrection, and my body I commit to the Earth to be decently burried, at the Discretion of my Executors, as near the Remains of my late Husband as may be, so as not to hurt the foundation of his Tomb, which was bestowed on him by my beloved Niece Mrs. **Sarah Frankland**.

Item. It is my Will that all my Just Debts and Funeral charges be paid and satisfied as soon as conveniently may be after my Decease, hoping that **Thomas Frankland**, Esquire, my said Niece's husband, (whose Mortgage on the said **Eleazer Allen's** Estate may perhaps go near to Swallow the whole) will not avail himself of that mortgage so as to cut off the just Demands of my other Creditors. For his and their Benefit, however, and to avoid the tedious process of Law and to express the Regard I have for some other Friends and the Justice I would do them, I think it incumbent on me to make this will. And it is my Will that all the Estate, real and personal, whereof I am possessed, except what is in this will specifically bequeathed, be sold by my Executors hereafter mentioned in the manner I shall direct, that is to say, all the produce of my plantation fit for sale, and all other produce of the Labour of **my Negroes**, such as tar, Turpentine,

Corn, and the like, all my remaining household Furniture {excepting plate, my wearing apparel and other things specifically bequeathed) and all the plantation stock of Cattle, horses and hogs, or such of that Stock as can be spared from Carrying on the Business of the plantation (which I would have continued until advice arrives from Mr. **Thomas Frankland** with Direction to my Executors [or his Attorney if he appoints one], how they are to proceed in regard to the Mortgage) to be sold by public Sale to the highest bidder, allowing for enhancing the Sale a proper Credit not exceeding twelve months upon bond and Security for Sums exceeding twenty pounds. But as to the Real Estate and **Negroes** it is my Will that they shall not be sold but at such Time and such place, either here or in South Carolina, and in such manner as shall be directed by the said **Thomas Frankland,** Esquire, his Executors or Administrators having left a Letter of Advice to him on that Subject, Duplicates of which I desire may be forwarded to him by my Executors immediately after my decease, as also a Copy of my Will. And I do fully impower my Executors to make Sufficient titles for all my real Estate which they shall sell according to the Directions and Intentions of this my Will. And if there be any Surplus of my Estate after paying all my Debts as aforesaid, I do, in that case, bequeath the following Legacies. But in case there be no Surplus of my Estate after paying my Debts the said Legacies will depend upon the permission or approbation of the said **Thomas Frankland**, his Executors or Adm'ors. The Legacies are Imprimis. To my beloved Niece, Mrs. **Sarah Frankland**, my Wedding Ring (Plain Gold) as a particular Mark of my affection and a memento of my Conjugal happiness, not doubting hers is equal, and may it be as lasting.

Item. To my beloved Niece, Mrs. **Mary Jane Dry**, I give and bequeath my Gold Watch, not of modern Taste but an excellent piece of Mechanism, the Gold Chain and all the Trinkets belonging thereto to be worn in remembrance of her affectionate Aunt, who living or dying wishes her happiness.

Item. To my beloved Nieces, the Daughters of my Sister **Moore**, viz., Mrs. **Sarah Smith** of Charlestown, Mrs. **Mary Harlston**, of the same place, and Mrs. **Ann Swann**, of Cape Fear, I give a mourning ring to each of them to be worn in remembrance of their affectionate Aunt, wishing to them and theirs a Series of many happy years.

Item. To my beloved grand Niece, Miss **Mary Frankland**, I give and bequeath my Silver chased Tea kettle and cream pot and Lamp, as also my walnut tree fineered Tea chest containing three pieces of plate chased as the Tea kettle, in the form of Urns for Tea & Sugar which I beg she will accept as a small Instance of my affection accompanied with my blessing.

Item. I give to my Grand Niece, Miss **Hariet Frankland**, my largest silver waiter as a small Instance of my affectionate remembrance of her, accompanied with my Blessing.

Item. I give to my Dear Grand Niece, Miss **Rebecca Dry**, as a small Instance of my Affection, a Dozen tea Spoons and Strainer, in a black Shagreen case, almost new, designed to accompany an eight sided silver coffee pot, put into her possession when I went to England in the year 1756 which I also give to her together with a Shagreen writing stand quite new to encourage her in that part of her Education, in which she seems to be making great progress within these late months.

Item. I give to my beloved Mrs. **Mary Jane Dry** my Silver sauce pan.

Item. I give to my beloved grand Niece Miss **Susanah Hasell** a Mohogony dressing table and a little gilt smelling bottle.

Item. I give to my beloved grand Niece **Mary Hasell** a little mohogony tea Chest — these I give as small tokens of my love and kind Remembrance of them attended with my Blessing.

Item. I give all the books of Modern taste which I shall die possessed of to my grand Nieces before mentioned — **Rebecca Dry** and **Susanah Hasell**, to be divided between them as equally as setts can be. And it is my further Request that the books thus bequeathed may be kept for their use and behoof only, not to be lent out and by that means the Sets may be broke before they can use them.

Item. It is my Will and desire that all my wearing apparel of what kind soever be immoderately put into the hands of my beloved Niece, **Mrs. Dry** and my much loved and esteemed Friend, Mrs. **DeRossett**, Senr., to be disposed of as in their Judgment shall seem meet.

Item. I give to my generous and constant Friend, **William Dry,** Esquire, a mourning Ring in Testimony of my Sense of his invarrying goodness to me.

Item. I Give to my loved and long esteemed Friend, Mrs. **DeRossett, Senr.**, my Silver Etice in a black Shagreen Case as a small Instance of my affection.

Item. I ordain that the said Mrs. **DeRossett** and Mrs. **Dry** have the care of all my private papers. It is also my Request that all **Mrs. Franklands** Letters, which they will know by the Indorsement, may be sealed up without opening and be sent to her in England by the first safe hand. As to all my other Letters to and from my several Correspondents abroad and in America as also what Miscellanies I have of the amusing kind I commit them entirely to their Discretion.

Item. It is my Will that my Letters and Mr. Aliens, of which there are several bundles, be kept sacred from the Eyes of any except these my two Friends whose inclination may perhaps lead them to peruse some of them, after this the fire will be the properest Repository for them and all the rest of my private Letters. The other Letters and papers relating to Business must be left with my Ex"ors after named.

Item. It is my Will that One Acre of Land round the Tomb of my said deed husband be reserved sacred for the use of our Cemetery or hurrying Ground by my Executors when the rest of the plantation of Lilliput shall be sold and I do require my Ex'ors to cause a proper pailing to be made round the said Tombstone. Lastly I nominate and appoint my Friends, **James Murray** ,and **William Dry**, Esquires, and **Henry Hyrne**, Gent., Executors of this my last Will in this province and in case of the Decease of one or two of them I do nominate and appoint first **Frederick Jones** of the Oak, Gent., and next **Benjamin Hyrne**, Gent., to supply the place of such Ex'or or Ex'ors deed and I do further nominate and appoint William Bampfield of South Carolina, Merchant, Executor of this Will as to that part of my Estate which lies in South Carolina. In Testimony whereof I have set my Hand and Seal unto this my last Will consisting of two Pages this 28th. Day of January In the Year of our Lord one thousand seven hundred and Sixty one.

Signed, Sealed, published and declared by the Testatrix, **Sarah Allen**, as and forher last Will and Testament in presence of us who at her Request and in presence of each other have subscribed our names hereto,

SARAH ALLEN (SEAL)
GEORGEMOORE ELIZ.
CATH. DEROSSETT
JAMES COLSON.

WILMINGTON 1 April, 1761. The within written will of Sarah Allen, deed., was duely proved before me by the Oath of George Moore, one of the subscribing Witnesses thereto: At the same time **James Murray** and **William Dry** qualified before me as Executors of the within written Will.— Let Letters Testamentary issue thereon to the said **James Murray** and **William Dry** accordingly.

ARTHUR DOBBS

These are to Certefy that **Henry Hyrne** Took the oath of an Executor to the within will before me the 21st February, 1763.

FRED'K GREGG. J. P.

++++++++++++++++++++++++++++++++++++++++++++++++++++++++++++++++++++++++++++

## John Arderne's Will

NORTH CAROLINA, SS. IN THE NAME OF GOD AMEN. I, **John Arderne**, of North Carolina, though in perfect health and strength of body, of thurough and Sound understanding of mind, praised be Almighty God for it; but considering ye great uncertainty of human life, ye many Contingencys of it, ye certainity of Death, have therefore made this my last will and testament, by it absolutely Revoking and disanulling all former Wills by me made, and declaring this only to be my last will and testament in maner and form following: Imprimis. I do in all humillity bequeath my Soul to God y't gave it, and my body to the Ground decently to be Interred as he I shall hereafter Appoint my Sole Execr shall think fitt, in hope and full assurance of a Joyful Resurection to Eternall life, through ye alone merritts and intercession of my Blessed Saviour Jesus Christ. And in relation to my worldly Estate; Since it is too often Seen through ye mercinary and Evil designes of many wicked men, to propagate their own Interest, many plain and interpretive Wills have had false, misterious construction put upon y'm, Directly contrary to ye Intent and designe of ye testator, I do therefore, hereby believing it as a Necessary introduction to ye particulars y't follow, and to prevent all cavells and disputes aft'r my death, most Slomnly declare in ye p'rsence of Almighty God, in Gen'er Terms, yt it is hereby my most true and Sincere intent & purpose to give and bequeath Every part and p'cell of my Estate, real and personall, whether in America, England, or any other part of ye world, unto my dearly beloved kinsman, **William Duckenfield**, Esqr., of ye Aforesd. Province, from whom I have Received ye greatest favours, and to whom I owe ye greatest respect of any person living upon ye face of ye Earth; I further Solomnly declare as a certain truth, as I hope for mercy at Gods hand hereafter, that were I worth Ten Thousand millions of money, and in ye same single state I am in, I would leave it Every farthing to my afores'd kinsman, but for forms sake I shall descend into ye particulars. I know myself to be possest of, and of w,t I have a right to in England, and may hereafter be possest of.

Item. I therefore hereby give and bequeath after my **death unto my most Dear and Affectionate Kinsman, William Duckinfield**, Esqr., all that **plantation** and tract of Land, called and known by ye name of **Salmon Creek**, as likewise all ye **negro, Indian, Molato Slaves** I am now in actuall possession of, and have right and title to, togeather with all ye of horses, Mares, Colts, Cattle, hoggs, young and Old, or any thing besides I have right and title to in America, England, or any other part of ye world, I hereby give and bequeath ye whole and Every part thereof, after my death, to my dearly beloved Kinsman, **Wm. Duckenfield**, Esqr. Item. I further give and bequeath unto my afores,d kinsman, a massy Gold ring, with ye Essines of Death Enamelled upon. it, with this Inscription Engraven: post moementum Eternitas, now in possesion of my very hon'ble Relation Sr. **John Crew**, of Ushkinton, in ye County of Cheshire, in England. Item. I likewise give and bequeath unto my afores,d Dear kinsman, **William Duckinfield**, Esqr., a Legacy of two Guineys, bequeath'd to me by my dearly beloved Relation and Choice friend, ye Exelent **Lady Crew**, now in ye hand and keeping of Sir **John Crew**.

Item. I likewise give and bequeath unto my Afores'd. dear kinsman, all y,t part of my household goods at Clayton bridge house, where my brother Ralph lives, in ye County of LanceShire and Parish of Manchester.

Lastly, I further appoint my dear and loving Kinsman **Wm. Duckingfield**, Esqr. to be my sole Exec'r of this my last will and testament, and to ye full confirmacon hereof, have hereunto set my hand and Seal, in ye prsence of three writing witnesses as ye Law Requires, this 22d of October, in ye year of our Lord

**JOHN ARDERNE.** (Seal)

Signed, Sealed and delivered in ye presence of

**HENRY LYTLE,**

**THO. ARNOLD,**

**GEO BLAINGE,**

+++++++++++++++++++++++++++++++++++++++++++++++++++++++++++++++++++++++++++++

### William Arenton's Will

IN THE NAME OF GOD, AMEN. I, **William Arenton**, of Craven County, and Province of North Carolina, Planter, being in perfect Sound mind and Memory, thanks be to God, but Calling to mind the uncertainty of this life, do make and Declare this to be my last will and Testament, in Manner and form following. & First, I Recommend my Soul unto the allmighty God who gave it, hoping for Pardon for all my Sins through the Merits and Mercy of Jesus Christ my Saviour and Redemer, and my body to the Earth, and as for my Temporal Estate which it hath pleased God to bestow upon me I Give and Dispose of the Same in Manner and form following:  Imprimis, my will and Desire is that my well beloved wife **Mary Arenton** have the use of the Plantation Whereon I now live during the time of her life.

Item. I Give and bequeath unto my well beloved wife **Mary Arenton** One third part of all My Estate of horses, Cattle & hoggs and Household Goods to her and her heirs for ever.

Item. I Give and bequeath unto my three Children, **Rebeccah, Mary and Leah Arenton**, all the rest of my Estate to be Equally Devided Amongst them when they Come to Age or Marriage.

Lastly. I Doe hereby Nominate, Constitute, Ordain and appoint my friend **Henry Shippard** Executor of this my last will and Testament, And I Doe hereby utterly Disallow and Make Void all and every Other will or wills, Legacys and bequests heretofore done or Made, Ratifying and Confirming this and no Other to be my last will and Testament.

In Witness Whereof he hath hereunto sett his hand and Seal
this 23d Day of January, 1761.

W. A. (His Seal)
Signed Sealed Published & Declared by the Said William Aren-
ton to be and Contain his last will & Testament in the Presence of us the Subscribers
**EDMUND HATCH**
his
**MARTIN X SHIPPARD.**
mark

++++++++++++++++++++++++++++++++++++++++++++++++++++++++++++++++++++++++++++

### David Bailey's Will

IN THE NAME OF GOD  AMEN. This sixth day of  October, Anno Dom. 1745. I,  **David Bailey**, of Pasquotank County, in the Province of No. Carolina, Esqr., being  not well in health,  but of perfect mind  & memory,  thanks be  given to  God there fore, calling to mind  the mortality of my body & knowing that  it is appointed unto all men once to  die, do make & ordain  this, as my last will & Testament, That is to say: Principally & first of all, I recommend my soul into ye hands of God that gave it, &c., and my Body to the ground, to be buried at the Discretion of my Exs. hereafter named. And as touching such worldy Estate wherewith it hath pleased God to bless me in this life, I give demise & bestow ye same, in  manner &  form following:

Impr. I  give &  bequeath to  my well  beloved Wife,  **Thamar Bailey**, all the Cattle up Pasquotank River, that I had by her; and also, all other Goods & Effects that were  properly her own before our intermariage,  also the sum of four hundred pounds Current paper money, to be paid to her by my Exs. hereafter named.

It. I give  & order that my **negro  fellow Andrew**, be sold at  a public Venclue, to help raise the afsd. money; & that my wife be i. debar'd the liberty of bidding for him (if she see Cause.) It. I Give

& bequeath to my well beloved Daughter, **Elizabeth Bryant, one negro wench named Joney**, also one Dutch Linnen wheel. It. I give & bequeath to my well beloved son, **Joseph Bailey**, the Plantation whereon he now dwells, together with all the land thereunto belonging, to him & his Heirs for ever; also four steers runing on ye sd. Land. It. I give & bequeath my **negro fellow called Jones**, to my son, **Joseph Bailey**, also my **negro wench called Moll**; also my **negro boy called Luke**;

also the one half of my Whip-saw; also one Steel-Trap; also one Corn Mill; also one Walnut oval Table besides what he has recvd. before. It. I give & bequeath to my well beloved son, **Benjamin Bailey, one negro boy called Mosee**; also Two yoke of Oxen; also my old Flat; also all the Steers clown ye River that shall be in being at my death. It. I give & bequeath to my well beloved son, **Benjamin Bailey**, ye Land & Plantation I bought of **Ebenezer Hall**, containing Two Hundred & six acres, lying in this County, to him & his Heirs for Ever. It. I give to my Daughter, **Sarah Snowdon**, the use & service of my **negro wench called Ruth**, during my ad. Daughter's life, and after her decease I give and bequeath the sd. **negro wench** called **Ruth**, and all her increase, to the Heirs lawfully begotten of my sd. Daughter **Sarah's** body; also three Ews & Lambs.

It. I Give & Bequeath to my well beloved son, **Robert Bailey**, my Land & Plantation, the Folly, to him & his heirs for Ever; also one **negro boy called James**; also the **one half of my negro Girl Called Doll**; also one feather Bed & furniture, wch is now down ye River; also one black mare, wch I Bought of **Joseph Lowry**, branded With E. L., Two Cows & Calves wch is down ye River; also one Case of Bottles; also the half of the new Schooner; also the half of my whip saw, one Steel Trap; one very large Iron Pot, one iron pot Trammel.

It. I give & bequeath to my well beloved Son, **Simon Bailey**, my plantation & **Land Called Piney Point**, lying at Core Sound, contianing Three hunched acres p. Patent, to him & his Heirs for Ever; also all my Cattle upon that Plantation of the Plantation mark, being a swallow fork in ye right Ear, the left Ear off; also **one negro fellow called Mustipher; also the other half of my negro wench called Doll**; also my Will & order is, That the increase of the sd. **negro Doll**, pass, the first child to my son, **Robert**, the next to my son, **Simon**, & so on, and if there be an odd one, the same to be Equally divided between them; also one bed & furniture, wch is in my Room at my son, **Joseph Bailey's**; also Two Cows & Calves, one young mare branded with D. B. & called Wren; also one small Trunk, & fifteen pounds in Gold & Silver in it of Virginia Currency; also all ye Hives of Bees on ye plantation abovesd; also Two Cows & Calves.

It. I give & Bequeath to my Daughter, **Tamar Bailey**, the work & service of my **negro Wench called Hannah**, during my sd. daughter's life, and after her decease, I give & bequeath my sd. **negro Hannah**, and all her increase, to the Heirs lawfully begotten of my sd. Daughter's body; also one bed & furniture, wch is down the River; also one young Mare called no-fail; one Trunk, one white Chest, one Case of Bottles, one Looking Glass, one Box-iron Heaters, Three Pewter Dishes, one set of Tea ware; also one Dutch Linnen Wheel, also one Woolen Wheel made at Core Sound; also Two Cows & Calves, one iron pot that I bought of Sarah Snowdon; one iron pot Trammel; also one young Horse called Button.

It. I give & bequeath to my second Wife's Daughter, **Miriam Overman**, one **negro Girl called Hagar** & her increase, to her & the Heirs of her body. It. I give & bequeath to my second Wife's son, **David Wallis**, the work & service of a young **negro Boy of mine, called Jeffrey**, towards his maintaining & bringing up, till he shall arrive to ye age of Twenty one years; but if the sd. **David Wallis**, shall happen to die before he Shall attain to that age, then the sd. **negro Jeffrey**, to return to me & my heirs; but if the sd. **David Wallis** shall live to the full age of Twenty one years, then the sd. **negro Jeffrey** is to be his for Ever.

It. I give & bequeath to my sons, **Joseph Bailey, Robert Bailey**, & my son in law, **Simon Bryant**, all my neat Cattle Sheep marked with a swallow fork in ye right Ear, the left Ear off; also all my Horses and Mares branded with D. B., wch are running upon the banks at Core Sound, Equally among them; also all the neat cattle upon Hunting Quarter, belonging to me, marked with a Poplar Leaf in ye left Ear. & a Crop & a slit in ye right.

It. I will, bequeath & strictly order, That all the rest & residue of my personal Estate, not mentioned in this will, and wch shall be found in this County, and within the Lord Carteret's line, be sold at publick Vendue to the highest bidder, and the monies thereby arising (my Wife's Legacy first discharged), to be Equally divided between my Children, Viz : **Elizabeth Bryant, Joseph Bailey, Benjamin Bailey, Sarah Snowdon, Robert Bailey, Tamar Bailey & Simon Bailey;** also for my Exs. to take care of my son, **Simon Bailey** & bring him up.

It. I nominate, constitute and appoint my son **Joseph Bailey,** and my son in law, **Simon Bryant,** Co-Executors of this my last Will & Testament, to see the same perform'd to the utmost of their power, utterly revoking, disannulling & making void all former or other Wills, Testaments, Legacies and bequests, formerly by me in any wise made, willed or be- queathed. Ratifying & confirming this & no other, as my last Will & Testament.

In Witness whereof, I have hereunto put my hand & Seal, the Day & year first afore written.

**DAVID BAILEY** (Seal).

Signed, Sealed, published, pronounced & declared by ye Sd. **David Bailey**, as his last Will & Testament, in presence of us the Subscribers:
**THOS. WEEKES, Jurat,**
**PATRICK BAILEY, Jurat,**
**JOHN BAILEY**.
No. CAROLINA. March the 29th., 1746.

++++++++++++++++++++++++++++++++++++++++++++++++++++++++++++++++++++++++++

### William Barrow's Will

IN THE NAME OF GOD AMEN, I, **William Barrow**, of ye pre- cinct of Hide, in ye County of Bath, in ye Prov. of North Carolina, being Sick & weak of Body but of sound and perfect mind & memory and Calling to mind ye Certainety of Death and not knowing when it may pleas ye Lord to Call mee out of this life do make and ordaine & appoynt this my last Will and Testament, in maner and forme following:

Imp: I give, devise & bequeath to my three Sons, **William, John & Richard Barrow,** my Plantation whereon I now live, Containing ffouerteen hundred Acres of land more or les, to be Equally devided between my afsd. three Sons, that is my Eldest Son **William Barrow** to have ye maner Plantation whereon I now live after my Wifes Dec: to be held of them& Every of them their heirs and assignes in fee simple for ever.

Itm. I give devise & bequeath to my Other three Sons, **Samuel, Joseph and James Barrow,** all my Tract of Land lying& being upon Broad Creeke Containeing one Thousand Acres of land more or les, to be Equally devided between my sd. three Sons namd: **Samuel, Joseph & Jams. Barrow** to be held of them, their heirs & assignes Severally, In fee simple for ever.

Itm. I give and bequeath to my Son, **William Barrow,** all and every part of my Smithe tools, and my longest Gun or fouleing peace to be at his disposall when he shall attaine to ye: age of one & twenty years.

Itm. I give and bequeath to my Son, **John,** all & Every part of my Coopers tooles, and my Shortest gun to be at his disposall when he shall attaine to ye age of twenty one years.

Itm. All the rest & residue of my Estate over & above ye legasies before given So Comeing & remaineing boath personall& reall, the one third part of which so riseing I give to my Loveing wife **Eliz. Barrow,** and ye remaineing part after her full one third part so taken oute I give & bequeath to my six Sons before named & to my two Daughrs **Ann & Sarah Barrow** to be Equally Divided among my sd. Six Sons & two Daughs. to be at their disposall, that in my sd. Six Sons afsd. as they shall respectively attaine to ye age of twenty one years & my two Daughs: to have at ye age of Eighteen Years or ye day of marriage.

Itm. My Will & desire is that my Lov. Wife, **Eliz. Barrow**, have the use and ocquepation of my plantation whereon I now live together with all houeses, orchards & all other Conveniances there unto belonging with oute Molestation or Incumbrance dureing her natural life and after her dec: then to myson, **William Barrow**, his heirs for ever more as afsd. that is, my will & desire is that my sd. three Sons, **William, John and Richard Barrow**, Shall not be hendered or debarred fron Seating on Conveniant parts of ye sd. Lands so given them when they shall attain Respectively to ye age of twenty one Years.

Itm. I doe appoynt my Loveing wife, **Eliz. Barrow**, and my Son, **William**, to be Joynt Execs. of this my last will & Testament as witness my hand & Seal this 8th. Day of Jan'ry, 1715.

**THOS. BONNER,**    **W. BARROW. (Seal)**
**THO. MARTIN,**
**JNO. PORTER.**

This may Certifye That on the 23d. Day of Octo., 1716. The above written will was proved by the Oath off **John Porter** before me,
**GALE,** Ch: Just

+++++++++++++++++++++++++++++++++++++++++++++++++++++++++++++++++++++++++++

## An Inventory of the
## Estate of Wm. Bartram

Acres

| | |
|---|---|
| To 1 peice of Land at the Wacanaw Lake Containing | 120 |
| To 1 peice of Land at the Lake known by Bartram Lake Con | 320 |
| Ditto to 320 Acres on Bartram Lake | 320 |
| To 1 peice on the Bluff at the Sugar Loaf Containing | 215 |
| To 1 peice of Land Called ashwood Containing | 640 |
| To Ditto 1 Peice on the No. Est side of the river Called ashwood Containing | 640 |
| To 1 peice of Land at Bartram Low or Lake Containing | 150 |
| To 1 peice at the white Marsh Containing | 120 |
| To 1 Peice at the White Marsh Containg | 100 |
| To 1 Peice at the White Marsh Containing | 100 |
| To 1 peice at the Mouth of Donohue Creek Containing . | . 3 |
| To 1 peice of land on the No Est side of the River containing | 500 |
| To 1 peice adjoining to Ashwood Containing | 150 |
| To 1 peice adjoining to Hezeck Davis Containing | 50 |

To 1 peice on plummers run to be taken at two thirds the Value

| | |
|---|---|
| To 2 peices on Carvers Creek & belonging to the Mill Containing of Land | 490 |

& Mills & Iron works & Utentials belonging to them

To 1 Lot in Wilmington bought of Kinny 23 feet front 33 feet    Back

To 1 Lot Leased to Burgwin      To 2 Lots from Isaac Hill

To other Lots the Deeds in one Keen Name

To 1 Lot in Campbelltown

To Doctor Books & Docter's Medicens & Vials & pots the Number unknown & articles to me

To Some Docter Instruments

To a percil of Docter Drugs the Article & Do Not known

1 Rifel Gun Ditto 1 Smooth Gun

1 Good Saddle Ditto 1 Midling Saddle      1 Silver Watch

1 Pair Silver Shoe Buckels Ditto 1 pair Nee Buckels
1 Stock Ditto 1 Hone    1 Hown harne & 2 razars & a Case
To a percil of Book Accounts for practise of Phisick
1 Iron Tea Kittle 1 Chest    1 Large Cutto knife
1 pair of Shot Moles    1 pair of Bullet Moles
To a percil of wearing apperil  To 1 Mouth peice for a Negro
To 1 Rat Trap    to 1 pair Iron Traces
To 1 Fleshing knife    To 1 Iron to Bake Bread
A Just & true Inventory taken by
      Thos. Robeson Junr Administrator
To the Best of my Knowledge
(Filed Nov. 17, 1772.)

++++++++++++++++++++++++++++++++++++++++++++++++++++++++++++++++++++++

## An Inventory of the
## Estate of William Bartram Senr Deceased
## Taken by the Administrators:

25 old Books of Diferent sorts & percil of other old Books
30 New pewter plates    18 old puter plates & 26 spoons
11 puter Bason    5 puter Dishes 1 Tin pan
14 Earthen plates    1 Salt Sellar & peper Box
3 Tea Kittles    4 Tea pots & one Coffee pot
12 Tea Cups & sassers    4 Candel Sticks & 1 pair Snuffers
3 Earthen butter pots & 1 pan   2 pair fire Dogs & 1 old one
2 pair fire Tongs & 2 Shovels    8 Iron Pot & 2 Iron Kittle
4 pair pot hooks 1 pot Tramel    1 Flesh fork & Skimmer
2 Skillets & Frying pan    1 Iron Spit & Gridiron
1 Iron trivet & bread Tester    6 Wine Glasses & one Decanter
12 Knives & Forks    2 punch bowles & 1 Case & Bottles
6 Beads & furniture 4 bead Steads
7 Chests & 11 Chairs & 14 Sickels
1 pair of Stillards & Scales & Weights
2 Brass Morters & 1 Iron Morter
3 Tables & 1 Safe & 4 Jugs
2 Wier Sives & 2 pair flat Irons
2 Looking Glasses & 1 Desk    3 pails 2 piggens & 1 tub
2 Churns & 2 Keelers    1 pair of hand Mill Stones 1 Grinding Stone & whet Stone
1 Avil Bellow & 2 Vices 3 hammers 1 Sledges & 2 Service plates
3 pair of tongs & a percil of files
1 Rost Meet hook & Melting Ladle    1 pair of Brass button Molds
1 pair of Spoon Molds    1 pair of Shot Molds
2 Big wheals & 2 Little Wheals
2 pair of Cards & 1 pair Tow Combs
2 Hackels & 1 pair wosted Combs    3 pair bar plow Irons
2 Flacks Iron without Colters    6 pair of Iron Traces
12 Weading hows & Six axes    3 Iron Wedges & 1 frow
1 Cross Cut Saw & 1 Tennent Saw
3 hand Saws 6 Chissels 1 gaug
1 Ads & 2 Augers & 2 old Cross Cut Saws
1 pair Timber wheals & 1 pair Cart wheals

2 Ox Chains & 1 Timber Chain      2 Grubbing hoes & 3 Spaids

1 Still & worm

1 Iron Cotton Gin & 1 Coffee Mill      6 old Gun Barrels

2 Iron Cart hoops & 3 small Boxes    3 old Guns & 1 Cookin Iron

7 Rasors & a percil of Snipe Bills

1 Good Mill Saw & 5 old Mill Saws

2 Cooper howels & 6 pair Bridel bits

1 Surveyers Cumpas & Chain

4 pair of Sturrip Irons & one odd one     1 pair of Money Scales

3 old Swords & 3 Trupers Pistols

2 horse Locks & 1 pair tooth Drawers

1 pair Dore hinges 1 pair of Window Ditto

1 Gun Lock & Staples & ring for Ox Yokes

6 Ox or horse Bells      1 piece & 1/2 of gert webing

1 Cag with some powder & a peice of Lead

1 Shoe Maker hammer & pinchers & Some other Shoe Maker Tools

1 old Steal Mill      1 Set of Brass for a Gun

8 New bells Not Brased      1 Mouth peice to put on Negroes

1 pair Iron hoppels for Negroes

1 hand vice & 1 piece of old Copper Kittle &    4 plow Clevis

1 Glue pot & a percil of Glue   2 puter quarts &   1 puter Tankerd

1 pair of Leather Bags   1 peice of old Crank & a percil of old Iron

5 Hogsheads & 2 Powdering Tubs 2 yards of Black Cotton Velvit

1 1/2 yards of Snuff Colered Velvit

63 head of hogs of Diferent Sorts      11 two year old Bulls

14 Barren Cows      4 three year old Bulls

8 year old heffers      34 Cows & Calves

8 two year old heffer      2 one year old Bulls

2 three year old stears      6 for year old stears

2 five year old stears      3 two year old stears

11 working Oxen      3 Stallions

5 Mairs      3 one year old Mairs

1 two year old Mair      1 Mair & Colt

4 plow horses      3 Riding horses

1 four year old horse      1 horse sold by W Bartram Junr

23 head of Sheep      2 Gaurges & 1 hand Saw 2 Chissels

3 Augors 2 Drawing knives      2 Ox or horse Bells

1 Curring knife & Steal

2 Flats one in the river the other in the Mill pond

1 old pair of Timber Wheals      1 old pair of Cart Wheals

4 Ox Yokes 1 pruning knife

3 horses      4 Barrels Locks instead of pad locks

1 Harrow with 10 Iron teeth

1 Iron Instrument to Make Lines or Ropes & a parcil of Gun Worms

1 Little Old Conno      1 two foot Scale

**11 Negro Men & Boys**      **8 Negro women & Girls**

**3 Negro Children**      **8 Negro Children Boys & Girls**

percil of Notes of hands & orders if Can be recovd to the Amount
of £143: 11: 1:1/4      To a proved Account £20: 14: 8

To 23 pounds in Cash

To a percil of Sundrey Book Account unSettled the Amount Not known
To Some horses & Mairs & Some Cattle Supposed to be runing in the woods the Number Not known
17 Thousand feet of Marchint Lumber
5 Thousand feet Marchantbb in town
**A percil of Slaves the number Not known**
About 240 Bushels of Indian Corn
9 head of Cattle killed for use
11 head of hogs killed for house use

The within is a Just & true Inventory taken by us to the best of our Knowledge

**Wm. Bartram**
**Thos Robeson Junr**

+++++++++++++++++++++++++++++++++++++++++++++++++++++++++++++++++++++++++++++++

## Thomas Bell's Will

IN THE NAME OF GOD, AMEN. I, **Thomas Bell**, of Albemarle County, Gentn., being of Sound and Perfect mind and memory, doe make, Ordaine, constitute and declare these presents to be and contain my last Will and Testiament, hereby revokeing & makeing Null and Void all former and other Wills by me heretofore made or declared.

Imprimis. I give devise and bequeath unto my Cousen, **William Bell**, and to his Heirs for ever, all my Tract of Land called Matthew's Point in Perquimains Precinct.

Item. I give devise and bequeath unto my Cousen, **Thomas Bele**, Son to my Brother, **John Bele**, and to his Heirs for ever Fifteen Acres of Land out of my Tract of Land joyning on Kendricks Creek, it being the Tract of Land on which I now live, and to be laid out according to the discretion of my Execut's hereafter named, so as to take in & include the **Plantation** that is cleared & the House now built at the Back Landing; Also Two hundred Acres of Land more to be laid out by my Executo's as aforesaid so as to joyne on the deep Runn & Swamp or division between my land and Mr. **Cullen Pollocks** & so as not to take in or include my Plantation that is Cleared at the deep Runn.

Item. I give devise and bequeath unto my Cousens, Ann & Jane, the Children of my Brother, **John Bell**, the Sum of Fifty Pounds (the currancy of this Country) to each, to be paid unto them Severaly as they shale arrive to full age or day of Marriage which shall first happen.

Item. It is my Will that my Executs. hereafter named or the survivor of them doe see that out of the profitts annualy arriseing by my Estate, they doe maintain & Educate m Cousins, **Thomas,** and **Anne,** Children of my Brother, **John**, in as handsome and good a manner as may be.

Item. Is my Will that ale the residue of my Estate boath real & personal be and remain unto my Loveing Wife, **Elizabeth,** dureing her life, and after her dcease unto my Cosen, **William Mackey**, & his heirs for ever. Provided & be it hereby understood that if my Cousen, **William Mackey**, shall depart this life before my Wife; or dye without Heirs lawfully begotten by him, that then all my said Estate boath real & Personal be and remain (after the Decease of my Wife) unto my Cousen, **Thomas Bell**, the Son of my Brother, **John Bell** & his Heirs for ever.

Item. It is my Will that no Sale be made of **any Slaves** or Stock, but that my Estate be kept intire as it now is as near as possible dureing ye life of my Loving Wife, **Elizabeth**, excepting my Sloop which I leave to the discretion of my Executors hereafter named to employ or dispose of as they shall think most proper.

Lastly, I doe make Nominate & appoint my Loveing Wife, **Elizabeth,** and Loveing Cousen, **William Mackey**, to be Executrix & Executor of this my Will & Teastiament whome I desire to see all Parts of this my Will performed.

In Testimony whereof, I, the said **Thomas Bell**, have hereunto put my hand & Seale this Eleventh day of December,

One thousand, Seven hundred & Thirty three.

THOS. BELL. (Seal.)

Signed, Sealed, Published & declared to be my last Will &
Testiament (being Interlined, with ye words [after ye Decease of my Wife]) in Presence of us.
SAML. DURRANCE.
W. DOWNING,
her
HANAH H GIRKIN.
marke

CHOWAN, Sc.                    January Court, 1733.

++++++++++++++++++++++++++++++++++++++++++++++++++++++++++++++++++++++++++++

### William Carr's Will

IN THE NAME OF GOD AMEN. I, **Willaim Carr**, of the County of Duplin, & Province of
North Carolina, Am Sick in Body, but perfect In Memory and of a Sown Judgment, Blessed be God
for It, and having Called to Mind the Scertainty of Death and of a future State, and that it is appointed
for all Men Onest to Die Do hereby Recommend My Soul to God, and my Body to the Earth to be
Buried at the Descration of my Executors, whome I shall hereafter Name, And in hopes of a Glorious
Res- urraction through the Merits of My Lord and Saviour Jesus Christ; Do hereby as far as Almighty
God Enabels me in this My present Condition, Do Renounce the World & the Things of this Life,
andby these Presents Do Constitute andOrdain, this to he my last Will & Testament, Revocking all
other Wills and Testament by me Made, Either by Word or Writing, and this only to Stand and remain
for my last Will & Testament: Therefore Doth Order, Settle & Leave what Woreldey Estate God bath
Blessed me with, In the following Manner, Viz:

Itam. I Order that all my Just Debts & Funeral Expenses be first Pay'd out of my Estate That
Almighty God hath Now Blist me with, And the rest of my woreldey Substance I leve and Bequeath
In the following Manner, Viz:

Itam. I Leave & Bequeath to my Beloved Wife, **Hannah**, The one third part of all my Moveable
Estate after my Lawful Debts & funeral Expences is pay'd, together with the Houses & plantation
where I now live to Such times as My Son, **Archibald** Carr, comes to ye age of Twenty one years,
and then the Sd. Houses & Plantation to be his for Ever. But In falure of him to ye Nixt Heir In Law
& so on; And the rest of my Goods & Chattles, after my Just Debts and Funeral Expenses is pay'd,
and the one Third of ye rest of ym. taken off to my Wife, as afsd., then ye remainder I leave &
Bequeath to beDivided Equaly In it's kine Amongs my other Children, Viz: **Archibald Carr, Jane
Carr**, & ye one that is yet unborn if it Should pleas God that it comes to the woreld; and In case that
any of ye children Should Die before that they arive to age; I order that the part of the Deceased shall
be Equally Devided Amongst the rest of the Surviving Children.

To Which Last Will & Testament, I Do hereunto set my Hand and fix my Seal, this fifth Day of
December, In the year of our Lord, One thousand, Seven Hundred and fifty Three; I order & appoint
my Beloved Wife, **Hannah,** Executor of this my Last Will and Testament.

WILLIAM CARR. (Seal)
Signed, Sealed, and Declared In presents of Us:
JOHN DICKSON.
WILLIAM MCREE.
SUSANNAH McALEXD.
NORTH CAROLINA, DUPLIN COUNTY, SS. October Court, 1754.

++++++++++++++++++++++++++++++++++++++++++++++++++++++++++++++++++++++++++++

## Thomas Clifford's Will

IN THE NAME OF GOD AMEN. I, **Thomas Clifford**, Esqr., late of Charles Town in South Carolina, but at present residing in New Hanover Precinct, in North Carolina, Do Make and declare these presents to be and contain my last Will and Testament:

Imprimis. I Will that all those Debts which I owe in Right or Conscience be truly and Justly paid by my Executrix hereafter named within some reasonable time after my decease.

Item. I Give, Devise & Bequeath unto my Loving wife, **Mary**, all the rest & Residue of my Estate whether Real or personal, to her and her heirs and Assignes for ever.

Hereby naming, Constituting and appointing my said wife, Mary, Sole Executrix of this my Last Will & Testament, Revokeing all other Wills by me heretofore made or Declared.

In Testimony whereof I have hereto put my hand and Seal, this Nineth day of October, Anno Dom., 1735.

**T. CLIFFORD** (Seal)

Signed, Sealed, published and Declared In presence of :

**M: MOORE.**

**ELIZA: SWANN.**

**E. MOSELEY.**

NORTH CAROLINA:

Personaly appear'd Maurice Moore, Esqr., one of the Evidences to the within Last Will and Testament, who being Sworn on the holy Evangeist of Almighty God, saieth, That he saw **Thos. Clifiord** sign, Seal a declare this to be and contain is Last Will and Testament, and that he was of sound mind and disposing memory, and that he saw **Eliz: Swann** and **Edward Moseley** sign as Evidences thereto at the same time.

**GAB. JOHNSTON**

+++++++++++++++++++++++++++++++++++++++++++++++++++++++++++++++++++++++++++++++

## Jean Corbin's Will

IN THE NAME OF GOD AMEN. I, **Jean Corbin**, of New Han-over County, Widdow and Relict of Francis Corbin, late of Cho-wan County, in the Province North Carolina, Esqr., being weak in body, but of perfect Sound & disposing Mind and Memory, do make this my last Will and Testament in Manner following: And first I resign my Soul in to the hands of my all merciful' God, in hopes of a Joyfull resurrection thro' the Mediation of a Blessed Redeemer; And as to my worldly Goods and Estate I Give, Devise, and Bequeath in manner following:

First. Whereas, by a certain Marriage Settlement, or Indenture Trepartite, bearing date the Twenty eight day of October in the Year of Our Lord one Thousand Seven hundred & Sixty one, and Executed between me and my said late Husband **Francis Corbin** and **Samuel** and **John Swann** Trustees named in the sd Indenture, I have an absolute and disposing right in and of a Moiety of **three plantations**, Tracts or parcels of land, Lying and being on the Eastermost Branch of Long Creek in New Hanover County containing in the whole Twelve hundred and Sixty Acres, Also One Other plantation Tract or parcel of Land, lying and being on the North East Side of the North West branch of Cape Fear River, Joining the upper side of the late Henry Simmon's Land; Also One Other Plantation Tract or parcel of Land containing One hundred & eighty Acres lying and being in Bladen County on the West side of the North west branch of Cape Fear River, Joining Mcknight's land; Now I Give Devise & Bequeath to **John Rutherfurd Junier, William Gordon Rutherfurd** and **Frances Rutherfurd** (Children of my good friend of my good friend **John Rutherfurd** of New Hannover County Esquire) and their respective Heirs and Assigns forever, to be equally devided between them, the Moieties of the said several Plantations Tracts or Parcels of Land. And it is my Will, Intention, and direction, that in the partition of the said Parcels of Land,

regard be had as well to the Value as the quantity, so that each Devision be in Value & quantity nearly equal.

Item. I Give and Bequeath to the said **John Rutherfurd Junior, William Gordon Rutherfurd,** and **Frances Rutherfurd,** All my **Negroe Slaves**, wch I hold and Possess or am entitled to, as well by Virtue of the aforementioned Indenture or Other- wise, (and not Otherwise disposed of by this my Will) and wch I may at the time of my decease, hold, possess have, or be entitled to, together with all my Stocks of Cattle Horses, Sheep & Hogs, with All my Plate, Houshold & Kitchen furniture,Plantation Tools, and implements of Husbandry of whatever kind or Sort they may be wch I shall die possess'd of.

Item. I Give and Bequeath to the said **John Rutherfurd Junier, Wm Gordon Rutherfurd,** and **Frances Rutherfurd** all arrears of money due or growing due to me, as my Jointure or annuity of One hundred & Twenty Pounds per Annum from the Death of my said late Husband, Francis Corbin, and provided to me, by the aforemention Marriage Settlement.

Item. I Give and Bequeath to my Good Friend **Thomas Holloway,** the **Use of my Negroe boy Exeter** (wch he now has in his possession) for and during the Term of his Natural Life,and after his decease I Give the said **Negroe** to **John Rutherford Junier, William Gordon Rutherfurd,** and **Frances Rutherfurd.**

Item. It is my Will and desire, that my old **Negroe fellow Peter**, who hath Long & faithfully Served me, be, at the time of my death Liberated & Set free, and it is my further Will and direction that my Executors herein named, pay him Eleven pounds proc
money pr Annum during his natural Life, as a reward of his fidelity, and for his Support and Maintenance.

Item. Whereas I have advanced & paid several sums of my own Monies, for and upon Amount of the Estate of my late Husband, **Francis Corbin,** wch said sums are still in Ar-

**JEAN CORBIN**

rear & unpaid to me; it is therefore my Will and desire that all the accts between the sd Estate & myself (wch shall be unsettled at my decease), be settled, as Soon as the same can be done; and the balances & monies due me thereon recov- ered; All wch balancies & Monies, I Give to the sd **John Rutherfurd Junier, William Gordon Rutherfurd** and **Frances Rutherfurd.**

Item. Whereas my good friend **John Rutherfurd** Esqr: has had, at different times the Labour & Service of several of my negroes Slaves; now my will and desire is, that no Accts. or charge, be made or brought against him for the Same And my Will & meaning is, that he be acquitted & discharged of & from any demand therefor; And Also that he be acquitted exonerated & discharged from all Other Debts, dues, demands, or Claims of what nature or kind soever wch I may have against him.

Item. It is my Will and direction that all my Just debts be first paid as soon as may be, either by the hire, work & La-bour of my Slaves, or by the Sale of so much of the most per- ishable part of my Estate, and wch may be of the best use and benefit to the sd **John Rutherfurd Junier William Gordon Rutherfurd** and **Frances Rutherfurd**; or by both, as my Exec- utors shall Judge necessary.

Item. I Give Devise & Bequeath to the sd **John Rutherfurd Junier William Gordon Rutherfurd** and **Frances Rutherfurd** All the rest residue and remainder of my real and Personal Estate, not herein particularly devised, of what nature or kind soever or wheresoever it may be found.

Item. And for the more Clear, and better Understanding of this my will, and to prevent disputes and contraversies thereon, I hereby declare my design to be, that all the Several Slaves, Stocks, Plate, houshold & kitchen furniture together with ever Other article or Articles, thing or things Devised, Given and bequeathed, or intended to be Devised Given and

298

bequeathed by this my Will to the said **John Rutherfurd Junier, William Gordon Rutherfurd** and **Frances Rutherfurd**, be equally divided among them, share and share alike, and in Case of the death of either of them, the Share to have fallen to such party, to goe to the Survivors or Survivor.

And further, my Will and positive directions are, that All the Lands, Stocks, Plate, houshold & kicthen furniture, to- gether with every Other Article or Articles Thing or Things, Devised, Given & Bequeathed by this my Will to the sd **John Rutherfurd Junior William Gordon Rutherfurd** and **Frances Rutherfurd** shall be, and remain in the keeping, and Under the direction Care & management of my sd good friend **John Rutherfurd** Esqr.; and after the payment of my Debts, he to receive all the profits, emoluments and benefits ariseing andaccruing therefrom, to enable him the better to Educate, Sup- port, and Maintain his said Children, without being further accountable for the Same, untill the Marriage of the sd **Frances Rutherfurd,** at wch time the said Frances to have her Share or Portion thereof; And the Residue or the Remainding parts or Shares, to continue and remain under the Care, direction and Management of the said **John Rutherfurd** Esquire, and he in like manner to receive all the profits, emoluments, and benefits ariseing and accruing from the sd residue or remaind- ing parts or Shares (to enable him to Educate, Maintain & Support the sd **John Rutherfurd Junier, & William Gordon Rutherfurd**) without being accountable therefor, for such time, and so long as he shall think proper; to retain & keep the same.

Lastly. I do nominate, constitute, and appoint, my good friends **Lewis Henry Derosset** and **John Rutherfurd** Esquires and Mr **Thomas Holloway** Executors of this my last Will, contained in Six pages, each page being Signed at the Bottom with my own hand; revoking all former Will and Wills by me heretofore made.

**JEAN CORBIN**

In Witness Whereof I have hereunto Set my hand & Seal
the 10th February 1775

**JEAN CORBIN** (Seal)

Signed Sealed & Published by the said **Jean Corbin** for and as
her last Will and Testament in the Presence of
**SAM ASHE     DANIEL MORGAN
DAVID MORGAN**

+++++++++++++++++++++++++++++++++++++++++++++++++++++++++++++++++++++++++++++++++

### Moses John DeRossett's Will

IN THE NAME OF GOD AMEN. I, **Moses—John DeRosset**, of Wilmington, in the province of North Carolina, practioner in physic and Surgery, being of sound and disposing mind and memory, do make this my last will and testament, in manner and form following, that is to say:

First of all, I order that my executors hereinafter named dopay all my just debts and funeral expences; Also I give, be- queath and devise all my estate, both real and personal, of what kind or quality soever, to my beloved wife, Mary, and to my daughter, **Magdalene-Mary** & my son, **Armand - John**,their heirs and assignes forever, to be equally divided among, them, share and share alike; and I do make my said wife exec- utrix, and my brother, **Lewis—Henry DeRosset** and my friends, **John DuBois, James Moore** and **Marmaduke Jones**, esquires, executors of this my last Will and testament, hereby revok- ing all wills by me heretofore made.

And I do also nominate and appoint my said executors to be guardians of my said son and daughter until they shall arrive at the age of twenty one years of age respectively. And in case both my children should die before they shall arrive atage, or the day of Marriage, then it is my will that my whole estate should belong to my said wife, to hold to her heirs and assigns forever.

In witness whereof, I have hereunto set my hand & seal & published this as my last will and testament, the thirtieth day of November, in the year of our Lord one thousand, seven hundred and sixty seven.

**MOSES JNO. DEROSSETT (Seal)**

Signed, sealed, published and declared by the above named testator as & for his last will and testament, in his presence, in the room where he was, & in the presence of each other: (the words "their heirs & assigns forever" being first interlined).

**ANN MOORE.**
**E. JUSTICE.**
**A. MACLAINE.**

WILMINGTON, the 1st Of March, 1768.

**Archibald Maclaine**, Esquire, one of the Subscribing Witnesses to the within Will personally appeared before me and made oath that he saw the within mentioned **Moses John DeRossett**, the Testator, Sign, Seal, publish, pronounce and declare this to be his Last Will and Testament; and that at the Time thereof he, the Testator, was of sound and disposing mind & Memory accordingto the best of this Deponents knowledge and belief.

**WM. TRYON**

+++++++++++++++++++++++++++++++++++++++++++++++++++++++++++++++++++++++++++++++++++

### Arthur Dobbs Will

IN THE NAME OF THE ALMIGHTY GOD AMEN. I, **Arthur Dobbs**, of Brunswick, in New Hanover, Governor and Captain General of the Province of North Carolina, in America, injoying a moderate state of health and having by the blessing of the infinitely perfect and good God the Father Almighty, a perfect and sound mind and memory, do make this my last Will and Testament in manner following:

First, I recommend my soul to the Almighty Triune God, **Jehovah Elohim** and his only Begotten son, Jesus Christ my God and only Saviour and Redeemer and to his Holy Spirit Blessed forever; and my Body to the Earth to be decently and privately interred, in an assured and full hope of a Glorious and happy Resurection with the Just, at the first Resur-ection and a Blessed immortality in the Heavenly Kingdom of Christ the Messiah, untill he shall deliverup his Mediatorial Kingdom to God his Father when he shall be all in all hisCreatures; and instead of immoderate Funeral Expenses, I desire that one hundred pounds, Sterling Money, maybe paid and distributed proportionally among the Housekeepers of the Parrishes of Ballynure and Kilroot in the County of An- trim, and Kingdom of Ireland, and one other Hundred pounds like Money among the Poore Freemen House keepers who reside within the County of the town of Carrick Fergus, in thesaid Kingdom, to be paid out of my Personal Estate which I may be intitled to at the time or my Decease out of my Demesnes at Castle Dobbs, or out of the arrears of Rents I re- served out of a Moiety of my Lands in that Kingdom during my Life, at the Discretion of my Executors hereinafter to he named; desiring that my Body may be Buried in the parish or place where it pleases God that I shall die: And as to the Disposition of the Worldly Estate which I may die possessed of, my funeral Espences and Debts being first paid, I give, devise and bequeath as followeth, that is to say:

First, I do confirm in the most ample manner the Settle- ment made on my son, **Conway Richard Dobbs**, on his Marriage in July, 1749, in which is included the several remain- ders and Fortunes to my Younger Children and to his and their Issue.

Item. I confirm unto my Younger Son, **Edward Brice Dobbs,** (over and above his fortune secured in that Marriage settlement, which I hereby limit and Ascertain to be One thousand pounds, Lawful Money of Ireland, is mentioned in my Marriage settlement upon my intermarriage with my first Wife) all the Lands in America, which are Specified in a Deed or Deeds which I made to him and his Heirs since my Setling at Brunswick; together with all the Slaves, goods & Chattles, therein mentioned.

Itim. I give, devise and bequeath unto my beloved Wife, **Justina Dobbs**, and her Issue, by me Begotten, in case she shall have any or be pregnant at the time of my Decease, all the **Slaves** and other Chattels which was or shall be hereafter given her by her Father.

Item. I give, devise and bequeath unto my said beloved Wife, all **my Slaves**, goods and Chattles, Plate, Money and other Effects of what Nature of kind soever in America (not already settled by deed upon my son, **Edward Brice Dobbs**), Which I now have or hereafter shall have at the time of my Decease, in which is included the money and Interest due, or which shall be due to me by the General assembly for theLands Called Tower hill, in JohnstonCounty, purchased from me by the public.

Item. I give, devise and bequeath unto my said beloved Wife, **Justina Dobbs** after the payment of my Debts, Funeral Charges, and Legacies, all arrears of Sallery which now are, or shall be due to me at the time of my Decease, by Virtueof my appointment by his Majesty to the Government of North Carolina.

Item. Whereas, I have a right to the Moiety of Two hun- dred thousand acres of Land, Granted to me by the Crown, in Sixteen Patents of Twelve thousand, Five hundred acres each, in Mecklenburgh (late Anson) County, as one of the associates of Huey and Crymble, the other Moiety having been settled by me upon my eldest son, Conway **Richard Dobbs**, upon his Marriage, I do hereby impower and direct my Executors, or Either of them, as soon as convenient may be after my Decease, to sell in parcells (to the present Occupants or to suchothers as shall incline to become purchasers), the said moiety of Lands, and that theMoney arising therefrom (except so much thereof as shall, together with the Money hereinbefore bequeathed to my said wife, make up the sum of Two Thousand pounds, Sterling Money of Great Britain) shall be laid out by my Executors in **Negroes** for the sole use and benefit of such Issue by me as my said Wife shall have living, or be pregnant with at the time of my Decease, and their heirs for- ever; And in case my said Wife shall have no Issue by me alive, or be pregnant at the time of my Decease, then, and in that case, I will and devise the said undivided Moiety of Land shall be and remain to my son, **Edward Brice Dobbs**, and his heirs, upon this special provisor, that he makes up and pays so much Money to my said Wife, **Justina Dobbs**, as together with the sums herein before bequeathed to her, shall amount to the sum of Two thousand Pounds, sterling Money of Great Britain, which I Will and Desire that my said beloved Wife may have and receive out of the Estate I shall die possessed of.

Item. I bequeath to each of my Children who shall be alive at the time of my Decease, fifty pounds Sterling.

Item. I bequeath to my beloved Brother, the Reverend Doctor **Richard Dobbs**, Twenty pounds Sterling, which two last Mentioned bequest is to buy them Mourning and Rings.

Item. Whereas, I am intitled to a Moiety of Twelve Thou- sand Acres of Land by a purchase from Mr. **Patrick Smith**, of Waterford, Merchant, (for which) for which a Patent was Granted to him as an associate of **Huey and Crymble**, Sub- divided from the Great Tract Number 4, the heirs or assigns of Mr. **James Benning,** of Lisburn, In Ireland, being intitled in equity, to the other Moiety of the said Patent. Whatever part of the same as may remain unsold at the time of my Decease, I devise to my Executors, to be sold for the payment of my Debts and Legacies herein bequeathed.

Item. I give and Bequeath unto my son, Conway **Richard Dobbs**, after his Discharging my Debts, Funeral Charges, and Legacies which shall be due in Europe at the time of my De- cease, all my Plate, Goods, Household Furniture, arrears Rents, and other Chattles whatsoever which are now belonging or hereafter may belong to me, at my Decease, which now are or hereafter may be at Castle Dobbs, in the County of Antrim, and Kingdom of Ireland.

Lastly, I do appoint my Beloved Wife, **Justina Dobbs**, and my Sons, **Conway Richard Dobbs** and **Edward Brice Dobbs**, my Residuary Legatees and Executors of this my last Will and Testament; hereby revoking all former wills by me here- tofore made.

In Witness whereof I have hereunto set my hand and seal,
this 31st. day of August, in the Year of our Lord, 1763.

**ARTHUR DOBBS** (Seal)

Sign'd, Seal'd, Publish'd and declar'd to be the last will and
Testament of the Testator in presence of:
**JAMES HASELL,**
**LEWIS DEROSSET,**
**JOHN SAMPSON.**

NORTH CAROLINA.  Wilmington, 24th, April, 1765.

Then personally appeared Before me **James Hasell** & **Lewis DeRosset** two of the subscribing Witnesses to the foregoing Will and made oath on the Holy Evangelists of Almighty God, that they saw **Arthur Dobbs**, sign, seal and publish the foregoing as and for his last Will and Testament;and that the said **Arthur Dobbs** was at the same time (to the best of their Knowledge and Belief) of a sound and disposing mind and Memory, and that they, the said **James Hasell & Lewis DeRossett**, together with **John Sampson,** subscribed their Names as Witnesses thereto, in the Presence of the Testator.

At the same time, **Justina Dobbs**, Executrix before mentioned, took the Oaths by Law appointed for Her Qualification. Let Letters Testamentary issue thereon accordingly.

**WM. TRYON**

+++++++++++++++++++++++++++++++++++++++++++++++++++++++++++++++++++++++++++++++

### John Dubois' Will

IN THE NAME OF GOD AMEN. I, **John DuBois**, of Wilmington, in the province of North Carolina, Esquire, being of sound & disposing mind and memory, do make this my last Will and testament in manner and form following, that is to say:

First of all, It is my Will that all my just debts and funeral expences be first paid.

Also, I give unto my eldest son, **Peter**, ten pounds sterling, which tho, he merits an equal proportion of my estate, will I flatter myself be more agreable to him (as he is already blessed with a plentiful fortune), than an equal distribution with my other children.

Also, I give unto my son, **Walter**, forty pounds, current money of the province of New York, a year to be paid him half yearly out of my estate by my executors hereinafter named during his natural life; I also give to my said son, Walter, my silver watch.

Also, I give and devise unto my son, John and his heirs and assigns my upper brick tenement in Dock street next to the house of **Wm. Campbell**, with the ground thereto belonging,
together with my plantation on Smith's creek containing three hundred acres of land. I also give unto my said son, **John**, my fowling piece, my silver hilted sword and my case of pistols, I likewise confirm unto my said Son, John, a large diamond ring which was formerly given him by captain **Dekan**.Also, I give and devise unto my daughter, **Magdalene-Margaret**, & her heirs and assigns, my middle brick tenement in Dock street with the ground thereto belonging. I also give unto my said daughter, two diamond rings which belonged to her mother.

Also, I give and devise unto my Daughter, **Margaret**, and her heirs and assigns, my lower brick tenement now occupied by Doctor **Eustace**, with the ground thereto belonging.

Also, I give and devise unto my son, Isaac, my wooden tene-ment in Dock street adjoining to the tenement where Doctor **Eustace** lives together with the small tenement thereto adjoin-ing & the ground belonging to the said two tenements, to hold to him, the said Isaac, his heirs and assigns forever.Also, I give and devise unto my beloved wife, **Jean,** the house in which I now live, with the lott of ground belonging thereto and all the houses and improvements thereon, together with the lott of ground adjoining, during her widow hood and after the expiration of that term, then to my daughter **Anna- Jean** and her heirs and assigns forever.

Also, I give and devise unto my son, **James,** my lott of ground in front street and running thence to the river with the two tenements, bake house, and all other houses and improvements thereon with their appurtenances, together with my land and the Wind mill erected thereon adjoining to Wilmington, to hold to the said **James,** his heirs and assigns forever.

Also, I give and devise unto my daughters, **Magdalene-Margaret & Margaret,** and their heirs and assigns my lott of ground on the North side of Market street between the house of **Alexander Ross,** deceased, and **Samuel Swann's** lott, share and share alike as tenants in common. Also, I give unto **Caleb Grainger,** son of Colonel **Caleb Grainger,** deceased, a monthly clock which I had with my third wife his aunt, but if the said **Caleb Grainger** should happen to die under age or unmarried, then I give the said clock to his brother **Cornelius.** Also, I give unto my beloved wife, **Jean,** all my silver plate, household and kitchen furniture and utensils, the said clock excepted. Also, All the residue of my personal estate in North Carolina not heretofore disposed of, I give and bequeath unto my beloved wife, Jean, and my children, **John, Magdalene-Margaret, Margaret, Isaac, Anna-Jean,** and **James,** to be equally divided among them by my executors herein after named. And whereas I am intitaled to a proportion of lands or personal estate, or lands and personal estate, in the province of New York, in right of my Grand-mother or other wise, I there-fore give and devise the said estate whether real, personal or both to my executors herein after named to be sold, and the money arising from such sale to be equally divided among all my children hereinbefore mentioned.

Also, It is my will and so the same is to be taken and under-stood, that the legacies hereinbefore given to my said wife be in full of her right of dower and all other demands on my estate, and if she pretends to claim her dower that, then, and in that case, I hereby give and devise the house and lotts where I now live to my Daughter, **Anna-Jean,** immediately after my decease, and the other legacies herein given to my said wife, in that case I give to my children, **John, Magdalene-Margaret, Margaret, Isaac, Anna-Jean** and **James,** to he equally divided among them.

Also, It is my will that my children, **John, Magdalene-Mar-garet, Margaret, Anna-Jean, Isaac,** and **James,** shall not be intitaled to the profits of the tenements & lands respectively devised to them, till each of them shall arrive at the age of twenty one years, or day of Marriage, but that the same shall be received by my executors herein after named and applied towards the education of my said children and the maintenance of my family, and improvement of my whole estate for the joint benefit of my said Last mentioned children and my wife.

And it is also my will, that the bake house divised to my son, James, be kept employed for the benefit of my said wife, and last mentioned children, & my boats and negroes kept employed in the usual manner for the same purpose, until my son, James, shall arrive at the age of twenty one years or the day of Marriage, and that such child or children who shall happen to marry, or may have arrived at the age of twenty one years, shall draw his or her proportion of the profits of the said boats and negroes.

And in case of the death of any of my said last mentioned children before such child or children shall have attained the age of twenty one years or day of Marriage, then it is my will that the share orshares hereby given to such child or children so dying, both real and personal, shall go to the survivor or survivors of my said last mentioned children, to be equally divided among them, if more than one and that such part of my real estate as shall go to any of my children by the death of the others or any of them shall, be held by such children as as a tenancy in common. And in case of the death of all my said last mentioned children before marriage, then I give and devise such part of my estate as is herein given to them, to my beloved wife Jean & her heirs and assigns forever.

And lastly, I do make, nominate and appoind my beloved wife, **Jean,** my sons, **Peter, Walter** and **John,** and my friends, **Lewis-Henry DeRosset** and **Moses-John DeRosset,** esquires, to be guardians of my children and their respective estates during their minority, and also executors of this my last will and testament: hereby revoking all wills by me heretofore made.

In Witness whereof I have hereunto set my hand to this my will, written on four pages of paper together with my sealand published the whole as my last Will and testament, this thirteenth day of September, in the year of our Lord, one thousand, and seven hundred and sixty seven.

Before publishing this my last will, I hereby order and direct that my said executors shall purchase out of the profits of my estate, able **negroes** in number four, fit to go in my boats, & that the number then on my estate shall be kept up by my said executors as often as necessary in case of death or other-wise. (The words "then on my estate" being interlined.)

**JOHN DuBois,** (Seal)

Signed, sealed, published & declared by the above named,
**John DuBois** as and for his last will and testament in presence of us whose names are hereunder written, who did each of us sub-scribe our names as witnesses thereto at his request, in his pres-ence, and in the room where he was (the words "of twenty one years" being first interlined in the third page.)

**J. EUSTACE.**
**EDWARD CHIVERS.**
**A. MACLAINE.**
WILMINGTON, April 9th, 1768.
**WM. TRYON.**

++++++++++++++++++++++++++++++++++++++++++++++++++++++++++++++++++++++++++++

### Alexander Duncan's Will

IN THE NAME OF GOD AMEN. I, **Alexander Duncan**, of Wilmington, Merchant, Intending, please God, going Soon for Great Britain & knowing the uncertainty of Human Life, in Case of my death do make this my Last Will and Testament for the ordering & Disposing of what Worldly Estate or Personal Interest which it has pleased God to Bestow upon me.

In the First place, I give and bequeath unto my Brother, **Robert Duncan,** if allive, the Sum of three hundred Pounds Sterling money, to him or his heirs; In case of his death or having no heirs, this Legacy to be divided equally between the Surviving Children of my Sisters, **Elizabeth Ronaldson**, Deceased, & **Margaret Henery**, now Supposed to be in Edinburgh, if not there, Let enquiry be made where my said Nieces & Nephews do Live; I Also Will & bequeath to Said Children of my said Sisters, as many as there may be of them, the sum of Seven hundred pounds Sterling, to be equally divided among them, Share & Share alike, to them & their heirs. These Legacys I desire to be made to **Alexander Purves,** Esqr., in Edinburgh; or to John Clark, Goldsmith there; in Case of their death, to Mr. **Thomas Smith,** Merchant there, as soon as my Executors Can, not Exceeding two years at Farthest.

I Give & Bequeath to **John Rutherfurd**, Esqr., of this Province, the Sum of One thousand pounds Sterling money, by him to be disposed of as he pleases, the same to be Remitted to his order in London, as soon as the Circumstances of my affairs will permitt, not exceeding three years, to him & his heirs.

My Will & Desire is also, that my Executors may within two years after my decease, if Circumstances will permitt, purchase four young **Negro Men** & as many **young Negro women** that are likely, which I desire them, my Executors, to make a present of to **James Moore**, Esqr., for his use during his own life; in case of his death before his wife the said **Negroes** are to decend to her, and their Increase to be willed & Disposed of as sheplease.

I Also give & bequeath to **Thomas Cunningham, Junior**, who has Lived with me with great fidelity, the sum of four hundred Pounds, Proclamation money, to assist him to follow Trade, if he pleases, which if he does, I desire That my Executors may procure for him in England, Credit to ammount of five hundred pounds, Sterling, for the payment of which they are to be his Security. To Ammount of the Four hundred pounds, Proclamation money, my Executors are to Remitt for him, it being the sum I give him & his heirs, the rest he to make payment of himself.

I Give & Bequeath towards the finishing, if finished, towards Adorning Wilmington Church, the sum of four hundred pounds, Proclamation money, to pay which the Executors of my Will are desired to make over to the Judge of the Superior court for the time Being, the ammount of that sum in some Sufficient Bond or note due to me at the time of my death, to be Recovered for this purpose.

I Give & Bequeath, **Frances Rutherfurd**, daughter of **John Rutherfurd,** Esquire, the Same Legacy as I have given to Colo-nell **James Moore**, above mentioned, in Case she returns to this Province & Marys here; But in Case of her Living in Europe & Marying there then I Leave to her four hundred Pounds, Sterling, to be paid to her when she Marys or is of Age, to her & her heirs forever.

I Give & bequeath to the Daughter of **John Walker**, a Car-penter in Wilmington, by his wife, **Isobell Walker**, being his Last Marriage, (this girl Lives or did Live at **Richard Lyons** at Cross Creek) if allive at my death, **three Negro Girls** to be purchased in Like manner as the Others I Leave above mention-ed, which Legacy is to be in Trust for this Girl till she Comes of Age or is marryed, with the Wife of **Thos. Cunningham**, in Wilmington, if dead, young **Thomas Cunningham** to take care of them for her use forever.

My desire also is, that the following Sums may be paid Soon after my Decease as a token of my friendship & Esteem for the following persons, either to purchase mourning Rings &c in Remembrance of me, at their option, or disposed of as they think proper, **Cornelius Harnett**, Twenty Pounds, Ster-ling, His wife the same Sum; **Mary Grainger**, widor of **Caleb Grannger** the same sum; Mr. **Maurice Moore** the same sum, His wife the same sum; Captain **John Forster** the same Sum, His wife the same sum; & to **Alexander Chapman** the same sum; All which is to be understood if these persons are allive at the time of my death and are in North Carolina.

Having an opinion of the good qualitys of **Arthur Benning**, of Wilmington, and Considering him as unfortunate in this part,
I will & Bequeath that my Executors make over to him for his Sole use if alive, the Sum of Five hundred Pounds, Proclamation Money, out of such debts in this Province as may be due to me at the time of my death, to him & his heirs or Assigns.

I Will and bequeath to **Robert Schaw**, my now Partner, after mydebts and the afforesaid Legacies are paid, one half of all the Outstanding Debts that may be my part in this Province or in America at the time of my Death, as also one quarter part of all the Ready Effects, or **Negroes** that are now my part in Company with him & Mr **Ancrum** to him and his heirs forever.

And Lastly, I give & Bequeath to **John Ancrum**, my now Partner, all the rest of my Real or Personal Estate not before given, to him & his heirs forever, Who with **Robert Schaw**, I Constitute & Appoint my Executors of this my will, to see it Executed as it means without any form of law, which they know I never Choose to have any thing to say to, on which Account I make this will more for their Government in the distribution of my Effects, than to have it conformable to law, & I desire that they may Construct it as such knowing this to be my hand writing without even a Witness as the Law in all Wills directs, therefore desire that they may agree in all things Like Brothers, Live together in Harmony to perform their friend's Will & Remember him only as he has deserved.Given under my hand as my Last Will and Testament at Wilmington, the 11th. May, 1767.

**ALEXR DUNCAN**

P: S: Mrs. **Elizabeth Hall** may be in Ordinary Circum-stances, in Case of her being so, my Will is that during her Continuance as such, that my Executors pay her yearly the sum of Thirty Pounds, Proclamation money, for her assistance.

NORTH CAROLINA.

The Within last Will and Testament of **Alexander Duncan**, deceased, was proved before me this 18 Day of May, in the Year of our Lord, 1768, by **Thomas Cobham** and **William Lord**, who swore that they were well acquanted with the Handwriting of the said **Alexander Duncan**, the Testator, and that they verily believe the said deceases Name, as well as the whole Body of the Will, is of his, the said Testators own proper Handwriting. The said **Thomas Cobham** and **William Lord** further declare, that they were both before and since the Date of the said Will, well acquainted with the said **Alexander Duncan** in his Life Time, and were often in his Company, & that they believe at the Time of the date the Said Will He was of sound and disposing, mind & Memory.

  **John Ancrum** and **Robert Schaw** the Executors therein named took the Oaths appointed for their Qualification.

  Ordered That Letters Testamentary issue thereon accordingly.

**WM. TRYON**

++++++++++++++++++++++++++++++++++++++++++++++++++++++++++++++++++++++++++++++

## Caleb Grainger's Will

    IN THE NAME OF GOD AMEN. I, **Caleb Grainger**, of New Hanover County, in the Province of North Carolina, Esquire, being in Perfect health and of Sound and Disposing mind and Memory, but knowing the Incertainty of human Life do make Ordaine and Declare this to be and Contain my Last Will and Testament, hereby Revoking all former And Other Wills by me at any time heretofore made.

    Imprimis. I give and Bequeath my Soul to Almighty God, the Giver of all things, hoping at the Last day to Inherit Eternal Life; And as to Such Worldly Substance wherewith it bath Pleased God to Bless me with, I Give, Devise, And Bequeath in Manner and form following, that is to Say:

    I Give, Devise and Bequeath unto my Loveing Wife, **Mary Grainger,** and to her heirs and Assign's for ever, one fifth Part of all my Personal Estate after My Just Debts is Paid off and discharges, Except what or Such Part as I hereinafter give and Bequeath to my Daughter, **Mary Grainger**, which Fifth Part as aforesaid is for and in Lieu of Any Thirds or Dower, She, my said wife, May Claim out of My Estate herein Devised and Bequeathed.

    Item. I Give, Devise and Bequeath Unto my son, **Caleb Grainger**, all my Houses and Lands on Smiths Creek, and the No. Et. River on the Northermost side of the Main or Kings Road that leads from Smiths Creek Bridge to Blakes Ferry, which said Land as aforesaid, I give, Devise and Bequeath unto him, my said Son, **Caleb**, his heirs and Assign's for Ever, But my will is that my said Son shall not sell said Land untill he arrives to or at the Age of Twenty five Years, which will be in the Year of of Our Lord One Thousand, Seven Hundred and Seventy three, on the 20th day of April.

    Item. I Give, Devise and Bequeath unto my son, **Cornelius Harnett Grainger**, all my Houses and Lands on Smiths Creek on the Southermost side of the Main Road that Leads from the Bridge to Blakes ferry, that is to say, all my Lands between said Road and Mr. **Sam'l Swanns** Land on said Creek, which said Land as aforesaid, I Give, Devise & Bequeath unto my said Son, **Cornelius**, to him, his heirs and Assigns for Ever. But my will is that my said Son, **Cornelius Harnett Grainger**, shall not sell said Land Untill he arrives to, or at, the Age of Twenty five Years.

    Item. I Give, Devise and Bequeath unto my son, **William Grainger**, all that Tract of Land on the Sound which I purchased from **Charles Harrison**, where I have Settled a New Plantation, to him, My son **William**, his heirs and Assign's for Ever.

Item. I Give, Devise and Bequeath Unto my Daughter, **Mary Grainger, Two Negro Wenches** and what Children they now have, or May hereafter have, the **Names of which Wenches is, Little Hager and Venice,** which **Said Negroes** as aforesaid, I give, Devise and bequeath to my said daughter **Mary,** to her, her heirs and Assigns for Ever. My farther **Will** is, that in Case either of said **Wenches Hager or Vence** should die before my said daughter comes to the Age of Seventeen of day of Marriage, that then, and in such Case my Executors shall replace such **Negro** or **Negroes** out of My General Stock of Negroes, and said **Negro** or **Negroes,** so replaced, to be **a Breeding Wench or Wenches.**

Item. I Give, Devise and Bequeath unto my Daughter, **Mary Grainger,** one Lott of Land in Wilmington, Containing Thirty feet front upon the Street, and the Common Debth of Lotts which I have sold upon said Street, Unto her, her heirs and Assigns for Ever; which said Lot as aforesaid my Will is shall be laid off and given to her, my said Daughter, by My Executors hereinafter Named, in Such Street or Part of the Town where they thing most Proper that is to say, where I own the Land: I also give, devise and Bequeath to my said Daughter, Mary, one Good Bed & Furniture, two Mahogany Tables, Six Mahogany Chairs, one Large Mahogany fraimed Looking Glass, and Such of my Plate as I shall leave a Listof Inclosed in my Will; all which things as aforesaid shall be delivered to her at the Age of Seventeen Years, or day of Marriage.

Item. My Will is that My Exec'rs sell my House and Land at Masonborough for the Use of my three Sons.

Item. My Will is that my Bridge on Smiths Creek, be keep in repair and in Case of a New One being wanted that it be built out of my Personal Estate, and that the Money Arising by the Rent of the Same go towards the Victualing, Clothing & Educating my Children, and that my wife have her Proportion of the Same dureing her remaining My Widdow.

Item. All the rest and Residue of My Estate, both real and Personal, I Give, Devise and Bequeath, Unto and Between, my three Sons, **Caleb, Cornelius (Harnett),** and **William Grainger,** to them Respectively, and to their several and Respective Heirs and Assign's for Ever, to be Equally Devided Between them, Share and Share Alike, by my Executors or the Sur-vivors of them, when or as soon as my son Caleb, shall arrive to the Age of (Twenty) Twenty One Years; and in Case of the death of either of My said Children, before they or either of them shall come of Age or Day of Marriage, that then, such Part of my Estate, both Real and Personal, hereby intended for such Child so dying, I give, Devise and Bequeath to the three surviving Children, to them, Their Heirs and Assign's for Ever, and in Case of the Death of any two of My said Children, before they shall come of age or Marriage that then such Part intend (that is to say of my Estate both real and Personal) for such Children dying I Give, Devise & Bequeath to the two Survive-ing Children to them their heirs & Assign's for Eever; And in Case any Three of my Children should die before they become of Age, That then Any Part of my Estate, both Real and Personal, intended for such three deceased Children, I Give, Devise and Bequeath to the One Surviving Child, to him or her heirs and assigns for Ever.

Item. It is my Will and Desire (after my Debts is Paid) that then my Executors Pay over and Deliver unto my Wife, **Mary Grainger,** all and every Part of my Estate herein Before given and Bequeathed unto her, and it is my Will, that my said wife have the Use of My Household goods until my son, **Caleb Grainger,** is of Age, she giving Security to my Executors (if required), to return the same in good Order, all that does not fall to her share, and I hereby begg and desire my Executors to take an account of my Plate, Other furniture, Stock of Cattle &c. My farther Will is, that after my Wife has had her **Share of Negores and Slaves,** that then the **Negroes and Slaves** remaining I do hereby Order, direct and Appoint shall be kept to work together or hired, wherever or which ever, my Executors shall think Most Advantagious and the Money arisingfrom their Labour and the rent of the Bridge, I would have laid out in board, Cloathing and Education of my Children, either in this Province or wherever my Executo s May thing most Propper, and if any Overplus Remain of the Profits Arising from the Negroes Labour, & Rent of the Bridge, as afores'd, that the same shall be laid out in buying young Negroes to add to the General Stock, for my Children.

Item. It is my farther will, that my Wife have the use of My Plantation till my Son **Caleb,** become of Age. Provided she remains my Widdow Solong, but She is not to have it Any Longer than her Remaining so.

Lastly, I _____ Nominate, Constitute and Appoint **Maurice Moore, Cornelius Harnett, Saml. Aâ€"e** and **Alexander Duncan**, Esquires, Executors to this my Last Will and Testament, And My Wife, **Mary Grainger**, Executrix dureing her Remaining my Widdow; hereby revoaking all other and former Wills by me at any time heretofore made, and Acknowledge this, Containing two Sheet of Papper, to be my Last Will and Testament.

In Witness whereof I have hereunto set my hand and Seal this day of in the Year of His Majestys Reign and in the Year of Our Lord, One Thousand, Seven hundred and Sixty Three

**CALEB GRAINGER** (Seal)

interlined, all the above before
sealing. **SAM'LL GREEN.**
**ANTH'Y WARD.**
**JOSEPH STOCKLEY**.

Account of Plate Left my Daughter, Mary Grainger.
  1 Doz. Table Knives & forks, Silver Handles.
  1 Doz. Desart Ditto Silver Handles.
  1 Silver Butter Boat,
  1 Do. Tea pott.
  1 Ditto Milk Pot.
  1 Dz Silver Salts & Shovels.
  1 Silver Salver.
  1 Set of Casters with Silver Tops.
  1 Soop Spoon, Silver
  Half a Dozen Silver Table Spoons, Tea Spoons
August 23d., 1760.

**CALEB GRAINGER**

(Turn Over) As it will be of no Real Service to my Friends, the giving of Scarfs &c (I desire that I be Buried in a Decent Manner and as a Mason), with a Plain Blacked Coffin, not Covered with Cloth, And that my Dear and ever Worthy Friend Mr. **Corn. Harnett** have purchased out of my Estate a neat Mourning Ring which I begg he may wear in remembrance of his Sinciar Friend & Brother,

**CALEB GRAINGER**

Feb'ry 16th., 1761.

I, the said **Caleb Grainger**, Do by these presents Codicil, Confirm & ratify my said Last Will and do give & bequeath unto the Child My wife, **Mary Grainger**, is now Pregnant with whether it be a Male or a female, his, or her heirs & Assigns forever, all my Moiety of the Land on Smiths Creek adjacent to the Saw Mill & Grist Mill now building by my friend, **Cornelius Harnett** & mysell, together with a proportionate part (with the rest of my children), of my personal Estate. It is also my Will that the said Saw mill, to wit, my Moiety, be com-pleated & finished by by Executors out of the Proffits of my Estate; the proffits arising from the said Mills, to go to the use of my Estate until the said child come of age or day of Marriage; and my will is that this Codicil be adjudged a part of my said Will.

In Witness whereof, I have hereunto Set my hand & seal
this fifth day of October, in the Year of our Lord, One thousand
Seven hundred & Sixth five.

**CALEB GRAINGER** (Seal)

MARY GRAINGER.
MARGARET DOUGLASS.
EDMOND FOYER.

+++++++++++++++++++++++++++++++++++++++++++++++++++++++++++++++++++++++++++++++++

### Thomas Moor's Will

WILMINGTON, 3d. february, 1735.

I, **Thomas Moor**, Late of New York, now in Wilmington, Being Sick of Body but sound of Judgment, Doe make This my Last Will and Testament.

In Primis, I appoint and Constitute **Cosmas Farquharson**, Doctor of Physic, my Sole Executor and Administrator of all the Debts, Effects and Moneys I Can Lay any Claim to in North Carolina, in Order that he, the said **Cosmas Farquharson**, may Remit the Same to New York to be Dispos'd off there as my former Will, in the hands of Mr. **Alsop** and **Carroll** there Directs, and this My Last Will and Testament Day And Date foresaid, I have signd, seald and Delivered in presence of :

THOS. MOOR (Seal)
Witness:
CALEB MASON.
SIMON PAYNE.
RD. HARTLEY.

At a Court begun and Held for the County of New Hanover on Tuedsay the 4th. Day of February, 1753.

+++++++++++++++++++++++++++++++++++++++++++++++++++++++++++++++++++++++++++++++++

### Roger Moore's Will

NORTH CAROLINA, NEW HANOVER COUNTY.

IN THE NAME OF GOD AMEN, the Last will and Testament of **Roger Moore**, of the Parish of Saint Philips. Imprimis, I doe give, Devise and Bequeath unto my Son, **George Moore,** and his Heirs forever the Following Tracts or Parcells of Lands, Vizt., All that Part of my Plantation Called by the Name of **Kendall**, Bounding to the Southward by the Creek that runs up to my Mill as far as there is a Post to be fixt about three Hundred yards up the Creek above the House where Gready Lately removed from; and from thence a Due west Line to be Continued as far my Lands runs up the Neck, and Bounded to the Northward by **Mr. Allens** Creek, with the Little Island of Marsh fronting the said Plan- tation in the River. And all Other my Lands bounding on the said Creek; and all Other my Lands Lying between the Thoro- fare and Black river, in the Neck known by the Name of Maultby's Point,with all my Lands on the Island Opposite; And One half of the Tract of Land in the fork of the river known by the Name of Mount Misery; the Same to be Divided in Such Manner as my son, **George**, shall think Properto Direct; and them my **William** to Take his Choyce, & that to be Done in One year After my Decease. And five Hundred Acres on the Northwest river, Lying Between the Lands of Mr. **Job Howes** and the Land that was Mr. **Dallisons**, Decd.; and all that Tract of Land I bought of Mr. **John Porter**, Decd., on the No. West River at or Near the Saxapahaw Old fields, being Three Thousand & Twenty five Acres; And the Lott of Land in the Town of Brunswick where Mr **Ross** at Present Dwells,being five Poles wide & runing from the river as farr as the Street before Doct. Fergu's House, with the Wharf and all Other Improvements thereon.

Item, I doe give unto my Aforesaid Son, **George**, **my Negro man Higate the Carpenter**, His **wife Rose**, with all her Issue

& Encrease.

Item, I doe give, Devise & Bequeath unto my son, **William Moore** & his Heirs for ever all that my **Plantation called Orton** where I now dwell, Joyning on Kendals, as its before Bounded by this my Will, with all my Land Bounded to the Southward on the Creek where My Mill now is, being in all about 2500 Acres; & also, 640 Acres at Rockey Point, bounding on Mr. Allens and the river, and the Remaining, half of Fifty five Thousand Acres in the Neck known by the Name of Mount Misery, and all the Tract of Land bounded by the River & Smiths Creek; and 5000 Acres at or near the Haw or Eno old Fields.

Item, I doe Also give, Devise, and Bequeath unto my Said Son, **William**, One full fifth Part of the Slaves I Shal Dye Possessed of; and its my Will that all my Slaves Shall in One Month After my Decease be Devided into five Equal Parts, as near as mybe, by himself and my Son **George**, when so done that my son; **William**, take his Chance by Lott for such his Part. And I doe Also give unto my said Son, **William**, all the Stock of Horses & Cattle. & Sheep that Shall Properly belong to & be on my Plantation Orton, at my Decease, with all my Plate & Household furniture, Hee, my son **William,** Paying to my son **George**, in Two years After my Decease, the Sum of One Hundred Pounds, Proclamation Money or the Value thereof.

Item, I doe give unto my Daughter, **Sarah Smith**, the Sum of five Pounds, being in full for her Fortune; She having Already recd. from me, with the Legacy Left her by Her Grand Mother, by my Computation, at Least £1600 Sterling.

Item, I doe give unto my Daughter, **Mary Moore**, the Sum of Eighteen Hundred Pounds, Proclamation Money, or the Value thereof, to be Paid Her, or sure'd to be paid Her, in Two years after my Decease; but on the Condition Only my Exors. then Taking a Release for the Legacy left her by Her Grand Mother, Mrs. **Sarah Trott**, and Also, that she Doe not Marry but with the Consent of my Exors. & her Aunt, Mrs. **Sarah Allen** or the Majority of them.

Item. I doe give unto my Daughter, **Anne Moore**, the Sum of Eighteen Hundred Pounds, Proclamation Money, or the Value thereof, to be Paid her, or sured to be paid Her, in Two years after my Decease; But on the Same Terms & Conditions as Her Sister **Mary** before Mentioned.

Item, I doe give unto my son in Law, Mr **Thomas Smith**, & this Heirs for ever, all that Lott of Land in the Town of Brunswick where Mr. **William Lord** at Present resides, Besides with the Building thereon.

Item, I doe give, Devise & Bequeath unto my sons, **George & William Moore**, and their Heirs forever, all the rest & Residue of my real & Personal Estate, to be Equally Divided Between them, After the Payment of all my just Debts & Legacys, but on these Conditions, that they, at the expence of my Estate, Maintain their Said Sisters, **Mary & Anne** aforesaid, untill their Legacy become Due, unless they shall Marry before, but Nevertheless, if my Two Sons Shall Choose to pay their Legacy Out of my Principal Estate, they shall be at their Liberty so to doe soe as not more then One third of the same be Paid to Each in Land; & the Lands & slaves to be Vallued to them by Indifferent Persons, to be Choose by each Party, & they on Oaths, there being Twenty Odd Thou- sand Acres of Land & Near Two Hundred & fifty Slaves, with the Stock of Horses, Cattle, &c., & besides the Debts Due To me not before Bequeathed in this my Will.

Item, I doe Devise & Bequeath unto my Dear beloved Wife, **Mary Moore**, all the Estate that was her own at the Time of Her Marriage, be it of any Nature and Kind Whatsoever, with the Profits arising Since Such her Marriage; as also the Saw Mill I entend to Build on BRice's Creek, with the Slaves & all Utensils that shall Properly Belong to them. And if it shal soe Happen that I shal Dye Before the said Mill shall be Compleatly finished, that She, my said Wife, is to have the work of my four Carpinters now at Nuce, until they be Compleatly Finished; and the aforesaid Land & Mill I doe give unto my said Wife, Hurs forever, & in full Consideration of her Dower & any Claim She may have by Law to any Part of my real & Personal Estate.

Item, it is my Will that each of my Daughters, **Mary & Anne,** Doe at their Marriage, take Each their Choyce of any One of the **House Slaves, Except the Negro wench Bess,** who I leave to Her Liberty to make Choyce of any One of my Children for her Master or Mistress.

Lastly, I doe Nominate and appoint my Two Sons, **George & William Moore,** Exors. to this my Last will & Testament, Revoaking all Other Wills herefore made by me.

In Testimony Whereof, I have hereunto Set my Hand &
Seal, this 7th. Day of March 1747/8.

**ROG. MOORE** (seal)

Signed, Sealed, Published &
Declared to be my Last Will &
Testament in the Presence of:

**WM. FORBES.**
**RICHD. QUINCE.**
**GEO. LOGAN.**

A Codicil to this my Last will & Testament: Whereas, it is Apparent from the Late Storm, that the Legacy I have Be- queathed unto my Loving Wife, **Mary,** The giving her my saw Mill and the Appurtenancys thereunto Belonging, may, Instead of being a Yearly Profit to her, Prove rather an Ex- pence, therefore I doe Absolute Declare that Part of my will soe much as relates to the Saw Mills and appurtenancys there unto Belonging to be Void and of none Effect; &, in Lieu of the Same, do give unto my said Loving Wife, **Mary,** One Hundred Pounds, Sterling Money, or the full Vallue thereof, to be Paid her Yearly by my Exors. During the Time she Does remain my Widdoe, and noe Longer, and the same to be in full for her right of Dower, & in full for any Claim or Demand of any kind Whatsoever She may have Legully to any Part of my Estate.

In Testimony Whereof I have here unto Set my Hand &
Seal, the 30th. Day of June, 1750.

**R. MOORE.** (seal)

++++++++++++++++++++++++++++++++++++++++++++++++++++++++++++++++++++++++++++++

### Edward Moseley's Will

NO. CAROLINA, SC.

IN THE NAME OF GOD AMEN, I, **Edward Moseley**, of New Hanover County, Esqr., do make and Declare these Presents to be and Contain my Last Will & Testament Rovoking all Other.

Imprimis, I will that all my Debts be well & Truly paid, within Convenient time after my Decease, Out of the Profits arising from the Labour of my Slaves.

Item, It is my Will that as soon as it well may be done After my Decease, a True and Perfect Inventory be made of all my Personal Estate, and that the Same be Returned upon Oath into the Secretary's Office, as also into the Office of the County Court of New Hanover, within Ninety Daies After my Decease.

Item, I give and Bequeath unto my Eldest Son, **John Moseley**, my **Plantation at Rockey Point**, where I Frequently reside, on the West side of North East Branch of Cape Fear River, Together with all my Lands Adjacent thereto, Containing in the whole about 3500 Acres, be the Same more or Less, To Have and To Hold the same to him, the said **John Moseley**, & his heirs male of his Body Lawfully begotten for ever. Andfor want of Such Heirs then to my Second Son, **Edward Moseley**, and his Heirs Male of his Body Lawfully Begotten for ever; and for want of Such Heirs, then to the next of my Sons as Shall Attain to the Age of 21 years, intail male as above men- tioned; and for want of Such to my right Heir infee Simple.

Item, I give to my Second Son, **Edward Moseley**, my Plantation where I formerly Dwelt in Chowan County, and the Lands adjacent thereto, Containing by estimation 2000 Acres, be the Same More or Less, To Have & to Hold the Same to him & the Heirs male of his Body Lawfully Begotten infee tail; and for want of Such, then to my Son, **Sampson Moseley**, & the Heirs Male of his Body Lawfully Begotten infee tail; & for want of Such, then to my Son, **James Moseley**, infee tail Male as above exprest; & for want of Such, Then to my Fifth Son, **Thomas Moseley**, and His heirs for ever.

Item, I give and Bequeath unto my Son, **Sampson Moseley**, and his Heirs and Assigns, all my Lands On the East Side of the North East Branch of Cape Fear River, Lying Between Holly Shelter Creek and the bald white Sand hills, Containing by Estimation 3500 Acres, be the Same More or Less.

Item, I give & Bequeath unto my Son, **James Moseley**, and his Heirs & Assigns, all my Lands on the East side of the North East Branch of Cape Fear River Opposite to my Rocky Point Plantation, Containing by Estimation 1650 Acres, be the Same More or Less.

Item, I give & Bequeath unto my Son, **Thos. Moseley**, & his Heirs and Assigns, all my Lands on the North West Branch of Cape Fear River, Vizt: 1280 Acres I had by the Will of **John Baptista Ashe**, Esqr., at Rockfish Creek on both sides the River; and 600 Acres on the East side of the North West branch of Cape Fear River, Near Opposite to the Lands Where-on Mr. Mitchell Formerly Dwelt.

Item, I give & Bequeath unto my Son, **John Moseley**, and his Heirs and Assigns, my Lot and Houses in Brunswick where my Habitation usually is at Present, After the Decease of my Loving Wife, to whom I give it During her Natural Life. I also give to my said son **John** & his Heirs and assigns, my **Plantation** below Brunswick, Commonly Called **Macknights.**

Item, I give and Bequeath unto my Son, **Edward Moseley,** and his Heirs and Assigns, my Lot & house in Wilmington; Also, 600 Acres of Land Opposite to Cabbage Inlet; Also 500 Acres of Land in Tyrrel, Commonly Called Coopers; & 450 Acres of Land in Tyrrel County, Commonly Called White marsh, all these to him & his Heirs & Assigns.

Item, I give and Bequeath to my three Sons, **Sampson, James** and **Thomas,** all my Lands on the East side of Cape Fear River on Part. whereof Mr. **Bugnion** dwelleth, to be Divided into three Equal Parts, as near as may be; **Thomas** to have his first Choice, and **James** the Next, the Division to be made by my Wife.

Item, I give to my Loving Wife, **Ann Moseley**, During her Natural Life, my Plantation at the Sound which I bought of John Hodgson, Wheron there is a Large Vineyard Planted; Also 3200 Acres of Land in EdgComb, Called Alden of the hill, be the Same More or Less, Lying on a Branch of Fishing Creek, by Some Called Irwins by Other Butterwood; Also 1650 Acres, be the Same More or Less, upon the West side of Neuse River, about Twenty four Miles above New Bern Town. With full Power to her by any Deed or will, to give the first Mentioned to all or any of my Children She pleases, to be held by Such in fee Simple, and the two Last Mentioned Tracks, Vizt: 3200 & 1650, to all, or any of my four Youngest Sons, as She shall think they best deserve or may most want the Same, in Such Proportion as She Shall think Proper, to be held by Such as she shall Appoint, the same in fee simple.

Item, I give and Bequeath unto my five Sons, **John, Edward, Sampson, James, & Thomas,** & their Heirs & assigns, to be held in Severalty; & to be Equally Divided, my Large Tract of Land in Edgcomb County, Called Clur, Containing by Estimation Ten Thousand Acres, be the same more or Less;& it is my Will that in Case Any of my Sons Shall Dye before they attain the Age of 21 Years, or Without Leaving Lawfull Issue, that then the Lands of Such so Dying Shall be Equally Divided Among the Survivours, to be held by them infee Simple, Except those first Mentioned Lands Given to my Two Eldest Sons in tail Male, which in Case of their Or either of their Death is to go as I have before exprest.

Item, It is my Will that no part of my Stocks, Houshold Goods, Slaves, or Other Personal Estate, be Sold for Payment of my Debts; but that the Same Shall be Paid Out of the Money's Arising by Crops or Other Labour of **my Slaves**; hereby Directing that what Products of the Labour of **my Slaves** Shall be in being at my Decease, the Same Shall go towards Payment of my Debts, and that **my Slaves** that work in the field or on Tarr Work &c, to be kept to Labour in Such Manner, on all, or any of my Lands as Shall best serve, to raise most Money for Discharge of my Debts.

Item, After my Debts are Paid by the Labour of my Slaves, I give and Bequeath unto my Dear & Loving Wife, **Ann Moseley**, these **21 Slaves** Following, Vizt: **Robin & his wife Dinah& their Children, Little Mustapha, Caesar & Jonathan; Kate & her Children, Willy & Abram, Simon, Gabriel, Jacob, Primus, Francis, Abigail, Hager, Phillida & her Two Children, Quashey& Billey; Drago & his Wife Nan; and Moll Statiras Daughter.**

Item, I give and Bequeath unto my Daughter, **Aner Moseley** these **Eleven Slaves**, Vizt: **Sarah, Mustapha's Wife; Hannah &her Two Daughters Phillida & Bessy; Cudger & his Wife Bolinder & their Daughters Betsy, Sarah & Lucy, Esther Simons wife; and Little Esther, Jennys Daughter.**

Item, I give & Bequeath unto my five Sons, **John, Edward, Sampson, James & Thomas**, these **56 Slaves**, to Wit: **Manuel & his Wife Maria & their Children, Manuel, Frank, Jenny, and Yauna; Robin & his wife Doll; Judith and her Sons, Henry, Tony, Tom & Ben; Jenny & her Sons, Andrew & Ned; Bacchus & his wife Yanbo & her Children, Jupiter, Sarah and hannah; Mat, a Cooper, & his wife Mercy, & their Children, Mat, Frank & Peggy; Jemmy & his wife Sarah; Tom a Cooper & his wife Jenny; Joe & his wife Doll, & their Daughter Dol; Jemmy & Cooper, Sambo & Cooper, Scipio, Roger, Sandy, Cook, Button, Cyrus, Peter, Zebedee; Flora & Diana, the Daughters of Dinah; Nancey & her Children, Alden, Jacob & Suckey; Cudgeo, Kates son Statara, Peg & her Daughter Sarah Membo; Belindas Daughter Jenny; Esthers Daughters, Cates Daughter Hagar.**

Item, I give and Bequeath unto my Loving Wife, **Ann**, my New Chaise Harness and the Pair of Bay Horses, Smoker and Toby, which I bought of **John Hull**, Esqr, for that use, I also give Unto her Out of my Stocks, Ten Cows & Ten Calves, Ten Steers of Differant Age's, & Twenty Sheep & the horse Spark.

Item, it is my Will that my said Wife have the Care, Tuition and GuardianShip of my Daughter, **Ann**; & in Case of her Death, then to my Honour'd Mother in Law, Mrs. **Susannah Hasell**.

Item, It is my Will that **the Slaves** now usually kept about the house, shall be kept in the same Employment for my Wifes easier Life, and Care of my Children, untill She Marries, or One of my Sons Arrives at Age of 21 Years, then they are to go to those I have before Bequeathed them.

Item, It is my Will that my Wife Shall have the Use of my Lot & houses in Brunswick; and also of my Dwelling house, Kitchen &c. at Rockey Point, untill She shall Marry or that One of my Sons Shall Attain in the Age of 21 years, She keeping all my Houses in Repair. And when Any of my Sons Shall Attain 21 years of Age, then my wife Shall have her Choice Whether She will Dwell in my houses at Brunswick or at Rockey Point; it is also my Will,that she may work so many of the Slaves on any of my Lands as she Shall choose, along with **my Childrens Slaves** for which She may Draw a Proportionable Part with **Such Slaves** of my Children as shall be thought most for their benefit to be worked with hers; The Barns to be for the Use of my Children as well as for my Wife.

Item, it is my Will that after my Debts are Paid, my Sons Slaves Shall be Employ'd on all, or any of my Lands, and no where else, in the Most Beneficial Manner that may be forthe Profit of my said Sons; and Annually Accts. to be rendered to the County Court of New Hanover, of the Profits Arising thereby, which Profits are to be Accompted for without Any Charge of Commissions, &a., Other than the Overseers Share. Nor shall my Children's Estate be made any way Less Under pretence of Commissioners, &c., But all that I have or shall leave them in this my Last Will is to go Clear to them, Except what shall be hereafter exprest Concerning my Sons Education.

Item, I give unto my Six Children all my Stock of horses Mares, Neat Cattle, Sheep and Swine, to run & encrease for ther Benefit; and I will that proper Slaves be Appointed for Managing thereof of, which increase & profit made thereby of Such as are necesarily to be sold or Killed at Proper Seasons, **Accot.** to be rendered to the County Court, for my chil- dren advantage, without Charges,

Deducting first thereout what may be necessary of such kind of Provision for house- keeping for my said wife & Children.

Item, It is my Will that the Profits Arising by the Labour of my Two **sons Slaves**, & their part of the profits Arising by the Stocks, be laid Out in purchasing **Young Female Slaves** to be Added to their **Stocks of slaves**; And it is also my will that if any of the **Female Slaves** given be my in this will shall breed, in Such Case I give the issue to go along with the Mother.

Item, When it shall be necessary to give all or any of my sons Other Education than is to be had from the Common Masters in this Province; for I would have my Children well Educated, it is then my Will that Such expence be Defrayed Out of the profits of Such Childs Estate & not Otherwise.

Item, I Recommend it to my Dear & Loving Life that one of my sons, as shall be Thought best Qualified for it, be bred to the Law, it being highly necessary in so Large a Family; and to him I give all my Law Books, being upwards of 200 Volumes, which are now or Shall be in My Closet at Brunswick, and are Exprest in a Catalogue of my Own hand Writing, in a Marble Cover Book in my Closet.

Item. I give to my Dear wife, Blomes History of the Bible in folio, 3 Volumes in folio of Arch Bishop Tillotsons Works, four volumes in Octavo of Dr. Stamhopes on the Epistles & Gospels, and all the Books of Physick.

Item, I give to my Daughter, Ann Humfries, 3 Volumes in folio on the Old & New Testament, and I will that my Exors. buy for her, the work of the Auther of the whole Duty of Man. I give to the Eldest of my Sons, that shall not Study the Law; Chambers Dictionary, two Volumes in folio; Locks Work, three Volumes in folio; Millers Dictionary; 2 Vol in folio, and LeBlond of Gardening in Quarto: And the rest of my Books, about 150 Volumes, to be Divided among my Other three Sons.

Item, I give & Bequeath unto my Eldest Son, John, my Large Silver Tea Kettle, Lamp, & Server for it to stand on, weighing in all about 170 Ounces. To my Son, Edward, my Large Silver Coffee Pot Pott; to my Son, Sampson, my Large Silver Tea Pot; to my Son, James, my Large Silver Tankard, & to my Son, Thomas, a pair of Large Square Silver Servers; my Cases of Knifes, forks, Spoons, Salts, Casters, & Other my Plate, to be Divided Between my wife & Daughter, my wife to have Two Thirds, & my Daughter One Third. Nevertheless, my wife to have the use of my Children's plate untill She shall Marry, or they respectively Attain to age of 21. But if any shall Depart this life before that Age, such Childs part of the plate or Other Personal Estate I shall & Hereafter in this will give to them, to be Equally Divided among my sons Surviving.

Item, in Case my Wife shall marry, or as Soon as Any of my sons Shall Attain to 21 years of age, which shall first Happen, I will that my household goods & Other Personal Estate not before by me given shall be Equally Divided into four Parts; One thereof to be for my Wife, the Other three Parts among my Six Children.

Item, As there are very Considerable Debts due to me I expect more than Sufficient to pay the Debts I owe, I leave it to my Wife either to Apply the Same for Payment of my Debts, or in Building for all or any Of my Son's as She shall think Proper, if she shall Choose to Apply it in Building, I would have the house at theVineyard Finished Fit for Use, and as She knows my mind with Regard to a handsome large Dwelling house to be built at Rockey Point, the Foundation whereof is Dugg, She may, if She pleases, Proceed thereon And use all the Materials Already Provided by me, And Also, the Sum of One Hundred Pounds Sterling, or the Value thereof in Products, yearly for Two Years, Out of the Labour of all my **Sons Slaves**, And all or any parts of the Debts Due to me.

Item. I give & Bequeath unto my very Good Friend, **Samuel Swann**, Esqr., Major **John Swann** & my Brother in Law, Mr. **Jas. Hasell**, Jr., the Sum of Ten Pounds Sterling, each, or in Products; hereby Requesting there Advice & Assistance in having this my Will fullfilled. And to Mr. **Jeremiah Vail** & Mr. **Alexander Lillington**, the Sum of Five Pounds Sterling, Each, or Value in Products; & to my Very Good Friend **Jas. Hasell**, Esqr., & to my Sisters in Law, Mrs. **Mary Vail** & Mrs. **Sarah Porter**, I give to Each a ring of two Guineas price; & to Each of the Children of my Sister in Law, Mrs. **Mary Vail** & of her sister Elizabeth, late the Wife of Collo. **Maurice Moor**, and to the Children of my Late Brother in Law, Mr. **John Lillington**, & to Colo. **Maurice Moor's** three youngest Children, I give to Each a ring of a Guinea price.

Item, I give to my Honoured Mother in Law, Mrs. **Susannah Hasell,** a ring of three Guineas price.

Item, the rest & Residue of my Estate, Real & Personal, I give to be Equally Divided among my Sons & the Survivours of them.

Lastly I nominate & Appoint my Dearly beloved Wife, **Ann Moseley,** & my Two Eldest Sons, **John & Edward**, to be Executors of this my Last Will & Testament (Containing in Eight Pages all of my Own hand Writing)

In Testimony whereof, I have Hereunto Set my Hand & Seal, this Twentieth Day of March, Anno Dom., 1745.

**E. MOSELEY**, (Seal)
Signed, Sealed, Published, &
Declared In presence of:
**ELEAZR. ALLEN.**
**ROGR. MOORE.**
**WM. FORBES.**
**MATT. ROWAN.**

August Court, 1749.

A Codicil to the Last Will and Testament of **Edward Moseley,**
dated March 20th., 1745. hereunto annexed.

To my Son **William**, born since my said Last Will was made, I give & bequeath my two round Silver Servers; Also, the tract of Land in my said Will mentioned, lying in Edgecombe County, called Alden of the Hill, containing 3200 acres, be the same more or less; Also about 300 acres more, contiguous thereto, which I have Entred in **Earl Granville's** office. To hold the same, about 4000 acres, to him & his heirs forever. It is also my will, that my said Son, **William,** shall have an equal share of the **Slaves** & personal estate left to be divided among my other five sons in that my will.

It is also my will, that if I shall have any more children, They shall be intitled to an equal part of my slaves & personal Estate left to my sons in that my Will mentioned, and that all my sons born or to be born, shall have an equal share or divi- dend of that my large tract of 10,000 Acres called Clur, mentioned in my said will.

I give to my dear wife Ann, **my negro woman named Jane**, for her better care & management of my children, she having been much employed about them.

I give to my Daughter **Nancy**, **Peggy's** youngest **mulatto child named Abram.**

**My slaves Mustapha, Cush & Moll** having behaved very well I order them to be free, but if it shall not be allowed them, Then it is my will that my executrix shall place them jointly or severally as they shall choose, on any of my lands, to make what they shall judge most for their advantage, rendering one tenth part of the profits to my executrix.

Lastly, I make my dear wife **Ann**, Executrix, and my two Eldest Sons, Executors, of this Codicil which I will shall be taken & deemed as a part of my last Will & Testament. In Witness Whereof, I have hereunto set my hand and seal this Nineth day of June, Anno Dom., 1748.

**E. MOSELEY** (seal)
Signed, sealed, published &
Declared in presence of:
**JOHN COCHRAN.**
**JOHN HANCOCK.**
**JOHN COOKE.**

N B, This Codicil is fixed to the Will by Mr. **Sampson's**
Seal (my Wife's Father) mine being lately lost.
NEW HANOVER COUNTY.   August Court, 1749.

+++++++++++++++++++++++++++++++++++++++++++++++++++++++++++++++++++++++++++++++

### John Paine's Will

IN THE NAME OF GOD AMEN. I, **John Paine**, of Wilmington, in the Province of North Carolina, Merchant, being sick and weak in Body, but of sound and disposing Mind, Memory and understanding, Do make, publish and declare this my Last will and Testament, in manner following, That is to say,

First, I recommend my soul to God who gave it and my Body I desire may be decently Buried at the discretion of my Execu-tors herein after named.

Item, I will, Order and direct that all my Just Debts and Funeral Expences may be paid by my Executors herein after named, so Soon as Conveniently may be after my decease.

Item, I Will, order & Direct that all my real Estate, Lands and Tenements be Sold by my Executors herein after named, if they shall think proper to sell & dispose of the same; And I do hereby Impower them in Case of sale, to give good and sufficient Titles in Law for the same to the purchaser or purchasers.

Item, I Give devise & Bequeath all my Estate whatsoever and wheresoever, unto my Loving wife, **Catharine Paine**; To my loving Daughter, **Catharine Musgrove Paine**, and to the Child or Children that my wife now goes with to be equaly divided between them, share and share alike, and to their heirs and assigns for ever; my Childrens Portions to be paid to them by my Executors when they respectively attain the age of Eighteen ------- years or day of Marriage which shall first happen; And if Either of my Children die before they Attain the age of Eighteen years or day of Marriage then, and in that Case, I give, devise and Bequeath the same to my sd. wife, Catharine, to the survivor or survivors of them, and their heirs & assigns; and in Case all my Children die, then I give, Devise & Bequeath all my Estate to my loving wife, **Catharine**, and her heirs forever.And whereas there is a Legacy of Nine hundred pounds, South Carolina Currency, directed & ordered to be by me paid, (by the Last will & Testament of my Mother, **Mary Brewton**, Deed.), to the Children of my Sister, **Elizabeth Arthur**, wife of **Francis Arthur**, now in Georgia, I do therefore hereby Will, order and direct that my Executors after named, Do pay or cause to be paid unto the said Children of my Sister **Elizabeth Arthur**, in Georgia, the said Legacy of nine hundred pounds, South Carolina Currency; together with lawfull Interest for the same till paid, and that the same be paid them so soon as may be after my decease.

Item, I Will, order & direct that my Executors herein after named, within three years after my decease, or sooner if con-venient, Do pay into the hands of the church Wardens of every county in this Province, thirteen pounds, proc. money, to be by them distributed amongst the poor Inhabitants of the said several & respective Counties.

Lastly, I appoint, constitute & nominate my Loving Wife, **Catherine,** Executrix of this my last will and Testament during the time she remains my Widow; and I direct that she may have the Tuition & Guardianship of my Children, Butin case she marry, then, I nominate, constitute & appoint my good Friends, **Maurice Moore & William Hill**, Executors of this my last Will & Testament, and desire they may take possession of my Childrens Estate if they think proper. And I do hereby Revocke all former &other wills by me at any time heretofore made, and declare this Only to be & Contain my last Will and Testament.

In Witness whereof, I have hereunto set my hand & seal at Wilmington, this ninth day of January, in the year of our Lord one thousand Seven hundred & Sixty Seven.

**JOHN PAINE**. (Seal)

+++++++++++++++++++++++++++++++++++++++++++++++++++++++++++++++++++++++++++++

316

### John Lillington's Will

IN THE NAME OF GOD, AMEN. I, **John Lillington**, of the County of Bath, in North Carolina, Gent., being Sick and weak of Body, but of Sound & perfect mind & memory, and Calling to mind the Sertainty of death and not knowing when it may pleas the Lord to call me out of this life, do make, appoint and ordain this to be my last Will and Testament, in maner and form following, that is to Say, after My Just & lawfull Debts are paid.

Impr's. I give bequeath & Devise unto my Loveing wife, **Sarah Lillington**, three of my **negro slaves, Named, Shippy & Jupiter, two men; and Marya, a woman**, to her proper use forever.

Item, I give, bequeath & Devise unto my Son, **Alexander,** one Thousand Acres Land being the one moiety of this parcel of Two thousand Acres of land whereon I now live, to be held of him, his heirs or assignes in fee simple forever.

Item, I give and Devise to my said Son, two of my Negro **Slaves, Named Danger & Jack**; also Tenn Cowes with Calves by their Sides, and Six Sowes and a Boar, and Six Ews and a Ram, all to be likely and good, and apair of hand mill Cullen Stones, and my large Family Bible, all to be delivered to my said Son, by my Executors hereafter named, when he shal attain to the age of Twenty one years, for his proper use forever.

Item, I give, bequeath & Devise unto my Eldest Daughter, **Elizabeth**, one of my **Negroe Slaves Named Roas, a wench**; also Ten likely good Cowes with Calves by their Sides, and One Feather Bedd, bolster and Pillow with a sute of Curten & Vallens, to be delivered to my said Daughter by me Exetrs.hereafter named, when she shall attaine to the age of Twenty one years or day of marryage, for her proper use forever.

Item, I give, bequeath, & Devise unto my Daughter, **Mary**, one of my Negro **Slaves Named Judy, a Guirl**; also Tenn Cowes with Calves by their sides to be likely & good; and one Feather Bedd, bolster & Pillows, with a sute of Curtains & Vallens, to be delivered to my Said Daughter by my Exec'tr hereafter named, for her proper use forever, that is to say, when she shall attain to the age of Twenty one years or day of Marryage.

Item, I give, bequeath & Devise unto my youngest Daughter, **Ann, one of my Negroes Named Moll**, a Guirl; also Tenn likely Mood Cowes with Calves by their Sides, and a Feather Bedd, bolster and Pilloes with a Sute of Curtains & Vallens, to be Delivered to my said Daughter by me Exesrs. hereafter named, when she shall attain to ye age of Twenty one years or day of Marryage.

Item, I give, bequeath & devise al the rest & Residue of my Estate not before mentioned and given (the better thereby to Inable my sd. wife to bring up my sd. Children in Schooling &c.) unto my afsd. Loveing Wife, for her proper use forever.

And lastly my will and desire is, that all my lawfull debt be paid out of the profits arriseing by the labour of my slaves before nominated & given, and that they be kep together under the Care and ordering of my said Wife, and so to re-maine untel all my debts be fully paid & discharged thereby.

I do hereby nominate and appoint my Loveing wife, **Sarah Lillington, Maurice Moore, John Porter** and **John Bap'a. Ash,** to be my Exers., Joyntly or Severally to doe and Execute all and every part of this my last will and testament. (Turn over)

In Witness whereof, I have hereunto Set my hand and Seal, this 19th day of March, Anno. 1721/2.

JOHN LILLINGTON (Seal)
Signed, Sealed & Delivered, in presents of us:
**PAT. MAULE.**
**SAMUELL COOPPER.**
the mark of
**JOHN I TRANTER**

NO. CAROLINA. BEAUFORT AND HYDE PRECINCTS, SCT.
At a court held for the said Precincts, at Bath Towne, on Tuesday

ye 2d. July, 1723 Pres't..........? Esqr. His Majesties Justices.

The Last Will and Testam't of Mr. **John Lillington**, dec'd, was by the Exors. therein named, Exhibited in this Court and proved by the oaths of **Sam'll Cooper & John Tranter**, two of the Witnesses thereunto, who also deposed yt they saw **Patrick Maule**, the other Witness evidence the same.

Ordered that notice be given to the Secretary of the Same & that it be Recorded.

**JNO. BAP'TA. ASHE**, Cler: Cur:

+++++++++++++++++++++++++++++++++++++++++++++++++++++++++++++++++++++++++++++++

## John Lawsons' Will

NO. CAROLINA. BATH TOWNE.

IN THE NAME OF GOD, AMEN, ye 12th. day of August 1708. I, **John Lawson**, of Bath Towne, in the Province of North Carolina, Gent., being of perfect mind & memory, thanks be given unto God therefore, calling to mind the mortality of my body & knowing that it is appointed for men once to dye, Doe make and Ordayne this my last will and testament, that is to Say, principally & first of all, I give a recomend my body to ye Earth, & my Soul to Allmighty God that gave it.

Impris., I give & bequeath to my Dearly beloved **Hannah Smith**, the house & Lott I now live in, to enjoy the sameduring her Naturall life & also one third part of my Personale Estate in No. Carolina to her own proper Use & behoofe & for her to dispose of ye Same as She Thinks fitt.

Item, I give ye remainder of my Estate, both Personall & reale, to my Daughter, **Isabella,** of Bath Town and to the brother & sister (which her mother is w'th Child off at this present) to them Equally to Enjoy (vizt.) that Each of them two shall Enjoy & inheritt alike an Equall part of all my Estate that I dye Possessed of, the Land to be parted &devided when they shall arrive att twenty one years of age or Marry. And if it shall please God that her Mother, **Hannah Smith**, shall have more than one Child at a Birth, which she is now with Child off, that then, every Child of hers by me shall Enjoy an equall part of my Estate.

And Doe hereby Constitute, make & Ordayne ye Commis' of ye Court of Bath County w'th Mrs. **Hannah Smith**, the Exr's. of this my last will and Testament all & Singular my lands tenem'ts & Messauges, & I doe hereby utterly disallow, revoke & disanull all & every other former Testaments, Wills, Legacy's & Bequests & Exrs. by me in any way before named, Willed & bequeathed, ratyfying & Confirming this & no other to be my last will & testament.

In Witness whereof, I have hereunto Sett my hand & Seal ye day & Year above Written.

**JOHN LAWSON**. (Seal)

Signed, Selaed, published & declared by ye sd. John Lawson,as his last will & testament in thepresence of us ye Subscribers:

**WM. W. HAWKOCK.**
**RICH'D SMITH.**
**JAMES LEIGH.**

+++++++++++++++++++++++++++++++++++++++++++++++++++++++++++++++++++++++++++++++

# Thomas Hewitt Will - 1776
## NC Archives, Onslow Co. Wills

*In the Name of God Amen.* I **Thos Hewitt** of the County of Onslow and Provence of North Carolina, planter, Being Very Sick and Weak in body [but] of Perfect Mind and Memory thanks be to God, and Calling to Mind the immortality of my body and Knowing that it is once [appointed?] for all Men to Die, do Make and ordain this my Last will & Testament in the Maner and form following ---

*First* of all I humbly commend my Soul to the Mercy of God my creator and my Body to the ground to be Decently buried at the Discression of my Exrs Here after Mentioned and as for Such worldly goods as god Hath Inabled me with I will and Dispose as followith ---

*Item* [First?] & my will and Desier is that all my Just Debts and Necesarey charges be first paid and Satisfied ---

*Item* I give and Bequeath unto my Son John Hewitt the Plantation Lying on New River, that I purchased of Mr. **John Morris**, to him and his Heirs Lawfully Begoten of his body and for the want of Such Heirs to come unto his brother **GoldSmith Hewitt** to him and his Heirs and assigns for Ever.

*Item* I give and bequith to my Son **John Hewit** the Hogs now Running on the Plantation to him & his Heirs & assigns for Ever ---

*Item* I give and & Bequith unto my Son **Goldsmith Hewit** the Plantation whereon I now Live after the Death of his Mother to him and his Heirs & assigns for Ever ---

*Item* I Lend unto my Beloved wife **Elizabeth Hewitt** the Plantation whereon I [now?] [____] Live During her Natural Live. I also Lend [____] for her Coffort [*comfort?*] and for the Support of my [younger?] children all my Moveable Estate until my Daughter [**Marey?**] **Hewitt** Shall reach to the age of Sixteen years old then all my Estate to be Equilly Divided Between my Beloved wife and my children hereafter Mentioned. **Christian[na?] Hewitt, Elizabeth Hewitt, Judah, Goldsmith** and **Mary Hewitt** to them their Heirs and assigns for Ever ---

Item My will will [*sic*] & Desire in Case my wife **Eliz^h Hewitt** Should [Marry?] and it apears to my Exrs here after Mentioned that there be any wast of the Estate that ~~they~~ [_____] Takes the Same in too his possession [_____] him surety for Making good the [_____] the aforeSd Time of the Division ---

*Item* Last of all I constitute and apoint my Beloved wife **Eliz Hewitt** and my True and Trusty friend **Reuben Grant** my Hole and Soul [*sole*] Exers of this my Last will & testament in Witness whereof I have Set my Hand and fixed my Seal this the first Day of Decr in the year of our Lord Seventeen Hundred & Seventy Six.

Snd Seald and ~~Delvd~~ Acknowledged by the the [*sic*] Testator as his Last will & Testament in the Presents of the Subscribers.

**Thomas [+] Hewitt**
**Stephen Hawkins**
**Petway Burns**

This will was proved by the Oath of [Petway?] Burns April Court 1777. Test **Wm Crayden**
Reuben Grant, Esq^r was Qualified as an Exc^r therein [hole]ned
Recorded.

+++++++++++++++++++++++++++++++++++++++++++++++++++++++++++++++++++++++++++

## Mary Hemingway Last Will and Testament

North Carolina State Archives: Records of Wills 1764-1954, pages 179-181, File Number 122, Last Will and Testament of **Mary Hemingway**, 12 October 1842.

IN THE NAME OF GOD, AMEN!

Know, all men, by these presents, that I, Mary Hemingway, of the county of Brunswick in the state of North Carolina, calling to Mind the Mortality of the flesh & that it is appointed unto all to die, do declare and constitute THIS, my Last Will & Testament in manner & form following, to wit:

1st, I commend my soul to Almighty God, who gave it, and my body to the earth to be decently buried by the side of the grave of my former husband **Joseph Hewett** & my grave to be covered with brick in like manner as his was and both to be enclosed in a brick wall, the expense thereof to be paid out of the legacy hereinafter bequeathed to my Nephew John Holden.

Secondly, my will & desire is that my **negro Man Slurry** and his **wife Nancy** for their long & faithful service to me, be placed in the possession & under the care of my nephew **John Wescoat** freed or exempted from the duties of a slave or servant during their natural lives. I also place in his possession **My negro Man Friday**, and two cows & calves for their support, after their death the said negro Friday to be the property of **John Wescoat**. My will is that John Wescoat come and take the two cows & calves before my stock is divided.

Third, I give & bequeath to **U. W. Rourk** one yoke of oxen before my stock is divided his choice.

Fourth, My will is that my stock of cattle hogs & sheep be equally divided half and half out of the one half I give **John Holden**, Junr. His choice of one yoke of oxen and two cows & calves & the remainder of that half to be equally divided among the surviving children & wife of **William Holden**, decd – **John Holden, Jr**. excluded.

5th. The remaining half of my stock of cattle, hogs & sheep I leave to the use of **Sarah Gause** during her natural life – I also leave her one half of my household & kitchen furniture at her death the remaining property to be equally divided among her daughters.

6th, I give to *my grand Nephew John Holden, Jr. my plantation, known by the name of the Taylor* Plantation. If the said John Holden should die leaving no lawful issue the said land to belong to John Holden, Senr.

7th, I give to my two grand Nephews, **Saml. Stanaland & Peter Thomas Stanaland** 250 acres of land lying between **Job Holden** and my seashore plantation well known by the **name of the Simpkins land – should Peter Thomas die leaving no lawful issue Saml. Stanaland** to inherit the whole reserving also to **Sarah Gause** their Mother a farming privilege during her natural life.
8th, I give & bequeath to my sister (?) Holden my horse & gig – should she not be living at my death I give it to Sarah Gause.

9th, I give to my niece **Mary Taylor** five hundred dollars in a note I hold against **Dr. S. B. Everett** – I give to my niece Mary Taylor, one silver ladle, six silver table spoons, six silver tea spoons all marked J H M, one scissors, silver chain.

10th – I give to my Nephew **William Wescoat** three hundred dollars in a note I hold against **U. W. Rourk**.

11<sup>th</sup>-I give to my niece **Elizabeth Robinson** one half of my household and kitchen furniture – also my **Negro woman Elcy** & **her boys Cuff & Henry** & her future increase if not disposed of otherwise.

12<sup>th</sup> – I give to my Nephew **Thomas Holden my boy Slurry.**

13<sup>th</sup> – I give to my grand niece **Lydia Mince my boy Robert.**

14<sup>th</sup> – I give my boy English to **U. W. Rourk & John Wescoat** share and share equal.

15<sup>th</sup> – I give to my grand niece **Molly Holland Robinson** a negro girl **Mary Ann, Elcy's** daughter.

**16<sup>th</sup> – I give to my grand niece Amelia Stephens** a Negro girl named **Rose, Charity's daughter.** I also give her two hundred & sixty dollars in a note I hold against **U. W. Rourk** – Should she die without issue **Ephraim D. Gause** to inherit the whole – should they both die without lawful issue **Lydia Mince** to inherit the same.

17<sup>th</sup> – I give to **U. W. Rourk** my ox cart and **my negro man named Rentz** – I also give to **Sophia Ruouk** my side saddle and bridle.

18<sup>th</sup> – I give to **Thomas H. Rourk my Negro boy named Whitfield.**

19<sup>th</sup> – I give to my nephew & **John Wescoat a negro woman named Charity** & **her son Fuller** with all her future increase if not disposed of otherwise.

20<sup>th</sup> – I give to my Nephew **Lewis Wescoat** my **negro girl named Beck** with all her increase if not disposed of otherwise.

21<sup>st</sup> – I give to my niece **Elizabeth Stanaland my Negro girl named Sarah, Elcy's daughter.**

22<sup>nd</sup> – I give to my niece **Sarah Cha???oy my Negro girl named Flora Jane.**

23<sup>rd</sup> – I give to my Nephew **John Holden, Senr.** 100 acres of Salt Marsh including the ford at Cedar landing j- also one note I hold against himself for one hundred and fifty dollars & the interest.

24<sup>th</sup> – I leave all the remainder of my property not otherwise disposed of Real & Personal, with **U. W. Rourk** and **John Wescoat** for the special purpose of paying all expense and charges of my burial and enclosing the graves as is directed in the first item, and defending my will. If any difficulty should occur and after all necessary expenses are settled, the residue thereof, if any remains I give to John Holden, Senr.

25<sup>th</sup> - & lastly I do hereby constitute & appoint my two trusty friends **U. W. Rourk & John Wescoat** Executors of this my last will & testament & moreover I do hereby revoke and make void all other wills or parts of wills heretofore by me made & declare this only to be my last will & testament – In witness whereof I the said Mary Hemingway have hereunto set my hand and seal this 13<sup>th</sup> day of October in the year of our Lord, 1842.

**Mary Hemingway**

Signed, sealed & declared by the Testator to be her last will & testament in presence of us who at her request & in the presence of each other have hereunto subscribed our names –
**James Bell            Robt. Woodside            Anthony Clemmons**
This is to certify that I annex this to my Will as a Codicil in the manner & form following –

In the 8<sup>th</sup> Item of my will where I have given my horse & gig & harness to Sister **Sarah Holden**, she being in a low state of health, I revoke that part of said will, and I now give to my Nephew **John Wescoat's** wife **Mary Wescoat** the said horse & gig & harness. I also give to **Sarah Gause** fifty dollars in cash or notes that may be on hand at my death. In the 16<sup>th</sup> item of my will where I have given a negro girl and two hundred & sixty dollars in notes to **Amelia Stephens & Ephraim D. Gause**, I now revoke that part where **E. Gause** is concerned & give the said girl and two hundred & sixty dollars to **Amelia Stephens** above.

In witness whereof I have hereunto set my hand & seal this 24 July 1843.

**Mary Hemingway**

++++++++++++++++++++++++++++++++++++++++++++++++++++++++++++++++++++

Brunswick County, NC Bibles
**William Hill and Margaret Moore Hill FAMILY BIBLE**

**Permission granted by: Donna Sherron**

**William Hill and Margaret Moore** were married at Orton, Brunswick Co. NC on the 29 th Sept. 1757 at noon, by Rev. **John McDowell.**
**William Hill** born 15 April 1737 O.S.
**Margaret Moore** born Dec. 1735 O.S.
CHILDREN
1. **Margaret Anna** born Charleston, South Carolina 5 Dec. 1759 and died 27 Dec 1759.
2. **John**, born Brunswick, 12 April 1761
3. **Henry Richardson**, born in Brunswick Co. NC, 7 Jan 1763 died 27 July 1764
4. **William**, born in Brunswick 16 May 1765 and died 11 Nov. 1769
5. **William Henry** born in Brunswick, 1 May 1767
6. **Nathaniel Moore** born Brunswick 1 Jan 1769
7. **Thomas**, born in Brunswick 28 Nov. 1770
8. **Maurice**, born in Brunswick Co. 15 May 1772 and died 4 July 1774
9. **Maurice Moore**, born in Wilmington, 10 Dec. 1775 and died.

**Thomas Hill and Susannah Mabson** married in Wilmington by **Thomas Hages** Esq. Oct. 15 1792
Their Children:

1. **Thomas,** born in Wilmington Aug. 21 1799; **Thomas** married **Eliza** ( Grant?)
2. **William Henry** born ( Horesport ? ) Nov. 11 1795
3. **Maria** , born at ( Torseport ?) May 22 1797
4. **Arthur** born at Horseport Feb. 25 1799
5. **Margaret** born at Horseport Jan 18 1801; Under **Margaret**'s name died in Wilmington  married **Thomas** ( Gains or Grant )
6. **Thomas** born at Horseport Dec. 10 1812
7. **Susan**, born at (Wyconbann ?) April 15 1814; **Susan** married a ( **Rubert**?)
8. **John Hampton** born  ( Hpas ?) born Apr. 21 1807; John Hampton married **Mary Ann Holmes** died at Goldsbro Feb. 19th 1893 at 11:30 A. M.;
9. **A boy** born and died at (Hpas ? ) 1810
10. **A boy** born at ( Heibron ? ) Sept. 1811 died immedally after his birth
11. **Eliza Alice** born Hipen ?  Dec. 4 1812. Eliza married John ( Haugern ?)

**Thomas Hill and Mary C. McConnaughey** were married, near Salisbury,. Rowan Co,. by Rev. **Thomas G. Haughton**, on the 8th Dec. 1858 at 10 A.M.
**Thomas Hill, eldest son of Dr. John Hampton Hill and Mary Ann Holmes.** He was born at Gilmore in Sampson Co., Oct. 26 1832, died Feb. 18 1906 at Goldsboro, NC.
**Mary Carolina McConnaughey,** dau. of **John Chambers** and **Carolina McConnaughey**, she was born at Oak Gear, Rowan Co., April 14 1840. Died Feb. 28, 1907 at Goldsboro, NC.

**John H. Hill** was the son of **Thomas Hill** and **Susan Mabson Hill.**
**Mary Ann Holmes** was the dau. of **Gabriel** and **Mildred Mabson Holmes.**
**James Chambers McConnaughey** was the son of **James** and **Anna Roberson McConnaughey**
**Carolina Hall** was the dau. of **Allmance** and **Annie Hwain Hall**

Children of Dr. **Thomas** and **Mary C. Hill**:
**James McConnaughey** born at Oak Gear, Rowan Co. 18 Sept. 1859 - died Jan 6 1927 Lenoir Co. NC
**Mary Ann** born at Lilliput, Brunswick Co. 18 Feb. 1861 - died Aug. 3, 1910.
**Theophilus Holmes** born at Oak Gear, Rowan Co., born Nov. 21, 1863.
**Thomas** born Keansville, Duplin Co.NC , Oct 8 1869 - died Goldsboro
**Caroline** born Salisbury, NC on Sept 7 1871 - died 25 Aug. 1872
**Maria Caroline** born Danville, MO., Feb. 10 1873 - died 14 Dec. 1898; Died at Goldsboro.
**Margaret Moore** born Danville, MO., May 27 1876 - died Oct. 25 1943
**John Yiamans** ( or **Yeamans**) born near Salisbury, NC,  1 July 1880 - died 2 Aug. 1882
**James McC. Hill** was married at Charlotte, NC, June 19 1895 to **Margaret Isabella Walker**, dau. of Capt. Mr. **John Mosely Walker**
+++++++++++++++++++++++++++++++++++++++++++++++++++++++++++++++++++++++++++++++++

*North Carolina Government, 1585 - 1974, A Narrative and Satistical History* by Thad Eure.

*Colonial Assembly:*

| | |
|---|---|
| **Robert Howe** | 1764-1775 |
| **Thomas McGuire** | 1764-65 |
| **John Paine** | 1766 |

| | |
|---|---|
| **William Davis** | 1769-1773 |
| **John Rowan** | 1773-1775 |

*Town Representatives from Brunswick:*

| | |
|---|---|
| **Maurice Moore** | 1766-1774 |
| **Park Quince** | 1775 |

*General Assembly:*

| | |
|---|---|
| Archibald Maclaine | 1777, 1780, 1782 |
| Alexius M. Foster | 1788, 1787 |
| Alfred Moore | 1782 |
| Joseph Eagles | 1783 |
| Benjamin Smith | 1784, 1792-1800, 1804-1810, 1816 |
| William Walters | 1784-85 |
| Dennis Hawkins | 1785, 1791-92 |
| Lewis Dupree | 1788 |
| Jacob Leonard | 1790 |

Note: Posted in the Wilmington Gazette on 14 March 1809, Jacob Leonard said: "Taken up, and now in my possession, an African man, about twenty-five years of age, five feet or nine inches high, spare made, has on a pair of plain blue trousers, a blanket & common blue negro cap & he can scarcely be understood, from which I infer that he has been but a short time in this country. He says his name is **WILL**, that his master's name is **PEE** (being dead) by signs he conveys the idea his master planted cotton and corn, and that he has a cotton machine. The owner of said negro is requested toc ome forward, prove his property and take him away, reasons to be assigned to the owner, why the subscribed has not committed the negro to jail. Jacob Leonard, Brunswick County, January 17th."

| | |
|---|---|
| Jacob W. Leonard | 1814-1815, 1817-1818, 1820-1822 |
| Jacob Leonard | 1828-1830 |
| William Wingate | 1801-1803, 1811-1813 |
| Thomas Leonard | 1811 |
| John C. Baker | 1819, 1822-26 |
| Benjamin R. Locke | 1826-1828 |
| William R. Hall | 1830-1834 |
| Maurice Moore | 1834-35 |
| Frederick J. Hill | 1835 |

| Name | Distict | Years |
|---|---|---|
| A. J. Jones | 19 | 1856-57 |
| John D. Taylor | 19 | 1860-61 |
| Salter Lloyd | 19 | 1866-67 |
| Edwin Legg | 13 | 1868-1870 |

| | | |
|---|---|---|
| G. A. Hill | 13 | 1872 |
| John N. Bennett | 13 | 1876-77 |
| Asa Ross | 13 | 1879 |
| S. P. Swain | 13 | 1885 |
| John N. Bennett | 13 | 1889 |
| George H. Cannon | 10 | 1897 |
| W. J. Davis | 10 | 1899-1900 |
| George H. Bellamy | 11 | 1903, 1907-1908, 1911 |
| Edward H. Cranmer | 10 | 1917 |
| Joseph W. Ruark | 10 | 1923-24, 1927, 1943 |
| T. H. Lindsey | 10 | 1931 |
| Samuel B. Frink | 10 | 1935, 1939,1951,1959,1971 |
| Rudolph Mintz | 10 | 1947 |
| Ray H. Walton | 15 | 1955-56 |

*Representatives:*

| | |
|---|---|
| William Lord | 1777 |
| Richard Quince,Jr. | 1777 |
| Lewis Dupree | 1778 |
| William Gause | 1778 |
| William Dry | 1778 |
| Joseph Greene | 1781 |
| Alfred Moore | 1781 |
| Dennis Hawkins | 1782-83 |
| William Waters | 1782-83 |
| David Flowers | 1784-85 |
| Jacob Leonard | 1784-85 |
| Robert Howe | 1786-878 |
| Lewis Duprey | 1787 |
| John Cains | 1788 |
| Benjamin Smith | 1789-1792 |
| William E. Lord | 1790-94, 1795-96 |
| Alfred Moore | 1792-93,1814, 1817-28 |
| William Wingate | 1793-96 |
| Abraham Bessant | 1794-95, 1796-1800 |
| George Davis | 1797, 1809 |
| Benjamin Mills | 1798-1802 |
| John G. Scull | 1801-03 |
| Thomas Leonard | 1803-10 |
| Maurice Moore | 1804, 1812-13 |
| Richard Parrish | 1805-06 |
| Thomas Russ | 1807-08, 18010-11, 1813-14 |
| Jacob W. Leonard | 1811 |
| Robert Potter | 1812 |
| John C. Baker | 1815, 1817-18 |
| Uriah Sullivan | 1815 |
| Edwin Mills | 1816 |
| William Simmons | 1816 |
| John Neale | 1819-20 |
| Francis N. Waddell | 1821-22 |

| | |
|---|---|
| Samuel Frink | 1822 |
| Jacob W. Leonard | 1823-25 |
| Haynes Waddell | 1824-25 |
| John Julius Gause | 1826-26 |
| Jacob Leonard, Jr. | 1826-28 |
| William L. Hall | 1828-29 |
| Marsden Campbell | 1829-30 |
| John J. Gause | 1825-26 |
| Benjamin S. Leonard | 1830-31, 1833-34 |
| Samuel A. Laspeyre | 1831-34 |
| John Waddell | 1832-33 |
| Abram Baker | 1834-35 |
| Robert M. McCracken | 1834-35 |
| William R. Hall | 1835 |
| Frederick J. Hill | 1836-41 |
| Armelin Bryan | 1842-43 |
| Henry H. Waters | 1844-47, 1848-49, 1852-54 |
| David D. Allen | 1848-49 |
| John H. Hill | 1850-51 |
| Gaston Meares | 1854-55 |
| Thomas D. Meares | 1856-61 |
| Daniel L. Russell | 1862-64, 1876-77 |
| Daniel L. Russell, Jr. | 1864-66 |
| D. C | 1866-67 |
| B. T. Morrell | 1868-70 |
| John A. Brooks | 1870-72, 1872-74, 1881 |
| John N. Bennett | 1874-75 |
| A. C. Meares | 1879-80 |
| W. M. Grissett | 1883 |
| D. B. McNeil | 1885 |
| S. P. Swain | 1885-87 |
| Rufus Galloway | 1889 |
| E. Hickman | 1891 |
| George H. Bellamy | 1893, 1913 |
| William W. Drew | 1895-97 |
| D. B. McNeill | 1899-1901 |
| W. H. Phillips | 1903 |
| C. Edward Taylor | 1905-11 |
| Dempsy L. Hewett | 1915-19, 1929 |
| Elijah H. Smith | 1921, 1925 |
| Marvin B. Watkins | 1923-24, 1927 |
| James W. Thompson | 1931 |
| Joseph W. Ruark | 1933, 1941, 1945 |
| Richard E. Sentelle | 1935-38 |
| Cornelius Thomas | 1939 |
| William J. McLamb | 1943 |
| Odell Williamson | 1947-49, 1953, 1963-66, 1967 |
| Harry L. Mintz, Jr. | 1951 |
| Kirby Sullivan | 1955-56 |
| James C. Bowman | 1957-59 |

Samuel B. Frink          1961
Thomas J. Harrelson 1971-74

# Bibliography

Alvaney vs. Powell.54 N. C., 35, 51 N. C., 233.

Ballagh. White Servitude in the Colony of Virginia. Thirteenth Series, Nos. VI. and VII.

Bassett, John Spencer, 1867-1928.  Ed. by Adams. Herbert B.; c. 1896 by the John Hopkins Press.
The Friedenwald Co., Printers,  Baltimore.

Bassett. The Constitutional Beginnings of North Carolina. ibid., Twelfth Series, No. III.

Battle. Address on the Life and Services of Brigadier-General Jethro Sumner. 1891.

Bernheim. German Settlements and Lutheran Churches of the Carolinas. 1872.

Biggs. A Concise History of the Kehukee Baptist Association. 1834.

Born in Slavery: Slave Narratives from the Federal Writers' Project. 1936-1938 These narratives were collected in the 1930s as part of the Federal Writers' Project of the Works Progress Administration (WPA) and assembled and microfilmed in 1941 as the seventeen-volume Slave Narratives: A Folk History of Slavery in the United States from Interviews with Former Slaves.

Brackett. The Negro in Maryland. 1889.

Brickell. Natural History of North Carolina. 1737.

Brunswick County Records, Conveyances. B, 84, 189, 327, 341, 368; North.

Bryan Tyson, The Institution of Slavery in the Southern States. pp. 9, 11.

Butler, Lindley S. North Carolina and the Coming of the Revolution. 1763-1776. Published by Theo. Davis Sons, Inc. Raleigh. 1976.

Carolina Cultivator. April, 1855, pp 59-60.

Cashman, Diane Cobb. Cape Fear Adventure. Windsor Publications. Chatsworth, California. 1982.
Colonial Court Records; Box 190; Folder "Corn Lists, 1715-1716"; Taxes & Accounts, 1679-1754.
North Carolina State Archives, Raleigh, N.C.

Col. Recs., I., 204, 720.

Col. Recs. II., 345.

Col. Recs. IV., 460.

Col. Recs. VI., 729-730 and 985-986.

Colonial Records of North Carolina. Compiled by Col. W. L. Saunders, ten volumes, 1886-1890.
Connor, Robert D. W. Cornelius Harnett;: An essay in North Carolina History. 1971, Books for Libraries Press (ISBN 0-8369-5647-8).

Connor, Robert D. W. Revolutionary Leaders of North Carolina. Reprinted 1971 from 1916 edition. (ISBN 0-87152-063-X) Chapter 3: pages 49-78. Biographical Directory of the United States Congress.

Crow, Jeffrey J. A Chronicle of North Carolina During the American Revolution. 1763-1789. NC State University Graphics. 1975.

Debates of the Convention. 1835.

Doyle. The English Colonies in America: Virginia, Maryland and the Carolinas.

Fiske. The Discovery of America. 1892.

Fiske, The Discovery of America. II., pp. 427 *et seq* 272.

Franklin, John Hope.  The Free Negro in North Carolina 1790-1860.  The University of North Carolina Press.  1943.

Fryer, Jack E., Jr.  The Coastal Chronicles.  Volume I.  Dram Tree Books.  2000.

Geza, Schutz.  Additions to the History of the Swiss Colonization Projects in Carolina.  NCHR. X. 134-35.1.

Goodman, Louis and Cooper, Alice Sawyer.  Daniel Lindsey Russell Governor of North Carolina.  1897-1901; A Family and Friends Memoir.  New Hanover Public Library.

Guion Griffis Johnson, 1900-1989.  Ante-Bellum North Carolina: A Social History.  Chapel Hill: University of North Carolina Press, 1937.

Hawks. History of North Carolina. 1858.

Hawks, History of North Carolina. II., 73, 205.

Holden, John F.  The Beginning and Development of Holden Beach.  New Hanover Printing and Publishing.  C. 2000.

Hooper, A. M.  Memoir of General John Ashe.  Wilmington, 1854; Uni Mag III, 366.

Horne, Robert.  Brief Description of the Province of Carolina.  (1666) An English Pamphlet Extolling the Virtues of the Cape Fear Region - in 1666.
2007 - J.D. Lewis, Internet.

Hurmence, Belinda.  My Folks Don't Want Me to Talk About Slavery. John F. Blair publisher, Winston Salem, NC.  C. 1984.

Hurmence, Belinda.  Before Freedom, When I Just Can Remember.  John F. Blair publisher, Winston Salem, NC.  C. 1989.

Johnson, F. Roy.  Tales from Old Carolina.  Johnson Publishing Company, Murfreesboro, NC. 1965.
Jones. Defense of North Carolina.

Journal. p. 459.
Landholding in the Colony of North Carolina. The Law Quarterly Review (London). April, 1895.

Laws of North Carolina. Revisions of 1715, 1752, 1765, and 1773.

Laws of 1741. Ch. 8, Ch. 24.

Lawson, History of North Carolina. pp. 73, 74;

Lee, Lawrence. New Hanover County...a brief history. NC Department of Archives, 1971.

Lefler, Hugh T. and Powell, William S. Colonial North Carolina, A History. Charles Scribner's Sons, New York, 1973.

Legislative Papers. Senate December 14, 1827.] Ann J. White Will. White *v.* Beattie, 16 N. C., 87

Legislative Papers. House, December 26, 1827.

Lower Cape Fear Historical Society. Latimer House Office. Wilmington, NC.

MacCubbin, Robert P. and Mawrtin, Peter. British and American Gardens in the Eighteenth Century. C 1984 by the Colonial Williamsburg Foundation.

MacMillan, W. D., III, "John Kuners," Journal of American Folk-Lore. XXXIX, 55-57. See also "One Time Picturesque Custom Peculiar Here," Wilmington News-Dispatch, June 4, 1925.

McLamb, Carol. Calabash Now and Then.
Memorial of the Citizens of North Carolina. MS in Joseph Brevard Diary, 1791.

Minutes of the Bladen, Brunswick, Duplin, and Wilmington-New Hanover County Committees of Safety. Wilmington (N.C.). Committee of Safety. May 20, 1775 - May 21, 1775 . Volume 10, Pages 24 - 29

Minutes of a Court of Magistrates and Freeholders in Brunswick County North Carolina, Magistrates and Freeholders Court. March 5, 1778, Volume 13, pages 375-376

Moore, Lewis T. Stories Old and New of the Cape Fear Region. Broadfoot Publishing Company, Wilmington, NC. 1956, 1999.

Narrative of some of the Proceedings of the North Carolina Yearly Meeting on the Subject of Slavery within its Limits, 1848. Published by the Committee for Sufferings.

New Hanover County Public Library. Wilmington, NC.

North Carolina Department of Cultural Resources Markers Web Page. The Southern States of America, Chapter III - North Carolina 1775 - 1861.

North Carolina General Assembly Minutes. November 6, 1769, Vol. 8, pages 141-143.

NC Court of Please and Quarter Sessions, April 5, 1768.

North Carolina Office of Archives and History. Online resources. Raleigh, NC.

Observer. Letter from Woodsides Hotel, Smithville, to the "Observer," Raleigh, October 4, 1878.

Phillips Moore Papers: L. V. Hargis to Phillips Moore. August 27, 1823.

Price, NC Higher-Court Records. Vol. V, p. 263. Mar. Court 1722.

Price, NC Higher-Court Records. Vol. V, p. 322. Oct. Court 1722.

Robinson, Blackwell P. The Revolutionary War Sketches of William R. Davie. NC State University Graphics. 1976.

Slavery and Servitude in the Colony of North Carolina.
Electronic Edition.

Smith, Elmer Lewis, John G. Stewart, and M. Ellsworth Kyger. The Pennsylvania Germans of the Shenandoah Valley. Publications of the Pennsylvania German Folklore Society. 26 (1962), 1-278.

South Carolina Gazette. July 28, 1733, February 2, 1734, May 18, 1735.

Star, May 5, 1826.

Steiner. History of Slavery in Connecticut. Johns Hopkins University Studies in Historical and Political Science, Eleventh Series, Nos. IX. and X.

Strachey. Travayle into Virgini. Published in Hakluyt Society Publications.

Triebe, Richard. Photographs.

Troxler, Carol Watterson. The Loyalist Experience in North Carolina. Publised by Theo. Davis Sons, Inc. 1976.

True Republican or American Whig. 1809 CE. Wilmington, NC. Transcribed by Joseph E. Waters Sheppard. Heritage Books. 2008.

Tryon, William. Letter to Wills Hill, Marquis of Downshire. September 15, 1769, Vol I, Page 71 of the Colonial and State Records of North Carolina.

U. S. Census Office, Century of Population Growth. p. 140.1.

Weeks. Church and State in North Carolina. Johns Hopkins University Studies in Historical and Political Science, Eleventh Series, Nos. V. and VI.

Wheeler, John H. (John Hill), 1806-1882. Reminiscences and Memoirs of North Carolina and Eminent North Carolinians. 15, lxxiv, Columbus, Ohio, Columbus Printing. Electronic Edition.

Wikipedia. Bartolomé de las Casas. Stamp Act 1765.

Willis, Eulis. Navassa, The Town and its People. C. E. Willis. 1993.

Young, Henry, Disposition regarding David Pollock, November 17, 1771. Vol. 9, Page 53 of the Colonial and State Minutes of North Carolina.

*Special Thanks to:*

**John Muuss, Photographic Artist.** Southport, NC. www.johnmuuss.com
Email: johnmuussphoto@yahoo.com

**Old South Tour & Carriage Company, LLC**
www.oldsouthtourcompany.com
Email: oldsouthtourcompany@yahoo.com

**Brunswick County Historical Society**
Shallotte, NC

**Lower Cape Fear Historical Society**
www.latimerhouse.org
info@latimerhouse.org

# INDEX

355

Printed in the United States of  America.

2887845

Made in the USA